1973

Melville's
Drive
To
Humanism

Melville's Drive To Humanism

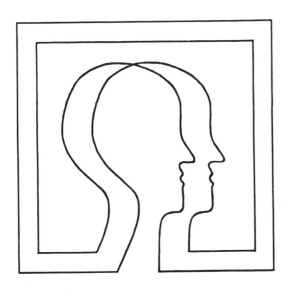

by Ray B. Browne

1971

Purdue University Studies
Lafayette, Indiana

PREFACE

CALL ME DIVER! might have been Melville's appropriate words to describe himself and his belief that man must make every possible effort to understand himself and the universe around him. It was this desire to plunge headlong, perhaps sometimes heedlessly, into the deepest water which, although it perplexed and alienated many of his contemporaries, makes Melville the single most provocative and appealing nineteenth-century American author to the confused but searching reader of today.

If Mark Twain was the Lincoln of literature, as Howells said, then Melville was the Shakespeare of American writers, more than Hawthorne whom Melville likened to the English playwright. Like Shakespeare, Melville was capable of the weakest accomplishment as well as of the strongest. He combined the searching, probing strength of the minds and hearts of Hawthorne, whom of all nineteenth-century American writers he most admired and resembled, Emerson, Thoreau, and others. He coiled together all their strengths and harpooned the universe. Melville was protean. He is all things to most men, especially to those who ponder the human situation and try to comprehend it.

His appeal has naturally stimulated a great flurry of critical and scholarly activity, especially in the last two decades, and will undoubtedly provide much more. His works are a vast armada of possibilities ready for the hunter to search out and make fast to. Hunting the white whale of Melville's works is a longer and more trying voyage than Ahab's for Moby-Dick, but the quest is more delightful and more rewarding. It is a lonely voyage, fraught with frustration, at times with hopelessness, and always with danger. But the end for all such hunters is a partial metamorphosis into Ishmael. For no one comes away from the long encounter with Melville without having gained greater knowledge of himself and the universe.

*It takes more than one individual to man a whaling vessel.
So, too, all scholarly and critical achievement in the study of
Melville is a part of the vast ocean of endeavor by predecessors.
Some efforts have been small waves, others mountains of
water crashing with penetrating force. All, to one degree or
another, have broken into the cliffs of Melville's meanings
and brought forth grains of knowledge and understanding.*

*In one way or another, such is the present work. I have
read all, or most, of the works on Melville. At times I may
seem to have ignored some studies, and at times to have
rejected them. Often I have approved and probably incorporated them silently more than I realize. Where I felt it
was warranted I have acknowledged them.*

*The particular books that I have found most stimulating
have been F. O. Matthiessen's* The American Renaissance,
William E. Sedgwick's Herman Melville: The Tragedy of
Mind, *Richard Chase's* Herman Melville, *Daniel Hoffman's*
Form and Fable in American Literature, *and Merlin Bowen's*
The Long Encounter. *Though I often differ considerably with
each, I found them all arresting and informative. The best
texts of Melville's works are, of course, the Northwestern-
Newberry Library edition now in progress.*

*I have also found informative and useful the comments—
and criticisms—of my former colleagues at Purdue: Darrel
Abel, William Braswell, Richard Crowder, Roland Duerksen,
Allen Hayman, Martin Light, Virgil Lokke, Barriss Mills,
C. E. Nelson, William Stafford, William Stuckey, Tom H.
Towers, and John Tuckey.*

*I am grateful to the Purdue Research Foundation for a
grant which allowed me to devote full time to this study
during a summer,* and to Nineteenth-Century Fiction *for
permission to use the chapter on* Billy Budd—*somewhat
changed—which first appeared in that magazine*

*I am most appreciative, however, to my three little
Ishmaels, Glenn, Kevin, and Alicia, and to my wife, Alice,
for the various kinds of assistance they rendered but I cannot
acknowledge.*

Ray B. Browne   Bowling Green, Ohio   June, 1970

CONTENTS

INTRODUCTION

Though not always consistently so, Herman Melville was
the most powerful American writer of the nineteenth
century. The reasons are twofold.

In the first place he felt very keenly the magic and
thrust of powerful language properly used. His awareness,
always acute, became especially sharp during the summer
of 1850 when, stimulated by the closeness of Hawthorne's
presence and literary accomplishment, Melville rediscovered
the richness of Shakespeare's language. Thereafter he was to
develop a rhetoric which when not carried to excess is
virtually unequalled in gusto, daring, and brilliance. The
depth and breadth, the comprehensiveness and incisiveness,
the suppleness and nimbleness of his language at its best—
in the most effective passages of *Moby-Dick*, for example—
can only make the reader marvel at Melville's complete
control; the reader feels that at Melville's best—to
paraphrase and modify a passage in *Moby-Dick*—he
linguistically attempted everything and achieved nearly all.
He tried all the instruments of a grand orchestra and
mastered most of them. Such an evaluation of Melville's
style is not invalidated by the fact that his language at its
worst—and too often it is at less than its best—is sound
and fury, fustian and bombast, appearance without substance,
skin without flesh and bone, goat's horn masquerading
as golden trumpet.

More important than language in contributing to
Melville's power, however, was the probing of his all-
curious mind into the unfathomable and unutterable
profundities of existence. As he once wrote to his friend
Evert Duyckinck, in approving of at least one element of
Emerson, "I love all men who *dive*." He approved of "the
whole corps of thought-divers, that have been diving and
coming up again with bloodshot eyes since the world

1

began." [1] This characteristic Melville recognized in Hawthorne, and was drawn to the older man like metal filings to a strong magnet.

In a review of Hawthorne's *Mosses from an Old Manse,* written between July and August 5, 1850, before he actually met the author, Melville praised Hawthorne for these very qualities. Hawthorne's "great power of blackness . . . derives its force from its appeals to the Calvinistic sense of Innate Depravity and Original Sin, from whose visitation, in some shape or other, no deeply thinking mind is always and wholly free." No thinking writer can brood on this world without taking Original Sin into the reckoning, and "perhaps no writer has ever wielded this terrific thought with greater terror" than Hawthorne did. He shares this quality with Shakespeare: "those deep far-away things in him; those occasional flashings-forth of the intuitive Truth in him; those short, quick probings at the very axis of reality." In Hawthorne are blended properly the two searching elements of humanity, the head and the heart, with which he, like Shakespeare, is master of the "great Art of Telling the Truth."

From his earliest period of intellectual maturity to his death, Melville pondered similar questions, which have plagued man since the beginning: the nature of the universe and man's role in it; whether there is an intelligence, love, or force behind the universe, and if so its purpose and ultimate aims.

One reason for Melville's constant probing was his own psychological and spiritual longing for something to believe in and cling to. Early in life he had been separated from the refuge of belief in Jehovah. As a searcher left with no external refuge, he more and more through the years turned in upon himself and the human race in his effort to make existence somehow intelligible and tolerable. His attitude on this subject throughout the last four decades of his life is pictured in the comments Hawthorne made in his *Journal*

1. Quoted in Merrell E. Davis and William H. Gilman, *The Letters of Herman Melville* (New Haven, 1960), p. 79.

upon seeing his friend for the last time, in Liverpool, in 1856:

> He stayed with us from Tuesday till Thursday; and, on the intervening day, we took a pretty long walk together, and sat down in a hollow among the sandhills, (sheltering ourselves from the high, cool wind) and smoked a cigar. Melville, as he always does, began to reason of Providence and futurity, and of everything that lies beyond human ken, and informed me that he had "pretty much made up his mind to be annihilated;" but still he does not seem to rest in that anticipation and, I think, will never rest until he gets hold of a definite belief. It is strange how he persists—and has persisted ever since I knew him, and probably long before—in wandering to and fro over these deserts, as dismal and monotonous as the sandhills amid which we were sitting. He can neither believe, nor be comfortable in his unbelief; and he is too honest and courageous not to try to do one or the other.[2]

Hawthorne's incisive observations about Melville's compulsive probing for absolutes are strengthened by Melville's own statements as revealed in his works (and letters and journals) through the years. These questions and answers in one way or another manifested themselves in all of Melville's writings from first to last.

Many of these subjects have been studied exhaustively by numerous critics. Other topics, however, have been underdeveloped or ignored. These are the topics I shall be primarily concerned with in this book. They are themes which express Melville's probing for answers to the questions about man and the universe, which demonstrate how Melville finally satisfied his need for an absolute to believe in. They reveal that Melville believed that the solution of man's problems lies not with any supreme power but with man himself, and they demonstrate Melville's

2. Quoted in Jay Leyda. *The Melville Log* (New York. 1951). 2:529.

3

recognition of the innate value and dignity of man—in other words, in "humanism": the examination and questioning of social institutions, especially as they impinge upon the natural rights of the individual; the good and possible evil generated in and by society; the validity of social institutions which make society operate in what Melville called the "forms" of life. Looking up above himself and finding no comforting power, Melville through the sheer power of intellect and will raised man to a super-human plane and found solace, if not pleasure, in his own creation.

Richard Chase said that Melville's "religion" should be called something like "skeptical humanism." Leslie Fiedler has termed it "tragic humanism," and Elizabeth Foster named Melville's attitude in *The Confidence-Man* "last-ditch humanism." All these adjectives are appropriate and suggestive, though none is sufficiently comprehensive or descriptive. Nor did these critics, or the numerous others who have touched on the subject, reveal the dimensions and fullness of Melville's humanism. He was perhaps less "skeptical" than Chase believed him and less desperate than Miss Foster thought, perhaps even less "tragic" than Fiedler believes, though surely not without the depth of tragedy. Indeed his works, especially those after *Pierre*, point up a less bleak attitude than is generally assumed he held, and in fact demonstrate a perhaps resigned but certainly hopeful belief in the future of mankind. Melville had found his own substitute for a non-existent absolute.

Fundamentally my examination in this book will center on Melville's profound concern with the various facets of this humanism. I shall branch out to other aspects of his works when they have not been adequately discussed by other critics. But essentially I shall always be concerned, whether the connection is explicitly made or only implied, with Melville's examination of the human plight and his affirmation of humanism.

As Melville's ideas generally persisted from the beginning of his literary career, so too did his techniques, though as he developed he executed them with greater sophistication and art, more organic development, and profounder symbolism. Besides his re-use of personal adventure, bolstered with a generous fattening taken from books on the same and similar subjects, which he increasingly used with great creative enrichment, these methods of work included organic use of folklore and frontier Crockett-like tall tales and humor, popular and folk songs, minstrel humor, and over- and understatement. These methods of development, because of their very nature, all helped to emphasize Melville's intended tie-in with his study of man and to give that thematic examination its great impact.

This volume is not a conventional book of general criticism or of biography-criticism. Instead, I have concentrated on one theme in all of Melville's works and have demonstrated its existence in each. In a way, then, this book is a series of essays on the individual works. Yet in the persistence of the theme and the study of its appearance, the essays do in fact constitute a whole. To have made the work more inclusive and more comprehensive would have doubled its size—which at this time I feel is unnecessary—and would have gone beyond my desires

ONE

BEFORE *MOBY-DICK:* THE MAGIC GROWTH OF A STRONG MIND

The phenomenon of Melville's growth in five short literary years (1845-50) and five books—*Typee, Omoo, Mardi, Redburn,* and *White-Jacket*—can accounted for only with the word *genius.*

Melville's genius, however, whatever else it might have been, was a product of a man reacting with a powerful mind and heart to the stresses and strains of the world around him. *Moby-Dick* could have been written by no other person than Melville, in no other country than America, and during no other period than the middle of the nineteenth century. For mighty forces were at work in this country at that time.

America was a nation of newly-realized power and purpose. After the War of 1812 she had begun to develop a self-awareness and a civilization all her own. Although the nation was still essentially agricultural, already the East was showing its potential industrialization. The lure and promise of the West pulled people in the great westering movement. All activity was energized by a philosophy of *laissez-faire* which invited man to dare anything with a strong hope of success. Society was democratic, people were patriotic, and most were optimistic. America seemed destined to fulfill every promise implicit in the term *New World.*

The most vital single ingredient in this cup of promise was, of course, Transcendentalism. Deeply rooted in the Renaissance and Reformation, Transcendentalism strove to deepen and enrich human experience. In its best impulses and forms, it did. In thinkers less than the strongest, and even in Emerson and Thoreau when they were not at their best, however, Transcendentalism was too easy in its optimism. It glossed over the realities of life; it looked toward a sunny dawn when its feet were deep in mire.

Opposing the optimism of the Transcendentalists was the realization, or suspicion, that dark forces controlled man. Man instead of being angelic was in fact Satanic, weighted down with Innate Sin and Natural Depravity. The various forces thrusting America toward her destiny were possibly malign, not always beneficent. All aspects of life had to be examined and understood.

Clearly, then, America in the middle of the century was more complex than it had ever been before. Life brought great strains on the thinking mind that endeavored to make order out of the contradictions, to render the complexities understandable. One easy answer to the baffling problem was to close the mind. Another was to open the mind only to those aspects which could be wished or explained away, or minimized, as the Transcendentalists did. The most difficult and painful answer came to those people who could and would with fully opened eyes, heads, and hearts front life in all its complexity, terror, and loneliness.

The power and will for this facing up to life and the penetration of it was the characteristic of Hawthorne that Melville immediately admired. In April 1851, Melville outlined in a letter to his new friend these qualities which meant so much to him:

> There is a certain tragic phase of humanity which, in our opinion, was never more powerfully embodied than by Hawthorne. We mean the tragicalness of human thought in its own unbiassed, native, and profounder workings. We think that into no recorded mind has the intense feeling of the visable truth ever entered more deeply than into this man's. By visable truth, we mean the apprehension of the absolute condition of present things as they strike the eye of the man who fears them not, though they do their worst to him . . . . He may perish; but so long as he exists he insists upon treating with all Powers upon an equal basis.

Independence of will and mind! The willingness, the
temerity, the necessity to explain God's workings when "God
cannot explain His own secrets"—these are the deeps that
Melville knew needed to be sounded:

> There is the grand truth about Nathaniel Hawthorne.
> He says NO! in thunder; but the Devil himself cannot
> make him say *yes*. For all men who say *yes*, lie; and
> all men who say *no*,—why, they are in the happy
> condition of judicious, unincumbered travellers in
> Europe; they cross the frontiers into Eternity with
> nothing but a carpet-bag,—that is to say, the Ego.
> Whereas those *yes*-gentry, they travel with heaps of
> baggage, and, damn them! they will never get through
> the Custom House.[1]

For Melville, man had to break through the apparent
and reach an understanding of life that balanced what truth
was in Transcendentalism with what there was in the opposite. Amalgamation of the conflicting forces did not make
Melville flash forth *yes* in lightning—he would never be one
of the *yes*-gentry—but it did allow him to affirm in a faint
light of hope which relieved what might otherwise have
been bleak black despair.

Melville's strength bursts forth in his great books, *Moby-
Dick* and most of those which followed it. But *Moby-Dick*
was not without its antecedents. Just as no man fails to
stand on the shoulders of his predecessors, as Francis Bacon
observed, most books grow from previous efforts. *Moby-Dick*
exploded from compression of the five books which preceded
it. They provided the trying-out of Melville's starts and
techniques, the testing of his methods and the development
of his ideas, just as surely as J. Ross Browne's *Etchings
of a Whaling Cruise* and others contributed their blubber
to the book.

Examination of these five books reveals the way and the
degree to which they demonstrate one of the main concerns

---

1. Quoted in Merrell E. Davis and William H. Gilman, *The Letters of Herman Melville*
(New Haven, 1960), p. 125.

that gripped Melville throughout his adult life—his
questioning man's role in the universe—and the way he
answered the question with an affirmation of his faith in
life. *Moby-Dick* and the books which follow it reveal a
continuation of this philosophy no matter how gloomy the
surface appearance. Melville's affirmation was not with
himself, not with God or the universe. Instead it was with
what William Ellery Sedgwick called the "destiny which
binds us all together" in one common fate—with, in other
words, belief in the value, dignity, and worth of the human
being and, beyond that, in the human race. Melville
believed, as William Faulkner was to say in his Nobel
Prize speech in 1950, man must and will prevail simply
because there is nothing else for him to do, and because
innately he is worthy of prevailing and has the qualities
by which he can ultimately triumph.

There is no other course and no greater hope. If Melville's
works contained no other elements—and there are
always multiplicities of numerous rich elements—this
affirmation of hope would make them as we shall now see,
rewarding experiences.

TYPEE: THE LURE OF EDEN

Typee (1846) was published just two years after Melville
returned from his voyage into the south seas. This voyage
had begun in 1841 on the whaler *Acushnet* and had
included the adventures Melville was to describe through
the next several books. *Typee* is more than a first book by
a romantic young writer. Melville, only twenty-two years
old and with a limited educational background, began his
race with the literary muse in a full dog-trot. *Typee* is a
rich, well-handled, firm book about a young man's
adventures in Eden—with his initial attraction and
eventual revulsion, with the author's realization that Edenic
life was too narrow, thin and incomplete to attract him
always—and is a well-informed comparison of civilized and

heathen cultures.[2] But, most germane to our purposes, it also contains the embryos of ideas about man and universe, man and man that would trouble Melville all his life. Though these ideas are still embryonic they demonstrate the bent, as well as the potential strength, of Melville's mind.

There were good reasons for the power and bias of this young mind. Melville was the son of two proud families whose fortunes had never prospered. His early years had been made difficult by the fact that after the early death of his father and the subsequent state of half-dependency cast upon the mother, Melville had been incurably scarred by his own fortunes. These reverses forced him to shorten sail on expectations and to be prepared for something less than the full-speed momentum enjoyed by his more prosperous though no more deserving fellow Americans. He was buffeted from one job to another, and finally pushed to the sea in order to support himself. He bitterly resented having to forego the development of his eager and profound mind in formal college. The whaling ship was his Harvard and Yale, as he said in *Moby-Dick*. Though he matriculated in the college of hardest knocks, in which graduates into success were fewer than those into failure, Melville's mind soaked up experience, and in reacting to it grew observant and strong.

One of Melville's strongest affirmations of humanism was his outrage at man's injustice to, and abuse of, his fellow man. Melville's mind was always near the boiling point on this subject , and he was eager to fight tyranny whenever he encountered it. He was quick therefore in *Typee* to rebel against the despotic captain of the *Dolly*, in a situation similar to that which had actually prevailed aboard the *Acushnet*, whose tyrannizing extended also to mistreatment of the sick, the captain believing the only cure for any man's complaints was the "butt end of a handspike."

The tyranny of such captains extends from their crews to the natives of the various islands, and Melville's dislike

2. For a general discussion of this broad topic see R. W. B. Lewis, *The American Adam* (Chicago, 1955).

of all forms of vicious behavior includes this mistreatment of primitives. In the eyes of "civilized" society, natives can be mistreated by all, petty trader or grand captain. But let these "savages" defend themselves, and Europe howls revenge.

Melville's attitude toward arbitrary and tyrannical power was again made manifest in a comparison of the institutions of the Marquesas Islands with those of Tahiti and Hawaii. On these other islands government had been despotic and extreme. It was death or disfigurement to approach the rulers. In the Marquesas, on the contrary, the king and the palace are of a "most simple and Patriarchal nature. . . and wholly unattended by the ceremonious pomp which usually surrounds the purple." There was little government exercised throughout the Typees, and social peace reigned. How was this accomplished? "It must have been by an inherent principle of honesty and charity towards each other." [3]

Another early and firm manifestation of Melville's humanism was his compulsive effort to find satisfactory answers to his numerous questions about religion. Even early he found little evidence of and satisfaction in the conventional concept of God and expectation in His religion on earth. Consequently, as early as *Typee* Melville tried to minimize the value of regular religion, to bring it down from heaven to earth, and to humanize it. He approvingly reports that religion on Typee was not overly valued. Sometimes, however, the natives' treatment of religious figures and rituals was more like that of an older brother for a juvenile, a father for a son, a superior for an inferior, or of a master for a servant. The degree to which the Typees have humanized their religion is revealed to Melville when Kolory, "Lord Primate of Typee," handles Moa Artua, "the baby-god," with the greatest affection and disdain, and Kory-Kory, Melville's companion, growing angry with a

3. For ease of reference for all readers and because of the numerous editions of Melville's works available and the brevity of each chapter, I give my references by chapters, not page number. These quotations are found in Chapter IV.

god's statue for falling on him, rigorously tweaks his nose. Melville, though obviously startled by such behavior, clearly approves of the act. Such assumption of equality with the gods is proper for man though surely it overturns Victorian standards of behavior.

Melville's treatment of sex in *Typee* also runs counter to Victorian standards. Melville tries to humanize sex, to naturalize it, to accord it its proper place in life but to strip from it its long skirts of prudery and its corsets of up-rightness. In this effort Melville treats sex in two ways. In the first, he refuses to include it, though in his shyness at stepping over the bounds of acceptability he sometimes becomes coy, even leering. There are, for example, the double veiled allusions to the relationship between Tommo (Melville) and his "favorite" native, the beautiful Fayaway. Only by reading between the lines—which is not diffi-cult—can a person penetrate the disguise and guess at the real relationship between this man and woman.

At other times Melville openly defies Victorian hypoc-risies about sex, though in *Typee* this usage is rarer than it will be in later books. In one instance, which looks forward to the open statements of *Moby-Dick* and the only slightly cloaked ones in *Pierre* and "*The Tartarus of Maids*," he minces no words, referring to the "flinty bits of biscuit which generally go by the name of 'mid-shipmen's nuts'" (CH. VI).

Humor, which may or may not be associated with sex, is the great democratizer. Nobody used it with greater grin or more obvious enjoyment than Melville. From his earliest works he used humor for its own sake with obvious relish, sometimes as a tickler—not infrequently with a leer; but primarily he used it as a lash to beat pomp and hypocrisy. Often he works out his humor in the style of the American frontier, that is, both "high" and "low" humor and with under-and overstatement. Sometimes sheer exuberance of spirit unleashes restraint so fully that all types simply cas-cade over themselves. In all uses, especially in those which

13

beat down sham and fraud, Melville demonstrates the commonness of all men.

The most superficial type which relies on verbal play and lightness of spirit is well illustrated in *Typee* when the author is describing the "five hideous old wretches" who live in the house in the highly tabooed "hoolah hoolah" ground. Melville notes that their toes, "like the radiating lines of the mariner's compass, pointed to every quarter of the horizon" (CH. XXIV).

Even broader humor is given as the *coup de grace* to a serious discussion of democracy and the comicality of royalty. Mowanna, the king of Nukuheva, and his "beauteous wife" are invited aboard the *Dolly*, as a proper gesture to their rank, But, as usual, royalty looks better and more serious from a distance than up close. The king has an appearance "certainly calculated to produce an effect," properly arrayed in all magnificence. But there is one "slight blemish." He has a "broad patch of tattooing stretched completely across his face, in a line with his eyes, making him look as if he wore a huge pair of goggles; and royalty in goggles suggested some ludicrous ideas," But his queen's behaviour is even more suggestive to Melville. On board the ship she is intrigued by an old salt who is tatooed all over. Approaching him, she caresses the tatoos, opening the bosom of his frock in order to investigate further—to the acute embarrassment of the French. Then she performed a gesture that Melville was to use later in *Redburn* and *Moby-Dick*, one straight from vaudeville and minstrelsy. The queen, "eager to display the hieroglyphics on her own sweet form, bent forward for a moment, and turning sharply round, threw up the skirts of her mantle, and revealed a sight from which the aghast Frenchmen retreated precipitately" (CH. I).

Melville's mind pulsated with man's love for mankind. One aspect of life on board the *Dolly* that made existence bearable was the friendly association, the comradeliness, of the sailors. Though the men varied in quality, at least they had humanity in common. When Toby and Tommo desert

ship they are aware of their separation from other people.
Being thrown away from their comrades, Toby, feeling this
loss more quickly than Tommo, wants the two companions
wandering in alien country, to keep "close together." As
they wonder about which tribe they will come across, the
cannibalistic Typees or the friendly Happars, they hope for
the latter, not only because they prefer not to be eaten but
also because the Happars will provide them with human
friendliness, something that the French and missionaries
would not give.

Melville's powerful affirmative response to the call of humanity is further revealed in the book when later he is talking against the anti-humanistic practice in civilized countries of developing "death dealing engines." He comments
on civilized man's "remorseless cruelty" in the United States
where people are too "chicken-hearted" to destroy man by
execution and yet resort to far greater cruelty by condemning
them "to perpetual solitude in the very heart of our population" (CH. XVII).

Melville's further commitment to the earth and to people
is half comically but altogether seriously flashed forth in his
comment to Kory-Kory, the native who acted as his man
Friday. When asked if he would not like to go to his heaven,
Kory-Kory responded in the negative. Melville ponders
Kory-Kory's desire to stay on this earth and "cannot sufficiently admire his shrewdness" (CH. XXIV).

Finally, Melville's bonds of comradeship have grown
quickly and strongly. Although he has lived among the alien
Typees only a few months, he leaves them reluctantly. All the
natives in this valley were one happy family "bound together
by the ties of strong affection." Therefore when the opportunity to flee his captivity comes he feels the compulsion to
go but also regret at leaving these people who have been
friendly with him and whom he never expects to see again.
Melville is therefore pulled between two opposing forces—
the romantic, exotic and ideal, and the unromantic, pragmatic and real. More important, however, he realizes the

evasiveness, the unengageability of life in this Garden of Eden. He feels that because he knows about his world outside this Eden he would in effect shirk his duty unless he returned to it, joined it, and engaged it in necessary conflict. The lure of greater engagement among larger armies and issues—with all of humanity—pulled Melville, though he came reluctantly from his paradise. Thus early and firmly are established the outlines of the humanism he is to develop later.

OMOO: YOUNG FURY LOOSED

Self-driven from paradise because, like Milton's Adam, he preferred humanity to isolation, engagement with the problems and, perhaps, triumphs of people rather than protection from them, Melville picks up in his second book, *Omoo* (1847), his theme of humanism. Its several facets were already clearly established in *Typee* and are advanced clearly and firmly in this book.

Omoo, a continuation of the author's adventures after he left the Typee valley on the English ship *Julia*, is superior to its predecessor. It lacks, to be sure, *Typee's* sustaining suspense of having characters cast on an island with natives who might be cannibals and the romantic idyl of living in a hidden valley with peaceful primitives. But *Omoo* is more powerful in ideas and meditation, in technique and development. The main themes of humanism are more richly evolved and they more firmly forecast Melville's later thinking about man's role in the world. The adventures are more roundly commented on, praise and criticism of various aspects of life are more fully developed, and the characters are more richly inked in, especially in the development of the hero—an effort that was to become through the years virtually an obsession.

Melville's reaction in this book against tyranny is just as instantaneous and far-reaching as it had been in *Typee*.

16 BEFORE *MOBY-DICK*

About one type of cruelty and tyranny—flogging—Melville's attitude is clear. With the nature of sailors what it was and the need for discipline great, Melville admitted the necessity of flogging in the American or English style, where a man or boy was not "punished beyond his strength." But Melville makes his position clear. "War being the greatest of evils, all its accessories necessarily partake of the same character; and this is about all that can be said in defence of flogging" (CH. XXIX).

Melville's humor is more widely and deeply developed in *Omoo* than it had been in *Typee*. Again it depends partially on understatement. Like sailors and soldiers everywhere and everytime, he found the food on the *Julia* unbearable. The barrels of pork "looked as if preserved in iron rust." The beef was tough and tasteless, and Melville "almost believed the cook's story of a horse's hoof with the shoe on having been fished up out of the pickle of one of the casks." The "shot soup" which they had every day consisted of "great round peas, polishing themselves like pebbles by rolling about in tepid water" (CH. III).

The humor depends more on overstatement, frontier-like exaggeration, a type of humor which through the years was to grow larger and more important in Melville's work in general and especially in his development of the theme of humanism. On board the *Julia*, as on all whalers that had long been at sea, rats and roaches were rampant. "The business of eating and drinking was better done in the dark than in the light of day." The sailors live among the vermin rather than the vermin among them.

The cockroaches were so numerous and brave that "every night they had a jubilee," and during the ten minutes of this jubilee when "no hive ever hummed louder," it was safer to be on deck than in the forecastle. Melville tells how a rat was found in the tin can of molasses which nevertheless tasted sweet, no matter how long the rat had been dead in it. Melville caps his account with a kind of crude working on the reference that he would bring to beautiful fruition in *Moby-Dick*, when Tashtego falls into the sperm of the spermaceti whale: "The creature certainly died a luscious death" (CH. X).

Another episode in *Moby-Dick* is humorously anticipated here in the account of the absence of whales. The mate, unconcerned, carelessly observes that soon the ship would be sailing through so many whales that lookouts would not be necessary and whales would be so numerous and tame that they would make "a practice of coming round ships, and scratching their backs against them" (CH. XII).

Doctor Long Ghost is a naval Davy Crockett, able to exaggerate with the best in the tradition of the American frontier. When, for example, Melville proposed that he and his wandering partner settle down in Tamai, Long Ghost burst into a Crockett-like harangue: "I'll put up a banana-leaf as a physician from London—deliver lectures on Polynesian antiquities—teach English in five lessons, of one hour each—establish power-looms for the manufacture of tappa—lay out a public park in the middle of the village, and found a festival in honour of Captain Cook!" (CH. LXV).

One of the obvious improvements of *Omoo* over *Typee* and an omen of the later development on Melville's works was making the book greater than life, turning it into the adventure of heroes and demigods. Melville does this in several ways. He makes it clear from the beginning that Doctor Long Ghost is unusual. He has all the hero's characteristics. His "early history, like that of many other heroes, was enveloped in the profoundest obscurity." He is a Kentuckian, one of the "tall men." Another superman was Lem Hardy, the Englishman who had gone ashore permanently and become the military leader of a tribe "and war-god of the entire island." His "campaigns beat Napoleon's." Like heroes everywhere, he was a foundling, he was friendless and scorned by everyone. Too, the monarch of Tahiti "claimed to be a sort of by-blow of Tatorroa, the Saturn of the Polynesian mythology, and cousin-german to interior deities." Further, the flight of Melville and Long Ghost is called a "hegira" in an effort to throw over it religious and heroic atmosphere and proportions.

In *Omoo* folklore plays an important function. It fleshes out the sinews of sailor life. The burial of two men at sea, for example, calls forth numerous tales. Though Melville says he does not believe them, he relates one told by the carpenter that struck him forcefully. Interestingly, this story, told without any moralizing, was to be developed later in *Moby-Dick* with great implications. In *Omoo* Melville tells only how after a fever aboard on a voyage to India, phantoms were seen in the yard-arms ends, and "voices called aloud from the tops." Sailors were nearly pushed from the rigging "by an unseen hand; and his shipmate swore that a wet hammock was flirted in his face" (CH. XII). This wet hammock was later used to great dramatic effect in *White-Jacket*.

In *Omoo*, too, Melville begins building and enlarging the supernatural wisdom of the Scandinavian oracle-like character that was to continue through most of his works. Here it is Van, a Finn. Finns, according to seamen, "are regarded with peculiar superstition" because they "possess the gift of second sight, and the power to wreak supernatural vengeance upon those who offend them." On the night after the burial of the two seamen, this remarkable man, Van, "laid his hand on the old horse-shoe nailed as a charm to the fore-mast" (forecasting the doubloon in *Moby-Dick*) and predicted that in less than three weeks "not one quarter of our number would remain aboard the ship," a prediction which "produced a marked effect" (CH. XII).

All effects in this book add up to an affirmation of Melville's belief in democracy. Perhaps nowhere is it better illustrated than in the account of the queen's consort being called "Pot Belly" because he "carried the

19

greater part of his person before him to be sure; and so did the gentlemanly George IV."

Thus *Omoo* carries on the earlier themes of *Typee*. It does not show Melville at his best, but it clearly reveals the themes of humanism which increasingly through the years will grip him.

MARDI: TORN BETWEEN TWO WORLDS

Mardi (1849), a transitional book between the kind Melville began with and could write easily and the type he wanted to create, is artistically a botch, as freakish as some of the birds he would later describe in the stories about the Encantadas, beautiful in their parts but grotesque when they tried to combine their parts into those of a real bird and fly. In this work Melville is an immature bird trying too soon to fly into abstract symbolism and merely getting confused.

Mardi begins as a conventional Melville tale of his experiences in the South Pacific, full of clearly narrated adventure, jokes, and humor, with comments of various kinds. But halfway through, it switches from actual voyage to voyage as technique—a quest for the maiden Yillah, who is only a shadow of a symbol. This abrupt shift can be explained only as the point at which Melville tired of writing the kind of narrative that had earned him the name of "the man who lived among the cannibals," and changed to that kind he wanted to do but, as he later complained to Hawthorne, would not pay.

The first half, the straight narrative, is direct and clear. The second portion, which swings into the symbolic quest, is weird, often unintelligible. The symbolism, though clear in outline, is confusing in detail because the individual symbols are too arcane, vague, and mystical to be followed or to be considered worth following. Ostensibly a voyage to try to locate the vanished maiden Yillah, obviously the goal of heart's desire, and a fending off of the bitch goddess Hautia, the technique allows Melville to travel throughout the world and to comment on all aspects of life. But *in toto* the episodes do not add up to a coherent pattern except as adventures strung out on a makeshift journey. In technique, further, Melville's plan, similar to that which was later used in *Clarel*, is to allow numerous speakers who accompany him, and who represent different biases and points of view, to voice opinions, with which the author sometimes agrees. But at times they change their opinions or contradict themselves, so that at any given moment it is virtually impossible to know precisely the author's attitude. Instead, Melville's opinion must be mined from the mother lode of interminable talk with which the book, a veritable volcano of verbosity, abounds.

Despite the book's flaws, however, humanism continues to be developed along lines we saw in *Typee* and *Omoo* and which we will see in later works. But this work differs in conclusion from all the others. It breaks out of humanism into anti-humanism, a false humanism, or false Prometheanism. Unlike *Moby-Dick*, to which it is in many ways close, which grows from anti-humanism in the person of Ahab to real humanism in the person of Ishmael, *Mardi* works through humanism and ends in the person of Taji—who is a forerunner of Ahab—in a conclusion quite the opposite of that of the later and greater work.

Mardi begins in and continues to the last concerned with the various strains of humanism which are developed in Melville's other books. There is here, as elsewhere, a strong vein of humor, both broad and narrow, which advances the theme. In the former kind, Jarl, the old illiterate Skyeman who accompanied Taji when he abandoned ship, can laconically drop droll remarks. "Man and Boy," he says, "I have lived ever since I can remember." Melville at another time can develop delightfully a joke through understatement. When Taji and Jarl are floating in their open boat and because their biscuits are so hard they are inedible they dip them into sea-water, Melville remarks: "This plan obviated finger glasses at the conclusion of our repast" (CHS. III, XIV).

Understatement is frequently braced with its opposite, developed with the gusto of an American frontier minstrel Jonathan Swift. Sometimes it depends on sexual grotesqueness for effect. Little Peepi, the ruler of Valapee, is only the flimiest cover for scatalogy. The little ruler, hardly ten years old, dressed only in a string of shells in his hair, rides "striding the neck of a burly mute, bearing a long spear erect before him to which was attached a canopy of five broad banana leaves, new plucked." To this lad, who supposedly "inherited the valiant spirits of some twenty heroes, sages, simpletons, and demigods," homage is paid in a curious way, in the court ceremony of the pupera, in which people trying to stand on their noses assumed the "erect posture, the nasal organ the base." The grotesqueness is further exaggerated in a minstrel comment on the way the island chiefs leave the presence of royalty "with their heads between their thighs so that advancing in the contrary direction, their faces might be still deferentially turned toward their lord and master" (CH. LXVII).

Folklore references also strengthen the humanistic fiber of the book. Omens play a great role here, as they do throughout Melville. In the little boat on the open sea, Taji and Jarl are followed by a shark and his retinue of remoras. The shark is killed, but the pilot fish then transfer to the boat, with one under the keel. Jarl looks upon this happening as a good omen, and "no harm will befall us so long as they stay." And they did follow "until an event occurred which necessitated their withdrawal" (CH. XVIII). Later, Somoa, the husband of the shrewish Annattoo with whom the travelers journey for a while, had his arm cut off by Annattoo but would not bury it at sea in the customary way. He hung it from the topmast because he felt that to bury it at sea would mean that "he must very soon drown and follow it" (CH. XXIV). Finally, Melville used folklore to enrich history, in the diverting tale called "A Nursery Tale of

Ballalanja's," which is a South Sea version of the old tale of nine blind men trying to determine the true characteristics of the elephant.

More important to the book's main theme are the various political allusions. In commenting on the real value of a man, and the sham value of a king on a throne, Melville is effectively ironic. Discussing Media, king of Odo, Melville rhapsodizes how a king on a throne is a "fine sight to see," looking "very much like a god." "Man lording it over man, man kneeling to man, is a spectacle that Gabriel might well travel hitherward to behold, for never did he behold it in heaven." A king sitting on his throne is "Jupiter nodding in the councils of Olympus, Satan seen among the coronets in hell" (CH. LX).

Melville turns from ridiculing King Media to examination of his land and rule, and his cursing of the citizens of this country. The people were "serfs. And few of them could choose but be the brutes they seemed." "Their men were scourged; their crime, a heresy, the heresy that Media was no demigod." Melville predicts revolution: "The pit that's dug for us may prove another's grave" (CH. LXIII).

The threat of revolution is developed further later. In Dominora they witness the revolt of the poor, crying for bread and for the elimination of landlords and of wrongs. When this revolt is subdued by traitors in their midst who wear masks for anonymity and deceit, Melville ironically remarks, "Thus our Lord Bellow rewards all those who do him a service, for hire betray their kith and their kin" (CH. XLVIII).

In Franko (France) another political revolution is likened to a bursting volcano. Babbalanja, probably speaking Melville's hope, says that perhaps the lesson of revolution in · Franko can benefit the future of Porpheero (Ireland): "It may be that Porpheero's future has been cheaply won" (CH. CLIII).

In America (Vivenza) Melville's sharpest criticism about politics is unsheathed. On the "helmeted female, the tutelar deity of Vivenza" are inscribed the words "In-this-re-pub-li-can-land-all-men-are-born-free-and-equal" and further down in print very minute, "Except-the-tribe-of-Hamo." Melville's attack continues when the travelers are told by a jingoistic native, "We are all kings here," which statement is commented on by the "hieroglyphical notices" on the porch of Congress which are "offering rewards for missing men, so many hands high" (CHS. CLVII, XLVIII).

Americans of the West (Hio Hio) hold the hope of America—an opinion shared by such people as Thoreau and Emerson. Against the South, Melville's criticism is bitter. Are the slaves men with souls? he asks. He denounces Nulli—Calhoun—and others without reservation.

But Melville was not a rabid revolutionary. He felt that restraint or caution at least, must be used: "Freedom is only good as a means, is no end in itself" (CH. CLX).

Closely tied in with the political statements are those affirming the importance of life. By quitting the ship *Arcturion*, Taji and his companion Jarl avoid death. On their luck Melville comments: "Life is sweet to all; death comes as hard." Again, on their open boat, Melville reaffirms his feeling about the finality of death: "There is but little difference in the manner of dying. To die is all" (CH. VII).

But *Mardi* is much more anti-humanistic than humanistic. Taji—Melville—is humanistic until he encounters Yillah. But Yillah is of "more than terrestrial origin"; after meeting her, Taji becomes obsessed with this demi-goddess and therefore becomes a monomaniac, like Ahab, denying humanism, even attempting to destroy it. Yillah is Taji's female savior, but unlike the Chola widow in sketch eight of "The Encantadas," who represents the real human savior through suffering, Yillah is the false savior and seduces Taji into his own destruction. At the end of the book, when all the adventurers have come to Serenia (serenity) and discovered that they would rather reside there than seek the illusive symbol further, Babbalanja correctly

characterizes Yillah to Taji: "She is a phantom that but
mocks thee." But Taji, mad with his monomania, will not
listen. He is "fixed as fate," "the hunter that never rests!"
And he drags his companions on, asserting more and more
his anti-humanism: "My heart grew hard like flint, and
black like night, and sounded hollow to the hand I
clinched . . . I prayed not, but blasphemed." Finally
abandoned by his companions; whom he of necessity cast
off, Taji in his supreme instance of anti-humanism becomes
his "own soul's emperor." His "first act is abdication." He
turns the prow of his boat out to its own destruction, still
pursued by the furies: "And thus, pursuers and pursued flew
on over an endless sea" (CH. CLXXIX).

REDBURN: INNOCENCE IN A CRUEL WORLD

As Melville's art and main theme in *Mardi* swung
radically, blasted by the uncontrollable convulsion of his
very nature, in *Redburn* (1849), his fourth book, the
pendulum returned to its wonted course, again arcing
through the various phases of Melville's concern with
man's life on earth. Melville also returned to the
techniques he had successfully employed in his first two
books, that of recounting actual experience in a way that
every reader could understand.

But, as usual with Melville's books, underneath the
surface of *Redburn* there is much more than meets the
casual eye. Artistically and thematically it is the most
successful of Melville's books to date, more searching,
more probing, more promising in its fuller examination
of the human plight than the earlier books had been.
Innocence is treated roughly by a cruel adult world, yet
innocence can but grow with experience, and in the process
shed constricting layers of naiveté which prevent
complete commitment of life and to humanity; and
complete commitment to and consequent examination of
and compassion for life are the only narrow straits
leading into full existence.

65084

Wellingborough Redburn is Melville's first attempt to portray the child, the naif, the innocent, receiving education through experience. As Taji, in *Mardi,* is a pre-study for Ahab, Redburn is an initial canvas for White-Jacket—who is a pre-study for Ishmael—though the degree to which Redburn is sophisticated is infinitely less than that achieved by White-Jacket or Ishmael. Redburn sets out on his trip, like Ishmael, troubled in mind. He is a youthful misanthrope, frustrated and a failure, and "there is no misanthrope like a boy disappointed." Unlike Ishmael, Redburn is a long time being educated out of his bigotry. He hates the people in their "comfortable house, [who] . . . were taking their sunrise naps heedless of the way-farer passing" (CH. II). When he goes to New York to catch the ship to Liverpool, Redburn, like Pierre later on, feels alienated. He sees pawnshop operators as "hook-nosed" and therefore rascally. As well as being against Jews, Redburn is also against Negroes, or at least aware of their difference. He hesitates to drink from a glass that a Negro has just used, though to a certain extent Redburn's reluctance springs from the fact that the Negro was drinking spirits and therefore had left a bad taste in the glass. Later on, the ship's Negro cook looks so "cross and ugly" that he frightens the boy. Subsequently, when miserable almost beyond endurance, Redburn complains that he is being mistreated by "vulgar and brutal men lording it over" him as if he were no better than "an African in Alabama" (CH. XIII). Redburn's feeling of alienation is carried to Liverpool, where in his outlandish hunting jacket he presented such a grotesque figure that people made fun of him—as the sailors had on the ship on the way over—and shunned him.

This book, as usual with Melville's writings, is strengthened with folklore and frontier exaggeration. On the trip over to Liverpool, Redburn superstitiously believes that his is an "ill-omened voyage," as indeed it turns out to be. More important, the book is flecked with jokes and frontier humor. In a fine understatement typical of heroes, Redburn says that he shakes his hair "out to windward over the bulwarks every evening." With his tendency to touch upon the sexual, a tendency that at times reaches almost the leering, Melville tells about Redburn climbing the ropes and exposing his underwear, his "table linen," to the gaze of the other sailors.

He swings from understatement to frontier exaggeration. He recounts how pigs have been used by ship's captains in dense fog to warn ships by their squealing and thus save the ship, "as geese saved the Capitol." With a flair for verbal gymnastics typical of frontier humor, Melville has Larry, one of the sailors, refer to "Crinkumcrankum whales" that "can't be cotched." Melville's most obvious and most effective touch of this kind of humor is the minstrel gesture—which he was to use with greater mystification in *Moby-Dick*—given at the end of the book, when the sailors show their contempt for their former captain by turning their posteriors at him in a kind of anal Shanghai gesture.

The most overriding theme in the book is Melville's development of love of humanity. Redburn begins in the pose of hating the human race but ends in its opposite. Melville's attitude is framed between the two limits of these attitudes. Jackson is a figure of anti-humanism, a study in depravity, later to grow into such figures as Bland and Claggart. He is also the figure bigger than life, the Satanic hero. Melville uses the classic and conventional folkloristic and mythological techniques to build him up. Jackson claims kinship with the great, saying he is a "near relation of General Jackson." Also he looks different, as heroes always do. He looks devilish: his eyes snap "something like a forked tongue." He is as dignified as Tiberius. Thus Jackson stands alone and friendless in the world. He tyrannizes the crew in an effort to disguise or compensate for his natural depravity and aloneness. The sailor world is therefore indifferent to his fate when his disease finally causes his death.

Opposed to the Satanic anti-humanism of Jackson, the book throughout fairly throbs with Melville's sympathy for the sailors of the world. But he sees them and all of life clearly and without blind preference.

Not wanting to whitewash the character of the average sailor, Melville states plainly that the majority are marked by "sensualism of character, ignorance, and depravity"; but their character results from the fact that "they are generally friendless and alone in the world." Melville's hope for the sailor is Christian humanism: "We feel and we know that God is the true Father of all, and that none of his children are without the pale of His care" (CH. XXVIII).

Emphasis on the "of all" is developed further only a few pages later. Turning to the figure of the parliament of us all, a figure that is to recur often in his works (notably in *Billy Budd*), Melville speaks of the symbol of the ships in the harbor at Liverpool: "In the collective spars and timbers of these ships all the forest of the globe are represented, as in a grand parliament of masts." Here, "under the beneficent spar of the Genius of Commerce, all climes and countries embrace; and yard-arm touches yard-arm in brotherly love" (CH. XXXIII).

Christian humanism again asserts the democracy of us all. Churches, Melville says, should "remind the commonest wayfarer of his heaven," and God should be equally accessible to and heard by "all of His children." One of Melville's most outraged blasts comes from the treatment accorded a mother and her two children found in Lancelott's-Hey. Driven there by cold and hunger, the mother huddles under the grating below the street with her two infants, one dead and other dying. They have been pushed out and kept away by the indifference of their fellow human beings, who are callous to the "endless wail of someone forever lost" issuing from the pit. Melville's indignation over the callousness becomes enraged: "Were they not human beings? A woman and two girls? With eyes, and lips, and ears like any queen? With hearts which, though they did not bound with blood, yet beat with a dull, dead ache that was their life." He ponders further: "Surrounded as we are by the pains and woes of our fellow-men, and yet given to follow our own pleasures, regardless of their pains, are we not like people sitting up with a corpse, and making merry in the house of the dead?"

The general misery of the world prompts him to pray, significantly, not to God, but to the earthly parents of us all: "Adam and Eve! If indeed ye are yet alive in heaven, may it be no part of your immortality to look down upon the world ye have left" (CH. XXXVIII).

Melville, though strongly pro-American, is not blindly xenophobic. He thinks that poverty in England may result from the lack of suffrage, and thus conditions are better in America. But not all is perfect in America. Conditioned as he was to American prejudice against Negroes, Redburn is astonished to see how much better they are treated in England; and the degree of this astonishment reveals the amount of change that has come over Redburn during the experience of this brief voyage: "At first I was surprised that a coloured man should be treated as he is in this town; but a little reflection showed that, after all, it was but recognising his claims to humanity and normal equality" (CH. XLI).

The ambivalence of man's treatment of man is further revealed in the fate of the emigrants on Redburn's ship, and all ships in general. Forced to huddle amidships in foul and closed quarters, often wet, nearly always hungry, never allowed to clean themselves, and subject to all kinds of resulting diseases, these emigrants are horribly exploited by the captain and ship-owners, brutalized by the sailors, and despised by the wealthier travellers on the ship. Melville rages over their mistreatment. He insists that these emigrants cannot be kept out of America. Equal to all, they have "God's right to come."

Melville rounds off his comment on the emigrants, on world-wide rights of people, and on justice in general: "We talk of the Turks and abhor the cannibals; but may not some of *them* go to heaven before some of *us?*" (CH. LVIII).

The theme here as throughout the book is fundamentally what it was in *Typee* and *Omoo*. Melville is still contrasting so-called civilized life with that of the rebuked infidel and the cannibal, insisting that theirs is no worse than his. In fact often theirs is superior. When superior, it rises above his because of its concern with the facts of life in a real world. Those people are not blind "to the real sights of this world"; are not "deaf to its voice"; are not "dead to its death." Melville is saying that the proper study of man is mankind, that the first love of man should be man. Only after man has conquered worldly travails will he begin to achieve his potential. Then Christianity will begin to accomplish its purpose, part of which is making us better citizens of this world.

WHITE-JACKET: THUNDER AGAINST TYRANNY

White-Jacket, (1850), published only one year after *Mardi* and *Redburn*, continues to center on Melville's actual adventures on a ship. This time he recounts his experiences on the frigate *Unites States*, on which he had sailed from Tahiti and on which he had remained fourteen months, finally to be discharged in Boston in the fall of 1844. *White-Jacket* is to *Redburn* what *Omoo* was to *Typee*. Less spontaneous, less threaded with narrative of adventure, less energized by innocence and naiveté, and more larded with long passages of sermonizing and exposition, it is nevertheless grander in design and richer in execution than *Redburn* was. The symbol of the hunting jacket which made Redburn stand out from the crowd, at times the object of opprobrium, has in *White-Jacket* matured into the infinitely more complex and powerful white coat which here also sets the wearer apart from the mass of humanity until its loss allows him to merge back into humanity as a whole. Increasingly in Melville's subsequent books, this contrast between the individual and the whole human race will become one of the major subjects. *White-Jacket* throbs with Melville's concern for the world, society, and for humanity.

Melville's techniques are essentially those he had used earlier and would use later. But there are modifications and shifts.

White-Jacket is less a book of frontier humor, jokes, and folklore in general than its predecessors were. Folklore in this book is used almost exclusively to develop the folklore-mythology concept of the hero. Here the nominal hero is Jack Chase, who had been the admired and beloved real figure on board the *United States* when Melville sailed on it. The importance of Chase as real person and symbol to Melville is revealed by the fact that Melville dedicated *Moby-Dick* to him later and drew upon him at least partially for the figure of Bulkington in that book and for the longer development of the main character in *Billy Budd*, as well as other partial portraits in other works.

Chase is the typical hero of mythology and folklore. He has all the characteristics, as Melville makes explicitly clear. He is the "noble first captain of the top," who is "loved by seamen, and admired by the officers." His hero's mark is the absence of a finger on the left hand. Another bit of evidence of his heroic quality is the feeling held by men in general that he must have been a "byblow of some British Admiral of the Blue." When he is brought back aboard the *Neversink* from the Peruvian ship to which he had deserted in order to aid in the "civil commotions of Peru, and befriend, heart and soul, what he deemed the cause of the Right" (as a folkloristic hero always does), he is metamorphosed into a Christ-like heroic figure. His shipmates divide "his laced hat and coat among them, and on their shoulders carried him in triumph along the gun-deck." Significantly, Chase is a man of the people, as heroes

31

invariably are, as he tells Lemsford the poet, distinguishing between the public and the people and associating himself definitely with the latter: "The public and the people! Ay, ay, . . . let us hate the one, and cleave to the other"

There are other heroes and would-be heroes on board the *Neversink*. Captain Claret tries to be one. He "deemed it indispensable religiously to sustain his dignity." But "apart from the common dignity of manhood, commodores . . . possess no real dignity at all" (CH. VI). Melville uses both the captain and the admiral in his demonstration of the triumph of humanism over its opposite.

Bland, the dastardly man-at-arms, detested as well as feared by all, is also of heroic proportions, with the obvious signs of his Satanic grandeur. He is "neat and gentlemanly" and "broke his bisquit with a dainty hand." "There was a fine polish about his whole person, and a pliant, insinuating style in his conversation that was, socially, quite irresistible." Except for Chase, whose companionability was one sign of his heroic stature, Bland was "the most companionable man in the mess." His mouth "was somewhat small, Moorish-arched, and wickedly delicate, and his snaky, black eye, that at times shone like a dark lantern in a jewellery-shop at midnight, betokened the accomplished scoundrel within." He avoided swearing and oaths. This Mephistopheles, as Melville calls him, this "organic and irreclaimable scoundrel, who did wicked deeds as the cattle browse the herbage, because wicked deeds seemed the legitimate operation of his whole soul," who "phrenologically" was "without a soul," points up both the hazards of the common sailors and their restraint. For despite the fact that Bland had abused and exploited them, when he was dashed from his pedestal of power into their midst, they forebore, though often under such circumstances sailors had served such scoundrels "as Origin served himself, or as his enemies served Abelard" (CH. XLIV), that is, by castration.

The most important theme in *White-Jacket*, however, is the conflict between the officers on the *Neversink* and the

sailors, or *the people*, as Melville calls them with emphasis.
Melville frames the discussion between two pictures—that
of the common man, the sailors, and that of the anti-
humanists, the officers.

The commodore and the other officers overemphasize
dignity, which is, they feel, necessary to the holding of
their offices. "True, it is expedient for crowned heads,
generalissimos, lord high admirals, and commodores, to
carry themselves straight, and beware of the spinal com-
plaint" (CH. VI), but Melville's irony cuts deeply. Captain
Claret is a "martinet," who causes all kinds of misery through
his use of forms and because he wants to "strike subjection
among the crew" (CH. VI). Claret flogs a boy, saying he
"would not forgive God Almighty" (CH. XXXIII). But Melville
later says, "conscious imbecility in power often seeks to
carry off that imbecility by assumptions of lordly severity"
(CH. XXXVI). In "all despotic governments, it is for the throne
and altar to go hand in hand" (CH. XXXVIII). Claret was "in-
dulgent to his crew, so long as they were perfectly docile."
Generally officers "scruple not to sacrifice an immortal man
or two, in order to show off the excelling discipline of the
ship. And thus do *the people* of the gun-deck suffer, that
the commodore on the poop may be glorified" (CH. XLVI).

Further, "constitutional monarchies and republics" always
"magnify the fiction" that the king can do no wrong, the
well-known "fiction of despotic states" (CH. XXXVII).

Contrasted with the commodores of the world and their
usurped rights and privileges are *the people* and their
natural rights. Melville takes up the case of the latter form
the very beginning, though he grants that a group of
sailors need discipline, for "were it not for these regula-
tions, a man-of-war's crew would be nothing but a
mob" (CH. III).

The political overtones of the book are thus clear from
the start. In describing the structure and personnel of a
man-of-war, Melville discusses the numerous anonymous and
lost persons who are on her, faceless until they are needed. But

33

"In time of tempests, when all hands are called to save ship, they issue forth into the gale like the mysterious old men of Paris during the massacre of the Three Days of September; every one marvels who they are, and whence they come; they disappear as mysteriously, and are seen no more until another general commotion" (CH. III). To a large extent Melville is here identifying these people with all the sailors, and with White-Jacket, Ishmael, and himself.

Jack Chase is both democrat and humanist. Though a "little bit of a dictator" in ordering his men around on the main-top, he believed that men were all "brothers." Chase's impulses were democratic. "Though bowing to naval discipline afloat, yet ashore he was a stickler for the Rights of Man and the liberties of the world" (CH. IV). He even deserts ship in order to fight for the liberty of Peru.

Melville criticizes the tyranny of the captains and the commodores as well as the foolishness of their practice by detailing the sham dignity accorded to the hours for eating on the man-of-war. Dining time is controlled by the rank of the diner. So "it will be seen that while the two estates of sea-kings and sea-lords dine at rather patrician hours—and thereby, in the long run, impair their direstive functions— the sea-commoners, or *the people*, keep up their constitutions by keeping up the good old-fashioned, Elizabethan, Franklin-warranted dinner hour of twelve" (CH. VII).

Conditions among the common lot of sailors are not best, but proper conditions can make such men better. In speaking against privilege, Melville thinks it is "a sweet thing" to observe officers admitting "human brotherhood." And the sailors perform just as well as the officers: "True heroism is not in the hand, but in the heart and the head." Consequently every "American sailor should be placed in such a position, that he might freely aspire to command a squadron of frigates" (CH. XXIII).

Melville thunders against flogging: "You see a human being, stripped like a slave; scourged worse than a hound. And for what? For things not essentially criminal, but only made so by arbitrary laws." Sailors should not be summarily punished. They should not be treated differently, "For him our Declaration of Independence is a lie." And a law should be "universal," and "include in its possible penal operations the very judge himself who gives decisions upon it." Flogging is "opposed to the essential dignity of man." He sounds his opposition in the "name of immortal manhood," and wishes "to God that every man who upholds this thing were scourged at the gangway till he recanted." "Conscious imbecility in power often seeks to carry off that imbecility by assumptions of lordly severity" (CHS. XXXIII, XXXV, XXXVI).

Melville is explicit here in a matter which will take on even greater importance in *Billy Budd*. Lord Nelson, whose name he continuously invokes, especially in *Billy Budd*, "was averse to flogging; and that, too, when he had witnessed the mutinous effect of government abuses in the Navy . . . and which, to the terror of all England, developed themselves at the great mutiny of the Nore" (CH. XXXVI).

Finally, as a conclusion and caution, Melville feels that the hope of the world lies in man himself. Here, as in *Moby-Dick*, his next book, Melville is ambivalent about the choice between individual man and collective men. Each has his role and function. From the captains and admirals and other despots of this world, there is no recourse. "We the people suffer many abuses." "Yet the worst of our evils we blindly inflict upon ourselves; our officers cannot remove them, even if they would. From the last ills no being can save another; therein each man must be his own saviour." But tied in with his belief and faith in the individual is the realization of the need for humanism: "Whatever befall us, let us never train our murderous guns inboard; let us not mutiny with bloody pikes in our hands." Then he turns to a kind of Christian humanism, which, however, seems out of character and more a public sop than a firmly held conviction. But it emphasizes both Christianity and humanity: "Our Lord High Admiral will yet interpose; and though long ages should elapse, and

35

leave our wrongs unredressed, yet shipmates and world-mates! let us never forget, that 'Life is a voyage that's homeward bound!'"(CH. "THE END").

Melville's explicit statements are strengthened with his symbols. The symbol of the white jacket is of paramount importance. The book begins with it. The first words are: "It was not a *very* white jacket, but white enough, in all conscience, as the sequel will show." White enough it surely was. A jacket made when Melville had no other, out of white sailor cloth, sewn into an outlandish utilitarian garment, it nevertheless set him off from all the other 500 men of the man-of-war. He was automatically and unthinkingly picked out from all crowds. "Let White-Jacket do it," became the favorite command. Thus, clearly, Melville's individuality became his plague, the price he had to pay for being an individual. Not painted black because the lieutenant would not allow paint, the jacket remains outstanding.

In this instance, as in others, *White-Jacket* is a pre-study for *Moby-Dick*. Falling into the water, from the starry heights of the main-most, White-Jacket almost sinks to the bottom. But he takes out his knife and rips his way out of the encumbrance, then rises rapidly to the surface and is saved. Newton Arvin believed this scene pictures Melville's suicidal complex, and an artistic release from it. But it has nothing to do with a suicidal complex. Rather it is a profound preoccupation with the role of man *vis-a-vis* God and society. The scene in which White-Jacket falls off the mast is closely paralleled in *Moby-Dick*, and Melville makes it clear there that the evil is too much individualism, too much Platonic brooding. Further, the rebirth scene is strikingly like that comic version of obstetrics when Queequeg is saved by the dexterous hand of Tashtego, though here White-Jacket performs his own obstetrical delivery. Most important is the parallel with Ishmael. Ishmael's education will consist of a death to individualism and, led by Queequeg, a rebirth, in the final chapter of *Moby-Dick*, into complete humanism. White-Jacket's experience, though less artistically satisfying and occurring earlier in the book, is likewise a death to individualism and a rebirth into humanity. After the jacket disappears, he becomes one of the anonymous mass, as he wanted to.

White-Jacket, then, though less aesthetically accomplished than the earlier works, particularly *Redburn*, is more obviously an explicit statement about Melville's major concern with the theme of humanism. *White-Jacket* is, in fact, the most powerful statement on the subject of any of the books before *Moby-Dick*. It is a final testing of the various instruments preparatory to the composition of that much greater book.

The five books antecedent to *Moby-Dick* constitute microcosmic trial heats for the macrocosm of the greater work. The composition of the infinitely more complex book could not come about until triggered by the rich mixture of Melville's experience in life and in writing books. But this miraculous event could not have matured into *Moby-Dick* had not Melville's mind been prepared for the "unfolding" of his very being which he said he experienced "every three weeks" after his twenty-fifth birthday and his lucky meeting with Hawthorne and rediscovery of Shakespeare. The central fabric of Melville's humanism which so strengthens *Moby-Dick* had been tediously and painstakingly woven during the composition of these five earlier books.

TWO

MOBY-DICK: MAN OVER SUPERMAN

Moby-Dick is the richest and most powerful "novel" written to date in America. Though not strictly a novel it is the nearest any writer has come to producing the great American novel, and it is the American epic. In it Melville says, "I try all things; I achieve what I can." Though perhaps he does not accomplish all he might have hoped, he does achieve a staggering amount. The result is a wonderful though sometimes startling combination, often of extremes—of the highest seriousness and the lowest jocularity, of the sublime and the grotesque, of deepest diving after truth and of surface comicality and boisterousness. A whale's head interlaced with thousands of tissues of "fragment spermaceti," it pulsates with a dozen—perhaps two dozens—veins.

    Moby-Dick is virtually all things to all critics, as the numerous books of criticism attest. Among other things it is a serious examination of the conflict between heart and head, of Transcendentalism and Yankee practicality and common sense; a direct examination of and attack on Emerson and Thoreau. It is a grab-bag of all kinds of folklore, used for development of one of the major theses. It throbs with frontier humor, especially of the ring-tailed roarer type. It is Shakespeare and the popular theater. It is a defiant, though sometimes masked, hooting at conventional sexual mores and taboos, a defiance Melville was to state at great length, though somewhat covertly, in later works, expecially in *Pierre* and "The Tartarus of Maids."

    Moby-Dick is a notable departure from Melville's earlier works, even from the first version of this book (finished in 1850 as "a romantic and fanciful account of the whale fishery," as a friend described it). But to a large extent it gathers together the strands of Melville's former books, especially those strands we have discussed above, and further comments on the major problems that troubled him during 1850 and 1851 in particular and were to haunt him for the next forty years. In texture and technique *Moby-Dick* is an obvious—sometimes painfully obvious—borrowing from and echoing of numerous authors, including Wordsworth and Coleridge, Thomas Browne, Swift, Smollett and Rabelais, Dante and Milton, and most notably Shakespeare, who profoundly influenced Melville during the summer of 1850, after the first version of *Moby-Dick* had been completed.

Primarily this leviathan of a book is, as Richard Chase eloquently argued, a serious dramatization of the conflict between Prometheus and Zeus, or hero against god. Ahab is the "false Prometheus," a perverter of real Promethean impulses. Ahab dares question the supremacy of God over man, the inviolability of his laws and the reason for their supremacy. Essentially, however, the book is an examination of the conflict between superman and mere man, or men. Melville suggests the eventual tragic failure of the Promethean impulse in the individual but its eventual triumph in massed Prometheanism in humanity—in democracy—in the person of Ishmael.

Here the triumph is more implied than explicit, and Melville will develop it more strongly in later books, but his attitude, though ambivalent, is clear. In a letter to Hawthorne written about the same time he was writing *Moby-Dick*, Melville approved in general of Goethe's philosophy "Live in All." But he equivocated about going all the way with Goethe; he felt sure that one must at times also live in the part. At this time Melville also said: "It seems an inconsistency to assert unconditional democracy in all things, and yet confess a dislike to all

mankind—in the mass. But not so."[1] The apparent
paradox in Melville's thinking at this time is plain. But the
seeming contradiction does not in fact exist. As we shall
see, in *Moby-Dick* Melville actually resolved the apparent
contradiction, building on his insistence on democracy
and working beyond it to love of mankind in the mass.
He was to come to faith in mankind in general, to the
consolation of triumphant humanism. The seedbed of
stronger statements on these subjects is obviously being
cultivated here. It is this level of the book that we
should examine first.

THE HERO AND THE MASS

The conflict between the individual and the mass, with
the ultimate triumph of the latter, is set immediately.
Ishmael starts out with "November in [his] soul," and
seeks a "substitute for pistol and ball" in the medicine of
universal man: He goes down to the sea. But there is
nothing unusual in this move. "If they but knew it,
almost all men in their degree, some time or other,
cherish very nearly the same feelings toward the ocean."
Ishmael sees people congregating from all over
Manhattan. From north, south, east, and west, both high
and low, "and all unite" as close to the water as
possible. The secret of life resides in water, and man
tries to read it. But Melville has people seeking the
secret *en masse.* To a certain extent people discover the
key to it not in the water but in their reflected image as a
group.

Melville makes it clear that he is looking at man both
vertically and horizontally, in the particular individual—the
hero, the out-standing individual—and in the mass.
Ishmael is not interested in identifying himself with the
Titans, with the aristocrats and supermen. He is insular
and naive, an Isolato. An apostle of individualism, he

---

1. Merrell E. Davis and William H. Gilman, *The Letters of Herman Melville*
(New Haven, 1960), p. 127.

thinks he is interested only in himself. He believes it is as much as he can do to care for himself, without assuming common interests with other people. He is another Redburn, but with greater potential. Like Redburn, Ishmael does not yet know how fully his humanism will grow and assert itself. It will take Queequeg, his cannibal friend, acting as catalyst to quicken and nourish the depths of Ishmael's latent true feeling.

Ishmael goes to sea as a "simple sailor, right before the mast" (CH. I). But he had unlimited vertical mobility. The fact that he can and will rise and become the hero through his humanism is revealed in the character of Bulkington. This man is drawn from the real figure of Melville's greatly respected former sailing mate Jack Chase—to whom *Billy Budd* will be dedicated—an embryo version of the savior-hero developed later in such figures as Bartleby and Billy Budd. Bulkington is a common sailor or began as one. But he is much more. He is "noble" in size and stance. He looks like "one of those tall mountaineers from the Alleganian Ridge in Virginia." He has a profound sense of the troubles of life. He is an intimation of Melville's thesis later developed that non-white people are superior to pure whites: Bulkington's "face was deeply brown and burnt, making his white teeth dazzling by the contrast"— he is a kind of mulatto-minstrel. Six feet tall, "with noble shoulders, and a chest like a coffer-dam," Bulkington stands aloof from the crowd, though the favorite of all the people (CH. III).

Bulkington figures little personally in this voyage. He is "but a sleeping-partner." But he is sufficiently developed for Melville to make his point; Bulkington is a symbol of what all men would like to be. He attracts them. When he is missed by his comrades in the Spouter-Inn, they raise the cry of "Where's Bulkington?" and rush out in pursuit of him. His magnetic qualities are even more heroic when we meet Bulkington for the second and last time, in the "six-inch chapter" which is his "stoneless grave." He is standing at the helm of the *Pequod* on this "shivering winter's night, as the

Pequod thrust her vindictive bows into the cold malicious waves," guiding her. Just returned from a four-year voyage, he must "unresistingly push off again for still another tempetuous term." He persishes in the "open independence" of the sea and is not driven by the "wildest winds of heaven and earth" which "conspire to cast" him on the "treacherous, slavish shore." This "demigod" thus triumphs: "Up from the spray of thy ocean-perishing—straight up, leaps thy apotheosis!" (CH. XXIII).

Bulkington's appearance, though brief, was necessary and sufficient for Melville to establish his thesis. Bulkington was a springboard for the development of other heroes, those of the people. This early disappearance and apotheosis was fundamental. Bulkington serves as a nexus between Ahab and Ishmael.

Ahab thinks himself a god, a Prometheus who can successfully challenge God. Like Milton's Satan he would rather risk loss of heaven than submit willingly to God's decrees. Ahab, no matter how admirable, is presumptive. He is an intruder, a destroyer. Bulkington, on the contrary, is, at least in Ishmael's mind, a "demigod," naturally noble. Much more than Ahab, Bulkington merits his ascent to heaven. But he is a common sailor, a man before the mast. His apotheosis, his rise to immortality, serves as a lodestone to Ishmael for his eventual salvation. As such Bulkington serves as a symbol that the common sailor is the true demigod, the superior of Ahab. It is the common sailor—not the presumptive would-be god—who will ultimately triumph. Thus Bulkington symbolizes one aspect of Melville's Christian humanism.

Before his apotheosis, however, the common man must suffer from the captains of the world. Ishmael, symbol of the ultimate triumph of man, is bossed around. He is ordered "to get a broom and sweep down the decks." But "What does that indignity amount to, weighed I mean, in the scales of the New Testament?" (CH. I). The rise of the common man is less difficult in the "scales of the New Testament" than in those of the Old. This is the feeling of the same Melville who wrote to

Hawthorne about the first of June, 1851, that there probably is a "slight dash of flunkeyism" in capitalizing the word *Deity*, and he cringed over doing it. In the same letter Melville said, "The reason the mass of men fear God, and at bottom dislike Him is because they rather distrust His heart, and fancy Him all brain like a watch." [2] In the New Testament a gentler God stands between this "watch" and man.

Melville's antagonism against God, which increased through the years, is revealed in two remarks he entered in the *Journal up the Straits*, his observations when he toured the Holy Land: Jehovah is a "terrible mixture of the cunning and awful," and "Hapless are the favorites of Heaven."

Ishmael, like Melville himself, is torn between training and instinct. He feels that he should defend himself against the charges of being too ambitious. He does snap back at his critics. The archangel Gabriel does not think any the less of him because of his getting a broom and sweeping the decks. "Who ain't a slave?" he asks humanistically. "The universal thump" of the captains of the world is passed around to all, he says. Therefore "all hands should rub each other's shoulder blades and be content." It is wise to be "on friendly terms with all the inmates of the place one lodges in" (CH. I).

Led by his humanistic instinct that the cheapest quarters are near the water, in New Bedford Ishmael had turned toward the poorer district of the city, where streets were dark and deserted. Melville at this point introduces one of his major themes, here as in later works: the innate superiority of non-white people over whites, a theme to be developed in this book in the person of Bulkington, as we have seen, and in the three harpooners, Tashtego, Daggoo, and especially Queequeg— and in later works, such as "Benito Cereno" and *Billy Budd*.

2. Davis and Gilman, *Letters*, p. 129.

Ishmael comes to a "low, wide building, the door of which stood invitingly open. It had a careless look, as if it were meant for the uses of the public." Readers of the later story "Temple Second" will catch the beginning of a satiric thrust. Significantly Melville calls this New Bedford church "the Trap" after he stumbles over an ash-can in the entrance. It is a trap for two reasons. Religion is a trap for all people. Furthermore, this building is a trap because it is a church for black people, a ghetto structure. In this theme Melville introduces the subject he is to develop more fully in later works, in "Benito Cereno," for example. These people are trapped because of their color. But they are not content to be trapped, and, as he says in the later story, are going to rebel.

The New Bedford passage makes the threat clear: "it seemed the great Black Paliament sitting in Tophet. A hundred black faces turned round in their rows to peer; and beyond, a black Angel of Doom was beating a book in a pulpit" (CH. II) The Negro's text was "about the blackness of darkness, and the weeping and wailing and teeth-gnashing there." The key to the passage is, of course, "blackness of darkness." Melville in his review of Hawthorne's *Mosses from an old Manse* (1850), written while he was broiling his whale in "hell-fire," had used the same words in approving the profundity of Hawthorne's work, saying that the strength of Hawthorne resides in his "power of blackness" and the "blackness of darkness; and even his bright gildings but fringe and play upon the edges of thunderclouds. . . . Those occasional flashings-forth of the intuitive Truth in him; those short, quick probings at the very axis of reality." The probing of this black minister reveals the deepest truth and inquiry of the human mind. These Negroes are searching for, and perhaps have found, a deeper truth than the whites know. But Ishmael, with all his properly biased intuitions, leaves the church, having found only "wretched entertainment" at this congregation. The contrast between this minister and congregation and

Father Mapple and his congregation later is startling.

Though Ishmael runs away from the incipient Negro rebellion, like Amasa Delano later in "Benito Cereno," he is not totally indifferent to man's injustices to man. When he sees before the Spouter-Inn a poor Lazarus on the curb-stone, his social protest bristles. He knows that "it's too late to make any improvements now. The Universe is finished; the copestone is on, and the chips were carted off a million years ago" (CH. II). But he does not accept or approve of the universe, which is turned topsy turvy. Rich and poor are, in fact, bound together, subject to the same "universal thumps," and neither should be distinguished from the other socially.

This theme is developed further in the Spouter-Inn, when Ishmael is confronted with the fate of sleeping with the cannibal Queequeg. Initially Ishmael's training causes him to protest. He declares that nobody likes to sleep with somebody else. Even sailors sleep in their "own skin" and hammock. But Melville's innate true humanism obtrudes. Ishmael recognizes that common sailors all sleep "together in one apartment," even as all people on earth do. As he broods over sleeping with the cannibal, Ishmael realizes that he "might be cherishing unwarrantable prejudices against this unknown harpooneer" (CH. III). And he relents, thinking that he will give the man a good looking-over before refusing to sleep with him.

Melville develops his humanism also along the strand of religion in the broadest sense of the word. He criticizes narrow Protestant religion and often God. Peter Coffin, the proprietor of the Spouter-Inn, attempts to explain to Ishmael why Queequeg is staying out so late at night. The narrowness of New Bedford toleration of the rights of others and of Coffin's indifference to human dignity is revealed in his remark that it would not be proper for Queequeg to be out selling "human heads about the streets when folks is goin' to churches" (CH. III).

45

Ishmael's trained reaction to the customs of others is not much different than Coffin's, as is later revealed when, having gone to the room in which he is going to sleep, he examines the poncho that Queequeg used in his religious services. Dressed in it he looks into a mirror and reacts violently, tearing himself out of it so fast that he almost puts a kink in his neck. The damage Ishmael does to himself points up Melville's feeling that such bigotry is harmful and therefore that all kinds of religion must be respected. This is further demonstrated later when Queequeg comes into the room. With his splotchy skin he frightens Ishmael almost to death. But Ishmael decides: "It's only his outside; a man can be honest in any sort of skin." Again, Ishmael's Protestant, insular reaction obtrudes when he sees Queequeg going through his religious practices with Yojo, the little figurine, who to Ishmael is a "little devil" of an idol. The fact is that both Queequeg and Ishmael hate the devil, as is revealed a little later when Queequeg discovers Ishmael and sings out, accusing *him* of being a devil. Melville hammers home the point he had set up earlier when Ishamael concedes after a few words with Queequeg: "For all his tattooings he was on the whole a clean, comely looking cannibal . . . the man's a human being just as I am" (CH. III). After this bit of self-enlightenment, Ishmael goes to bed and "never slept better in my life."

The next chapter, "The Counterpane," carries on Melville's thesis. The bedspread represents, like Melville's conventional use of hearth and home, all the comforts of civilization and home, or at least conventional civilization and home. It also represents conventional Christian religion. Melville subtly compares heathen cannibal religion with good Nantucket Presbyterianism. The counterpane is "a patchwork, full of odd little particolored squares and triangles; and this arm of his tattooed all over with an interminable Cretan labyrinth of a figure, no two parts of which were of one precise shade . . . looked for all the world like a strip of that same patchwork quilt. Indeed, partly lying on it as the arm did when I first awoke, I could hardly tell it from the quilt, they so blended their hues together" (CH. IV) The mystical experience of this correspondence is pointed up by Ishmael's recounting an experience from his youth that this counterpane—blended with the heathenism—reminded him of. As a child once he had been sent to bed in the middle of the afternoon and awoke feeling a "supernatural hand" placed in his. He believed that the horrible spell could be broken if he could but say a word. Finally the spell disappeared.

Now the situation is similar. The setting is to a large extent the same, counterpane and all. This time it is a "pagan arm thrown round" him. Ishmael wants to move Queequeg's arm and "unlock his bridegroom clasp," but the cannibal hugs him as though "naught but death should part" them. This is then Melville's symbol of the death of prejudice, or the mystical birth of tolerance and universal brotherhood. It was almost like being reborn from prejudice into tolerance, or a marriage into true brotherhood, for Queequeg and Ishmael seem "married."

To emphasize the degree of this rebirth, of this marriage, and the naturalness of one spouse watching the other dress, Ishmael tells, obviously with Swiftean humor and seriousness, Queequeg's quaint customs in putting on his clothes. The cannibal's ablutions are a parody of Christian rites, but just as good and equally effective.

"The Chapel" had set the stage earlier for development of Melville's feelings about religion. Nearly all "moody fishermen" visit the Whaleman's Chapel before going off whaling. Out on the Sunday morning when he is in New Bedford in his bearskin, Ishmael escapes from the storm by darting into the chapel. There he finds "a small scattered congregation of sailors, and sailors' wives and widows. A muffled silence reigned, only broken at times by the shrieks of the storm." Each worshipper sits apart from the others, "as if each silent grief were insular and

incommunicable." There is a sharp contrast between
this white man's church and that of the Negroes that
Ishmael had earlier visited. Here only a few people attend;
there many, a regular "parliament," were present. Here
everybody sits apart from the others, isolated in his grief;
there all apparently sat together, sharing their troubles.
Differing from the people at the Negro church, these whites
all seem pygmy versions of Ahab—his monomania, like
their grief, is incommunicable.

There is, however, one person in the white church who
is not insular: Queequeg. He has a great deal in common
with the Negroes of the other church, at least in not being
accepted by the whites and in not being of their color and
culture. He notices the entrance of Ishmael because he is
illiterate and cannot read the "frigid inscriptions" of the
Christian ritual on the walls. Queequeg is sociable because,
pagan that he is, he is not grieving. Melville snaps at the
Christian religion—and indeed all such religions—by
remarking on those people whose loved ones died at sea:
"What deadly voids and unbidden fidelities in the lines that
seem to gnaw upon all Faith, and refuse resurrections to
the beings who have placelessly perished without a grave."

Melville continues his criticism of religion: "But faith, like
a jackal, feeds among the tombs, and even from these dead
doubts she gathers her most vital hope." But Ishmael
refuses to believe such gloomy religion. He thinks that
the body is not the proper place for the soul. So, happy and
jolly, and with a peculiar mixture of Ahab and Stubb, he
adopts an attitude of Christian fatalism: "and come a stove
boat and stove body when they will, for stave my soul,
Jove himself cannot." This flouting of God's power
parallels a statement Melville made about this time to
Hawthorne, praising him when he "insists upon treating
with all Powers upon an equal basis." For "take God out of
the dictionary, and you would have Him in the street."[3]

3. Davis and Gilman, *Letters*, p. 125.

The entrance and behavior of Father Mapple in the church, along with his sermon, continue Melville's criticism and his insistence on humanism. Mapple comes in alone, not having used any man-made means of traveling in the storm. To have used such a conveyance would have been an admission by Mapple that he had to depend upon his fellowman. As soon as he enters, he isolates himself from the congregation by climbing up to his crows-nest of a pulpit, then deliberately dragging "up the ladder step by step, till the whole was deposited within, leaving him impregnable in his little Quebec." In contrast the black minister at the Negro church had made no effort to isolate himself. Ishmael realized that Mapple's act "must symbolize something unseen," that "by the act of physical isolation, he signified his spiritual withdrawal for the time, from all outward worldly ties and connections? Yes, for replenished with the meat and wine of the word, to the faithful man of God, this pulpit, I see, is a self-containing stronghold—a lofty *ehrenbreitstein*, with a perennial well of water within the walls."

Melville then presents a preview of the ship Ishmael is going to sail on, the *Pequod*, and its owners, Bildad and Peleg, and their peculiar Christian behavior; he previews also the bigotry of religion in general as well as his own comment on the voyage, and a forecast of Ahab's doom: "The pulpit is ever this earth's foremost part; all the rest comes in its rear." The pulpit leads the world, "is the prow." The symbolism seems clear. The pulpit is the forward part of the ship as it plows through the sea and life. It receives the brunt of the world's rebuffs. It travels blindly and unchangingly. When, for example, Ishmael goes on board the *Pequod* with his determination to see the world, he is asked by Captain Peleg to look over the weather-bow and report what he sees. Ishmael tells Peleg that he sees only water, and the captain responds that all the world is the same: "Can't ye see the world where you stand?" (CH. XVI). Bulkington, however, the epitome and hope of the common man, does not stand at the bow of the

49

ship. During the brief span in which we see him, he is at the helm, guiding and directing the course of his peers. Thus Melville is saying that positions of greatest importance in this world are not those that are the most conspicuous and seemingly significant.

Father Mapple is a religious Ahab. He too is tyrannical. He directs the congregation to do as he does not do. He orders them "to condense," as Ahab commands his ship's crew to encircle him around the doubloon. Mapple is also a confidence man, and likes to do things for public observation. He takes himself seriously, and Melville ironically says that a man of Mapple's known piety could not be doing things for theatrical effect only. But Melville does doubt Mapple's sincerity, as he doubted that of all ministers. In a letter to Hawthorne, about June 1, 1851, Melville had said: "Truth is the silliest thing under the sun. Try to get a living by the Truth—and go to the Soup Societies. Heavens! Let any clergyman try to preach the Truth from its very stronghold, the pulpit, and they would ride him out of his church on his own pulpit bannisters."[4] Mapple is not ridden out of town. On the contrary, he is famous for his sermons, his brand of truth—and respected by all the other bigoted Protestants around, such as Bildad and Peleg, for example. Mapple's heart cannot be of unadulterated purity, for purity is impossible. Solomon, as Melville says later, is "the truest of all men," and "Ecclesiastes the fine hammered steel of woe," but, as Melville commented in his famous letter to Hawthorne written while he was working on this book: "It seems to me now that Solomon was the truest man who ever spoke, and yet that he a little *managed* the truth with a view to popular conservatism."[5]

Mapple offers a prayer "so deeply devout that he seemed kneeling and praying at the bottom of the sea." This cannot be an unmixed compliment because only a while before, Ishmael had decided that "in looking at things spiritual, we are too much like oysters observing

4. Davis and Gilman, *Letters*, p. 127.
5. Davis and Gilman, *Letters*, p. 130.

the sun through the water" (CH. IX). Mapple's famous sermon, itself monomaniacal, is a direct parallel to Ahab's Promethean monomania, as we will see it develop through the book, though we have not, of course, yet seen Ahab. Though seeming a proper antidote to Ahab's poison, the sermon germinates anti-humanism. Mapple says that to obey God we must disobey ourselves, "and it is this disobeying ourselves, wherein the hardness of obeying God consists." Jonah, the sermon runs, disobeyed God and tried to flee from his God-appointed task. Jonah thought that men could help him escape God's wrath. Mapple paints both Jonah and the captain of the ship that took him to Joppa as con men, each trying to bilk the other. The sea "rebels" against bearing Jonah, and the storm rises. When the sailors discover that it is Jonah that the sea is after, they, quite contrary to the captain's behavior, are humanistic. They want to save themselves without tossing Jonah into the sea. But the captain cannot understand this kind of behavior. He forces the men to cast Jonah out. Mapple draws his moral, exactly paralleling Bildad's self-contradictory words later: "Sin not, but if you do, take heed to repent of it like Jonah." Then, isolated in his tower of self-righteousness, "Mapple leaned over towards the people" and emphasized his Ahab-like pride by "bowing his head lowly, with an aspect of the deepest yet manliest humility." Then he said: "Shipmates, God has laid but one hand upon you; both his hands press upon me." He says that he would like to exchange places with the congregation, but since he has been appointed by God to point out the lessons of "the living God," he cannot become one of the multitude. Like Jonah, Mapple must "preach the Truth to the face of Falsehood." His method is tyrannical: "Woe to him who seeks to please rather than to appall."

Mapple's reward for Christianity is exactly Bildad's— gain and profit—though he calls it "Delight." "Delight is to him—a far, far upward, and inward delight—who

51

against the proud gods and commodores of this earth, ever stands forth his own inexorable self." "Delight—topgallant delight is to him, who acknowledges no law or lord, but the Lord his God, and is only a patriot to heaven." Mapple then waves a benediction, and the congregation depart, leaving him "alone in the place." Melville's purpose here seems to be to point out the danger inherent in Mapple as it will be later in Ahab. Mapple's sermon is strongly anti-humanistic. Though he preaches to the people, he is isolated from them. He is not one of them and, like Ahab, cannot ever become one of them. He is left alone when the people depart on their moody and scattered, but earthly, ways.

Melville's dislike of this sermon and of Mapple's behavior is demonstrated in the kind, gentle and humanistic Queequeg. He had left the chapel while Mapple was preaching his hard, unrelenting, and despotic Christianity, "before the benediction some time." Now he was sitting at the inn. "One hand was holding close up to his face that little negro idol of his; peering hard into its face, and with a jack knife gently whittling away at its nose, meanwhile humming to himself in his heathenish way" (CH. X). Queequeg is exactly the opposite of Mapple. Puzzled by Mapple's hard-hearted Christianity, Queequeg is studying his god to see if he is of such a nature. Instead of taking another man's word about the nature of God, Queequeg is digging into the truth himself. To see if his god is so ironwilled and jealous as Mapple says the Christian God is, Queequeg is whittling at his nose, altering his appearance, and not suffering at all, meanwhile "humming to himself in his heathenish way," singing his own hymns. The scene is as earthily humanistic as a similar one in *Typee*, when Kory-Kory, Melville's heathen friend, not finding the behavior of his god to his liking, buffets him around. Heathen treatment of the gods, Melville is saying, is superior to that of the Christians.

Queequeg's superior religion, along with his person and behavior, is further highlighted. Whereas Mapple wanted to be alone, ascended to his pulpit, and engaged in his insular Christianity, Queequeg, a humanist, gladly gives up his religious practices for human fellowship, at least in this instance. When Ishmael comes into the inn, Queequeg lays his idol aside. The difference between the simple religion of Queequeg and the complicated one of Mapple is emphasized in the Swiftean satiric jab of having Queequeg examine the Bible.

He counts the pages of the huge book, stopping always at fifty and "looking vacantly around him, and giving utterance to a long-drawn gurgling whistle of astonishment." But despite subscribing to a simple religion that would fill only one fifty-page book, Queequeg has a great soul, and is of a "simple honest heart." "He looked like a man who had never cringed and never had had a creditor," and he was "George Washington cannibalistically developed." Queequeg is then superior to Mapple, for he has qualities that the minister does not possess. Mapple has cringed a great deal, before God if not before man, and might well have had creditors.

As Christian and cannibal sit, Ishmael more and more appreciates Queequeg, saying, "I felt a melting in me," a feeling that he had not experienced in the presence of cold and detached Father Mapple. "No more my splintered heart and maddened hand were turned against the wolfish world. This soothing savage had redeemed it." As they smoked, "any ice of indifference towards me in the Pagan's breast . . . soon thawed . . . out, and left us cronies," and they became "bosom friends."

The importance of this passage is emphasized by comparison with a letter Melville wrote to Hawthorne, about November 17, 1851, in spontaneous appreciation of Hawthorne's favorable comment on *Moby-Dick*. The sentiment is exactly that of Ishmael's feeling for his friend Queequeg: "I felt pantheistic then—your heart beat in my ribs and mine in yours, and both in God's."[6] Melville has an "infinite fraternity of feeling" with Hawthorne.

Queequeg prepares for his idolatrous religious service. He had been magnanimous enough to attend the services of the Christians. At first Ishmael, as Christian, is frightened at the prospect of heathenish worship. But soon Ishmael sees that to worship with Queequeg is to follow the dictates of the true God. In an act which runs directly counter to Mapple's sermon, he turns "idolator," and worships with the pagan. In so doing he points up the falsity of Mapple and to a lesser extent of Peleg and of Bildad also. After worshipping together the Christian and the pagan are brothers. They do not separate, as Mapple's congregation had after worshipping with him. Instead they go to bed together. Ishmael's comments assert the true purpose of religion: the establishment of the brotherhood of man.

But Melville's criticism of religion is directed against Queequeg's as well as against Mapple's, though more against the latter than the former. Yojo, Queequeg's heathen god, is good and bad, just as the Christian God is. Queequeg's trusting him completely parallels the trust that Christians place in their God. Queequeg had consulted Yojo about his future, and the little god had said that if left alone, Ishmael would choose the right ship. Queequeg's feeling for Yojo was, with the exception of the familiarity of feeling and the candor of expressing that feeling, rather like that of Christians for their God. He was a "rather good sort of god, who perhaps meant well enough upon the whole, but in all cases did not succeed in his benevolent designs" (CH. XVII). In the broadest and best terms, Yojo was successful in choice of ship, considering what the voyage did for

6. Davis and Gilman, *Letters*, p. 142.

Ishmael. But in another sense, he erred as badly as the Christian God did in allowing His worshippers to ship on the *Pequod.*

Ishmael is led by the cannibal god to the *Pequod,* of course. This vessel is a "cannibal of a craft, tricking herself forth in the chased bones of her enemies." Both the captains whom Ishmael meets first are full of "insular prejudices, and rather distrustful of all aliens, unless they hailed from Cape Cod or the Vineyard." Both are well-to-do and retired. Both are practical Yankees who know that "religion is one thing, and this practical world quite another." They were successful because they cannibalized upon the world. They exploited aliens—cannibals—but did not like them. Ahab depends on cannibals in the person of harpooners. The whalers cannibalize upon the whales, trying out their oil and even eating them at times. And Ahab in a spiritual cannibalizing eats the souls of his crew.

Significantly it is the practical Yankee Captain Peleg who characterizes Ahab. Christian that he is, Peleg knows about God, and therefore believes that Ahab is "a grand, ungodly, god-like man," who is "above the common." Having said these things, Peleg, in an effort to allay Ishmael's fears, tries to humanize Ahab. He insists that tough, "stricken, blasted, if he be, Ahab has his humanities." But the sincerity of this remark, or the way Melville meant it to be taken, is indicated in Peleg's remarks leading up to it. His touchstone of Ahab's "humanities" is that he has a wife and child. On the basis of this fact virtually alone, Peleg advances what may be merely his way of duping Ishmael: "Hold ye then there can be any utter, hopeless harm in Ahab?" (CH. XVI). As Ahab's monomania bloats on the voyage, the reader more and more questions Peleg's wisdom or the honesty with which he made this statement. Though in the narrow sense of the word, Ahab is not really one of Melville's bachelors (those people who isolate themselves from life), in a larger sense he has not committed himself to humanity, and therefore is a bachelor.

In criticizing Queequeg's religious ritual in the chapter entitled "The Ramadan," Melville is castigating all religions, and trying to point out the superiority of humanism. Queequeg is nobler than the Christians. But he behaves peculiarly in his Ramadan. The nuisance of the whole business is emphasized. Ishmael tells Queequeg that his religious exercises are "stark nonsense," and against "common sense." But Ishmael gets nowhere. Queequeg is a typical man of typical religion: "Because, in the first place, he somehow seemed dull of hearing on that important subject, unless considered from his own point of view; and, in the second place, he did not more than one third understand me, couch my ideas simply as I would; and, finally, he no doubt thought he knew a great deal more about the true religion than I did."

Moby-Dick is a book about gods and men, heroes and commoners. To a certain extent, at least, all people on the Pequod are heroes. It is a heroic ship on a heroic voyage. Ahab is heroic. But so are the common sailors. In the end the point of the voyage has been clearly to reverse the roles of the men on the ship. Ahab, the ostensible hero, has been destroyed and thus reduced in stature. Ishmael, the commonest of the commoners, has been apotheosized as a symbol of the rise of the common man.

The course the book is going to take is made clear from the very beginning. The ship sails on highly symbolic Christmas day, the supposed birthday of the greatest Commoner of all. Captain Peleg further points out the heroic qualities of the sailors when he calls them "sons of bachelors," that is bastards; bastardy, or something akin to it, is a common attribute of heroes.

The chapter called "The Advocate" advances Melville's insistence upon the heroic aspect of the common sailors. They are better than martial commanders, "whom the world invariably delights to honor." These common whalers have the courage to attack the whale, God's most glorious creature—in fact, God Himself. It was the whaleman who established "eternal democracy" in South America. There is the greatest dignity in whaling, Melville insists. "Drive down in presence of the Czar, and take it off to Queequeg." Taking whales is more honorable than taking cities, as captains of old used to do and be glorified for. Ishmael particularizes one kind of glory that he personally derived from whaling. Ahab has been to college. But if Ishmael ever does anything worthwhile, and leaves valuable manuscripts, he will ascribe "all the honor and the glory to whaling; for a whale-ship was my Yale College and my Harvard." This remark has two functions. It elevates whaling to heroic proportions, and it humanizes and democratizes Yale and Harvard, mixing the students of those schools with commoners throughout the world.

As everyone and everything deserves a good laugh, Melville cannot avoid the greatest democratizer of all, humor. He ends his paean to the glory of whalers, their heroic and dignified qualities, by pointing out with a straight face that "a king's head is solemnly oiled at his coronation, even as a head of salad." And the only kind of oil used is "sperm oil in its unmanufactured, unpolluted state, the sweetest of all oils." "Think of that, ye loyal Britons!" he apostrophizes, "we whaleman supply your kings and queens with coronation stuff!"

In a continuation of his theme of the conflict between the hero and the common man, Melville points out how Starbuck failed to become the hero. Although he was a brave man, he was without the spiritual bravery needed to "withstand those more terrific, because more spiritual terrors, which sometimes menace you from the concentrating brow of an enraged and mighty man." But though Starbuck did not have the

57

individual courage to outstare Ahab, as a member of the human race he did not suffer abasement. Such a sight Ishmael could not report, because although "Men may seem detestable as joint stock-companies and nations," man, democratic man, has a dignity "which, on all hands, radiates without end from God: Himself!" (CH. XXVI).

Of the three officers on the *Pequod* Starbuck was the grandest, but Stubb was not much lesser. Like Derwent or Rolfe in *Clarel,* Stubb was "neither craven nor valiant." He was, as Ahab says, the other half of Starbuck. Where Starbuck was careful and reserved, Stubb was reckless and indifferent to danger, always good-humored. Flask, the third mate, was a vulgar hero, but heroic also. He was the Mike Fink and Davy Crockett of the crew. Like the frontiersman and typical American humter, he killed merely for the fun. And like Fink and Crockett, he lacked reverence for the god-like quality of the whale.

Ahab is of course obviously the "supreme lord and dictator" on the ship. Though heroic in appearance, grandeur, and power, he is a false hero. Instead of advancing humanism and democracy, he flouts it and attempts to destroy all such impulses. Instead of being altruistic, selfless, willing to suffer for the people, he is egoistic, selfish and wants only to democratize those above him.

There is about him "an infinity of firmest fortitude, a determinate, unsurrenderable wilfulness." Like all of Melville's heroes, and heroes throughout folklore and mythology, Ahab was marked "with a crucifixion in his face; in all the nameless regal overbearing dignity of some mighty woe." He was a "khan of the plank, and a king of the sea and a great lord of Leviathans"

But these attributes only aggrandize his stature and therefore make all the more tragic his failure to be heroic; and in so doing make all the more heroic the ascendancy of Ishamel over Ahab. Though Ahab is thought by some to have his touch of humanity, it is a selfish, egocentric touch, because he is capable of abusing his men—all of humanity—as is evidenced by his telling Stubb to "down dog, and kennel" (CH. XXIX).

"The Specksynder" is one of the key chapters in the development of the theme of democracy and humanism. All captains walk the decks of their ships with "elated grandeur," Ahab included. Ahab hides behind forms to do his work, and at times exceeds their authority and thereby becomes dangerous, for "through these forms that same sultanism became incarnate in an irresistible dictatorship."

"The Cabin-Table" also advances the theme of democracy. It tells how the officers go to eat, and how Ahab lords it over them. Flask is the last to begin to eat, and since he must quit when Ahab is finished, he gets precious little to eat. Melville moralizes: "There's the fruits of promotion now; there's the vanity of glory; there's the insanity of life!"

Sharply contrasted with the table of the officers are the eating habits of the harpooners. They are the real heroes of those people who dine in the captain's cabin. Though they dine "like Lords," theirs is a table of "almost frantic democracy." Such frenzy, however, breeds nobility in the real sense. Daggoo, the magnificent Negro, is the lordliest of all these diners. He is wonderfully abstemious, not to say dainty, a "noble savage." Melville rounds off other harpooners, into the realms of the religious and mythical: "Not by beef or by bread, are giants made or nourished."

In development of the theme of humanism the doubloon is one of the important symbols in the entire book. As Melville says, "Some certain significance lurks in all things." The scene is used here, as the lone pine is used in *Clarel*, to isolate various individuals and give levels of interpretation of them and their character. The importance of the doubloon is highlighted at its installation in the chapter called "The Quarter-Deck." By nailing the doubloon to the mast, Ahab intensifies his

59

stature as a superman. After having called the men together to witness his nailing it to the masthead and after exacting shouts from the crew, Ahab bestows magic on the gold piece, "slowly rubbing the gold piece against the skirts of his jacket, as if to heighten its lustre, and without using any words was meanwhile lowly humming to himself, producing a sound so strangely muffled and inarticulate that it seemed the mechanical humming of the wheels of his vitality in him." Ahab's is black magic, and Starbuck recognizes it as such. The first mate accuses Ahab of blasphemy. In reply Ahab smites his chest—symbolically the seat of humanism—which is "vast, but hollow." The extent of his heroic blasphemy is emphasized in his own words: "Who's over me?"

Ahab's act is anti-humanistic. The doubloon was "set apart and sanctified to one awe-striking end," and all the "mariners revered it as the white whale's talisman." Little wonder then that monomaniacally egotistic Ahab sees in it the symbol of himself: "The firm tower, that is Ahab; the volcano, that is Ahab; the courageous, the undaunted, and victorious fowl, that too, is Ahab." But though the entire crew had earlier madly joined in the ritual of making the doubloon magical, they now begin to denigrate it, to make it normal. In this act they again assert the importance of humanity to Melville.

Stubb, who according to Ahab represents half of humanity—and who is, as we shall see, a pre-study of Derwent and Lesbian in *Clarel*—decides that the doubloon represents nothing more portentous than fun. To him, "Oh, jolly's the word for aye." As various other commentators approach the doubloon the magic surrounding it is further removed. In humanizing the symbol they add a new kind of importance. To Flask it represents 960 cigars. The old Manxman thinks of it as a voodoo sign. Stubb comments on the commonness of men: "All sorts of men in one kind of world, you see," but, as Ishmael had earlier said in the Spouter-Inn, "all sleep in the same dormitory." Queequeg sees the doubloon as a sexual symbol, finding "something there in the vicinity of his thigh." Pip in his wonderful double talk, his parsing of a verb, finally reduces the symbol to the "ship's navel," and thence to a folk jig and vaudeville song. In so doing he ties it in with, and enriches, the theme of the popular theater which, as we shall see in the next section, is another theme which Melville uses to accomplish his purpose in the book.

"Sunset," another of the key chapters in the book, further develops Ahab's Titanism. Ahab soliloquizes that his crown is too heavy, this "Iron Crown of Lombardy." He is "gifted with the high perception," but lacks the "low, enjoying power." Therefore he is "damned, most subtly and most malignantly! damned in the midst of Paradise." In other words, it would be good to live on this earth but Ahab lacks the democratic spirit heeded to enjoy it. After this momentary weakness for things of this world, Ahab reassumes his heroic qualities, bragging that he has made all the various wheels revolve, and he is demoniac. He is blasphemously anti-god. He curses and slashes at the "great gods," and in so doing perhaps unconsciously allies himself yet again with humanity, an alliance that is only momentary at this time, but as we shall see will be one of his final motions in life. Now he challenges the gods to alter him: "Come, Ahab's compliments to ye; come and see if ye can swerve me. Swerve me? ye cannot swerve me, else ye swerve yourselves! man has ye there."

Starbuck comments, Hamlet-like, on Ahab's speech, saying that Ahab would be a "democrat to all above; look, how he lords it over all below!" Against this anti-democracy Starbuck asserts his own Christian humanism. He stands midway between Ahab and Ishmael. Starbuck calls on God to help him fight Ahab's Prometheanism. Ishmael however, rises above religion, and triumphs over anti-humanism with humanism alone. Humanity collectively can triumph over all adversaries, mortal or immortal, and prove their heroic qualities. Moby-Dick the whale is God incarnate.

61

By extension, therefore, any whale is god-like, or at least heroic. A whale is ubiquitous and very nearly immortal. Yet men linked together can triumph over Leviathan, not when they are keeled along the monomaniacal individualism of Ahab, but when they are federated together. Though no whalers can overcome Moby-Dick himself, together they can slay lesser whales; and in overcoming these heroic god-like monsters, the whalers * prove their own heroic qualities.

This thesis is advanced in the chapter called "The Honor and Glory of Whaling." Only a hero—"a Perseus, a St. George, a Coffin"—can slay a whale. Common whalers therefore belong to royalty. As whaler-hero, Ishmael, like all heroes, has the right to claim "heroes, saints, demigods and prophets," as antecedents.

One of the most awe-inspiring chapters in the book is "The Grand Armada," in which an account is given of thousands of whales joining together into vast meadows of masses, "as if numerous nations of them had sworn solemn league for mutual assistance and protection." Thus early, like Tennyson, Melville envisions a League of Nations, an organization to bind together individual members. Significantly these individuals are the god-like whales. In this conceit Melville accomplishes two goals: He elevates the nations of the world—and therefore the human beings—to superhuman status, and he further emphasizes the need for companionship and association.

One of the most explicit sections about democracy and humanism is the chapter "Fast-Fish and Loose-Fish." Here Melville reduces to absurdity the laws about ownership of whales: "A Fast-Fish belongs to the party fast to it," the law reads, and "a Loose-Fish is fair game for anybody who can soonest catch it." From this simplistic legalese Melville radiates out to philosophizing about the rights of the poor and of countries. He comes down to particularize about American thoughts on stealing Mexico. From this particular he goes on to the rights of man. Melville's conclusion is a

warning that if one is not careful his rights will be stolen
from him by oversimplified law tailored to fit those people
in power, the wealthy.

Melville's humanism is further developed tellingly in the
person of little Pip and in his fate in the open sea. Pip "loved
life, and all life's peaceable securities." He is destroyed by
Stubb, but Stubb is actually a humanist, as we have seen,
though a rather practical Yankee one. Because of his
propensity for making money, Stubb abandons Pip when he
jumps for the second time from the whale boat. Being
abandoned causes Pip to go insane. Pip becomes "another
lonely castaway" in the open sea. "The awful lonesomeness
is intolerable. The intense concentration of self in the middle
of such a heartless immensity, my God! who can tell it? Mark,
how when sailors in a dead calm bathe in open sea—
mark how closely they hug their ship and long coast along
her sides" (CH. XCIII). This "intense concentration of self in the
middle of such a heartless immensity" simply must be
radiated out and diffused into humanity. Melville indicates
that man must have company to live in this world.

The intensity of Melville's feeling about humanism is
perhaps nowhere better revealed than in the famous chapter
entitled "A Squeeze of the Hand." As Ishmael and his
companions squeeze the knots in the sperm, he blends
spiritually as well as physically with all people, and he
becomes, as it were, Everyman: "I squeezed that sperm till
a strange sort of insanity came over me; and I found myself
unwittingly squeezing co-laborers' hands in it, mistaking
their hands for the gentle globules. Such an abounding,
affectional, friendly, loving feeling did this avocation
beget; that at last I was continually squeezing their hands,
and looking up into their eyes sentimentally; as much as to
say—Oh! my dear fellow beings, why should we longer
cherish any social acerbities, squeeze hands all round; nay,
let us all squeeze ourselves into each other; let us squeeze
ourselves universally into the very milk and sperm of
kindness." The power of this feeling is revealed in the

letter Melville wrote to Hawthorne, already quoted, in which he confessed to his friend that "your heart beat in my ribs and mine in yours, and both in God's."

Further power is given the passage as it is echoed later, when Ahab, on the third day of the chase of the white whale, takes a backward wistful glance at the humanity he rejected years earlier in his monomania and then turns to Starbuck momentarily for the hand of fellowship: "Starbuck, I am old;—shake hands with me, man." Melville explicitly makes his point: "Their hands met; their eyes fastened; Starbuck's tears the glue." The poignancy of this passage, as well as the one it echoes, is increased by the realization that on the preceding day, after the whaleboat had been swamped by Moby-Dick, Ahab had revealed his great need for his fellowman: "Aye, aye, Starbuck, 'tis sweet to lean sometimes, be the leaner who he will; and would old Ahab had leaned oftener than he has."

The sinking of the *Pequod* rounds off the theme of humanism that has been manifest throughout the book. The meeting of the *Rachel* by the *Pequod* helps develop this final statement. The *Rachel* is the most important ship Ahab and his crew meet. The captain of this ship has lost a child, one of the captain's two sons aboard, and he begs Ahab to help search for the boy. He paraphrases Christ in his entreaty: "Do to me as you would have me do to you." But Ahab, now in a frenzy, will have nothing to do with this human plea; nor with any human practice. He even flees from the common practice of burying the dead.

After this build-up Ahab and his crew chase Moby-Dick. On the third day Ahab is yanked from the whale boat by Moby-Dick. The crew, the common people, finally rebelling against Ahab's tyranny over them, are not concerned with the loss of him. Instead of commenting on that, they turn immediately away from him, the tyrannical individual, and back to humanity, back to their ship: "The ship? Great God, where is the ship?" they gasp.

Ahab causes the destruction of everything—himself, the ship and all his fellowmen—by the relentless exercise of his

god-like pride. His pride is strong enough to bring about
the overthrow, if not of the white whale, then at least of
God. For the ship in its sinking drags heaven down with
it, in the form of the bird-of-heaven which sinks with
the ship:

> A sky-hawk that tauntingly had followed the main-
> truck downwards from its natural home among the
> stars, pecking at the flag, and incommoding Tashtego
> there; this bird now chanced to intercept its broad
> fluttering wing between the hammer and the wood;
> and simultaneously feeling that ethereal thrill, the
> submerged savage beneath, in his death-grasp, kept his
> hammer frozen there; and so the bird of heaven, with
> archangelic shrieks, and his imperial beak thrust
> upwards, and his whole captive form folded in the flag
> of Ahab, went down with his ship, which, like Satan,
> would not sink to hell till she had dragged a living
> part of heaven along with her, and helmeted
> herself with it.

Significantly it is Tashtego, the heroic whaler-
commoner, who is last seen on the *Pequod*. Earlier he had
stood near Ahab, his "head . . . almost on a level with
Ahab's heel." Now, however, Tashtego lives longer than
his former captain. Though he is lost, his last gesture,
unlike Ahab's, is a reaching upward toward heaven.
Tashtego does outlive Ahab and he does reach toward
heaven, but it was necessary for him to die, for at least two
reasons. First, his fruitless gesture toward the sky indicates
that heaven has indeed disappeared, as Stephen Crane later
felt, or at least is no longer succor for man. Second, Tashtego
must die because the only person who can survive the
destruction of the world is that man who has risen up to
the stature of "immortal manhood" through the mixture of
the good qualities of paganism, Christianity, and all other
religions: Ishmael. Because of his brotherhood with
Queequeg, and all it has taught him, Ishamel is saved
with the cannibal's help, though Queequeg is present only
in the symbol of his death, his coffin.

Over the destruction of the ship "the great shroud of the sea rolled on as it rolled five thousand years ago." This is a second flood. From it there emerges a new race, with hope for mankind. The *Rachel*, searching for a child, picks up Ishmael floating on his lifeboat. This mother will love and properly care for the newly discovered representative of the human race. Now educated, with the proper breadth and depth of understanding and love for his fellow man, Ishmael will carry on the hope and promise of humanity.

THE POPULAR THEATER MOTIF

In developing his major topic of concern with the problems of humanity, Melville threads the various chapters of the book with a strong fiber of popular theater. There is in *Moby-Dick* both light and heavy legitimate drama— Shakespear's Lear and Fool—but there is also use of the popular theater which constitutes a minor but significant theme that informs both the Shakespearean elements and by other aspects.

By "popular theater" is meant the various kinds of theater in the middle of the nineteenth century which appealed to people in general as distinguished from the "legitimate theater." Burlesques, extravaganzas, farces, variety acts, melodramas, and most significantly, of course, Negro ministrels are included. Although both white- and blackface shows were the same with different colored faces, Melville generally separated them, especially to emphasize the importance of the blackness of the latter;[7] therefore here they are usually distinguished.

Melville's use of this popular theater was especially fortuitous for his purposes. The popular theater is antipathetic to the more "aristocratic" and "heroic" legitimate theater. It is also complementary to the legitimate theater; therefore, in a book covering all

7. On this subject in general see Harry Levin, *The Power of Blackness* (New York, 1958).

elements of all mankind, both halves of the theater should be included. The popular theater is the voice of the common people. It is the theater of the frontier, and a strong element of the frontier, as we shall see, stengthens *Moby-Dick*. It is also strongly laced with folklore, which Melville used to develop his theme. Finally, Melville used the popular theater because he liked it; he was an earthy, common, "popular" person; in using this element he revealed a good deal about his own nature, and helped underscore the purposes of his book. [8]

Melville knew the popular theater well. It was everywhere around him. As Constance Rourke commented: "Through the 40's and 50's the spirit of burlesque was abroad in the land like a powerful genie let out of a windbag." [9] This powerful genie was another of the devices used by people to democratize the land; it was a pin used to prick pretensions and stuffiness, sham and fraud.

Melville was always interested in the "spirit of burlesque," as Matthiessen said. This is clearly demonstrated in his early, sophomoric exercises in the Albany *Microscope* and his nine "Authentic Anecdotes of 'Old Zack,'" which were published in *Yankee Doodle*. Had Melville not learned about it from the stage itself, he would have got a thorough knowledge of the popular theater from the various songbooks of the day. He was a lover of songs and singing. While on the *Acushnet* he and Toby Greene whiled away "many pleasant moonlight watches" telling "yarn and song till 'eight bells,'" Toby reminded him after being discovered alive. [10] Melville wrote to Hawthorne, furthermore, at the time that *Moby-Dick*

<hr>

8. Despite the large body of scholarship on *Moby-Dick* by writers interested in the breadth and depth of Melville's subject matter and technique, this element has unfortunately been sorely underdeveloped. For the best treatments see Daniel G. Hoffman. *Form and Fable in American Fiction* (New York, 1961); Richard Chase, *Herman Melville* (New York, 1949); F. O. Matthiessen, American Renaissance (New York, 1941); Constance Rourke. *American Humor* (New York, 1931).

9. Rourke, *American Humor*, p. 155.

10. Jay Leyda, *The Melville Log* (New York, 1951), 2:632.

was being burningly set to paper, that his picture of heaven included "humorous and comic songs."[11] Finally, Melville would have learned about the comic theater from his fellow sailors and whaling men. On whaling ships the dog-watch was generally spent in singing and dancing. Whaling men carried pocket songsters (small songbooks) on their long voyages.[12] In addition to songs, these books contained skits and passages of stage humor. Melville is known to have been interested in such books and to have consulted them.[13]

On the popular stage there was a general lack of seriousness, a broad humor, a knowing wink at the audience, all of which are characteristics of *Moby-Dick*, and qualities that Melville obviously enjoyed.

The influence of the popular theater is not always obvious. Sometimes it is subtle and intricate. But it is never extraneous, because all elements in the book are functional. Further, this influence explains why in *Moby-Dick* Melville sounds at times like fantastic Shakespeare, when, as Matthiessen felt, he is "lumbering" and his "humor runs thin." But Melville knew what he was doing, however much his readers do not.

That *Moby-Dick* is theatrically oriented Melville makes clear at the very beginning; that it is framed in drama is pointed out in the "Epilogue" which begins, "The drama's done." In the beginning, in "Loomings," Melville sandwiches Ishmael's name on "the bill" between an announcement of an election for the U. S. Presidency and a battle in Afghanistan. Ishmael wonders why he was put down for a whaling voyage, when others were given

11. Leyda, *Log.* 1:423
12. See one of the books that Melville drew on heavily for *Moby-Dick*, J. Ross Browne, *Etching of a Whaling Cruise* (New York, 1846), p. 111. For the extent to which Melville used *Etchings* see Howard P. Vincent, *The Trying-Out of Moby-Dick* (Cambridge, Mass., 1949).

13. Merton M. Sealts, Jr., "Melville's Reading," *Harvard Library Bulletin*, 2, no. 3 (Autumn 1948): items 407, 411.

"magnificent parts in high tragedies, and short and easy
parts in genteel comedies, and jolly parts in farces."
Melville demonstrates that he knows the theater from top
to bottom when he says that Ishmael's going a-whaling
"came in as a sort of brief interlude and solo between
more extensive performances," which was common
practice on the stage of the day. In these words
Melville implies, at least, that the voyage will be more
popular theater than serious play.

The second hint of the popular theater motif—that of
minstrelsy—comes in the next chapter when Ishmael has
just arrived in New Bedford and, wandering around the
cold street looking for a cheap lodging he strays through
a door of a Negro church, and finds the "great Black
Parliament sitting in Tohpet." Discovering his mistake, he
hastily backs out, muttering to himself and revealing the
bent of his mind if not his overt purpose: "no entertainment" in this place. Ishmael's comment serves as
another indicator of the callowness of his mind at this
point. He is ambivalent in his feeling about people in
general, at times callous, at other times concerned, and
at times he does not fully appreciate the implications of a
situation or of his own remarks.

Melville uses popular theater references to contrast the
Negro church and its preacher with Father Mapple and
his church. The setting, the worshippers, and the
ministers are striking contrasts, as we have seen. The
former represents centripetal forces in humanity, the
latter centrifugal and atomistic forces. The Ishmael who
before could not instantly recognize the power of the
Negro purpose quickly identifies the accomplishment,
meant or unintended, of Father Mapple's church. When
Mapple ascends his rope ladder and pulls it up behind
him, thus isolating himself in his "little Quebec,"
Ishmael, pondering this act for some time, lets his mind
wonder to the theater—popular or serious—for he
cannot believe that the preacher, "who enjoyed such a

wide reputation for sincerity and sanctity," could be accused of "courting notoriety by any more tricks of the stage." But Melville's comments are ironic. He means that Mapple is capable of every trick of the stage.

The popular theater motif is carried on when Ishmael applies to the *Pequod* to sign up for the whaling voyage. Captains Peleg and Bildad are stereotyped characters straight from the popular stage. They shout, they use extravagant gestures, their language is overly dramatic. Peleg even threatens standard minstrel violence: "Dost see that leg?" he asks Ishmael. "I'll take that leg away from thy stern, if ever thou talkest of the marchant service to me again." Ishmael expects at least the 275th lay as his earnings for the voyage and would not have been surprised had he been offered the 200th. But when Peleg asks Bildad what lay Ishmael should be given, Bildad answers with the face of the popular theater straight man: "'Thou knowest best,' was the sepulchral reply,'the seven hundred and seventy-seventh wouldn't be too much, would it?'"[14] The two captains even engage in stage horseplay: "Out of this cabin, ye canting, drab-colored son of a wooden gun—a straight wake with ye!" shouts Peleg, making "a rush at Bildad, but with a marvellous oblique, sliding celerity, Bildad for that time eluded him."

This atmosphere is further maintained when Queequeg is brought aboard to sign up. Bildad, impressed with the promising harpooner, wants to engage him. Though nobody else has trouble understanding and pronouncing his name, Peleg, with a touch of the popular theater, mauls it almost beyond recognition: "We must have Hedgehog there, I mean Quohog, in one of our boats." In this carelessness about the human and personal dignity of this individual, Peleg reveals yet again his contempt

14. A "sepulchral" voice was one of the most well-worn techniques of the popular stage. See for example "De Darkey Tragedian," *The Ethiopian Drama*, N. 92 (New York, 1874). On the general subject see Carl Wittke, *Tambo and Bones* (Durham, 1930).

for persons other than himself and those in his immediate circle.

In *Moby-Dick* events usually come in doubles, one backing and commenting on the other. So Chapter XXIX ("Enter Ahab; to him, Stubb") is backed by Chapter XXXI ("Queen Mab"). In the latter Stubb recounts a strange dream he had after being insulted by Ahab. In this dream he was kicking away at a pyramid when "a sort of badger-haired old merman, with a hump on his back, takes me by the shoulders, and slews me round. 'What are you 'bout?' says he. Slid! man, but I was frightened. Such a phiz! but, somehow next moment I was over the fright. 'What am I about?' says I at last. 'And what business is that of yours, I should like to know, Mr. Humpback? Do *you* want a kick?'" Stubb's reference and his slang reintroduce Peleg's threat to kick Ishmael, and the popular theater motif, which is carried on in Stubb's further report: "By the lord, Flask, I had no sooner said that, than he turned round his stern to me, bent over, and dragging up a lot of seaweed he had for a clout—what do you think I saw?—why thunder alive, man, his stern was stuck full of marlinspikes, with the points out." This bawdy gesture is an indication of the common man's contempt for the man in authority, the captains of the world. It had already been used to indicate just such contempt at the end of *Redburn,* when the sailors, having been paid off or cheated out of their wages, all encircle the captain and turn up their rears to him.

The parallel here with *Romeo and Juliet* is obvious. But this sailor-version *anus dentatus* is not from the legitimate stage presentation. Rather the parallel must be to the tradition of the popular theater adaptation. Shakespeare was the most popular single author in American popular theater, and he was the most influential playwright on Melville during these months. There were hundreds of books of songs and jokes, gags and conundrums, burlesques and travesties in which he was used in every conceivable way. *Romeo and Juliet* was one of the most widespread.[15]

The closest known parallel to Melville, which was also. too extreme for presentation—at least to a mixed audience—is the somewhat later burlesque, "The Royal Nonesuch" in *Huckleberry Finn,* in which the King cavorts around the stage naked, "painted all over, ring-streaked-and-striped, all sorts of colors as splendid as a rainbow."

"The Cabin-Table" (CH. XXXIV) which gives the account of the order of precedence in which Ahab and the mates descend to the table to eat, is, as we have seen, a severe attack on privilege and the privileged. Much of the impact of this attack comes from Melville's use of popular theater to burlesque propriety. When Flask, "the third Emir," is alone on deck before being called down he performs as though on the popular stage. "Tipping all sorts of knowing winks in all sorts of directions, and kicking off his shoes, he strikes into a sharp but noiseless squall of a hornpipe right over the Grand Turk's head," then brings up "the rear with music." But he "ships a new face" before stepping into the presence of Ahab "in the character of Abjectus, or the Slave."

The thrust of "The Quarter-Deck" (CH. XXXVI). one of Melville's most effective and dramatic scenes, is intensified by the use of popular stage techniques and material. Ahab has gathered the men around him and nailed the golden doubloon to the mainmast, forcing the men madly to pledge allegiance to him and to the destruction of the white whale. The three mates have been stared down. Starbuck, the first mate, stands alone on the stage, soliloquizing: "My soul is more than matched; she's overmanned; and by a madman!" As he thinks further, his reveries are interrupted by "(A burst of revelry from the forecastle)," as the stage direction gives it. "Oh, God!"

15. See my article "Shakespeare in American Vaudeville and Negro Minstrelsy." *American Quarterly,* 12 (Fall 1960). 374-391.

meditates Starbuck, "That revelry is forward! mark the unfaltering silence aft." Then in the next chapter, as dusk approaches, Melville shifts the scene to Stubb, the thoughtless, jolly mate, who will go to his destruction, he says, laughing. The shift is a minstrel version of the knocking at the gate in *Macbeth* and serves somewhat the same purpose. It interrupts the intensity of the scene so that the reader can feel the full pressure, and it is a stage direction pointing to the next chapter. Stubb's interrupter consists of a popular song:

> We'll drink tonight, with hearts as light,
> To love, as gay and fleeting
> As bubbles that swim, on the beaker's brim,
> And break on the lips while meeting.

In the next chapter ("Midnight, Forecastle") the revelry which so shatteringly interrupted and commented on Starbuck's reverie earlier in the day has now peaked. Whalemen are singing and talking about girls. They want a "jig or two." For their musician they call upon Pip, an amateur Negro minstrel who at home "in his native Tolland County in Connecticut . . . had once enlivened many a fiddler's frolic on the green; and at melodious eventide, with his gay ha-ha! had turned the round horizon into one star-bellied tambourine." Here Melville, significantly, mentions the one musical instrument particularly symbolic of minstrelsy. Melville's further description of Pip is trite and so directly contradictory to his real feeling about the Negro that it can only be interpreted as pointing up Pip's "staginess": "With that pleasant, genial, jolly brightness peculiar to his tribe, which ever enjoy all holidays and festivities with finer, free relish than any other race."

Pip reluctantly agrees to play his tambourine. But the minstrel activity is interrupted by lightning and a squall. All hands tumble up to save the ship, leaving Pip alone to comment on the scene and predict the future. The thought of the white whale makes him "jingle all over

73

like [his] tambourine." The fact that Melville treats
little Pip with such respect here and elsewhere evidences
his real feeling for this little boy and for the Negro in
general. That Melville would treat this whole potentially
frivolous and possibly absurd scene with utmost
artistic and aesthetic respect reveals how fully he called
upon all aspects of life to drive his point home. In this
particular scene the minstrel motif is left in suspension to
be picked up and intensified later.

The motif is carried on in the powerfully dramatic
chapter called "Stubb's Supper" (CH. LXIV) in which
Stubb, having killed his whale, demands a whale steak.
Hoffman says that the cook's sermon is "comic in the
frontier fashion."[16] In fact, both the cook and the sermon
are more from Negro minstrelsy, as for example are the
stage directions: "This old Fleece, as they called him,
came shuffling and limping along, assisting his steps with
his tongs, which, after a clumsy fashion, were made of
straightened iron hoops." Fleece's exhortation is a
minstrel mock sermon, the dialect that of the Negro
stage: "Your woraciousness, fellow-critturs, I don't blame
ye so much for; dat is natur, and can't be helped; but to
gobern dat wicked natur, dat is de pint." Fleece's speech
is fundamental to a full meaning of the book. It is an
answer to Mapple's earlier anti-humanistic sermon.
Fleece's is thoroughly humanistic: to him all creatures
are brothers and are to be understood and forgiven their
failures. Fleece's sermon likewise takes the reader back
to the Negro preacher in New Bedford and his example
of brotherly love. Mapple's sermon has been weighed
against two others—both black, and one a Negro
minstrel version—and in both cases been found wanting.

Melville is not always serious about his popular stage.
As a laugh is a mighty good thing, as he said, so too he
probably thought that burlesque for its own sake is

16.   Hoffman, *Form and Fable*, p. 250.

worthy. Several examples, any way, seem to advance such a notion.

One occurs when the *Pequod* meets the *Rose-Bud* and Stubb conspires with the Guernsey chief-mate of the latter ship to relieve the Frenchman of the blasted whale which is tied alongside. In a veritable comedy, the chief mate mistranslates everything that Stubb says, in a scene which can only be looked upon as burlesque at its best—or worst.

Another example of burlesque humor is developed in the next chapter, "Ambergris" (CH. XCII). Melville is in a sportive mood about the paradox of this sweet substance coming from the bowels of the whale. Earlier, he had found humor about the bowels irresistible. In "The Pequod Meets the Virgin" (CH. LXXXI). for example, Stubb is chasing a "huge, humped old bull," the spout of which is "short, slow, and laborious; coming forth with a choking sort of gush, and spending itself in torn shreds, followed by strange subterranean commotions in him, which seemed to have egress at his other buried extremity, causing the waters behind him to upbubble." Stubb cannot resist referring to what must have been a whaler's joke but was typical of all burlesque humor: "Who's got some paregoric? He has the stomach ache. Adverse winds are holding mad Christmas in him, boys. It's the first foul wind I ever knew to blow from astern."

Melville's delight in the subject continues into the chapter on ambergris. He says that one cause for the creation of the substance is supposed to be dyspepsia. "How to cure such a dyspepsia it were hard to say, unless by administering three or four boat loads of Brandreth's pills, and then running out of harm's way, as laborers do in blasting rocks." From this joke, Melville turns to another which must have been even more common among sailors. Among whalers unnatural sexual relations were endemic, and jokes about copulation between man and whale must have been numerous. Melville says: "I have forgotten to

75

say that there were found in this ambergris, certain hard, round, bony plates, which at first Stubb thought might be sailors' trousers butons.''

Such a joke would have been merely the salt-water version of the type of humor ubiquitous on land, circulated for example in the numerous Crockett almanacs, which Melville had published in, and probably on the burlesque stage. In the Crockett *Awl-Man-Axe* for 1839, for example, there is the joke about ''the height of folly,'' which is, ''being so tall that you are obliged to climb a ladder to shave yourself.''[17] This type of joke is still a favorite genre of folk humor today. A widespread example is: ''Do you know what the height of folly is? A flea crawling up an elephant's leg with rape on his mind.'' That Melville was not above such humor is evidenced by his references in other books, and to his use of it in the climactic third day of the chase of Moby-Dick. As the *Pequod* sinks beneath the waves, Stubb, resigned to death, still thinks of life, and says, ''For me, off shoes and jacket to it; let Stubb die in his drawers! . . . cherries! cherries! cherries! Oh, Flask, for one red cherry ere we die!'' Flask, misunderstanding the sexual implications, merely replies: ''Cherries! I only wish that we were where they grow.''[18] In view of the fact that in ''The Cassock''(CH.XCV), the whole chapter is built on what must have been rough sailor humor, on ''the grandissimus, as the mariners call it,'' which is ''longer than a Kentuckian is tall,'' it is a serious oversight not to take his references to ''cherries'' in their sexual sense.

Pip's idiocy, which resulted from his being abandoned in the sea by Stubb, is picked up and developed in the chapter entitled ''The Doubloon'' (CH.XCIX). This chapter is the quintessence of the book. It is the first climax, the

17. Chase, *Melville*, p. 72

18. For a different interpretation of the cherry references, see Alan Heimert, ''*Moby-Dick* and American Political Symbolism'' *American Quarterly*. 15 (Winter, 1963), 498-534. Heimert would connect this reference with George Washington.

projection of the conclusion. It is built, as many others
are, on humor of the popular stage, on the kind that
Rosenberry called "dramatic-structural": "The artist . . .
deploys his comic forces to expose the vital interplay of
character and situation and performs the successful act
of creation that fuses the disparate elements of comedy
and tragedy into a balanced work of art."

One of the important series of themes in the book has
to do with the physical, visceral, sexual, and circular.
The last mentioned develops the book around the figure
of a center, of roundness. Sometimes the references are
used for fun and jokes, sometimes for satire, sometimes
for gratuitous shock. Generally they emanate from a
conception of the belly as the microcosm of the world,
the center of things, as the focal point. Usually the working
of this motif is political and humanistic, as well as artistic,
and is used for yet another of Melville's controls and methods
of development. Because this motif is closely tied in with
popular humor and theater, it is appropriate that it be discussed at this point.

To Melville, God is the center of the world, "that democratic
dignity which, on all hands, radiates without end from God;
Himself! the great God absolute! The centre and circumference
of all democracy! His omnipresence, our divine equality!" But
Melville means more than he says here.

This "center" radiates from the religious in several ways;
in one it goes into the superstitious, incantatory, and magical.
When the Spanish sailor insults Daggoo and they prepare to
battle, for example, the other sailors draw a ring for the com-
batants. The situation then develops both religiously and
politically. The old Manx sailor, the wiseman of the ship, the
Delphic oracle, comments: "Ready formed. There! the ringed
horizon. In that ring Cain struck Abel. Sweet work, right work!
No? Why then, God, Mad'st thou the ring?" Manx apparently
thinks, and says ironically, that God approved, or tacitly
allowed, the murder of Abel by Cain. Politically the Spaniard
represents here, as he will in "Benito Cereno," the old order—
a Cain-like old order—because he tried to enter the ring with

a knife against Daggoo, the noble, heroic, natural Abel, who carries no knife.

The terror of the circle, as well as the peace found at its heart, is well illustrated in the grand armada of whales into which the sailors are pulled when they are dragged from "the circumference of commotion" into "the innermost heart of the shoal, as if from some mountain torrent we had slid into a serene valley lake." From this situation Ishmael later introduces a prefiguration of his own salvation, springing forth from the grave of his fellowmen, from the center of both destruction and salvation: "But even so, amid the tornadoed Atlantic of my being, do I myself still for ever centrally disport in mute calm: and while ponderous planets of unwaning woe revolve round me, deep down and deep inland there I still bathe me in eternal mildness of joy."

The doubloon chapter further enriches the circle motif. The coin itself is a magic circle, "set apart and sanctified to one awe-striking end." Melville points at its importance: "Some significance lurks in all things, else all things are little worth, and the round world itself but an empty cipher, except to sell by the cartload, as they do hills about Boston, to fill up some morass in the Milky Way." The capitol of Ecuador, whence the doubloon came, is the "middle of the world, and beneath the great equator." After Ahab's reading of the coin, Starbuck, the Christian humanist, sees in it "this vale of Death," in which "God girds us round."

The symbol of the doubloon is reemphasized when all hands stand around the coin with their "eyes centrally fixed" on it, eager for the call to turn their ship toward the line, the equator, to seek out the white whale. Later Ahab tells Pip, "Thou touchest my inmost centre, boy; thou art tied to me by cords woven of my heart-strings." Ahab's dreadful injury to his groin is invested with the magic of the circle. His "temporary recluseness" on shore before the sailing of the Pequod was attributed to "that

timid circle the above hinted casualty . . . invested itself
with terrors, not entirely underived from the land of
spirits and wails."

These circular spirits and wails strengthen Queequeg
in his illness. Near death, his "eyes, nevertheless, seemed
growing fuller and fuller . . . and mildly but deeply
looked out at you there from his sickness, a wondrous
testimony to that immortal health in him which could not
die, or be weakened. And like circles on the water, which,
as they grow fainter, expand; so his eyes seemed
rounding and rounding, like the rings of Eternity."

At times the center can be deceptive, seeming to offer
salvation when in fact it does not. Crazy Pip thinks it will
save him. When in "The Cabin" (CH. XCIX). Pip in his
madness is bewailing the loss of Pip, he says, "Here,
then. I'll seat me, against the transom, in the ship's full
middle, all her keel and her three masts before me." But
he is dragged down to destruction when the ship sinks.

The circle figure is also used to build up the terror and
size of the whales. In the first days of the killing, when
the first right whale is harpooned, he, pierced by the
irons from two boats, goes "round the stern of the ship
towing the two boats after him, so that they performed a
complete circuit." And thus, Melville says, "round and
round the *Pequod* the battle went." The symbol is
continued in the battle with Moby-Dick. On the first day
of the chase, after smashing Ahab's boat, the whale
"swam swiftly round and round the wrecked crew,
sideways churning the water in his vengeful wake, as if
lashing himself up to still another and deadlier assault."
And "so revolvingly appalling was the White Whale's
aspect, and so planetarily swift the ever-contracting
circles he made, that he seemed horizontally swooping
down upon them." The whalers in the other boats dare
not interfere with Moby-Dick's activities. They remain "on
the outer edge of the direful zone, whose centre had now
become the old man's head." Only the bigger ship, the
Pequod, the symbol of humanity and the world itself, is

able to come in and break up "the charmed circle," and part the whale from the whalers.

The circle figure is used also to contrast Ahab's nature with mere man's: "In an instant's compass, great hearts sometimes condense to one deep pang . . .; for even in their pointless centres, those nobler natures contain the entire circumference of inferior souls."

By slight extension the circle is the viscera, the bowels, the umbilicus, procreation and death and resurrection which, again, numerous quotations illustrate. In "The Grand Armada" (CH. LXXXVII), the whaleman were "in that enchanted calm which they say lurks at the heart of every commotion. And still in the distracted distance we beheld the tumults of the outer concentric circles. . . ." In this stillness Queequeg and Starbuck see "long coils of the umbilical cord of Madame Leviathan, by which the young cub seemed still tethered to its dam." Further, "some of the subtlest secrets of the sea seemed divulged to us in this enchanted pond. We saw young Leviathan amours in the deep." When squeezing out the sperm in "A Squeeze of the Hand" (CH. XCIV), fingers begin "to serpentine and spiralize." In the chapter called "The Fossil Whale" (CH. CIV), Melville says: "Since I have undertaken to manhandle this Leviathan, it behoves me to approve myself omnisciently exhaustive in the enterprise; not overlooking the minutest seminal germs of his blood, and spinning him out to the uttermost coil of his bowels." Finally, as the *Pequod*, battered by Moby-Dick, sinks beneath the waves, "concentic circles seized the lone boat itself, and all its crew, and each floating oar, and every lance-pole, and spinning, animate and inanimate, all round and round in one vortex, carried the smallest chip of the Pequod out of sight" (CH. CXXXV).

But out of this circle Ishmael was resurrected: "Round and round, then, and ever contracting towards the button-like black bubble at the open of that slowly wheeling circle, like another Ixion I did revolve. Till, gaining that vital centre, the black bubble upward burst; and now . . . rising with great force, the coffin life-buoy shot lengthwise from the sea, fell over, and floated by my side" ("Epilogue").

Because of these various feed-ins the doubloon chapter is overwhelmingly important. The significance of the chapter is developed by its setting, that of the popular stage. Stubb stands by, hidden, while various members of the crew soliloquize. Each shapes the symbolism of the doubloon into his own likeness. The last to speak is Pip: "Here's the ship's navel, this doubloon here, and they are all on fire to unscrew it. But, unscrew your navel, and what's the consequence? . . . Cook! ho, cook! and cook us! Jenny! hey, hey, hey, hey, hey, Jenny, Jenny! and get your hoe-cake done!"

Vincent and Mansfield have remarked on the omphalos symbolism or the reference to the navel as being the center of life and being. But there is more. Melville had said earlier: "There are certain queer times and occasions in this strange mixed affair we call life when a man takes this whole universe for a vast practical joke, though the wit thereof he but dimly discerns, and more than suspects that the joke is at nobody's expense but his own" (CH. XLIX). Here Melville is carrying this serious joke forward. He is working in the common popular theater joke of the day that if you unscrew your navel your rear end will fall off.[19]

The setting is clear. Pip ends his speech with a shuffle, while singing "Jenny, get your hoe-cake done," a minstrel song immensely popular at the time, as Williard Thorpe has recognized.[20] This practice of having patter ended with a shuffle was, of course, the very fiber of minstrelsy. An illustration with a bit of Shakespeare, ending with the most famous of the "jump" songs, will be informative:

19. John D. Seelye, "The Golden Navel: The Cabalism of Ahab's Doubloon." *Nineteenth-Century Fiction*, 14 (March 1960), 350-355.
20. Willard Thorpe, ed. *Moby-Dick or the Whale* (New York, 1947), p. 408.

Oh! tis consummation
Devoutly to be wished,
To end your heartache by a sleep;
When likely to be dished,
Shuffle off your mortal coil,
Do just so,
Wheel about and turn about
And jump Jim Crow.[21]

With the minstrel aspect firmly established, Melville
carries on the popular theater motif while having the
Pequod meet, in the next chapter, the *Samuel Enderby*.
This is a zany ship, straight from a 19th-century *Hellzapoppin*.
The captain has lost his arm to Moby-Dick, and wears an
ivory one. Ahab is brought to the deck of the *Enderby* by
sitting on a blubber-hook, surely as undignified an entry as
he could have had. As soon as Ahab touches the deck, the
other captain approaches: "and Ahab, putting out his ivory
leg, and crossing the ivory arm (like two sword-fish blades)
cried out in his walrus way, 'Aye, aye, hearty! let us shake
bones together.'" Never before has Ahab had a "walrus"
voice, and never has he been hearty. The zany captain is
companioned with other fantastics. His name is Boomer,
his surgeon's name is Bunger, his first mate's name is
Mounttop, and the others, who are unnamed, probably have
similar appellations. Rosenberry recognized that these
people are straight from the stage. The significance of the
confrontation between these men and Ahab is portentous.
They are lighthearted. Boomer is not sorry he lost his arm
to Moby-Dick; he is delighted that he lost no more. But
Ahab is dark and terrifying. Here on the same stage popular
theater faces tragedy, and tragedy stalks away to its ruin.
Boomer's arm remains intact. But Ahab quits the *Samuel
Enderby* so precipitately that he half splinters his leg and
has it replaced.

Back on the *Pequod,* Ahab sends for the carpenter to
build a new leg. Here Melville reverses his usual order of

21. See my article, already cited, p. 382.

having light comedy follow serious drama; instead he has the carpenter, standing before his vice-bench trying to be serious while making a man, burlesqueing his own seriousness by sneezing in the middle of every stroke of work and every half thought. His feelings are callous and indifferent, but he turns to lighthearted banter: "If I but only had the time, I could turn him [Ahab] out as neat a leg now as ever (*sneezes*) scraped to a lady in a parlor." This is obviously Shakespeare, but more Shakespeare spoofed than given straight.

We next see mad Pip when he wanders in to talk to Queequeg, who, as all believe, is sick unto death and is testing the comfort of his newly built coffin. Pip draws near, and "holding his tambourine" says: "Poor rover! Will ye never have done with all this weary roving?" The words are probably a paraphrase of those of the chorus of a widely sung sea-song generally called "A-Roving!":

> A-roving, a-roving
> Since roving's been my ruin
> I'll go no more a-roving
> With you, fair maid.

Then Pip shakes his tambourine and says: "Rig-a-dig, dig dig! Now, Queequeg, die; and I'll beat ye your dying march."

In Starbuck's replies to Pip, Melville carries on the popular theater motif by echoing *Julius Caesar:* "I have heard that in violent fevers, men, all ignorance, have talked in ancient tongues." After another dozen lines Starbuck listens to Pip again. Pip "wildly" picks up the *Caesar* and develops it further: "Form two and two! Let's make a General of him! Ho, where's his harpoon! Lay it across her.—Rig-a-dig, dig, dig, huzza! Oh for a game cock now to sit upon his head and crow. Queequeg dies game! mind ye that; Queequeg dies game!"

22. William M. Doerflinger, *Shantymen and Shantyboys* (New York, 1951), p. 51. Melville's lines are also close to Byron's "So We'll Go No More A-Roving." Byron was well-known to Melville.

In developing his burlesque Melville interweaves several aspects. Earlier he had said that Stubb "would hum over his old rigadig tunes while flank and flank with the most exasperated monster." Here Pip quotes these words to contrast his own cowardice with Queequeg's bravery. Queequeg's bravery is, of course, Caesar's: "Cowards die many times before their deaths: The valiant never taste of death but once." This passage in *Caesar* contains words which, further, make a microcosm of the whole of *Moby-Dick*: "What can be avoided whose end is purpos'd by the mighty gods?"

Perhaps the neatest mixture in this passage is Melville's play on the Roman custom of reading the entrails of birds and beasts as auguries, and the popular theater—and general—tradition of the "Game Cock of the Wilderness," a usage which could hardly have escaped the attention of contemporary readers.

When we see Pip again, Melville is reintroducing the joke about the navel (CH. CXXV). Now just before the three-day battle with Moby-Dick begins, Ahab is battling the elements. He orders the Manxman to heave the log, but the Manxman fears that the line will part. When he does throw it, the line does part, and as Ahab stalks away, the Manxman remarks: "Where he goes now; to him nothing's happened; but to me, *the skewer seems loosening out of the middle of the world!*" (my emphasis). At this point Pip appears, riveting together the significance of the earlier joke and the fate of the ship.

The grand ending of the book—the "Epilogue"—blends all elements. The joke about the navel, which by now has become a motif, is given a final comment. Melville returns to his circle-center theme. Ishmael swirls "towards the button-like black bubble at the axis of that slowly wheeling circle," until from it springs his salvation, his resurrection, the coffin on which he rides to safety and immortality. He is resurrected from the belly button of the world.

Moby-Dick is a many-stranded rope, intricately wound. Melville's use of material from the popular theater, and the

many ways he interweaves it with allied material,
strengthen the fiber of the book as a whole. No other
American—not even Hawthorne—has taken material
intrinsically so slight and threaded it so thematically
and profoundly into a work of art which demonstrates so
profoundly the philosophy of humanism.

FOLKLORE: BLOODSTREAM
OF HUMANITY

Melville's use of folklore in this book is the most extensive of all American creative writers, including Hawthorne's. Hawthorne's was extensive and effective, and much
of his greatness, critics agree, results from his probing "human nature in the mass," or what he called, "the depths of
our common nature." One major technique by which Hawthorne did his probing was extensive use of international
folklore motifs. But in too many instances his development
of these motifs was awkward, mechanical, and essentially
two-dimensional, something like articulated skeletons, capable of moving but lacking all flesh and blood.

   Melville's development was superior for obvious reasons.
He was more nearly of the folk. His Harvard and Yale, the
Acushnet, was in many ways a folkschool; equally important, he did not lose the folklore that pulsed through him
in the sophisticated processes of formal schooling. Furthermore, he delighted in folklore. Rambunctious by nature
when relaxed and enjoying himself, he was a great teller of
tales. Toby Green reminded him once how the two had
whiled away "many pleasant moonlight watches . . . with yarn
and song till 'eight bells'," and Melville collected the now-
famous Agatha story and suggested that Hawthorne write
it. In *Moby-Dick* Melville uses his folklore to establish a
broader base and richer development for the book than would
have been possible without it. Thus he provides at the same
time more "truth" and more enjoyment. Most important,
however, Melville's use of folklore, the blood-stream of

humanity, deepens the roots of development for the triumph of humanism.

Melville's belief in the power of folklore is revealed in this work in two remarks. Always skeptical of everything but seldom dismissing out of hand anything that comments on the human situation, he questions: "Are you a believer in ghosts, my friend? There are other ghosts than the Cocklane one, and far deeper men than Doctor Johnson who believe in them." Later, Melville discusses how some Nantuckers distrust the story of Jonah, as "some skeptical Greeks and Romans . . . doubted the story of Hercules and the whale, and Arion and the dolphin; and yet their doubting those traditions did not make those traditions one with the less fact, for all that"(CH. LXXXIII).

Melville begins working in folklore early in the book, at the Spouter-Inn, turning to folk wisdom to ground his authority on an appeal to highest authority. He is trying to fathom various and illusory meanings of the dark and greasy picture on the wall. He advances numerous theories and possible explanations as he demonstrates the complexity of truth, the "sublimity about it that fairly froze you to it." In the final analysis, however, Ishmael the naif, the innocent, the folkfigure, concludes that the symbol is clear. The drawing pictures a ship in a great hurricane with a whale impaling himslef on the three mast-heads. The message is that nature and God in the whale descending from above are trying to destroy the ship of mankind but are unable to succeed. Ishmael makes clear that his interpretation is that of the folk: a final theory of his own, "partly based upon the aggregated opinions of many aged persons with whom I conversed upon the subject"(CH. III).

The wall opposite this picture is developed folkloristically also. On the wall are the weapons of white whalers, rusty, broken, and deformed. Their weapons, like white people's lives, are supported by myths and lies of one kind or another: "Some were storied weapons." One story is of Nathan Swain who "did kill fifteen whales

between a sunrise and a sunset." Another story about
a harpoon "so like a corkscrew now," shows the
ubiquitousness of the whale, how he traveled from the
Javan seas to the Cape of Blanco. This story is capped
off by the belief that the iron traveled forty feet in the
whale, from the tale to the head, like a restless needle
sojourning in the body of a man (CH. III).

Melville uses proverbs and folk-like proverbs freely to
illustrate or prove a point. Sometimes they are integral,
sometimes peripheral and comic. In examining the
amazing character Queequeg and proving his superiority
over other men, Melville discusses philosophers in
general and the intuitive philosophy of Queequeg,
rounding off his comment: "So soon as I hear that such
a man gives himself out for a philosopher, I conclude
that, like the dyspeptic old woman, he must have
'broken his digester'" (CH. X). Later the mad prophet
Elijah, talking with Ishmael and Queequeg, discounts the
real need of a soul, by giving a proverb: "A soul's a sort
of a fifth wheel to a wagon" (CH. XIX).

Proverbs are most widely used when the various
sailors are in the forecastle at midnight before the squall.
The setting itself is folkloristic. These sailors are nervous
because they can sense the coming of the storm. The
Long Island sailor reveals his nervousness in two good
American proverbs: "Hoe corn when you may," and "all
legs go to harvest soon." The Danish sailor attests to the
seaworthiness of the ship in the storm with a proverb:
"So long as thou crackest, thou holdest!" In the near-
fight between Daggoo and the Spanish sailor, each
combatant belittles the other with proverbs. Daggoo
curses the Spaniard with "white skin, white liver!" to
which the latter responds with "big frame, small spirit!"
(CH. XL). Even Ahab in his flight from all restraint against
his coming battle with God in the whale cries out
against Pip that there is too much in him that is cursing
his malady—"like cures like." Then he clinches the
proverb in his own repetition: "Oh! spite of million

87

villains, this makes me a bigot in the fadeless fidelity of man!—and a black! and crazy!—but methinks like-cures-like applies to him too; he grows so sane again"(CH. CXXIX).

Less often Melville uses folk comparisons, similes, and metaphors to strengthen the fiber of his book. In describing the try-works, the terrifying open-mouthed flame, he says it "smells like the left wing of the day of judgment." In contrast, the product of that fire, the whale oil, is "as sweet as early grass butter in April" (CH. XCVI).

Folklore is used to build up character. Melville begins by saying that whaleman are as superstitious as other sailors, "unexempt from that ignorance and superstitiousness hereditary to all sailors." He continues: "No wonder then that ever gathering volume from the mere transit over the wildest watery spaces, the outblown rumors of the White Whale did in the end incorporate with themselves all manner of morbid hints, and half-formed foetal suggestions of supernatural agencies, which eventually invested Moby-Dick with new terrors unborrowed from anything that visibly appears." Melville then quotes both Olassen and Povelson about the terror of the sperm whale, and builds on their exaggerated statements: "yet in their full terribleness, even to the bloodthirsty item of Povelson, the superstitious belief in them is, in some vicissitudes of their vocation, revived in the minds of the hunters." "So that overawed by the rumors and portents concerning" Moby-Dick, many whalemen thought that the sperm whale cound not be "hopefully pursued" by "mortal man," though some of the sailors "without superstitious accompaniments, were sufficiently hardy not to flee from the battle if offered." But one of the "wild suggestions" was that Moby Dick was "ubiquitous," and "nor, credulous as such minds much have been, was this conceit altogether without some faint show of superstitious probability." One belief was that the whale had found the "nor' West Passage." This and other beliefs, "these fabulous narrations are almost fully equalled by the realities of the whalemen." Some whalemen went even further in their superstitions, "declaring Moby-Dick not only ubiquitous, but immortal." There was enough in the earthly make and incontestable character of the monster to strike the imagination with unwonted power" (CH. XLI).

The old Manxman—the oracle and shaman of the ship—engages in white voodoo or magic to tell when and under what conditions the whale will be encountered. In an obvious echo of *Macbeth*, he gives out information taught to him by the "old witch in Copenhagen" that, "If the White Whale be raised, it must be in a month and a day, when the sun stands in some one of these signs" (CH. XLII).

Folklore is used to emphasize the whiteness of both the whale and the squid. Indicating the terribleness of the whale, Melville caps off his portrait with: "Nor even in our superstitions do we fail to throw the same snowy mantle round our phantoms; all ghosts rising in a milkwhite fog." According to legend and folklore few whale-ships ever beheld the white squid, and "returned to their ports to tell of it" (CH. LXXV).

Twice folklore is used, both times with tongue-in-cheek frontier exaggeration, to describe the whale. "The Right Whale's head bears a rather inelegant resemblance to a gigantic galliot-toed shoe. Two hundred years ago an old Dutch voyager likened its shape to that of a shoemaker's last. And in this same last or shoe, that old woman of the nursery tale, with a swarming brood, night very comfortably be lodged, she and all her progeny." In describing the hare-lip of the right whale, Melville facetiously remarks, reaching to one of the most widespread folk beliefs about birthmarking, that "probably the mother during an important interval was sailing down the Peruvian coast, when earthquakes caused the beach to gape" (CH. LXXV).

Folklore is also widely used in characterizing Ahab. Ahab is keenly aware of folk practices in dealing with sea weather. The proper way to "kill a squall, something as they burst a watersprout with a pistol" is to allow your ego full range and "fire your ship into it!" Folk analogy caps off Ahab's character delineation: "He lived in the world, as the last of the Grisley Bears lived in settled Missouri. And as when Spring and Summer had departed, that wild Logan of the woods, burying himself in the hollow of a tree, lived out the winter there, sucking his own paws; so, in his inclement, howling old age, Ahab's soul, shut up in the caved trunk of his body, there fed upon the sullen paws of its gloom!" (CH. XXXIV).

The poignancy of Ahab's Prometheanism is revealed folkloristically. In the powerful scene between himself and the carpenter, Ahab orders the carpenter to build a man, and especially to build another leg which when he mounts he "shall nevertheless feel another leg in the same identical place" where he should have his real leg. The carpenter replies "Truly sir, I begin to understand now. Yes, I have heard something curious on that score, sir: how that a dismasted man never entirely loses the feeling of his old spar, but it will be still pricking him at times. May I humbly ask if it be really so, sir?" To which Ahab, with great regret, responds, revealing the degree to which he has ceased being a mere man and has become in fact demonic: "It is, man. Look, put thy live leg here in the place where mine was; so, now, here is only one distinct leg to the eye, yet two to the soul. Where thou feelest tingling life; there, exactly there, there to a hair, do I" (CH. CVIII).

The character of Fedallah and his eventual usurpation of Ahab's soul is boiled in the cauldron of witches' brew and demonism. From the moment he goes aboard the *Pequod* in Nantucket, we know that he is a devil. This picture is enlarged upon by superstitious Stubb and Flask after a right whale has been killed and made fast to the ship opposite the sperm whale. They remember that Fedallah who knows "all about ships' claims" has said that after the head of a sperm whale has been hoisted on the starboard and a right whale's on the larboard the ship can never afterwards capsize. Fedallah knows "all about ships' charms" because he is the devil. According to these two men, Fedallah coils his tail in his pocket or in the "eye of the rigging," and wears oakum stuffed in the toes of his boots (CH. LXXIII). Ahab wanted him aboard so that like Faust and numerous other such dealers throughout folk history, he could make a bargain with him. Ahab makes the bargain, blending his soul with that of Fedallah in the famous scene where one shadow overmatches the other, and subsequently grows more and more demonic. When talking to the carpenter about building him another leg, Ahab touches on demonic creation, like Bannadonna later in "The Bell-Tower," by asserting that he will "get a crucible, and into it, and dissolve himself down to one small, compendious vertebrae." This flaming demonism grows stronger, when later Ahab brings to the blacksmith for his use in forging the magical harpoon the "nail-stubbs of the steel shoes of racing horses," "the best and stubbornest stuff. . . Blacksmiths ever work," which will "weld together like glue from the melted bones of murderers."

The demonism increases in tempo and significance as the barbs for the harpoon are made magical through ritual. Ahab takes the characteristic oath: he will "neither shave, sup, nor pray," until the whale is destroyed. The points are then tempered in "pagan" blood drawn from "three punctures made in the heathen flesh," like the brew from Macbeth's witches, all blessed—or cursed—with the demonic chant: "Ego non baptizo ten in nomine patris, sed in nomine diaboli!" "deliriously howled" by Ahab. These demoniac activities are further emphasized when Ahab gets false heaven's blessings in stretching the new tow-line until it "hummed like a harp-string," with which he bound pole and iron together "like the Three Fates." All ritual is capped off by the "wretched laugh" of Pip, the approval of a mad boy (CH. CXIII). Ahab grows as demon, drawing upon ritual, after the thunder has turned the needles of the compass. In

91

correcting them, Ahab performs like a magician, or witch-doctor. He exercises his "subtile skill" in a manner to "revive the spirits of his crew." "Abashed glances of servile wonder were exchanged by the sailors, as this was said; and with fascinated eyes they awaited whatever magic might follow." Only Christian Starbuck fails to be mesmerized. By the time Moby-Dick is sighted, Ahab has become the devil as dog, one of the oldest and most popular forms for Satan. Probably drawing from "Ethan Brand," Ahab sniffs out Moby-Dick like a "sagacious ship's dog."

Melville employs folklore in the form of omens to reveal the degree to which Ahab has gone insane. On the first day of the chase of the hated whale Starbuck uses the wrecked boat as an ill omen. Ahab rejects both the object as an omen and the idea of omens as such: "If the gods think to speak outright to man, they will honorably speak outright: not shake their heads and give an old wives' darkling hint." But the next day his madness has raged to the point where Ahab actually believes in omens, or uses them to sway the sailors to his evil purpose. After the boat has been wrecked a second time, Ahab rails: "Believe ye, men, in the things called omens? Then laugh aloud, and cry encore! For ere they drown, drowning things will twice rise to the surface; then rise again, to sink forevermore. So with Moby-Dick—two days he's floated—tomorrow will be the third."

The superiority of Queequeg over white men and their superstitions and religion is demonstrated through folklore. After the cannibal harpooner has been measured for his coffin, the Long Island sailor says: "Oh! poor fellow! he'll have to die now." But Queequeg, as though he were overturning such superstitions, gets well. It is Pip who cures him. While Queequeg is lying in his coffin, testing to be sure it is a comfortable place, Pip approaches and renders the last rites, in a minstrel

parody of Christian practice. Starbuck, paraphrasing
Shakespeare, builds on the situation by stating that he
has heard that men in "violent fevers," "all ignorance
have talked in ancient tongues," and have thus shown
amazing wisdom. Pip reveals the depth of his wisdom
in stating that Queequeg "dies game." "To all this ritual
above and about him, the cannibal "lay with closed eyes,
as if in a dream." But though half dead while these
Christian practices were being carried out, Queequeg
rallied, saying that he could live or die as he willed.
Melville's point is apparently that Queequeg here, as
elsewhere, passes through Christian belief and practice in
death and thereafter rose to a higher humanism.
Thereafter he strove "in his rude way" to copy parts of
the twisted tattooing on his body, the grotesque figures
and drawings, onto the coffin, tying in this scene with the
earlier one on "The Counterpane," in which Melville
made it explicit that the heathenish symbols of the
cannibal blend in indistinguishably with the symbols of
Christian religion.

Finally, Melville employs folklore to heighten and
intensify the drama of the final destruction of Ahab and
his world. On the crucial third day (magic in both
Christianity and folklore), as the captain sets out from the
ship for the last time, he is twice-warned though folk
wisdom of his impending doom. In the first place, the
"first sharks that had been observed by the *Pequod* since
the White Whale had been first descried," suddenly
appear and, aware of their coming feast, follow Ahab's
boat. "Whether it was that Ahab's crew were all such
tiger-yellow barbarians, and therefore their flesh more
musky to the senses of the sharks—a matter sometimes
well known to affect them—however it was, they seemed
to follow that one boat without molesting the others." In
other words, as in folk belief that like cures like, sharks
here are going to "cure" the shark-like devils on Ahab's
boat.

Ahab, ever more aware of hovering disaster, experiences a phenomenon well established in folk belief—premonition of death through extra sensitivity: "Oh! my God! what is this that shoots through me, and leaves me so deadly calm, yet expectant,—fixed at the top of a shudder! Future things swim before me, as in empty outlines and skeletons."

This folklore is used just as richly and fully here as the popular theater was used, as we saw in the preceding section. In Melville more than in any other American writer folklore was accorded its great importance in the life of man.

RAMPAGING FRONTIER HUMOR

Closely tied in with the folklore *per se* is a powerful muscle of popular frontier humor of the Davy Crockett-Mike Fink variety. Melville, as Chase and Hoffman have well shown, was closely connected with this kind of humor. He first began his writing by doing sketches for the Crockett-type magazines.

Moby-Dick is of course in concept and execution the most monstrous frontier exaggeration, the greatest joke, of all. The whale, the aquatic equivalent of the White Steed of the Plains, is bigger than life; Ahab is a Titan; God is grander than Himself. The rhetoric, the sheer power of the language, is, as Matthiessen says, a grand, explosive jest. The world of the book is, as Melville affirms, a vast joke. In blowing his book up to proportions larger than life, Melville achieves a result that at times is a jarring mixture of the grand and sublime and the grotesque and ridiculous, seemingly in places almost a wrenching away from the main thrust of the book. But the momentum, the sheer power of motion, carries Melville's point across. This particular point is that through frontier humor, as well as folklore in general, Melville grounds his metaphysic on reality, his rhetoric on the vernacular and every day. Thus the frontier exaggeration helps democratize the whole book, and expands the base on which is developed the main theme of humanism.

The humor operates on several levels, from the understatement to the ridiculously gargantuan, from the straightfaced to the uncontrollably guffawing.

Understatement starts with the beginning of the book. Ishmael is telling about how people all over Manhattan are attracted to the water, from all directions and kinds of streets. He rounds off his statement with a quiet slide into a ridiculous question: "Tell me, does the magnetic virtue of the needles of the compasses of all those ships attract them thither?" After he has found his way into the Spouter-Inn in New Bedford, a new shipload of men from the Grampus are heard rioting down the street, and Peter Coffin, the proprietor, says in the most natural and matter-of-fact manner, "Hurrah, boys; now we'll have the latest news from the Feegees," as though anybody could possibly care for this latest bulletin. Later Coffin, who is good at this Yankee straightfaced humor, explains where Queequeg is and why he has not returned to the inn. Coffin has correctly read Ishmael as a greenhorn. The humor is rather extended and probably not worth the space needed to work it out. Ishmael says:

"Do you pretend to say, landlord, that this harpooner is acutally engaged this blessed Saturday night, or rather Sunday morning, in peddling his head around the town?"
"That's precisely it," said the landlord, "and I told him he couldn't sell it here, the market's overstocked."
"With what?" shouted I.
"With heads to be sure; ain't there too many heads in the world?"

Later when Ishmael has finally consented to sleep with Queequeg, he insists that the cannibal must extinguish his pipe because Ishmael does not want to sleep with a man smoking in bed. "It's dangerous. Besides, I ain't insured." Somewhat later when Queequeg is telling Ishmael about the one time he had been afflicted with dyspepsia, the evening after his father had gained a great victory over his enemy and had slain and eaten many of the enemy, Ishmael shudderingly protests, saying that he remembers well when on such an occasion he had seen such food, properly garnished, "and with some parsley in their mouths, were sent round with the victor's compliments to all his friends, just as though these presents were so many Christmas turkeys."

Some of the jokes are almost grotesque and are in poor taste even for this *omnim gatherum*. Such for example is the minstrel business with Queequeg and Ishmael when they come aboard the *Pequod* early in the morning and find nobody astir. They discover a man asleep below decks, and Queequeg acts with a cruelty that is out of character for him. Ishmael suggests that they should "sit up with the body." Queequeg then feels of the man's buttocks, and having discovered that it is "soft enough" perches quietly down there. When Queequeg states that sitting thus will not hurt the man's face, Ishmael protests: "'Face!' said I, 'call that his face? very benevolent countenance then; but how hard he breathes, he's heaving himself; get off, Queequeg, you are heavy, it's grinding the face of the poor.'" Equally weak, devoid of almost every spark of humor, is the account given in the chapter entitled "The Tail," when Ishmael says that if you cannot understand the tail of the whale, how can you expect to understand his head, how understand his face "when face he has none?" "Thou shalt see my back parts, my tail, he seems to say, but my face shall not be seen."

Other jokes are strained so much that they have no remaining tensile strength. When, for example, Ishmael has been describing "The Whale as a Dish," he says that some "young bucks among the epicures, by continually dining upon calves' brains, by and by get to have a little brains of their own, so as to be able to tell a calf's head from their own heads; which, indeed, requires uncommon discrimination. And that is the reason why a young buck

with an intelligent looking calf's head before him, is
somehow one of the saddest sights you can see. The head
looks sort of reproachfully at him, with an 'Et tu Brute!'
expression" '(CH. LXV). Later in the same discussion,
Ishmael answers the charge that it is indecent for Stubb to
eat his whale steak by the light of the whale oil lamp: "But
Stubb, he eats the whale by its own light, does he? and that
is adding insult to injury, is it?"

Somewhat in the same category is the comment about the
taste of plum-pudding, that part of the whale's skin that
adheres to the blubber. When Ishmael once "stole behind
the foremast to try it, it tasted something as I should
conceive a royal cutlet from the thigh of Louis le Gros
might have tasted, supposing him to have been killed the
first day after the venison season, and that particular
vension season contemporary with an unusually fine
vintage of the vineyards of Champagne." In the same vein
is the statement when Ishmael is talking about the dignity
of whaling and of whalers, in "Nights and Squires," and he
says that "a king's head is solemnly oiled at his coronation,
even as a head of salad." In both instances the point,
though weakly developed, is to equalize commoner and king.

In many ways the most typically American and most
satisfying of the frontier jokes are those that are obviously
sheer exaggeration, whether extended or contracted, and
are developed in the usual frontier style. This type begins
with the very first page of the book, with the long list
of extracts from the history of the whale, itemized by the
sub-sub librarian. After this listing, examples are numerous.
When Ishmael in the Spouter-Inn hesitates to sleep with
Queequeg and decides to try the benches, the proprietor
cannot spare a tablecloth for a cover but he does try to
plane down the knots, to soften the bed. Later, in the huge
bed that he occupies, Ishmael complains that the mattress
is "stuffed with corncobs or broken crockery." Seeing
Queequeg naked for the first time, Ishmael concludes that
the cannibal had been in "a Thirty Years' War and just
escaped from it with a sticking-plaster shirt."

In New Bedford, Melville has great fun exaggerating the bonyness of parts of the city which frighten an observer, and the oiliness, so much an outgrowth of the whaling industry that fathers "give whales for dowers to their daughters." These examples of the long-bow are followed soon by one of Melville's lengthiest shots. He tells how Queequeg was once given a wheelbarrow to transport his goods from ship to boarding house and, having put his things in the barrow, then assumed he was to pick up the contraption and carry it across his back.

On Nantucket, Ishmael uses frontier similes and metaphors to describe how desolate the island is. The Islanders, among other things, have to "plant weeds there," they carry pieces of wood "like bits of the true cross in Rome," and the Nantucketers are "so shut up, belted about, every way inclosed, surrounded, and made an utter island of by the ocean, that to their very chairs and tables small clams will sometimes be found adhering, as to the backs of sea turtles." Melville then accumulates another mountain of metaphors demonstrating how these Nantucketers have conquered the sea, "like so many Alexanders." He tops off the pile by saying that, "With the landless gull, that at sunset folds her wings and is rocked to sleep between billows; so at nightfall, the Nantucketer, out of sight of land, furls his sails, and lays him to his rest, while under his very pillow rush herds of walruses and whales."

Mrs. Hussey, the landlady of the Try Pots, is the recipient of typical anti-feministic frontier humor. A shrew who speaks no more than is necessary, she is done out of extra food by Ishmael. Melville exaggerates the fishiness of the Try Pots until the smell is almost overwhelming. Served fish for breakfast, dinner, and supper, the guests look for fish bones coming through their very clothes. Mrs. Hussey binds books in shark-skin, the milk tastes fishy, and the cow even marches along through the sand "each foot in a cod's decapitated head, looking very slipshod, I assure ye."

The chapter called "Cetology" is humorously inspired. Melville divides whales, "according to magnitude," into "three primary Books (subdivisible into Chapters), and these shall comprehend them all, both small and great—into folios, octavios, and duodecimos." This magnificent whimsy is capped off by the marvelous statement that the horn of the narwhale "would certainly be very convenient to him for a folder in reading pamphlets." Later Melville rounds off his examination of the pictures of whales (CH. LVII) by raising his eyes upward and in frontier exaggeration, as heroic as the sum of his pictures, in a kind of folk apotheosis he tests the reality of heaven: "With a frigate's anchors for my bridle-bitts and fasces of harpoons for spurs, would I could mount that whale and leap the topmost skies, to see whether the fabled heavens with all their countless tents really lie encamped beyond my mortal sight!"

Stubb's supper of whale meat is gargantuan in the extreme—Mike Fink swallowing the world, or God. Stubb, despite being at times warmly humanistic, is essentially a Mike Fink, developed with all the characteristic trappings. Fedallah, Ahab's harpooner, is a frontier demon blown into the proportions of the supernatural. He is the Wandering Jew, or Satan, so old that if you took all "the *Pequod's* hold, and string 'em along in a row with that mast, for oughts, do you see; well, that wouldn't begin to be Fedallah's age."

The whale quite naturally lends itself to frontier exaggeration. Melville holds it up and examines it fully while turning it around, as it were, before our very eyes. The sperm whale has a "great Kentucky Mammoth Cave" of a stomach. The right whale "bears a rather inelegant resemblance to a gigantic galliot-toed shoe." But it is a "very sure looking fellow to grace a diadem." The right whale is a Stoic, the sperm whale a Platonist. The sperm whale does not offend by having a nose that should be pulled, since he has none. The right whale has such a large mouth that Jonah might easily get into one of his hollow teeth, but Melville remembers in the nick of time that the right whale is toothless.

Melville tells of the articulated skeleton of a whale of gigantic proportions: "like a great chest of drawers, you can open and shut him, in all his bony cavities—spread out his ribs like a gigantic fan—and wing all day upon his lower jaw. Locks are to be put upon some of his trap-doors and shutters; and a footman will show round future visitors with a bunch of keys at his side. Sir Clifford thinks of charging twopence for a peep at the whispering gallery in the spinal column; threepence to hear the echo in the hollow of his cerebellum; and sixpence for the unrivaled view from his forehead." In talking about the size of the whale's skeleton Melville cautions: "But as the colossal skull embraces so very large a proportion of the entire extent of the skeleton; as it is by far the most complicated part; and as nothing is to be repeated concerning it in this chapter, you must not fail to carry it in your mind, or under your arm, as we proceed, otherwise you will not gain a complete notion of the general structure we are about to view." The best way to consider a whale's spine is "with a crane, to pile its bones up on end," when they will look like "Pompey's Pillar." Such a mighty fish must be described with a mighty vocabulary, one similar to Dr. Johnson's, himself a lexicographer with an "uncommon personal bulk." "No great and enduring volume can ever be written on the flea, though many there be who have tried it," but the mighty whale is fit subject for a mighty book.

One of the most successful bits of frontier humor develops from the quiet Edenic picture of the nursing whales in the chapter called "The Grand Armada," when the mother whales are seen with umbilicus cords still stretched between them and their babies. In a footnote Melville expounds on the nursing habits of whales, then switches to the quality and taste of whale's milk, in a twist so absurd that it is the work of genius: "When by

chance these precious parts in a nursing whale are cut
by the hunter's lance, the mother's pouring milk and
blood rivallingly discolor the sea for rods. The milk is
very sweet and rich; it has been tasted by man; it might
do well with strawberries."

Many of the men are frequently pictured as heroic. But
the ship's carpenter is twisted into a humorous shape.
"If his superiors wanted to use the carpenter for a screw-
driver, all they had to do was to open that part of him,
and the screw was fast: or if for tweezers, take him up by
the legs, and there they were."

The good whaler *Bachelor* is subject for much sexual
allusion and many jokes, not the least of which is the
frontier-like sexual allusion about the ship being so full of
oil that "indeed everything was filled with sperm, except
the captain's pantaloons."

Finally, the character of Ahab that has been growing
into mammoth and heroic proportions throughout the
book is capped off with Crockett-like self aggrandizement
when on the second day of the chase after the white
whale Ahab finally stares down Starbuck, and in words
and stance, which under other circumstances could be
translated into similar acts of the gamecock of the
wilderness, says: "Ahab is for ever Ahab, man . . . I am
the Fates' lieutenant; I act under orders . . . Believe ye,
men, in the things called omens? Then laugh aloud, and
cry encore!"

SEX: BLENDING OF INDIVIDUALS

Melville's allusions to sex are at times more obvious,
more flagrant, and more boisterous than they had been in
the earlier works and more than they would be later,
except in *Pierre* and the short story, "The Tartarus of
Maids." In *Moby-Dick* they are used with a certain
defiant thumbing of the nose at Victorian taboos and
respectability; it is as though Melville were testing to see

101

how far he could use sex as a subject for profound study, and was preparing for the more overt treatment in subsequent works.

Moby-Dick is to a large extent a book of marriage, of the sexual blending of one thing or person into another both physically and spiritually. The theme of marriage—intercourse—is begun early. At the Spouter-Inn the proprietor, Peter Coffin, describes the bed that he has assigned to Ishmael and Queequeg as a "nice bed: Sal and me slept in that ere bed the night we were spliced. There's plenty of room for two to kick about in that bed." It is the bed in which their children were conceived, thus a fitting place for the "marriage" of Ishmael and the pagan harponner. And "married" there they are. The next morning Queequeg's arm is thrown over Ishmael "in the most loving and affectionate manner." Ishmael says, "You had almost thought I had been his wife." The cannibal has a "bridegroom clasp" on Ishmael and is hugging him in a "matrimonial sort of style." The marriage is, however, more spiritual than physical, for from this "union" comes a full understanding of the innate dignity and value of each man, and an inseparability that only death will interrupt.

This inseparability is carried on and demonstrated very effectively in the monkey-rope that ties the two together, a line running from the waist of Ishmael on the ship to that of Queequeg standing on the whale. While thus linked they are "inseparable twin" brothers. They are "wedded"; "an elongated Siamese ligature" unites them. It is interesting that the improvement on the idea of the monkey-rope, that the two ends of the rope be tied to the persons' wasits, in what is obviously a sexual linkage, was a refinement developed by Stubb, the Crockett-like Prometheus, humanist, and sensualist.

Melville makes three sexual references to sperm, playing on the obvious double meaning of the word. One is in the suggestive chapter "A Squeeze of the Hand," in which through the magic of the sperm in which he is working, Ishmael's physiology and spirit reach out to embrace the whole of mankind. Another is that of the ship named the *Bachelor* which is full to the top with sperm, as bachelors always are in Melville, full because they refuse to use it in committing themselves fully to life. Finally there is the obvious joke about the *Virgin* which has no sperm in her at all.

The gargantuan dimensions of the whale provide some heroic sexual jokes. Melville says: "If hereafter any highly cultured, poetical nation shall lure back to their birth-right, the merry May-day gods of old; the great Sperm whale shall lord it"—i.e., shall be sexually omnipotent. One of Melville's most extravagant, inspired, and amusing developments is the marvelous Pantagruelian delivery of Tashtego from the head of the sperm whale by Queequeg with a skill and thoughtfulness worthy of any surgeon. About to extract Tashtego, Queequeg discovers that the Indian is going to emerge a "breeches baby," and therefore he forces him back into the "womb" and manipulates him until he can deliver him in the normal fashion.

Melville enjoys this bit of joking so much, in fact, that he labors it with a final gratuitous observation: "Midwifery should be taught in the same course with fencing and boxing, riding and rowing." "Yes, it was a running delivery, so it was."

Later, in speaking about "The Grand Armada," Melville dwells at length upon sexual habits of whales. In "Schools and Schoolmasters" Melville speaks at length on how the "notorious Lothario" cannot be kept out of the whale's bed, "for, alas! all fish bed in common." "These Grand Turks are too lavish of their strength, and hence their unctuousness is small." These "Grand Turks" contrast with Melville's bachelors, on land and sea; like the committed men who pour out their "unctuousness" in living life fully, these whales are lighter for their engagement with life.

In "The Cassock" the whale's penis provides Melville with an extended joke that mixes frontier humor and sex as god: the penis is "longer than a Kentuckian is tall, nigh a foot in diameter at the base, and jet-black as Yojo, the ebony idol of Queequeg. And an idol, indeed, it is; or rather, in old times, its likeness was." Melville then catalogues various such idols. To end the account of how men use the skin of this organ for the mincer's protective coat, Melville finishes off his joke of this "grandissimus," as the mariners call it, by himself referring to it as the mincer's "full canonicals of his calling," and "what a candidate for an archbishoprick, what a lad for a Pope were this mincer." In the misspelling of "archbishoprick," Melville is obviously punning. In referring to the Pope, he may in fact be echoing a current lewd joke against the Pope. Later Melville returns to the same subject and discusses how the small whale or dub is hoisted to the deck so that his "grandissimus" can be skinned to provide his "poke or bag: to make sheaths for the barbs of the harpoons, and for the heads of the lances," here contrasting the original use of the instrument with the destructive, warlike abuse invented by men.

The *Rachel*, the ship that eventually discovers and saves Ishmael from drowning, approaches the *Pequod* and in so doing provides a sharp contrast with the demon-possessed ship. The *Rachel*, though she has lost one of her boys, is a ship with great masculinity and future. All her spars are "thickly clustering with men." At this time the *Pequod* is "making good progress through the water," but the winds desert her now as the fish had earlier deserted her; "the boastful sails all fell together...." She is deprived of any future. of any hope of the development of man. She cannot give birth to children, she is a parody of a womb, of the life-giving impulses: "the boastful sails all fell together as blank bladders that are burst, and all life fled from the smitten hull." The *Pequod*, under the dominance of the false Promethean

Ahab, is both anti-woman and anti-humanity; a monster that in trying to produce life can only abort.

The richly orchestrated chapter "The Symphony," coming as it does just before the three-day chase of the whale, is a cloaked account of intercourse between the "feminine air" and the "masculine sea." "Aloft, like a royal czar and king, the sun seemed giving this gentle air to this bold and rolling sea; even as bride to groom. And at the girdling line of the horizon, a soft and tremulous motion—most seen here at the Equator—denoted the fond, throbbing trust, the loving alarms, with which the poor bride gave her bosom away."

Before the storm there are overt references to girls by the sailors. On one occasion Melville asks if the queen is a "mermaid, to be presented with a tail? An allegorical meaning may lurk there." May indeed! In another brand of his joke he measures the size of the female whale as not more than half a dozen yards around the waist.

Often Melville develops the symbol of man's virility and fecundity. When the various men approach and soliloquize about the doubloon, Queequeg, the most positive force for the fathering of humanism, approaches and sees in the doubloon "something there in the vicinity of his thigh." In describing the fossil whale, Melville wants to be "omnisciently exhaustive in the enterprise; not overlooking the minutest seminal germs of his blood, and spinning him out to the uttermost coil of his bowels."

Ahab's hatred is at least partially the result of his sexual wound, caused by a stake that "all but pierced his groin." The captain's trouble is developed further later in "The Symphony" which is, as we have seen, a record of intercourse. Ahab's sexual fire has obviously burned out. The spy is oblivious to old Ahab's "close-coiled woe"! From the first encounter between Ahab and *Moby-Dick*, the whale swims away triumphant, like Jupiter "with ravished Europa."

105

The symbol of the de-sexed Ahab helps develop the steeling of his anti-humanism. On the second day of the chase, when his leg has been splintered, Ahab for a moment weakens his iron will and seeks fraternity with Starbuck, admitting that it is "sweet to lean sometimes." But he almost immediately recovers his hard heart. He orders Starbuck to master the boat so chase can be made after the whale. The first mate protests, and offers a helping hand: "Let me first help thee towards the bulwarks, sir." But Ahab in his haughty detestation of the weakness of man's feeling for man is touched deep in his very being: "Oh, oh, oh! how this splinter gores me now! Accursed fate! that the unconquerable captain in the soul should have such a craven mate."

Thus lacking completely the generative and love-inducing elements of sexual impulses, Ahab goes to his doom, and takes down with him all the self-destructive, non-generative bachelors of the world associated with him.

But not all are lost. All the sexual allusions, references to the viscera and the bowels, to belly-buttons, sexual organs, intercourse, and productivity finally meet and in a short well-rounded organ-toned conclusion to the voyage of evil open up promise. The theme of death, destruction, resurrection, and rebirth joins with and blends into all the sexual allusions to open up the promise contained in the Epilogue.

The Epilogue brims with sexual allusions. Ishmael is slowly pulled toward the "creamy pool" of the "vortex." He is drawn "Round and round, then, . . . towards the closing pool," ultimately reaching the "button-like black bubble at the axis of that slowly wheeling circle." Gaining the "vital centre," he is saved by the "coffin life-buoy" that "shot lengthwise from the sea." Finally it is the *Rachel*, which when she was last seen had been the very symbol of fecundity as well as of hope, with her masts—phallic symbols—covered with clinging men that finds and saves Ishmael. On her there is hope for growth into manhood, promise of bachelordom being supplanted by total commitment to life, and encouragement in the belief that sexual symbols promise a future.

THREE

PIERRE: "SCISSORS OF FATE"

Pierre: or the Ambiguities was written during the late
summer, fall, and winter of 1851-52, just after *Moby-Dick*
had been finished, when Melville was still driven by the
furor which had charged him while he was composing his
"whaling voyage." In subject matter Melville turned in
his new book from the sea to the land, from whaling to
what he described in a letter to Mrs. Hawthorne as
"a rural bowl of milk," to a domestic romance, which, as
Leon Howard says, Melville thought would warm the
hearts of women. But despite the fact that Melville had
changed his setting markedly, the theme of *Pierre* is
consistent with those of *Moby-Dick* and Melville's other
works. This book continues Melville's probing into the
fate of man *vis-a-vis* man and God, and here as elsewhere the author reveals his commitment to humanity
and to humanism.

The setting of the new book, though strikingly like the
Berkshire countryside around Arrowhead, is ostensibly a
baronial estate in upper New York called Saddle
Meadows. The action centers around the nineteen-year-
old idealist Pierre, his love for a goddess-like young
lady named Lucy Tartan, and his renouncing her for the
dark beauty Isabel, who, it turns out, apparently is his
half sister. As a consequence of his relations with
Isabel, Pierre is disinherited by his mother, who is one
of the important characters in the book. He takes
Isabel to New York masquerading as his wife, and
eventually all people with whom Pierre is closely associated are destroyed.

Melville uses much material from his own family and
that of his wife, the daughter of a justice of the

Massachusetts Supreme Court. But here, as was always the case, Melville transmuted his borrowings into his own particular kind of art and philosophy. The result is a book which, even after seeing it in proof, Melville insisted would be popular. In a letter to his English publisher he described it as "possessing unquestionable novelty, as regards my former ones,—treating of utterly new scenes and characters;—and as I believe, very much more calculated for popularity than anything you have yet published of mine—being a regular romance, with a mysterious plot to it, and stirring passions at works, and withal, representing a new and elevated aspect of American life."[1]

During the writing of *Pierre*, Melville's disposition seems on the surface to have been rather relaxed and his spirits high. He had got *Moby-Dick* off his chest—or back—and having finished that "wicked book" felt "spotless as the lamb," as he wrote to Hawthorne.

But this lightness was less real than seeming. Melville had anguished over the "wicked book." At its conclusion he felt light-headed, almost giddy. Apparently, however, the strain had dry-rotted his philosophic outlook more than even he recognized. Reception of *Moby-Dick* had been much less than he had hoped for. Now he was firmly committed to writing for a living, his second son had just been born, he was in debt to his publisher and earning very little money, and he felt he could never write the kind of books he wanted to produce. The anxieties resulting from these strains, perhaps half unconscious, probably caused him to put up a brave front, even to himself, and to cloak his intentions in his usual irony, or in self-delusion. For he must have known that *Pierre* was not "a rural bowl of milk" "very much . . . calculated for popularity." *Pierre* is as far from such a book as the published *Moby-Dick* is from the "whaling voyage" he apparently finished in the summer of 1850

1. Leon Howard, *Herman Melville* (Berkeley, Calif.), p. 193.

before falling under the fertilizing influence of Hawthorne and Shakespeare.

Pierre is in some ways a continuation of *Moby-Dick*, in its further study of the titanism of the earlier work. But *Pierre*, somewhat like *Mardi*, is a transitional book, beginning themes and methods of treatment which forecast Melville's later works. Despite superficial appearances, the tone is more somber, less ebullient, than that in *Moby-Dick*. It is not a spring idyll, an American *Romeo and Juliet*. It is instead a satiric treatment of the subject, a kind of minstrel version of *Romeo and Juliet*, with the author detached from and disdainful of the action, or at least of the actors, especially in the beginning of the book. Melville disapproves of Mrs. Glendinning and Mrs. Tartan, of Pierre and of Lucy. In their exclusiveness, unawareness, and indifference to the world, these characters, to Melville, pervert nature. All four are overly proud, though Pierre and Lucy less than their mothers. All four fall. One of the themes of the book is the anachronism of pride and hereditary privilege. It is a demonstration that these must disappear in America. The book is therefore a picture of the birth and growth of democracy.

Though Melville may have set out to write a book that would sell in England because it would appeal to English snobbishness about aristocracy, as Howard says, he probably still remembered that his English publisher would never believe that an American who had sailed before the mast could write such a fine book as *Typee*. Further, anybody who was as rabidly democratic as Melville was during these years could not approve—or even tolerate—snobbery. On the other hand he was probably grimly amused that a book might appeal to snobbishness when it in fact demonstrated the decline and fall of the institution it apparently praised. This is the appeal of wearing nobnailed boots into the parlor, of wearing sailor's togs into the baronial hall.

Pierre is a study of the descent of Superman, of Prometheus. Thus it is the humanizing of the gods, in the same way *Israel Potter* is. But the world of the descended gods—the demi-gods—is sterile. Pierre is aristocracy's *Gotterdammerung.* All persons who are above average, all those having anything to do with nobility, are doomed. Pierre is the last direct male descendant of his noble house. With his own hand he destroys the final person of the name of Glendinning. The world tumbles about the head of these supermen and women.

From these shambles emerges the overriding theme that was to take on even greater urgency in Melville's next book but one, *The Confidence- Man. Pierre* carries Ahab's "humanities" one step further, and urges the necessity of humanism in a world of "horrible and inscrutable inhumanities," though the book does not harden into the flintlike grimness of *The Confidence-Man.*

Lucy perishes without issue. So does Isabel. The only possible trace of any future in the world resides in a kind of side-blow, that of the commoners. Delly Ulver has shown herself capable of having children. Her child is born a bastard, in precisely the way that Isabel is born a bastard to Glendinning. Though Delly's child dies, Melville seems to be pointing out that the future lies with the children of the Delly Ulvers, that is, with common people. As such *Pierre* promises the future of democracy.

Tied in with this testament of democracy there is perhaps a kind of regret that life must be as it is. God cannot be shaken from His throne. Superman has descended to cohabit with citizens of this world. Titanism is restricted to the earth. There is still value in the heroic. But the heroic now lies with the meek, the democratic. This idea Melville was to exploit later, in such works as "Bartleby," *Billy Budd,* and many others. Although people may be less than perfect, there is hope

111

for them. Life has "some burdens heavier than Death."
Therefore the best must be made of the situation. This
is perhaps a resigned, but surely not a hopeless, humanism.

I. COMPLEXITIES OF SEX

Melville may have thought he was writing a
conventional domestic novel in *Pierre*. But his use of sex
is so unusual, and of such Freudian depths, that the
conclusion seems unavoidable that here, as in "The
Tartarus of Maids" and elsewhere, he was trying to
reveal, perhaps while cloaking, some of his feelings
about the complexities and dangers of sex.
"Unconscious" is one of his favorite words in this book.
Among the main characters, all persons are sexually
abnormal, or are frustrated for some reason from normal
sexual life.

First, of course, the attachment between Mary
Glendinning and her son is quite unusual. Mrs.
Glendinning is forced to sublimate her sensuality,
and has had to for years, since her husband's death
long ago. She is too prudish and Puritanical to engage in
sexual activity outside marriage, and is too snobbish to
marry again, since she sees her dead husband as the
symbol of the perfect man the memory of whom would
be smirched by a second marriage. But obviously her
sexual drives are strong. She has therefore sublimated
her desires by symbolic copulation with her son. She is
young and beautiful, and makes a point of appearing
before her son only when she looks her youngest and
most enticing. She is a woman from whom "youth had
not uncoiled from her waist." In the light of Melville's
later use of the word in relation to Pierre and Isabel
(as well as that in *Moby-Dick*), "uncoiled" must be
read in its sexual sense. Mary Glendinning teases Pierre
by having him comb her hair, put on her necklace, button
her dress and robe for her. She is a woman for whom

"a reverential and devoted son seemed lover enough."
But "seemed" is an ambiguous word, and "lover" she
undoubtedly felt in the sexual sense.

Further proof that Mary Glendinning is a sexual
tease is the treatment she has accorded the Reverend
Falsgrave, her pastor, through the years. She has set him
up in this particular pastorate because he is physically
attractive. She has teased him and flirted with him
through the years to make him think she is interested in
marrying him. He has proposed once. She refused, but
tentatively, not finally. Falsgrave therefore continues to
pay her court and to hope for eventual success.

Mrs. Glendinning's real sexual nature comes out on
two occasions when her pretenses are down. When, for
example, it becomes clear that Pierre has "married"
Isabel, Mrs. Glendinning lashes out at her, calling her,
"slut" (XII, 2). Even more revealing, when Falsgrave
tries to calm her, she attacks him, saying that he is not a
man, deriding his virility, as though it were his fault
that she has been sexually frustrated all these years.

Lucy, who is sexually cold and indifferent—or
immature—but not insensitive, recognizes Mrs.
Glendinning's abnormal lust and is terrified by it. In a
revealing scene, Lucy comes over to Saddle Meadows
one afternoon to see Pierre and interrupts him and his
mother talking about his marriage to her. This suggestive
setting is broken by the entry of Lucy, who has brought
some strawberries for the two.

These are obviously unusual strawberries. Lucy bought
them from "the strangest little fellow," who exhibited
preternatural knowledge of her wishes. Both Pierre and
his mother recognize the fellow as extraordinary. Pierre
calls him "little rascal," and Mrs. Glendinning says he is
a "very sagacious little imp." Strawberries are, of course,
conventional sex symbols. They were sacred to Frigga,
wife of Odin, who rules over marriage and home.
The strawberry is also a plant of Venus. That they meant
something sexual to Melville is demonstrated in

Moby-Dick in the magnificent chapter on "The Grand
Armada." Discussing "young Leviathan amours in the
deep," Melville footnotes extra information about the sex
habits of whales, including suckling habits, ending with
this ludicrously irrelevant but for that reason significant
sentence: "The milk is very sweet and rich; it has been
tasted by man; it might do well with strawberries."

Lucy in offering her strawberries to both Pierre and his
mother senses something peculiar in the ensuing
conversation: "I was audacious enough to think as much,
cried Pierre, "for you *and* me, you see, mother; for you
and me, you understand that, I hope." To which Mrs.
Glendinning responds, "Perfectly, my dear brother." At
this familiarity, Lucy blushed, and being keenly
embarrassed remarked, "How warm it is, Mrs.
Glendinning," and departed, realizing that she had
surprised the two "talking over some private affair"
because "both looked so very confidential."[2]

Mrs. Glendinning wants Pierre to marry Lucy because she feels that this young girl is her intellectual
and sexual inferior. Lucy is patronised because the
"resplendent, full-blown Mrs. Glendinning" sees no
competition in the "delicate and shrinking girlhood of
young Lucy," and Mrs. Glendinning "could not but
perceive, that even in Lucy's womanly maturity, Lucy
would still be a child to her."

Pierre, it is clear, is sexually precocious, a young colt,
and manages to control himself only through much
physical activity and by sublimation. His mother has
observed this sensuality, his passionate nature. And she
urges him to marry Lucy since the two of them have
nothing to do but moon around all day firing his passion.
Lucy, for her part, being the very essence of spirituality,
knows nothing of the physical implications of marriage.
Indeed, at this time she is emotionally incapable of

2. References will be made by book and section number, rather than by page number,
because of the numerous editions of Melville's works. This quotation is from Book III,
Section III, which will be abbreviated as (III, 3).

sexual intercourse. But Pierre certainly knows about sex. His forthcoming marriage will be "Pluto stealing Proserpine; and every accepted lover is" (III, 3). In other words, every marriage is physical, a rape.

Isabel, in her physical attractiveness, served as a sexual catalyst. Pierre's memory of the first chance viewing of her face kindled "he could not tell what mysterious fires in the heart at which they aimed." "The long, dark locks of mournful hair would fall upon his soul, and trail their wonderful melancholy along with them; the two full, steady, over-brimming eyes of loveliness and anquish would converge their magic rays," and "when once this feeling had him fully, then was the perilous time for Pierre" (III, 2).

When first Pierre and Isabel met in the house of the Misses Penny, and from that time onward, the stirrings in him that she had engendered soon burst into open flame.

Pierre has grown up reading about Spenserian nymphs, but later "all these delicate warmths should seem frigid to him, and he should madly demand more ardent fires" (I, 1).

Pierre is a book of ambiguities, as the name tells us— of reality and seeming reality. These dualities are carried out sexually also. Lucy represents one kind of female, Isabel the other. Each has a charm for Pierre, and each is actually confused by Pierre into the other, or he is forced to alter his own personality and desires to conform with the seeming girl.

Lucy Tartan, Pierre's first, pastoral love, is a combination of many things. She is light and lightness; she is joy. Sexually, however, she is an illusion. Pierre is fascinated by her in his pre-lusty days, when she represents everything beautiful and spiritual. Lucy is interested in Pierre the faun, but not in the satyr sexually attracted to her. Pierre's feelings are ambiguous. He recognizes himself as the worldling, as Romeo about to seduce Juliet against her will. Pierre's love for Lucy is "profane" because it "mortally reaches toward the

heaven" in her. The contrast between him and her is
startlingly set forth in Melville's figures. As Pierre
approaches Lucy's house, like Romeo in the garden, he
"lifted his eyes," and "fixing his glance upon one upper,
open casement there," he sees "upon the sill of the
casement, a snow-white glossy pillow" and a "trailing
shrub has softly rested a rich, crimson flower against it."
But the "rich, crimson flower" is doomed to make no
other indentation, for when Pierre shakes the casement
shrub, "he dislodged the flower, and conspicuously
fastened it to his bosom" (I,1).

The inviolability of Lucy is brought out even more
graphically later on. When Pierre and Lucy are out
walking, they sit down on a bank. Clearly the situation
invites a seduction. Pierre, with Lucy's hand in his,
"seemed as one placed in linked correspondence with the
summer lightnings; and by sweet shock on shock, receiving
intimating foretastes of the etherealest delights on
earth." Pierre then falls on the grass beside Lucy. She
loves him, in her own way. But like the goddess that
Pierre calls her ("Thou art my heaven, Lucy") she
realizes all too well that this love can be no more than
Platonic. With him beside her on the grass, Lucy looks
down and "vibrates," and "from her over-charged lids,
drops . . . warm drops." She charges Pierre with being
"too ardent and impetuous." She is, she says, "in the
bud" that April showers have nurtured. Fearing that she
can never unfold for Pierre, she gets him to swear that
"no such flower may untimely perish, ere the June
unfolds" (II, 5). When Pierre makes the promise, her
apprehensions are not settled: "Thou art young, and
beautiful, and strong; and a joyful manliness invests thee,
Pierre; and thy intrepid heart never yet felt the touch of
fear;—But—" she says and must be taken home,
apparently weak with the realization of her own
inadequacy.

The Platonic aspect of Lucy is further emphasized
when Lucy and Pierre are in her aunt's cheerful parlor,

and Lucy wants to drive away "the last trace of sadness from her"; so she sends Pierre to her room to fetch her blue portfolio. Pierre approaches the room as though it were a shrine. "He had never entered that chamber but with feelings of a wonderful reverentialness. The carpet seemed as holy ground." He felt he should bow. He turns to see the bed, "the spotless bed itself, and fastened on a snow-white roll that lay beside the pillow. . . . Then again his glance fixed itself upon the slender, snow-white, ruffled roll; and he stood as one enchanted. Never precious parchment of the Greek was half so precious in his eyes. Never trembling scholar longed to unroll the mystic vellum, than Pierre longed to unroll the sacred secrets of that snow-white, ruffled thing." Back in the parlor with Lucy, Pierre calls her "angel" and is transfigured because he has "just peeped in at paradise."

In eying the two beds, the "real one and the reflected one," Pierre is seeing Lucy in the Platonic sense. But he wants to "unroll the secrets of that snow-white, ruffled thing" in the sexual sense. The reference to Greek parchment draws to mind immediately the paper image of the vagina in "The Tartarus of Maids," (II, 6). Pierre realizes that Lucy is not of this world yet, and cannot be his. The scene is a travesty of a bridal scene. Lucy in bed and married is only a bundle covered with a bedspread, enough to cause a reflection in the mirror. There is grim irony in her saying to Pierre that she is entirely his. She is, as far as she can be, for she is actually incapable of being his.

The travesty of this marriage scene is furthered later on. When Pierre goes to Lucy's house to inform her of his "marriage" to Isabel, he is unnecessarily harsh. The scene exactly parallels the earlier marriage bed-side scene. This time, after having been absent from her for forty-eight hours, he has no thought of the sanctity of her bedroom, but dashes straight into it, finding Lucy in bed.

117

Surprised by his knock on the door Lucy is "overwhelmed with sudden terror," and gives a "cry of groping misery, which knew not the pang that caused it," as he came in. In the physical overtones here, Lucy, as usual, is caught up and ground down between the sexual demands of this world and her inability to respond to them. In a scene paralleling both *Romeo and Juliet,* which Pierre has been naming all along, and *Othello,* Pierre sits down on the bed "and his set eyes met her terrified and virgin aspect" (XI, 2).

The other side of sex—and the psychological depths of incestuous longings—are revealed in Isabel. Richard Chase is correct in seeing her as symbolizing several layers of physical attraction. She is Bell, she is voluptuousness, she is allurement, she is the dark Madonna. As Pierre thinks back over his first meeting with Isabel, he sees her "impassioned, ideal Madonna's face." And as he thought about her, "another sense was touched in him," "the emotions he experienced seemed to have taken hold of the deepest roots and subtlest fibres of his being," and he recognizes this feeling as "infatuation."

Pierre is half aware of his strength and weakness, Isabel's sexual allurements. He knows that "womanly beauty, and not womanly ugliness, invited him to champion the right." Melville points out the value of humanism—as distinguished from the exquisiteness of worldly heavenliness—when Pierre while approaching Isabel's cottage has the "strangest feelings, almost supernatural" pounding in his system. This is a crisis in Pierre's life something like that in Huck Finn's when he is torn between the desires of turning Jim in or letting him remain free. Pierre's feelings are *almost* supernatural, but remain human and natural. His worldliness—his earthiness—is emphasized further. Just before seeing Isabel, Pierre feels "the sun-like glories of god-like truth and virtue . . . still shine eventually in unclouded radiance, casting illustrative light upon the sapphire throne of God." When he sees her at the cottage "holding the light above her supernatural head," Pierre is over come with "spiritual awe." He stands, or thinks he stands, on worldly and bestial earth, with her above him. If she is indeed celestial, Pierre is able to drag her down, to humanize her, as he had not been able to humanize Lucy.

Their incestuous—or merely sexual—longings are immediately overwhelming. But more for Isabel than for Pierre. He had no reason for fearing her lack of worldliness. On the contrary, he has reason for fearing her receptivity. The very first night he goes to her cottage, she is ready to receive him sexually. He clasps

her in his arms and "felt a faint struggling within his clasp; her head drooped against him; his whole form was bathed in the flowing glossiness of her long and unimprisoned hair (VI, 1). Later, more sexually aroused, he looks satyr-like at her beautiful ear and lovely hair. Pierre so far has not consciously lusted after Isabel, but clearly he cannot think of her as his sister. He is too much aware of the "Nubian power" of her black eyes. Intimations of incestuous longing are almost overwhelming in the section of the book where Isabel tells the second part of her story to Pierre. Though the girl protests that there is no "sex in [their] immaculateness," she knows otherwise. Her "wild plaints" "carried with them the first inkling of the extraordinary conceit, so vaguely and shrinkingly hinted at in her till now entirely unintelligible words" (VIII,2). The situation, her person, the magical guitar that she plucks— all nearly overpower Pierre. Though she protests only sisterly love for Pierre, Isabel speaks so often of sex, as in referring to the "twin-born softness of [woman's] breasts," that so lusty a colt as Pierre could not fail to understand.

119

Pierre in his anguish decides what he must do. Wanting to "hold his father's fair fame inviolate," and "determining not to shake his mother's lasting peace by any useless exposure of unwelcome facts," he means to announce that he and Isabel have already been secretly married, and thus to extend to her a "brother's utmost devotedness and love." But sexually Pierre does indeed cross "the Rubicon," as Melville calls the chapter, for at the next meeting he and Isabel commit incest in spirit if not in fact. In close and violent embrace, each responsive, Pierre "would not let go her sweet and awful passiveness." Then Melville continues, with all the sexual implications of the word "coiled" that he unleashed in *Moby-Dick.* Pierre and Isabel "changed; they coiled together, and entangledly stood mute" (XII, 1).

Sexually the book reaches a crescendo when Lucy joins Isabel and Pierre in New York. Lucy has now been signally metamorphosed. In the past she has been divine to Pierre, a goddess, and he infinitely beneath her. She is still "angelicalness" and "transparently immaculate" in heart. But her and Pierre's roles have been reversed. All she can see is the heavenly and angelic Pierre, and her only desire is to serve him, and through him Isabel.

Isabel recognizes immediately the changed Lucy. Suffering has humanized her. She is now sexually receptive. Pierre also recognizes her newly awakened sensuality. He begins to look upon her "with an expression illy befitting their singular and so-supposed merely cousinly relation." She is now a human being. The myth of Enceladus is justification for Pierre's incest and for his rebellion against heaven.

II. DECLINE OF ARISTOCRACY

Another important theme in the book centers around Melville's detestation of snobs and aristocrats. Their decline is necessary to the working out of the book. Melville states at the beginning that he has gone to great length to set up the "richly aristocratic tradition" of Pierre because it is important for the career of Pierre and especially for the last chapter.

Melville's attitude toward the English was always ambivalent, though throughout life he cared more for them than for other Europeans. Some aspects of the English he approved of, others he tolerated, others he revolted against—especially their social snobbery, their seeming indifference to the poor. In *Pierre* Melville may have been trying to write a novel that would appeal to English snobbery, as Howard says, but if so he was attempting foolery on the same scale as that perpetrated by Stubb on the captain of the *Rose-Bud*, for *Pierre* is savagely anti-aristocratic, snapping at it in both England and America.

Melville's attack is manifest from the beginning. Ironically the book is dedicated to Mount Greylock, a real and genuine majesty, not that created by man for the exploitation of man. In setting up Pierre as a silly lad, the son of an "affluent, and haughty" mother, Melville points out his own pro-democratic bias: "indeed the democratic element operates as a subtile acid among us; forever producing new things by corroding the old" (I, 3). This changing of old things into new creates a new kind of pedigree, and American degrees then can be compared not unfavorably with English. There is no need for Americans to try to out-British the British. The English peerage is cursed universally by the bar sinister. Scarcely any English title can trace a "direct unvitiated blood-descent" before Charles II, and those that can would be from the "thief knights of the Norman." Melville then loosely parallels Juliet's question about the value of a name, to make his point: "the empty air of a name is more endurable than a man, or than dynasties of men; the air fills man's lungs and puts life into a man, but man fills not the air, nor puts life into that" (I, 3).

Continuing his theme about names, he concludes: "All honour to the names then, and all courtesy to the man; but if St. Albans tells me he is all-honourable and all-eternal, I must still politely refer him to Nell Gwynne." Interestingly, the English have been able to keep their peerages alive only by drawing upon the commoners, infusing them into their ranks.

Melville continues his attack on titles, and especially American trading in such absurdities. "Whatever one may think of the existence of such mighty lordships in the heart of a republic, and however we may wonder at their thus surviving, like Indian mounds, the Revolutionary flood; yet survive and exist they do, and now owned by their present proprietors, by as good nominal title as any peasant owns his father's old hat, or any duke his great-uncle's old coronet." Americans can just as legitimately claim "long pedigrees are bastards."

Melville further criticizes the undemocratic pretensions of the society of his day. Pierre might be a downy-cheeked aristocrat, Melville says, but give him time and he will be a "thorough-going Democrat . . . perhaps a little too Radical altogether to your fancy." Here with double irony Melville is echoing his letter to Hawthorne in which he speaks of his thorough-going democracy, and he is perhaps obliquely chiding Hawthorne for not having been receptive to the extravagances of his radicalism.

The old order of American aristocrats and snobs, as typified by Mrs. Glendinning, Melville excoriates unrelentingly. She "was a noble creature" "formed chiefly for the golden propensities of life," "bred and expanded . . . under the sole influences of hereditary forms and world-usages"—like Captain Vere in *Billy Budd*. "Infinite haughtiness" had fashioned her, and "a haughty Ritual" finished her. She is "pride's priestess," similar to Ahab. She calls herself a "pride-prisoned woman." She hates "plebeian" blood. Mrs.

Tartan is similar to Mrs. Glendinning. She too is pride-poisoned, and learns nothing from Mrs. Glendinning's terrible mistake in disinheriting Pierre and dying of a broken heart; Lucy too is disinherited. The Reverend Falsgrave stands half-way between aristocracy and democracy. Pretty much a sycophant, he toadies to Mrs. Glendinning's whims and snobbery; she calls him a "splendid example of the polishing and gentlemanising influences of Christianity upon the minds and manners."

Falsgrave is attacked openly by Melville, not just through Mrs. Glendinning. He is a handsome man, "nobly robust and dignified; while the remarkable smallness of his feet, and the almost infantile delicacy, and vivid whiteness and purity of his hands, strikingly contrasted with his fine girth and stature." Through Falsgrave Melville attacks American snobbery, as being more false and vicious than European: in America, where "of a hundred hands, that drop a ballot for the Presidency, ninety-nine shall be of the brownest and the brawniest. . . this daintiness of the fingers, when united with a generally manly aspect, assumes a remarkableness unknown in European nations" (V, 4).

III. HUMANIZATION OF THE HERO

Throughout the book Melville is concerned with Titanism, the hero, superman in society, and with the humanization of this hero. In *Moby-Dick* superman Ahab found the world so alien to his nature, so inferior to him, that he could not conform, and he was consequently broken. In later works—"Benito Cereno," *The Confidence-Man*, and *Billy Budd*, for example—the shift in theme is from Titanism to the descent of superman, as it is especially developed in *Israel Potter*, thence to the growth of the hero from the ground up toward heaven. The beginning of this new emphasis is clearly visible in *Pierre*.

123

From the beginning of this book we are observing superhuman people in a superworld. Saddle Meadows, the ancestral acres of a heroic family, is unnaturally wonderful and idyllic. The characters are hardly of this world. Melville reminds us that in the Heroic Age the gods descended to love earthly women: "Did not the angelical Lotharios come down to earth, that they might taste of mortal woman's Love and Beauty?" Pierre has sprung on both sides of the family from heroes. His mother wants and expects him to be a "haughty hero." He is so sprightly that he seems a "youthful Magian." He and Lucy are "fair god and goddess" (II, 4). The horses Pierre drives are divine steeds. Pierre is, in other words, a god trying to seduce Earth—Lucy. But he is unable to because although she is warm to a point in love, thereafter she turns cold. She is frightened of love and unable to carry it through to its natural climax.

Pierre loves the memory of his heroic and perfect father. Isabel is also a heroine. Her superhuman qualities are emphasized by the fact that she is a bastard Glendinning, an illegitimate; thus Melville builds her character through the age-old mythological and folkloristic characteristic of heroes being illegitimate or having something unusual about their birth. As we shall see, the fact that Isabel is also half French is significant in the development of Melville's theme.

Pierre's misfortune as a youth is that he is a son of his family. He is therefore enmeshed in the myth of their heroic qualities, unable to believe that he is merely mortal clay. His mother especially has deluded him. When he is brooding on her "immense pride" he is somewhat repelled and "staggered back, and only found support in himself," but unconsciously he strengthens his own sin of pride, for he then "felt that deep in him lurked a diving unidentifiableness, that owned no earthly kith or kin." Later when he realizes that he must sacrifice himself to duty, he thinks his duty "unselfish

magnanimities," and he is "almost superhumanly prepared" to sacrifice those he loves: "Thus in the Enthusiast to Duty, the heaven-begotten Christ is born;
and will not own a mortal parent, and spurns and rends
all mortal bonds" (V, 5). Pierre thinks: "May heaven
new-string my soul, and confirm me in the Christ-like
feeling I first felt" (V, 6). Melville here is distinguishing
between heaven-begotten Christianity and humanism,
with a denial of the former and an affirmation of the
latter.

In his final resolution to cling to Isabel and cast off
all other aspects of his former life, Pierre is as a "vulnerable god" that cuts off all retreat. Having told
his mother about his intended marriage, Pierre is
chased from the house. Leaving his home he stumbles
and falls on the portico, and is thus "jeeringly hurled
from beneath his own ancestral roof" (XI, 3) into the
world of the common man. He is humanized. But this
humanization was inevitable. Melville says that he will
treat Pierre honestly, and he therefore cannot be a hero.

Thus at the end of the book there is no surprise when
Pierre feels in him "the thews of a Titan . . . cut by the
scissors of Fate" (XXV, 3). And the fable of Enceladus can
be comforting (XXV, 5). But the new battle and warrior
are nobler than the old. Melville compares the new Pierre
with his nobler ancestors, to the glory of the younger:
"more glorious in real tented field to strike down your
valiant foe, than in the conflicts of a noble soul with a
dastardly world to chase a vile enemy who ne'er will
show front" (XIX, 2).

Isabel is in many ways both the most heroic and the
least heroic of all the main characters. She is most heroic
because she has the characteristic bastard strain. But she
is also least heroic for two reasons: because she is associated
with the French, who in Melville's mind were symbolic of
revolution, which generally was given his approbation
though he did not approve of the extremes to which they

generally carried their revolutionism; and because she
is the most democratic of all the characters. She is the
fallen angel who, like Eve, drags down into humanity Pierre
and Lucy, and thus serves as a stepping-stone, a transition,
from Titanism to democracy, from the heroic to the
humanistic.

IV. RISE OF THE COMMON MAN

Closely tied in with the Titanism, the descent of
superman, is its opposite, the rise of the common man.
Melville shows this by an obvious denial of the efficacy
of Christianity and the affirmation of its opposite.

He makes clear at the beginning that fate—chance, as
he says in most books—controls our lives, and thus plans
often go awry. Though disappointment is likelier than
gratification of expectations, people should not worry. As
he had written to Hawthorne during the composition of
Moby-Dick that he felt Solomon the wisest of men and
Ecclesiastes the truest of all books, he states here that
"Grief, not Joy, is a moraliser."

The anti-religious theme is brought out early, in the
persons of the Misses Penney. They are deaf and therefore
do not go to hear the Reverend Falsgrave preach anymore.
"While with prayer-books in their hands the Reverend Mr.
Falsgrave's congregation were engaged in worshipping
their God, according to the divine behest, the two Miss
Pennies, with thread and needle, were hard at work in
serving him" (III, 1), sewing for poor people.

Falsgrave himself is sufficient reason for the Penneys to
turn from God. He is a confidence man, a fraud, a person
who pretends religion but whose only real concern is his
own well-being. Two instances illustrate his character.
When Mrs. Glendinning savagely attacks Delly Ulver and
her seducer Ned, Falsgrave to a certain extent defends the
girl. But he very carefully does not jeopardize the coziness
of his relationship with his patroness. He is found wanting

when, as this scene progresses, the conversation becomes more hazardous. Pierre takes up the broader question of what should be the relationship of siblings, one legitimate and one illegitimate. That this question, or the situation, is extremely important is made manifest by Melville's symbolism, at times almost too labored. As Pierre tries to mouth the question, Falsgrave lightly but maliciously quips that Pierre has no tongue; the symbol anticipates the same voicelessness of Billy Budd when he is faced with his profound question voiced by a more sophisticated but similar confidence man, Captain Vere. Mrs. Glendinning adds to the seriousness of the situation by telling Falsgrave that his "cup is empty." When Pierre does ask the question, Falsgrave equivocates. Twice he is asked, twice tries to evade an answer; and each time symbolically his "surplice-like napkin" drops from the clergyman's bosom, revealing a "cameo brooch, representing the allegorical union of the serpent and dove" (V, 4). Obviously such a man is to be taken for the true shepherd by only the most credulous.

The fate of Christianity in this world, its change to something more useful, is revealed in the description of the Church of the Apostles, the house in which Pierre and Isabel live when they arrive in New York. Originally erected with nobel and pristine purpose as well as with towering architecture, the church through the years was overrun by business, eventually abandoned to it, and finally was metamorphosed into a home for artists and the poor. The church has now gone through its cycle, a cycle which parallels the development of Melville's humanistic impulses. The church, having served its purpose, gave way to business—especially legal business—which lasted for a while. Now the church serves its ultimate purpose; it houses the "glorious paupers," from whom Melville "learns the profoundest mysteries of things," and who have "lived and died in this world." Theirs is a "fundamental nobleness," and a "fundamental honour" no matter how much hooting there is from the "fools and pretenders of humanity, and the impostors and baboons among the gods" (XIX, 1).

Pierre has a long way to go from hero to commoner, and though Melville begins early in Pierre's metamorphosis, Pierre never in fact fully achieves his humanism. From the first he is blinded by his own vanity, becomes giddy with his own egotism (V, 5). In his egotism Pierre attempts in a manner almost like that of John Donne in his Divine Sonnets to make God swear on Himself that he will be true.

But in the grand style of the heroic, Pierre has the subtle beginnings of his own humanizing, for "though charged with the fire of all divineness, his containing thing was made of clay" (V, 6).

The catalytic agent for the development of humanism in the book is of course Isabel. She brings about the humanizing of the aristocrats because she is half aristocrat herself, and because she is also half French. She pinpoints the Ulvers of the world who, after the death of the aristocrats and the half-aristocrats, will inherit the earth. She is the fallen angel, the child of sin, who introduces Promethean fire of humanism to the earth.

In the long account of her childhood given to Pierre she tells of being orphaned and thus isolated from humanity and human love: "I feel that there can be no perfect peace in individualness" (VI, 4). When she was adopted with another child, she became aware of the "beautifulness of humanness." Later she tells how, protected by a single woman, she "thanked—not God, for I had been taught no God—I thanked the bright human summer, and the joyful sun in the sky," thus reversing the usual concept, and flashing forth humanism into the sky. Though she feels that she and all people are "in a world of horrible and inscrutable inhumanities," Isabel feels her "humanness among the inhumanities" (VI, 5).

Pierre wavers constantly in his gradual growth toward humanism; he acutally achieves it only a moment before his death. After his first interview with Isabel, he turns against humanity, mistakenly as Melville states:

> He could not bring himself to confront any face or house; a ploughed field, any sign of tillage, the rotted stump of a long-felled pine, the slightest passing trace of man was uncongenial to him. Likewise in his own mind all remembrances and imaginings that had to do with the common and general humanity had become, for the time, in the most singular manner distasteful to him (VII, 8).

The irony is that while Isabel has sought to unite herself with humanity, Pierre is seeking to disunite himself.

Like Ahab he remains long rebellious against the bonds of his humanity. A "vulnerable god," he fights to avenge his own lot. But Melville's sermonizing against such foolishness is both long and explicit, probing as it does the "dark, mad mystery in some human hearts, which, sometimes, during the tyranny of a usurper mood, leads beloved bond, as a hindrance to the attainment of whatever transcendental object that usurper mood so tyrannically suggests." Melville's censoriousness is clear, as is his subject of approval:

> Then the beloved bond seems to hold us to no essential good; lifted to exalted mounts, we can dispense with all the vale; endearments we spurn; kisses are blisters to us; and forsaking the palpitating forms of mortal love, we emptily embrace the boundless and the unbodied air. We think we are not human; we become as immortal bachelors and gods; but again, like the Greek gods themselves, prone we descend to earth; glad to be uxorious once more; glad to hide these god-like heads within the bosoms made of too-seducing clay (X, 3).

Again emphatically he makes the point in describing the Church of the Apostles. After the disappearance of the church aspects of the building, which probably inclined the members to an atomistic existence all the time except when they attended sermons, the poor people who finally inherited the building became a truly Christian organization in name and spirit though perhaps not in intent. They ceased being individualistic and uncommitted to the welfare of the group. Named the Apostles, they became clannish and "began to come together out of their various dens, in more social communion; attracted toward each other by title common to all"—that of *Homo sapiens.*

Another humanizing influence paralleling that of Isabel is Charlie Millthorpe. Millthorpe is the opposite of Pierre. A long-time boyhood friend who lived in poverty on Saddle Meadows, he too was, like Pierre, descended from heroes of England, tracing their "origin to an emigrating English Knight." Charlie's father was as noble in appearance as Pierre's father had been. "The delicate profile of his face, bespoke the loftiest aristocracy." Pierre loved Charlie but condescended to him. Millthorpe was an enthusiast like Pierre, and intended to be a great man. But unlike Pierre who in his enthusiasm became irresponsible to his family, Charlie upon the death of his father became a second father to them, and saddling himself with the obligation, though he would have preferred to remain a bachelor, shouldered for the time the burdens of being a family man. It is Charlie, whose misfortunes of having to shift for himself in getting an education parallels Melville's own, who gets Pierre to move into the Apostles.

In the Apostles, Pierre meets one of the significant figures in the book, Plotinus Plinlimmon. He is obviously a "supernatural" man, a demi-god, one of many Melville planted throughout his works. He has all the characteristics. His origin is unknown. He does not work with his hands, or read a book, or write anything. His influential pamphlet *Chronometricals and Horologicals,* written down imperfectly by students, cannot be found by Pierre when he wants to reread it. He has tremendous impact on Pierre, and begins to "domineer" over him. Plotinus tells Pierre by his looks to stop trying to write. He is a loner, his face was "a face by itself"; "it did not respond to anything." "Now, anything which is thus a thing by itself never responds to any other thing. If to affirm, be to expand one's isolated self; and if to deny, be to contract one's isolated self; then to respond is a suspension of all isolation"(XXI, 3).

His pamphlet *Chronometricals and Horologicals* is one of the important keys to Melville's message in the book. It teaches that there are two kinds of time in this universe, heavenly and earthly, God's and man's. The two do not synchronize because each is set for different readers. God's time is not meant for man, nor should man try to set his watch by God's clock. In other words, Plinlimmon says that there are things intended for heaven, and things intended for earth, and man should be content with his own clock. Man must live an earthly existence while on the earth, saving heaven for heaven. The pamphlet does not, however, "involve the justification of all the acts which wicked men may perform. For in their wickedness downright wicked men sin as much against their own horologes, as against the heavenly chronometer" (XIV, 3). Thus Melville does not justify the acts of such wicked men as Jackson, Bland, Claggart, or Captain Vere.

The pamphlet teaches instead that while on earth a person should live as fully and happily as possible:

> A virtuous expediency, then, seems the highest desirable or attainable earthly excellence for the mass of men, and is the only earthly excellence that their Creator intended for them. When they go to heaven, it will be quite another thing. There, they can freely turn the left cheek, because there the right cheek will never be smitten . . . A due appreciation of this matter will do good to man. For, hitherto, being authoritatively taught by his dogmatical teachers that he must, while on earth, aim at heaven, and attain it, too, in all his earthly acts, on pain of eternal wrath; and finding by experience that this is utterly impos-

131

sible; in his despair, he is too apt to run clean away into all manner of moral abandonment, self-deceit, and hypocrisy (cloaked, however, mostly under an aspect of the most respectable devotion); or else he openly runs, like a mad dog, into atheism.

In other words, Plinlimmon's advice is similar to Mr. Strether's to Chad in James' *The Ambassadors*—to live while you can before the opportunity slips away. The tragedy is that Pierre is too monomaniacal to understand and heed Plinlimmon's advice. But it was not altogether worthless to Pierre, because while he was looking for the pamphlet in order to read it a second time and try to understand it, the writing was serving a utilitarian human service, because it was lost in the lining of Pierre's coat and was helping in its way to keep him warm. And Melville suggests further that although Pierre thought he did not understand the pamphlet at all, he in fact did: "I think that, regarded in one light, the final career of Pierre will seem to show, that he *did* understand it (XXI, 3).

In most lights, however, Pierre does not understand the pamphlet. He does not, for example, ever become fully one of the Apostles. He never becomes, in other words, fully humanized. He remains half-committed, until at the very end when in his madness over the letter written to him by Glendinning Stanly and Frederic Tartan he wishes for the fraternal last embrace with them. But in his cold fury to slaughter these men, he reverts to his former isolation from the human race. Up until the very last his feelings about humanity are ambivalent.

In his quarters in the Apostles during the last days he drives himself to finish his book, forcing himself beyond the limits of endurance. But he needs the association of the human race. Like Hepzibah and Clifford in *The House of the Seven Gables,* Pierre needs to get out. He longs for the wholeness of life— "Land and Sea." More and more he walks in the streets to escape the reminder of his failure. But in the streets he asserts his detachment from people, from the "incessant jogglings of his body against the bodies of the hurrying thousands." And he dashes, with a "dark, triumphant joy," to deserted streets proud of the fact that all others have "crawled in fear to their kennels" to escape the inclement weather. He alone, like Ahab, dares face the elements.

Eventually, he wavers for a while, desiring to fraternize in the low-class "secluded and mysterious tap-rooms," where with cap pulled over his eyes he can observe if not associate with the "social castaways." Finally, however, he turns with "distaste" from these fellow men, and wanders through lonely streets. This final disavowal of human ties is his last, for he is seized by an "all-pervading sensation"; he "did not have any ordinary life-feeling at all." "The very blood in his body had . . . rebelled against his Titanic soul." As a result he loses control of his eyes, source of all important symbols in Melville (XXV, 3).

One day while in this state of "semi-unconsciousness, or rather trance," Pierre has the remarkably significant and revealing vision of Enceladus, the "phantasmagoria of the Mount of Titans," standing above Saddle Meadows, which was known locally as "the Delectable Mountains." In the development of this vision is disclosed the strength, horror, tyranny, and collapse of Titanism, and Melville's total commitment to the earth and humanism.

From the distance the mount looks virginally pure, holy, and beautiful, covered with the white amaranth throughout the year. But the beauty cloaks evil, for the amaranth, though beautiful, is worthless as feed, since the cows will not eat it, and yearly it spreads over otherwise useful land, stealing away useful pastorage. This holy mountain is, furthermore, beautiful only from a distance. When seen close up, its beauty and symmetry give way to "horrible glimpses of dark-dripping rocks, and mysterious mouths of wolfish caves," and concealing forests. This home of the gods is a chaos of broken and piled rocks, fierce and cutting streams, all "hideous repellingness" in "barbarous disdain" "stark desolation; ruin, merciless and ceaseless."

On the other side of the mountain, however, in the midst of the "sterile inodorous immortalness of the small, white flower," the amaranth, you might still "smell from far the sweet aromaticness of clumps of catnip, that dear farm-house herb," which would be mixed with "old foundation stones and rotting timbers of log-houses long extinct," from which the farmers had been chased by the relentless and inexorable advance of the amaranth. Melville makes his symbol quite explicit: "The catnip and the amaranth!—man's earthly household peace, and the ever-encroaching appetite for God."

On the side of the mountain is Enceladus the Titan, "the most potent of all the giants, writhing from out the imprisoning earth, endeavoring to advance against the gods of higher up." Originally almost completely bound in the earth, the rock had been only half freed by man—some students—but then had been abandoned. Finally it loses its arms through nature's force, and lies ignominious among the other Titans. In Pierre's dream, however, all the Titans rise up and batter the "precipice's unresounding wall." Enceladus himself "hurled his own arched-out ribs again and yet again against the invulnerable steep." Then as Pierre shouts to the Titan, it turns and Pierre sees himself in place of Enceladus.

The vision has its immediate implications. Enceladus was twice the son of incestuous union, that of Coelus and Terra which birthed Titan, and that between Titan and his mother Terra, Enceladus' parents. Thus the conflict of Enceladus (Pierre) to try to regain his "paternal birthright even by fiery escalade." But the assault was useless and futile. Though Pierre knew the fable well and recognized what it meant to him, he failed to understand the implications and the moral, and therein caused his own doom. Pierre did not "leap the final barrier of gloom; possibly because Pierre did not wilfully wrest some final comfort from the table; did not flog this stubborn rock as Moses his, and force even áridity itself to quench his painful thirst."

Had Pierre leaped the barrier he would have realized that "to grim Enceladus, the world the gods had chained for a ball to drag at his o'erfreighted feet;—even so that globe put forth a thousand flowers, whose fragile smiles disguised his ponderous load." Affirmation of this disguise is Melville's realization and declaration of the value of humanism in this world. Pierre's tragedy is his failure to recognize the mitigating flowers. But realize it he cannot. He is unable to join the human race (XXV, 4).

Near the end of the book, after having received the note from Stanly and Tartan, Pierre, wondering what "wondrous tools Prometheus used," chooses pistols to slay his cousin and Lucy's brother. Thus armed he stalks into the street. His position *vis-a-vis* the other people in the street is significant. On one side of the street are the "haughty-rolling carriages and proud-rustling promenaders," and "two streams of flossy, shawled, or broadcloth life unceasingly brushed by each other, as long, resplendent, drooping trains of rival peacocks brush." On the other side of the street are the poor people, the "porters, waiters, and parcel-carriers of the shops (XXVI, 5). But Pierre will not associate himself with either group. He has been lowered from the ranks of the former and is unwilling to accept that of the latter. He is still a loner. Still blind Enceladus and proud Ahab. Like Ahab attempting to destroy his tormentor, Pierre succeeds in slaying one—his cousin— by shooting him.

Immediately seized by the people he had scorned a moment before, he is taken to jail. There he is followed by Lucy and Isabel. Isabel inadvertently admits that she is Pierre's sister, and Lucy dies of horror at the incest Pierre and his "wife" have committed. Then both Pierre and Isabel commit suicide by drinking a drug that Lucy had carried in her bosom. But this *Romeo and Juliet*-like event is not Melville's final word. Fred Tartan rushes in and discovers Lucy dead and the other two dying. Falling beside Pierre he speaks to him in very humanistic terms. He calls him his "old companion, Pierre;—school-mate— friend." Pierre, roused by these declarations of fraternity, human love, and association, responds humanistically, just as Ahab did before being destroyed by the white whale. Pierre opens his hand for "one speechless clasp!" and dies holding the hand of his former friend and companion.

To clinch his point of Pierre's last-gasp conversion to humanism, Melville employs two symbols. He resorts to Biblical language in a gesture of sanctifying Pierre's death: Isabel in her death throes comments on Pierre's hand shaking and death: "All's o'er, and ye know him not!" (XXVI, 7). Then follows Melville's final clincher: "Isabel's whole form slipped sideways, and she fell upon Pierre's heart, and her long hair ran over him and arboured him in ebon vines." Significantly it is Pierre's heart, the superior half of the heart-head dichotomy into which Melville divided human existence, that is finally recognized and emphasized. Furthermore, Pierre is sepulchered in the symbol of sex, that of Isabel's body and wonderful, sensuous black hair.

Sex had seduced Pierre away from the isolation of his haughty home and heroic existence, away from the other-worldliness of the holy Lucy. Sex had finally humanized Lucy. It had especially humanized Isabel. After a long and terrible struggle it had finally brought Pierre to the fraternal clasp with a fellow human being.

Thus sex is in *Pierre* another of the many agents by which Melville advances the development of his major theme of humanism in Pierre the character and in the book as a whole. The book is perhaps an overly lurid and ex-aggerated part of the jigsaw puzzle of Melville's complete work. But in picturing the author's mind on the subject of man and humanism, it fits in perfectly.

FOUR

ISRAEL POTTER:
METAMORPHOSIS OF SUPERMAN

Melville's next novel, *Israel Potter: His Fifty Years of Exile* (1855), is his most underrated work. The re-written version of what Melville called "a little narrative of . . . adventures, forlornly published on sleazy gray paper . . . now out of print," this book is vastly changed from the original. Here, as in "Benito Cereno," *Moby-Dick*, and other works that draw heavily on printed sources, Melville telescoped or extended, emphasized or played down sections in order to make his points and develop his themes. Because this work came after the relative failure of *Moby-Dick* and the catastrophic reception of *Pierre*, when Melville's literary and personal fortunes were at their lowest, it is especially significant as an index to the author's thinking during these years. That the book continues to affirm Melville's belief in humanism is therefore especially significant.[1]

Simply told, the book is the story of a Berkshire mountaineer named Israel Potter, who as a young man wants to marry a certain girl but is frustrated by his father and runs away from home to seek his fortune. After proving himself on land and sea he returns to discover that his sweetheart has married another man. At news of the battle of Lexington, Potter answers duty's call. Wounded at Bunker Hill, he is hospitalized but returns almost immediately to assist in the fortification of Prospect Hill. Later he is captured by the British and sent to England to be imprisoned. His adventures thereafter are enough to break a dozen men. He escapes his captors and is recaptured. He has chats with King George and comes

---

1. The best full-scale study of *Israel Potter* to date is Arnold Rampersad, *Melville's "Israel Potter": A Pilgrimage and Progress* (Bowling Green, Ohio, 1969).

137

to respect and even like the monarch. He works with Horne Tooke and other "friends of America." He visits Paris and Benjamin Franklin. He sails with John Paul Jones, and participates in the attempt to burn Whitehaven and in the battle between Jones' *Bon Homme Richard* and the British *Serapis*. He encounters Ethan Allen in prison. Finally escaping the British officials, he buries himself in London for forty-five years. At the age of eighty, urged by his son whom he has told of the "fortunate Isles of the Free," Potter returns to America, in time to undergo other disappointments and to die.

In this novel Melville ponders over the matter of human liberty. He had grappled with monstrous tyranny in his earlier works, in for example, *Redburn, White-Jacket,* and *Moby-Dick,* and had baldly stated to Hawthorne his opposition to it. In *Israel Potter* Melville studies the topic in the eighteenth century, the period of revolutions of the common man against oppression, as he is to do later in "Benito Cereno" and *Billy Budd.*

In this novel as in "Benito Cereno" and *Billy Budd,* Melville demonstrates the triumph of the common man. But his technique differs. Richard Chase is partly right in saying that Melville's works develop Prometheus' effort to bring fire to the earth. *Israel Potter* shows that supermen and mere men cannot exist apart from one another. All men are the same and therefore must live together. The mixing of the superman and the common man results in a metamorphosis of the former into the latter. By the end of the book the superman of the beginning has disappeared and been replaced by the common man.

That the book deals with supermen becomes evident at the beginning. Israel was born in the eastern Berkshires, a section of the world as remote as "some terrace in the moon." Here as the eye "sweeps the broad landscape beneath, you seem to be Bootes driving in heaven." In mountain valleys one has "scarely the feeling of the earth." One realizes that the "very Titans seem to have been at work here," and the people have performed "herculean undertakings." This is the land of giant nature. The eagle soars, the hawk sallies from his crag "like a Rhenish baron of old from his pinnacled castle." Paganism and Christianity are combined. There is a "St. Peter's of these hills," the great purple dome of Taconic; and the "twin summits of Saddleback" are the "two-steepled natural cathedral of Berkshire."

The original settlers came into this region because they believed that high land is healthier than low. They were "a tall, athletic, and hardy race, unerring with the axe as the Indian with the tomahawk; at stone-rolling, patient as Sisyphus, powerful as Samson" (Ch. 1). Potter, of this stock, is the true mountainman, the backwoodsman, who to Melville always symbolizes a kind of superman. In what is one of Melville's deftest uses of Shakespeare, he refers to *Anthony and Cleopatra* to make Potter a Caesar in homespun: "He chose rather to plough, than be ploughed" (Ch. 3).

The other main characters are supermen also. Sir John Millett, the first Englishman to befriend Potter in England, is a "true Abrahamic gentleman." King George III is a superman because "strange and powerful magic resides in [his] crown" (Ch. 5). Franklin is a "household Plato" who has a "touch of primeval orientalness" and "the incredible seniority of an antediluvian." He is "the apostolic serpent and dove," who seems to be "seven score years old," and to whom "supernatural lore must needs pertain" (Ch. 7). Jacob, Hobbes, and Franklin are "practical magians in linsey-woolsey" (Ch. 8).

John Paul Jones, thinking himself a god, threatens to "rain down on wicked England like fire on Sodom" (Ch. 10). He is "like David of old" (Ch. 15), "an elemental warrior" (Ch. 16). The battle between the *Bon Homme Richard* and the *Serapis* is "akin to the Miltonic contests of archangels" (Ch. 19); Potter, while clinging to the tip of the yard on the *Richard*, "hung like Apollyon" (Ch. 19). Ethan Allen, whom Potter sees a captive at Pendennis Castle is a Green Mountain giant. Hoffman is certainly correct in saying that Allen was in Melville's day "half-legendary" and

139

folkloristic. He has "leopard-like teeth"(Ch. 21). He seems
"just broken from the dead leases in David's outlawed cave
of Adullam" (Ch. 21). With a voice like Stentor's and all
heroic figures, he blasts "wasp-waisted" officers backwards
"as from before the suddenly burst head of a steam boiler"
and snaps their spines (Ch. 21). He is a version of an early
and idealized Davy Crockett:

> Allen seems to have been a curious combination of a
> Hercules, a Joe Miller, a Bayard, and a Tom Hyer. . . .
> Though born in New England, he exhibited no trace
> of her character. He was frank, bluff, companionable
> as a Pagan, convivial, a Roman, hearty as a harvest.
> His spirit was essentially Western, for the Western
> spirit is, or will yet be (for no other is, or can be),
> the true American one (Ch. 21).

Melville was to develop Crockett as a symbol of the West
more fully in *The Confidence-Man*. In this symbol, this
spirit, Melville sees cause for both exaltation and fear.
Though it is the only spirit that can be truly American,
there is fear that "intrepid, unprincipled, reckless, pred-
atory, with boundless ambition, civilized in externals
but a savage at heart, America is, or may yet be, the
Paul Jones of nations," as he says in *Israel Potter* (Ch. 19).

As a superman in linsey-woolsey, Potter's role is to
demonstrate that as democratic god he can associate with
other heroes and reveal the mutual dependence of man and
superman. Melville shows that Potter's age is that of the last
of the demigods. Superman is being humanized through the
growth of democracy.

In the Berkshires, during the easy times of spring and
summer, "the heart desires no company but Nature." But
in fall and winter, mists and snow make these mountains
nearly uninhabitable. December snows drift "to the
arm-pits," and "as if an ocean rolled between man and
man," intercommunication is often suspended for weeks
and weeks. This is the terror of such a life. Even our giant-
like ancestors realized that they had to abandon the

mountains. "By degrees . . . they quitted the safety of this
sterile elevation, to brave the dangers of richer though lower
fields" (Ch. 1), leaving untenanted houses and mountain
tops showing "an aspect of singular abandonment." Further,
there were great stone walls built of rocks of such size that
"the very Titans" seemed to have been at work on this
"herculeanean" accomplishment now obviously falling into
disrepair. This turning to lower ground was inevitable
and desirable.

All the latter-day supermen in the book are democratic.
Franklin, "grown wondrous wise," is a "pocket congress
of all humanity" (Ch. 7)—Melville here uses one of his
favorite figures of speech for all-encompassing and all-
inclusive humanity and democracy. King George, though
largely controlled by the institution of which he is a part,
is personally good-natured and magnanimous, and acts
"like a true man" (Ch. 14). John Paul Jones is "citizen
and sailor of the universe" (Ch. 10). He does not mind
having as a "hammockmate a full-blooded Congo" (Ch. 11).
His arm is covered with tattooing "such as is seen only
on thorough-bred savages" (Ch. 11). In other words, like
Ishmael when he realizes it is better to sleep with a good
cannibal than a bad Christian, and like Queequeg, the
dignified and democratic pagan, Jones here equals the
humanistic qualities of both civilized and uncivilized
man. Jones wears on his face a "look of sagacious, humane
meditation . . . as if pondering upon the chances of the
important enterprise: one which, perhaps, might in the
sequel affect the weal or woe of nations yet to come"
(Ch. 11). Ethan Allen hates all that smacks of English
aristocracy. Lord Howe is to him a "toad-hearted king's
lick-spittle of a scarlet poltroon; the vilest wriggler in God's
worm-hole below" (Ch. 21).

Potter himself is interested in "such momentous affairs
as the freeing of nations" (Ch. 10). To him there is no
difference in rank between people. He is in no way awed by
the great and wise Franklin, nor by King George; to

141

the latter Potter says, "I have no king," and his natural dignity causes George to comment grudgingly, "Very stubborn race, indeed—very-very-very" (Ch. 5). Jones and Allen are recognized by Potter as only his equals. Further, as Potter says after he has just escaped from the house of the defunct Squire Woodcock and is changing clothes with a scarecrow in a field, there is a "difference between the contents of the pockets of scarecrows and the pockets of well-to-do squires" but clearly, as the tone indicates, not in the flesh of the two (Ch. 7). As Potter had said earlier,

"While we revell in broadcloth, let us not forget what we owe to linsey-woolsey" (Ch. 3). Some Englishmen who are non-soldiers are to Potter, with obvious contempt in the statement, "a sort of crafty aristocracy" (Ch. 25). Finally, like Melville commenting on the universality of all kinds of people in his questioning in *Moby-Dick* of who is not a coward, slave, and cannibal, Potter destroys all rank in his query, "Who ain't a nobody?" (Ch. 23).

Melville's demonstration of the equality of men is furthered by another way he treats the supermen in the book. That is, his attitude toward them is ambivalent. Although he obviously respects and likes them, he can be also mischievous, flippant, and irreverent.

Melville clearly likes Franklin, for example, yet he cannot restrain from making fun of him. Melville's humor and irony in this are so subtle, as they are to be in the later *Confidence-Man*, that they at times go unnoticed. When Potter first enters the Paris apartment of Franklin, he is clearly in the presence of a superman. Franklin is dressed in a "rich dressing-gown . . . curiously embroidered with algebraic figures like a conjuror's robe, and with a skull-cap of black satin on his hive of a head," and "the man of gravity was seated at a hugh claw-footed old table, round as the zodiac." He is a medieval necromancer. Though the room buzzes with flies, the "sapient inmate sat still and cool . . . absorbed in some other world of his occupations and thoughts" (Ch. 7). This is a man whose initial appearance, if the scene were played straight, would be dramatic. But Melville parodies the effect. Instead of placing Franklin so that his appearance would be overwhelming, as it should be, Melville turns him around so that Potter is denied the full effect. Franklin has his back to the visitor and will not turn around: "But when Israel stepped within the chamber, he lost the complete effect of this; for the sage's back, not his face was turned to him." The diminution of superman is neatly accomplished. Melville's technique is the same, though to a lesser degree, that he used in *Typee, Redburn,* and *Moby-Dick* when he burlesques people by having them, or others, expose their backsides.

Melville cuts Franklin down also by quipping about the old man's obsession with thrift. When Potter arrives in Paris, Franklin hands him some money for his needs, saying that it can be paid back in America. Potter returns it in a few minutes, however, and remarks, "No interest, Doctor, I hope" (Ch. 9). Later Franklin economizes on the cost of Potter's stay in the French house by taking out all the extra-cost items such as the Otard, sugar, and colored soap. Potter dryly urges him to be more exhaustive: "Oh, you better take the whole furniture, Doctor Franklin. Here, I'll help you drag out the bedstead" (Ch. 9).

The other heroic characters in the book are cut down to human dimensions also. King George, though a "magnanimous lion," stammers, as of course he did in life. But he is completely de-heroized by being denied his Kingship, when Potter tells him, "Sir, I have no king." John Paul Jones is reduced by one blunt remark. The great captain is ranting to Franklin and Potter about his prowess on the seas; he says, referring to himself in the heroic third person, "Paul Jones never was captured," and demands of Potter, "Did your shipmates talk much of me?" Potter's reply is curt: "I never heard the name before this evening" (Ch. 10). Ethan Allen, though a superman, is like "some baited bull in the ring," a "Patagonian-looking captive," whose "whole marred aspect was that of some

143

wild beast." Though gallant to the ladies, he has a "bovine forehead" (Ch. 21).

Melville's greatest art in diminution is reserved, however, for God. In bringing God down, Melville to a certain extent and clearly on purpose raises Potter to the stature of a demi-god. But more important, Melville is stripping God of His superiority and making Him not much above mere human beings, surely not something to be worshipped. In this way at least, Melville has a quarrel with God, as Thompson has argued.[2]   God is whimsical, especially with commoners. Potter is "planted, torn up, transplanted, and dropped again, hither and thither, according as the Supreme Disposer of sailors and soldiers saw fit to appoint" (Ch. 13).

Twice Melville cuts God most deeply by use of parody, both times of the Resurrection. When Potter is secreted in the chimney room of Squire Woodcock, which had formerly constituted a "portion of a religious retreat belonging to the Templars," Melville uses Biblical language to tie in this scene with the Resurrection. In this religious sanctuary Potter waits for release from his "coffin-cell of the Templars." Squire Woodcock promises to come for the "disintombment" as soon as possible, on the third day at the latest. While waiting, Potter, like countless Christians before him suffers: "Here, in this very darkness, centuries ago, hearts, human as his, had mildewed in despair; limbs, robust as his own, had stiffened in immovable torpor." Like their hope in eventual release, his expectations are vain. The scene is reminiscent of the sixteen hours the youthful Ishamel spent in his room waiting for his "resurrection."

Melville echoes Biblical language. "'This is the morning of the third day,' murmured Israel to himself; 'he said he would at the furthest come to me on the morning of the third day.'" When Woodcock, the dead god, fails to resurrect Potter on the third day, on the fourth Potter

2. Lawrence Thompson, *Melville's Quarrel with God* (Princeton, 1952).

resurrects himself. Significantly he is reborn a squire. He finds the spring that operates the chimney door and emerges (Ch. 12).

He finds that the squire is dead and the room hung with funeral drapings. As Potter emerges from his coffin-like room "by degrees he began to feel almost as unreal and shadowy as the shade whose part he intended to enact." Potter becomes Woodcock by dressing in the squire's clothes. So garbed, he emerges from the room, and the servents all believe he is the resurrected squire. The widow falls into a dead faint at the sight of him. Significantly she falls "crosswise before him," and he being a god "forced to be immutable in his purpose . . . solemnly stepping over her prostrate form, marched deliberately on" (Ch. 13).

The single overriding theme of this novel, as is the case with so many of Melville's works, is the necessity of man's faith in the human race in this man-of-war and godless world. This theme is strikingly developed in *Israel Potter* in events which now take place.

Outside the house, "the whole scene magically re-produced to our adventurer the aspect of Bunker Hill, Charles River and Boston town, on the well-remembered night of the 16th of June," when the first major stroke was made against tyranny in favor of the common man. Now, "acted on as if by enchantment," Potter realizes that he must be reborn as a human being. Suddenly he sees "a man in black standing right in his path . . . one out-stretched arm, with weird intimation pointing towards the deceased Squire's abode." The stranger seems "something more than humanly significant," not a "living man." But Potter, "the phantom of Squire Woodcock," with something of his "intrepidity returned," firmly marches "straight forward towards the mysterious stranger" (Ch. 13).

This "mysterious stranger" turns out to be a scarecrow. Potter changes his godly raiment for the sorry, human clothes on the scarecrow, and in so doing introduces one of the most grotesque—and not completely satisfactory—scenes in literature outside of sheer farce.

The morning after Potter has taken on the clothes from the scarecrow, a farm-laborer carrying a pitchfork approaches the spot where the scare-crow formerly stood. Thinking that the scene should not be changed, Potter assumes the position and stance that the scare-crow had had. When the laborer has passed by, Potter runs away as fast as he can. But looking around he sees that the laborer is coming back. Potter then freezes again in the stance of the scarecrow, pointing at the advancing man with his up-lifted arm, trying to frighten him. But this implacable human being approaches, puzzled by the apparent supernatural happenings, but determined to get at the truth. Potter now, in trying to escape, attempts to become Satan. "Israel as a last means of practising on the fellow's fears of the supernatural, suddenly doubled up both fists, presenting them savagely towards him at a distance of about twenty paces, at the same time showing his teeth like a skull's and demoniacally rolling his eyes" (Ch. 13). But the man is not frightened. He advances slowly, presents the end of his pitchfork to Potter's eye, and finally forces the scarecrow to take his heels. This Satan, this "apparition," is chased away by the laborer and a dozen others from an adjoining field who join in the rout. Scarcely any stronger statement could be made of man's triumph over the supernatural.

Melville's strongest affirmation of his belief in man rather than in God, and his sharpest travesty of God's creation of man, comes later when Potter, finished with his wartime adventures, has come to the neighborhood of London and gets a job at a brickyard. Melville makes it clear that this situation must be paralleled with the Biblical account of man's creation. Potter becomes both a buryer and a creator: "Half buried there in the pit, all the time handing those desolate trays [of brick mud], poor Israel seemed some gravedigger, or churchyard man, tucking away dead little innocents in their coffins on one side, and cunningly disinterring them again to resurrectionists stationed on the other." The creators—the dozen workers in this section—are whimsical, like God. Obviously influenced by the gravedigger in *Hamlet*, they are indifferent to their vocation, with its "helterskelter slapping of the dough into the moulds." These "muddy philosophers" feel that "men and brick were equally of clay." "'What signifies who we be—dukes or ditchers?' thought the moulders; 'all is vanity and clay.'" Melville extends the comparison between bricks and men: "brick is no bad name for any son of Adam; Eden was but a brickyard; what is a mortal but a few luckless shovelfuls of clay, moulded in a mould, laid out on a sheet to dry, and ere long quickened into his queer caprices by the sun? Are not men built into communities just like bricks into a wall?" Man "serves" bricks, as "God him, building him up by billions into edifices of his purposes. Man attains not to the nobility of a brick, unless taken in the aggregate" (Ch. 23).

In a scene strongly reminiscent of Hawthorne's "Ethan Brand," Melville has Potter sitting before the mouth of the kilns philosophizing while "a dull smoke—a smoke of their torments—went up from their tops" (Ch. 23). Melville now broods on how much man must commit himself to life, a question that is present to a greater or lesser extent in all his books, and a point on which he severely criticized Emerson for his failure to descend from his Olympian heights to mix with the mass of mankind. This question, instead of the one raised by James E. Miller on this point—that the fire equals evil or misfortune—seems more nearly correct.[3]

There are three kinds of bricks taken from the kiln. Those nearest the fire have been broken by the heat. This would seem to be a statement that although heat is beneficial to clay, necessary for the development of

3. James E. Miller, Jr., *A Reader's Guide to Herman Melville* (New York, 1962).

bricks, too much can break them. Those bricks furthest
from the heat are "pale with the languor of too exclusive an
exemption from the burden of the blaze" (Ch. 23); here
Melville is commenting on those persons who are too
detached from life, as he felt Emerson was, to live it fully.
Only those bricks which are in the middle are the good
ones. Not broken by life's poverty and adversities, not
detached and therefore indifferent, but truly and completely
and democratically committed, they are the best bricks for
the wall of humanity.

The religious implications of the scene as a continuation
of the preceding one are clear: "These kilns were a sort of
temporary temples constructed in the yard, each brick
being set against its neighbor almost with the care taken by
the mason" (Ch. 23). But the bricks last longer than the
temples, for once the bricks—men—are formed, down
come the temples "in a tumbled ruin," and the bricks
are sent off to mix with and to serve humanity.

Melville's message—his leveling of God and man and
the democratic mass—is made explicit at the end of this
chapter. Paralleling the fate of the American Israel with that
of his Biblical namesake, now "bondsman in the English
Egypt," Melville concludes that men are all the same
regardless of time or nation in which they live: "'What
signifies who we be, or where we are, or what we do?'
Slap-dash! 'Kings, as clowns are codgers—who ain't
a nobody?' Splash! 'All is vanity and clay'" (Ch. 23).

Melville's feeling that men are the same throughout
time and space does not extend to the belief that all
countries are the same. He will modify this feeling in
Clarel. Now, however, as it had been throughout most of
his earlier works, America is the hope of humanity, "the
Fortunate Isles of the Free." England represents the
opposite, at least to a large extent. Potter quits his job at
the brickyards and goes to London, "entering, like the
king, from Windsor." But though he can enter a city from
the same side as the king, not every man in London is yet

a king, Significantly, Potter enters on fifth of November,
Guy Fawkes day, when a man tried to destroy one symbol
of English institutions, the Houses of Parliament. To Potter,
London represents "that hereditary crowd—gulf-stream of
humanity—which, for continuous centuries, has never
ceased pouring, like an endless shoal of herring, over
London Bridge" (Ch. 24). Here, as in *Clarel,* Melville has his
man join the stream of humanity.

London Bridge, over which the stream of humanity
flows, epitomizes the evil of anachronistically insti-
tutionalized England. The Southwark entrance has
been the place through the ages on which "the withered
heads and smoked quarters of traitors, stuck on pikes"
have been used to tyrannize the people and keep them
in their place. The scene thunders with the same cry of
outrage as that at the end of "Benito Cereno," as well
as elsewhere in Melville's works, when Babo's head
piked above the street is the white man's ultimate in
self-degradation.

In London, where he wanders for forty years, Israel
knows "that being of this race, felicity could never be his
lot" (Ch. 24). It is not. Melville drags Israel through every
possible adversity, "wrangling with rats for prizes in the
sewers," "crawling into an abandoned doorless house . . .
where his hosts were three dead men, one pendant,"
fathering eleven children only to bury ten, jostling with
thousands for bare subsistence, warming himself and his
remaining son "over a handful of reignited cinders
(which the night before might have warmed some lord)"—
words and scene paralleling closely the left-over food being
fed the poor in "Rich Man's Crumbs." Finally Potter flees
England and returns to America, largely because his son
"felt added longing to escape his entailed misery" (Ch. 25).

Potter's return and fate in America rounds out Melville's
theme. Back in this country, on the Fourth of July he
discovers that most of the country's gratitude consists of
raising monuments, such as the one on Bunker Hill. A purse

is raised for him, however, and he, "the bescarred bearer of a cross," returns with his son to the mountains of his youth. There all traces of the Potters have disappeared. Inquiring from a stranger who is plowing, Potter discovers that the man is in fact plowing up the last remains of the Potters' old homestead. This man reports that the Potters have "gone West." In an agony of remembrance of his lost life Potter says to the laborer, "Plough away, friend."

In this sentence Melville reintroduces one of the main themes of the book. This is a reawakening of his earlier statement when like a plebeian Caesar he would rather plow than be plowed. Now he is willing to stand aside and allow the plowing by others. But the statement is not one of desperation. Though Potter has been denied a pension by "certain caprices of law," though "his scars proved his only medals," and though his name faded "out of memory," and though "he died the same day that the oldest oak on his native hill was blown down," the book does not end in despair. Rather, as in *Hamlet* and *Caesar*, there is hope in the fact that Potter leaves a son behind him.

Furthermore, there is some satisfaction in the fact that man can endure the hardships that Potter suffered for eighty years. There is hope in sheer animal endurance. Most important of all, however, is the obvious moral of the book, that men must stick together. Here, as in *The Confidence-Man*, which Melville will publish two years later, is the author's statement of the need for humanism joining all men—high and low, rich and poor—into a wall against adversity.

A word should be said about Melville's style in this book. It has none of the rhetoric that sometimes blemishes *Moby-Dick* and often mars *Pierre*. Instead it is fast, direct, and restrained. When necessary Melville gallops through or around material but never trips the reader. Having purged himself of most of his surfeiting of literary allusions and mannerisms, he here can paraphrase the Bible or Shakespeare with great dexterity, as we have seen. Furthermore, Melville uses a whiplike prose which forecasts its finer use in his next book, *The Confidence-Man*. Through all, there is a sure-handed poetic tone that reveals how confident Melville felt in his use of the material, as the following section from the fight between the *Bon Homme Richard* and the *Serapis* reveals:

> Not long after, an invisible hand came and set
> down a great yellow lamp in the east. The hand
> reached up unseen from below the horizon, and set the
> lamp down right on the rim of the horizon, as on a
> threshold; as much as to say, Gentlemen warriors,
> permit me a little to light up this rather gloomy
> looking subject. The lamp was the round harvest moon;
> the one solitary footlight of the scene. (Ch. 217-8).

All in all, this book about the wandering American Israel must be placed among the top half dozen of Melville's works.

FIVE

THE GREATER SHORT STORIES:
"BARTLEBY" AND "BENITO CERENO"

In the summer of 1853, Melville turned from long books to shorter tales. His reasons were largely economic. An unwell farmer at Arrowhead, he needed sources of income more remunerative than his books. Magazines, though their payments were rather small, provided him with sums which would supplement his other earnings.

In shortening and narrowing the scope of his writings, however, Melville did not at all alter his purpose or the inclusiveness of his range of vision. The short stories are merely, as Richard H. Fogle says, microcosms of the universe, and Melville's purpose in them is still unrelenting examination of the basic reasons for and explanations of the universe. Though shifting his subject and focus he is still primarily concerned with man and God and man and man.

Artistically Melville's accomplishment differs only slightly in the short story from what it does in the longer works. Several of these shorter works, to be sure, are weak. But two—"Bartleby" and "Benito Cereno"—are among Melville's most superb achievements.

"Bartleby," Melville's first effort in the genre, was from the beginning an unqualified success in public reception. More important, artistically it must rank as one of the author's finest works. Low-keyed and understated, it is in fact one of Melville's firmest affirmations of man's invincibility.

"Benito Cereno," unlike the earlier story, was not immediately recognized as being as powerful as it is. George William Curtis, when the story was sent to *Putnam's*, commented: "Melville's story is very good. It is a great pity that he did not work it up as a connected tale instead of putting the dreary documents at the end.—They should have made part of the substance of the story. It is a little spun out—but it is very striking and well done. And I agree with Mr. Law that it ought not to be lost." [1] Despite this approval the story had not begun to be published three months later, apparently because of the feeling that it, especially the ending, was not sufficiently worked up.

In his opinion of the story Curtis was better business-man than critic. Indeed he should not have wanted to "lose" the work. Melville had found a "story of reality" which was "instinct" with "significance" in Chapter 18 of Captain Amasa Delano's *Narrative of Voyages and Travels* (1817), and he had richly developed the possibilities. Although the ending is still criticized as being merely tacked on, it is in fact artistically one of the more powerful elements of the story, as we shall see. It is the ending which helps give the story the tremendous timely impact that makes it among Melville's shorter works second only to *Billy Budd*, though its overall effect is not as universal as that of "Bartleby."

THE AFFIRMATION OF "BARTLEBY"

"Bartleby, the Scrivener" (*Putnam's*, November-December 1853), one of Melville's most provocative and significant stories, is a multi-leaved allegory containing various meanings for various readers. Scholars have discussed the real people upon whom Melville modeled his tale. [2] Critics have seen the plight of Melville himself after the near

1. Leon Howard, *Herman Melville* (Berkeley, Calif., 1951), p. 221.

2. The best single volume of essays on "Bartleby" was the 1965 Melville symposium edited by Howard P. Vincent, *Bartleby the Scrivener* (Kent, Ohio, 1966). For discussion of the real people that Melville might have modeled on, see Jay Leyda, *The Melville Log*, 2:515-516, and *The Complete Stories*, ed. Jay Leyda (New York, 1945), p. 455; Howard, p. 208; also Egbert S. Oliver, "A Second Look at 'Bartleby'," *College English* 6 (May 1945):432.

failure of *Moby-Dick* and the catastrophic reception of
Pierre;[3] the battle between absolutism and free will;[4] the
destructive power of irrationality;[5] the crushing im-
personality of the business world, best illustrated in the
character of Bartleby as the "psychological double for the
nameless lawyer-narrator."[6] The most searching and
revealing, however, has been that criticism which has
centered on the story as a work of art and has seen it not as
"utter negation," as Matthiessen said it was, but as an
affirmation of Melville's belief in the ultimate victory of
humanity—always one of his major themes—with Bartleby
as hero and *avator examplar* of humanity's final triumph.
But Leo Marx and Marvin Felheim, the main proponents
of this last view, failed signally in developing this theme
as fully as they might. [7]

Another aspect of the story has been virtually ignored:
here, as in his works in general, Melville uses mythology
and folklore to further his meaning, and study of these
aspects is necessary for a full understanding of the story.
Melville's use is so complex, however, that it is impossible
to unravel the skeins, and all themes must be developed
concurrently.

Bartleby is a copyist who goes to work for a Wall
Street lawyer. At first he labors submissively. Soon, however,
he "would prefer not to" do certain tasks, and eventually

3. Richard Chase, *Herman Melville* (New York, 1949), pp. 147-149; Newton Arvin,
Herman Melville (New York, 1950), pp. 242-244.

4. R. H. Fogle, *Melville's Shorter Tales* (Norman, Okla., 1960), pp. 14-27.

5. Charles G. Hoffman, "The Shorter Fiction of Herman Melville," *South Atlantic
Quarterly* 52 (1953): 420-421.

6. Ronald Mason, *The Spirit above the Dust* (London, 1951), pp. 190-192; Mordecai
Marcus, "Melville's Bartleby as a Psychological Double," *College English* 23 (February
1962): 365-368.

7. Leo Marx, "Melville's Parable of the Walls," *Sewanee Review* 61 (1953): 602-627;
Marvin Felheim, "Meaning and Structure in 'Bartleby'," *College English* 23 (February
1962): 369-376. A similar study that arrives at a conclusion different from mine is
John Gardner, "*Bartleby*: Art and Social Commitment," *Philolgical Quarterly*, 43, 1
(January 1964): 87-98. His conclusion: "To understand that the narrator is at least as
right as Bartleby, both on the surface and on symbolic levels, is to understand the
remarkable interpenetration of form and content in the story."

refuses to do any work at all. Because he will not work, Bartleby finally is sentenced to the Tombs, the New York City prison, where he soon dies.

The minor characters—Turkey, Nippers, and Ginger Nut to a lesser degree—are *humors* characters in the Dickensian manner. Turkey, the sixty-year-old white-haired Englishman, is extremely painstaking and methodical, and is an excellent worker in the morning. At noon, however, he drinks heavily, and for the remainder of the day is "too energetic," with "a strange, inflamed, flurried, flightly recklessness of activity about him." But he is always submissive: "with submission" is his favorite response, even when he is firm in refusing to do what his employer demands.

Nippers, the other copyist, another Englishman (Turkey's "compatriot," as Melville calls him), is about half Turkey's age. He has the same general characteristics as Turkey, but his complement the older man's. "Their fits relieved each other, like guards," says Melville, and this "was a good natural arrangement, under the circumstances." Both men are flawed; each is only half a man.

In these two characters there is much political overtone. Indeed it is difficult not to read into them the two facets of the English national character, the Anglo-Saxon and the French. Turkey is a florid-faced, stolid, differential "dependent" Angle-Saxon. Nippers, on the contrary, is French-like, with a "brandy-like disposition."

Like the French he is impatient with legal documents. His "indigestion" causes him to grind his teeth, gives him "occasional . . . grinning irritability," and causes him to hiss his curses. Nippers is a "ward-politician," with broad political implications. He cannot get his writing table to suit him. "He put chips under it, blocks of various sorts, bits of pasteboard, and at last went so far as to attempt an exquisite adjustment, by final pieces of folded blotting-paper." But despite all manipulations and all angles, the table would never satisfy. "The truth of the matter was, Nippers knew not what he wanted." Nippers' plight can

155

only remind one of the eternal French proclivity of trying to improve their political constitution, and of being unhappy with the whole idea of having controlling institutions.

The only Americans in the law office, beside Bartleby, are Ginger-Nut and the lawyer. The former is a lad "some twelve years old," whose father, "a carman," was "ambitious of seeing his son on the bench instead of a cart, before he died." Like his employer, Ginger-Nut can get along with all kinds of people; he is largely without humors. Politically he represents youthful America, trying to make a success in life.

These characters are more, however, than mere people and political symbols. Melville says that theirs are names "the like of which are not usually found in the Directory." They are nicknames, "deemed expressive of their respective persons or characters." Such names are also folkloristic and mythological. Melville urges the reader to associate Turkey and Nippers with myth and folklore, with Gawain and Lancelot, as Fogle recognizes.

One example of Melville's urging is his medieval terminology. On some afternoons Turkey's face "flamed with augmented blazonry," and one afternoon his boss criticized him for "moistening a ginger-cake between his lips, and clapping it on to a mortgage, for a seal." In the *Morte Darthur* Gawain's strength waxes in the morning and wanes in the afternoon while Lancelot's increases in the afternoon and wanes in the morning. Gawain was the older—the earlier—hero of Arthurian legends until the younger Frenchman, Lancelot, supplanted him as leading hero of the Round Table.

Perhaps Melville's veiled references could be dismissed as mere coincidence if it were not for his obvious use of the momentous wrestling match between Gawain and Lancelot. In this match it was clear that Gawain—a solar myth, as Fogle says—derives his strength from the earth, and Lancelot realizes finally that the only way he can defeat the other hero is to pick him up and hold his feet above the ground until his strength ebbs. Nippers too is a wrestler. In his paroxysms he "would sometimes impatiently rise from his seat, and stooping over his table, spread his arms wide apart, seize the whole desk and move it, and jerk it, with a grim, grinding motion on the floor, as if the table were a perverse voluntary agent, intent on thwarting and vexing him." Further evidence that this wrestling match was on Melville's mind is revealed when, later on, the lawyer is thinking of his temptation to toss Bartleby out of the office and says: "When this old Adam of resentment rose in me and tempted me concerning Bartleby, I grappled and threw him" which statement in context is more a Gawain-Lancelot than a Biblical reference.

The militaristic and aggressive language of these two characters is also thematically significant. When the lawyer chides Turkey for his sloppiness and tries to dismiss him, for example, Turkey says: "I consider myself your right-hand man. In the morning I but marshall and deploy my columns; but in the afternoon I put myself at their head, and gallantly charge the foe." On another occasion, of an afternoon, Turkey strikes "a pugilistic" position and wants to "step behind his screen and black [Bartleby's] eyes for him." Nippers wants to kick Bartleby out of the office.

Another important symbol in the story is the color green. Leo Marx is correct in seing it as a symbol of growth. This color is, of course, important in connection with Gawain, in his adventures with the Green Knight, in the heroic tale. Further, when the lawyer first hires Bartleby he senses that the young man is superior to the other scriveners, and feeling that he can grow to the business successfully the lawyer places Bartleby near him behind a green screen.

Marx is correct again in paralleling Melville's words with those in a letter he wrote to Hawthorne about this time, in which he talks about the "silent grass-growing mood in which a man ought always to compose," and the further passage: "I am like one of those seeds taken out of the Egyptian Pyramids, which, after being three thousand years a seed and nothing but a seed, being planted in English soil, it developed itself, grew to greenness, and then fell to the mould."

Another aspect strengthens the green motif. Fogle rightly calls Bartleby a "melancholy Thoreau." "Bartleby," like many of Melville's works, tests the strength and weakness of Transcendentalism. Thoreau was at this time generally in Melville's thinking. For example, "The Apple-Tree Table" story was probably already on his mind, and in its final version it derives in parts at least from *Walden*.[8] Although Melville omitted the *Walden* passage from his story of the peculiar table, he significantly incorporated the color green. This passage roughly parallels Melville's use of the color in "Bartleby," and for comparison needs to be quoted in full. In the conclusion of *Walden*, Thoreau says that the egg of the bug that develops and eats through the table "has been buried for ages under many concentric layers of woodenness in the *dead dry life of society*, deposited at first in the alburnum of the *green and living tree,* which has been gradually converted into the semblance of its well-seasoned *tomb*" (my italics).

Green merges, of course, into the real conclusion of "Bartleby." But it also blends into another significant theme—that of the tomb.

"Bartleby" is a grimly ironic study of who will be saved must first be lost. As the story opens, the lawyer and copyists are already in this tomb but do not know it. At one end of the office there is "an unobstructed view of a lofty brick wall, black by age and everlasting shade," the square of which "not a little resembled a huge square cistern." Though the lawyer is undoubtedly ironic when he says that there is no need of a "spyglass to bring out its lurking beauties," he is unaware of his own blindness when he looks at the other view from his windows. At

8. Douglas Sackman, "The Original of Melville's Apple-Tree Table," *American Literature* 11 (January 1940): 448-451; Frank Davidson, "Melville, Thoreau, and 'The Apple-Tree Table'," *American Literature* 25 (January 1954): 478-488. All quotations in this chapter, given in the text, are from the Leyda edition of *Complete Stories.*

this end his quarters "looked upon the white wall of the interior of a spacious skylight shaft, penetrating the building from top to bottom." But the lawyer, with a straight face that reveals his spiritual blindness, says, "This view might have been considered rather tame than otherwise, deficient in what landscape painters call life." Obviously the only hope of life to be seen anywhere is this light.

When Bartleby comes to the offices, he is assigned a corner on the lawyer's side of the door, separated from his employer by "a high green folding screen." He has a side window "which originally had afforded a lateral view of certain grimy backyards and bricks, but which, owing to subsequent erections, commanded at present no view at all." But the unobservant lawyer scarcely feels called upon to comment on the really significant aspect of this view, that "a light came down from far above, between two lofty buildings, as from a very small *opening in a dome*" (my italics). The symbolism is explicit: the lawyer fails to notice this great light and therefore has no hope of communication with heaven; but Bartleby has over him the dome of heaven, and viewing it becomes a monomania with him. The logic of this interpretation is strengthened by the fact that in two other short stories written during these years Melville used exactly the same kind of symbol. In "The Apple-Tree Table," a story of the conflict between science and religion, the narrator finds in an attic filled with insects and cobwebs a skylight which despite the physical difficulties he finally manages to open and discovers it to be a window to heaven and nature. In the first of "The Two Temples," the narrator is "delighted by catching sight of a small round window in the otherwise dead-wall side of the tower" he is ascending. The window actually opens into hell, but its use closely parallels that of the window in "Bartleby." In "Bartleby" there is an obvious parallel with the fact that in mythology— and in many of Melville's other stories, *Billy Budd*, for example —heaven acknowledges the presence of a hero.

Surrounded by the green of promise on one side and by the light of heaven on the other, Bartleby grows into his tomb and toward eventual resurrection. Marx misunderstands what the dead wall really is, though he is right in placing great stress on it. When Bartleby is in his little office, especially after he has given up all copying, he stands "looking out, at his pale window behind the screen, upon the dead brick wall"; he "did nothing but stand at this window in his dead-wall revery." But he is always looking out—at the light coming through that small opening in the dome. When the lawyer asks why he will not write any more, Bartleby answers: "Do you not see the reason for yourself?" Bartleby recognizes that the time for his passion, entombment, and resurrection is upon him, and his eyes are turned from this world to the reality and nearness of the next. The lawyer notices that Bartleby's "eyes looked dull and glazed," but unobservant man that he is, he mistakenly assumes that Bartleby has been working too hard. Several times before, the lawyer has commented on Bartleby's deathly appearance. His "form appeared . . . laid out . . . in its shivering winding sheet"; he has a "cadaverously gentlemanly nonchalance"; a "cadaverous triumph"; he gives a "cadaverous reply." In the Tombs—his own sepulcher—surrounded by "the eyes of murderers and thieves," Bartleby is tempted by Satan in the form of the grub-man, but he resists all blandishments and lies down against the wall and dies.

The message of the story, obviously, develops through the two main characters, the lawyer and the unwilling copyist. The former characterizes himself at the beginning as a man about sixty years of age who, conservative and remarkably unimaginative, from youth on "has been filled with a profound conviction that the easiest way of life is the best." Without any real ambition, he is "an eminently *safe* man" whose "first grand point," said John Jacob Astor, is "prudence," He does a "snug business in rich men's bonds, and mortgages, and title deeds." He believes in charity— because it is a "wise and prudent principle."

The lawyer is governed by the philosophy of expediency. He is unwilling to face an issue and solve it under any circumstance.

In trying to cope with the passive resistance of Bartleby, the lawyer will use any excuse rather than face the crisis. The first confrontation he skirted because his "business hurried" him. He threatens "terrible retribution very close at hand," but postpones it because it is nearly dinner time. He even rationalizes his cowardice into predestination, and "Bartleby was billeted upon [him] for some mysterious purpose of an all-wise Providence." Like Captain Vere, when he was faced with the crisis of Billy Budd and resorted to books for guidance, the lawyer was brought to his persuasion by having consulted "Edwards on the Will" and "Priestly on Necessity."

The lawyer is not a monster. But all his goodness is suspect. His compassion develops slowly. Realizing that Bartleby lives all the time at the Wall Street office, which "of a Sunday is deserted as Petra," the lawyer begins to have "for the first time in my life a feeling of overpowering stinging melancholy," because the "bond of a common humanity now drew me irresistibly to gloom." But still his feelings toward Bartleby are mixed. The copyist's "pallid haughtiness" "awed" him. And the "scrivener had ascendancy" over him.

Further, the lawyer is not above playing cat-and-mouse with Bartleby. He thinks he can get rid of the copyist by *assuming* "the ground that depart he must." This technique "charmed" him. But his "vanity got the better of my pity." He liked the "with submission" statements of the other copyists. When Bartleby "prefers not to" do something, the lawyer "burned to be rebelled against." He "felt strangely goaded on to encounter him in new opposition—to elicit some angry spark from him answerable to my own."

Regardless of the several ambiguities about the lawyer, one thing is sure. He is more concerned with the attitude

161

of society toward him than he is with his own comfort. Just as he has never drawn down "public applause" he is determined not to cause censure. His private ordeal with Bartleby ramifies in his own mind into a public issue. He consults Turkey and Nippers, and even Ginger-Nut, about what should be down with the recalcitrant copyist. Later, after he has tried to "assume" Bartleby away, the lawyer walks down the street, hears strangers betting on the outcome of the election and automatically thinks they are talking about Bartleby. He thinks that "public" opinion can pacify tempers. He knows, later on, that his professional reputation is threatened by Bartleby's presence, yet he cannot "dishonor" himself by ousting the copyist. He is "fearful of being exposed in the papers." It is, finally, public pressure that makes him flee from Bartleby, even from the city.

But Bartleby, "the incubus," cannot be sloughed off. Like an albatross around the lawyer's neck, he goes with his employer everywhere, in spirit if not in body. The new tenants of the old Wall Street office that the lawyer has abandoned come to the new quarters to complain that something must be done about Bartleby, for whom, says society, the lawyer is "responsible." Several days later the landlord of the old offices returns with more news. Bartleby has been turned out of the rooms but is still haunting the hallways. Public pressure on the lawyer becomes irresistible. "Everybody is concerned; clients are leaving the offices." These are facts, but what the landlord considers the most terrifying aspect of his report, apparently, is sheer propaganda: "some fears are entertained of a mob," he says. Melville's irony here is deep. There is, in fact, no reason to believe that the mob is forming—if indeed it is forming at all—to threaten Bartleby. On the contrary, the fear entertained by the landlord is that the mob will *protect* the scrivener, and in so doing might destroy property. This is demonstrated by the fact that when Bartleby is forcibly ejected and taken to the police station, he is accompanied by the "mob" of "compassionate and curious by-standers." Under this great public pressure the lawyer returns to reason with his former employee, only to abandon him when all "common sense" has failed to influence Bartleby.

The personal anguish experienced by the lawyer in regard to Bartleby comes partially from the fact that, perhaps without being fully conscious of it, he feels like a father toward the younger man. Sixty years old, he is a bachelor, as Melville's uncommitted men generally are. He has remained single because he is constitutionally if not physically—as well as temperamentally—unable to become a husband and father. He is drawn toward the son aspect in Bartleby. He hires the copyist in the first place immediately upon his application because he recognizes that Bartleby needs a father. Bartleby is a "motionless young man, pallidly neat, pitiably respectable, incurably forlorn." Partially at least for these reasons the lawyer assigns him "a corner by the folding doors," in order "to have this quiet man within easy call." But though the lawyer may think and act like Bartleby's father, he is not. Fogle is wrong in seeing the lawyer as a kind of god and Bartleby's superior. Quite the contrary.

The most important character in the story is, of course, the scrivener. He is one of Melville's several studies of the naif, the innocent man in the world of innate evil, the kind that was to mature in Melville's surer hands into Billy Budd. The main difference between Bartleby and Billy is that Melville had not learned by the time he wrote the earlier story to universalize the type into world myth. Instead there are the efforts—successful, to be sure—but Bartleby comes out more like mere Christ than like the universal hero-savior of world folklore and mythology. The difference, however, is one of degree; the outlines are clear.

Bartleby's origins are shrouded in mystery. Either he does not know his parentage or prefers not to talk about it. Probably he is illegitimate, or has something miraculous about his birth, as is the case with all heroes. Like the typical hero, again, he is alone; he does not have a

163

"single relative or friend." "He seemed alone, absolutely alone in the universe. A bit of wreck in the mid-Atlantic." He is essentially sexless.

He is a complete naif. He never reads anything, and is a natural man. He is an ascetic, for he almost never eats; indeed, he seems to be fed by some supernatural means. Completely self-sufficient, as heroes are, he does not care for human society. As long as he is not forced to do something against his will, or to associate with society, he is compliant.

Further, and here the parallel with Billy Budd is close, the lawyer thinks Bartleby will act as a peacemaker. He is "glad to have among my corps of copyists a man of so singularly sedate an aspect, which I thought might operate beneficially upon the flighty temper of Turkey, and the fiery one of Nippers."

Again, like Billy and heroes in general, Bartleby has a tragic flaw, his inability to conform. His "eccentricities are involuntary," and therefore incurable.

Melville invites the reader to dwell on Bartleby's supernatural qualities. Not only is he unusual in appearance and extraordinary in habits—both characteristics of the hero—but is "like a very ghost, agreeable to the laws of magical invocation," and at times an "apparition."

Like all heroes, also, Bartleby is a revolutionary. Though he is quiet until pushed, Bartleby has an explosive character, as the lawyer recognizes. Melville undoubtedly had Thoreau in mind here, as Marx says, and believed that "one lone intransigent man can shake the foundations of our institutions." But the copyist is not merely intransigent. He is a positive revolutionist. Melville makes this explicit when he likens Bartleby to that "mettlesome poet, Byron" who was the very symbol of revolution.

Bartleby's end is in keeping with Melville's theme of the power of the hero, of his death and resurrection. Accompanied by the compassionate citizenry he goes to jail, his place of entombment and resurrection. The lawyer follows him to the Tombs, or, as he significantly corrects

himself, "to speak more properly, the Halls of Justice."
Justice is to be given to Bartleby. In his passion,
Bartleby is no longer negative. The lawyer approaches his
back and speaks to him. But Bartleby is not sufficiently
concerned even to look around. To the lawyer's call, he
responds, "I know you . . . and I have nothing to say to
you." The lawyer, trying to lighten Bartleby's suffering,
calls the surroundings to the scrivener's attention: "And
see, it is not so sad a place as one might think. Look, there
is the sky, and here is the grass!" There has seldom been a
more poignant, all-knowing, and superior statement than
Bartleby's response: "I know where I am." No longer a
victim, even in appearance, Bartleby is master of the
situation.

Melville's description of the yard where Bartleby dies is
significant: "The surrounding walls, of amazing thickness,
kept off all sounds behind them. The Egyptian character
of the masonry weighed upon me with its gloom. But a
soft imprisoned turf grew under foot. The heart of the
eternal pyramids, it seemed, wherein, by some strange
magic, through the clifts, grass-seed, dropped by birds,
had sprung." Bartleby has crept over to the base of the
heavy wall, lain down and died. But his is not the
ordinary posture of the dead, "His knees drawn up, and
lying on his side, his head touching the cold stones," and
his eyes open. This the fetal position, but is also
suggestive of the picture of the crucified Christ taken
from the cross and laid down.

This theme is made manifest and broadened in the
lawyer's last statement about Bartleby. The grub-man [9] (the
tempter) looks at the dead form and says, "He's asleep,
ain't he?" To which the narrator replies: "With kings and
counselors." Melville is saying that the dead man will rise
again—as all heroes do: this is indicated by the fact that
Bartleby's eyes are open.

9. The grub-man probably derives from Hawthorne's "Ethan Brand."

165

It is a serious mistake to overlook the parallel words in the lawyer's description of the prison yard and those in "The Apple-Tree Table" and in the first of "The Two Temples," mentioned above. More important, however, is the parallel with Melville's long philosophical poem *Clarel.* In the poem, Mortmain, a deeply heroic figure, after having separated himself from the other pilgrims, rejoins them at the Dead Sea and rails against Anti-Christ; the position he sits in is strikingly similar to that of the dead Bartleby:

> Hands clasped about the knees drawn up
> As round the cask the binding hoop—
> Condensed in self, or like a seer
> Unconscious of each object near,
> While yet, informed, the nerve may reach
> Like wire under wave to furthest beach.
> (II. xxiv. 14-20)

Later he dies, with an eagle's feather on his lips, and his eyes on the palm of the monastery Mar Saba, the symbol of the hope of immortality:

> So undisturbed, supine, inert—
> The filmed orbs fixed upon the Tree.
> (III. xxxii. 29-30)

In "Bartleby" form is important, as has been partially recognized. Thus the postcript is especially significant. Artistically it rounds off the story, bringing it full circle. The lawyer began his tale by saying that although he could write "divers histories," about scriveners in general he knew almost nothing about Bartleby. But he promises to relate "one vague report," which "will appear in the sequel."

This "vague report," which has a "certain suggestive interest," is, as Felheim says, a "choral comment." As such it universalizes the subject and the conclusion. Bartleby, it is shown, has already triumphed over death once; he has survived the dead letter office, which, Melville says, sounds like "dead men," where the hopes of men were buried.

Since Bartleby is released from this "death," is triumphant, we have a symbol of his being Christ or the Savior. But the symbol is developed one step further. Bartleby equals the Savior, who is universalized into humanity, for the story ends on the words "Ah, Bartleby! Ah, humanity!" This is the statement of Melville's humanism clear and resounding.

In this insistence the conclusion parallels in purpose the newspaper account and the ballad which conclude *Billy Budd,* and, turning Billy into folklore and mythology, project him as the hero and the hope of salvation for the common man.

"Bartleby," although not completed with as great sophistication as the later work, is also ended in hope. Leo Marx is correct in saying that the story is "exceptional in its sympathy for and hope for the average man." But it is not the lawyer who is typical humanity; his salvation is not promised. The lawyer is *man in authority,* like Captain Vere in *Billy Budd,* who despite his common bond with and professed sympathy for the common man cannot fully understand or empathize with him. Bartleby is the hero and savior of the "mob" of "compassionate and curious bystanders" who accompany him to the tomb—of, in other words, the common man.

"Norfolk Isle and the Chola Widow" is even more revealing than *Billy Budd* as a parallel statement to the meaning of "Bartleby." It was published only a few months after the account of the scrivener. The account of the long suffering of the Indian widow Hunilla ends with her "passing into Payta town, riding upon a small gray ass; and before her on the ass's shoulders, she eyed the jointed workings of the beast's armorial cross." Melville's message is abundantly clear in this picture of a female savior, for it is through her that he worships humanity: "Humanity, thou strong thing, I worship thee, not in the laurelled victor, but in this vanquished one."

"Bartleby" is then another story—and a superb one—of this heroic endurance that Melville worshipped. It is, furthermore, a kind of first chapter to a book that is going to pick up where the short story ends and, with an entirely different approach and attitude on the author's part, demonstrate what happens in a world that through rejection separates itself from the savior. As such, "Bartleby" is prerequisite to a full understanding of *The Confidence-Man*, which in its own grim and ironic way is also an affirmation of Melville's humanism.

POLITICAL SYMBOLISM IN "BENITO CERENO"

"Benito Cereno" (*Putnam's*, October-December 1855) is fundamentally, but not exclusively, concerned with the problems of American society during the early explosive 1850's, as some criticism of the story lately has demonstrated. Of such criticism the most suggestive is that of Joseph Schiffman and of Max Putzel. The latter sees the story as treating "problems of freedom and law which accompany man in his evolution from primitive barbarity to civilized and organized barbarity." The former, more specifically, feels the story "in some ways" is "a fossil relic of the stress and strain that America experienced over the slavery issue in the 1850's." Schiffman continues, citing evidence: "In answer to *Uncle Tom's Cabin*, fourteen pro-slavery novels were published between 1852 and 1854. These novels argued that the Negro 'is not fit for freedom, knows himself an inferior, and in the majority of cases prefers to remain a slave.' In these ante-bellum tracts, 'A thinking Negro is unusual.'" [10] Both Schiffman and Putzel vastly under-develop their theses.

Such a man as Melville, who believed that slavery is "against Destiny," who on numerous occasions expressed his firm belief in the equality and brotherhood of man, could not silently countenance such an attitude—not the man who wrote to Hawthorne of his "ruthless democracy," of his uncondi-tional democracy in all things," the man who kept his motto, "Keep true to the dreams of thy youth," pasted to the inside of the

---

10. Joseph Schiffman, "Critical Problems in Melville's 'Benito Cereno'," *Modern Language Quarterly* 11 (September 1950): 317-324; Max Putzel, "The Source and the Symbols of Melville's 'Benito Cereno'," *American Literature* 34 (May 1962): 191-206.

writing box on which he composed *Billy Budd* in the very last year or two of his life. [11]

"Benito Cereno" is, then, another in the long line of Melville's works which examine the affairs of man with the purpose of offering suggestions for improvement so that man's lot, his world, his future, and his fate can be improved. The story is in every way a practical object lesson in affirmative humanism, perhaps narrower than Melville's usual statements but nevertheless unmistakable in direction.

For this comment on American society, Melville chose for a subject a chapter from Amasa Delano's *A Narrative of Voyages and Travels,*[12] enlarging the original from about fourteen thousand to some thirty-four thousand words. In his expansion Melville eliminates or minimizes certain parts and enlarges or invents others, tooling the material to suit his own purposes. He contrasts the Old World with the New, the American South with the North, white with black society. But his real purpose is to demonstrate the evil and the potential danger of black slavery, and to broaden that problem into the burning issue of universal freedom for all mankind. His development is in terms which are, in the broadest and deepest sense of the word, political.

In examining the story we must be careful to consider also the other works Melville was writing or probably brooding over during these years, for all are other strands in the same thesis.

Significantly, Melville changes the date of Delano's *Narrative* from the nineteenth century back to the end of the eighteenth, the time of two general revolutions—a period that he was to re-use later in another treatment of the same subject in *Billy Budd.*

The American ship *Bachelor's Delight,* captained by Amasa Delano, has put in at a "small, desert uninhabited island" near the southern tip of Chile to take on water. On the morning of

---

11. Melville's comment on slavery was in his prose supplement to *Battle-Pieces.* Quotations on democracy are in Merrell E. Davis and William H. Gilman, *The Letters of Herman Melville* (New Haven, 1960), pp. 126-131. For the quotation on the dreams of youth see Merlin Bowen, *The Long Encounter* (Chicago, 1960), p. 217.

12. Boston, 1817.

169

the second day she is joined by another ship in need of water, the Spanish *San Dominick*, apparently captained by Benito Cereno. Thus the Old World and the New have met because of their common need for water, which Melville later calls "this republican element, which always seeks one level." The setting of this meeting is portentous. It is a gray dawn: "Everything was mute and calm, everything gray." The sea seemed "fixed." Over the leaden sea "flights of troubled gray fowl . . . skimmed low and fitfully . . . as swallows over meadows before storms. Shadows present, foreshadowing deeper shadows to come."

The meaning seems clear. Here in a *southern* setting in America, though South America to be sure, the political study begins. The problem—slavery—is the same that Melville probed in "The Bell Tower." In that earlier story, writing against the background of the Italian Renaissance of three hundred years earlier, he demonstates, by implication at least, that America, in a potential second Renaissance, is being frustrated because of man's enslavement to a machine-complex and because a dictator is trying to split the people and the nation asunder. Here in "Benito Cereno," Melville is demonstrating that in the morning of America's existence, the dawn of her Renaissance of the hopes of man, slavery is portending catastrophe.

The two ships are sharp contrasts in political symbolism. The *Bachelor's Delight* is a "large sealer and general trader" with a "valuable cargo." It is always well-ordered and shipshape. It is the New World, ever successful and apparently with an untroubled future. The *San Dominick* seems to the American captain a "Spanish merchantman of the first class, carrying negro slaves, amongst other valuable freight." But something is wrong with this "very large" and "very fine vessel." She has shown no colors, she has almost wrecked herself trying to come into the harbor, and under close examination she reveals herself to be in a state of ruinous decay and neglect, a ghost and rotting ruin.

White in Melville's works in an equivocal color. In *Moby-Dick* it symbolizes an inscrutable mask through which man must break in order to see reality. In *The Confidence-Man,* with which in several ways "Benito Cereno" is closely connected, the mute, who is dressed in "cream colors," is felt by some critics to be the archetype of the confidence man, if not one himself, in that he serves to soften up victims for the working of the actual crooks. In "Benito Cereno" too, white is a deceptive mask. The *San Dominick* appears to be a picture of decay and decadence. Her "spars, ropes, and great part of the bulwarks, looked woolly." "Her keel seemed laid, her ribs put together, and she launched, from Ezekiel's Valley of Dry Bones." "Battered and mouldy, the castellated forecastle seemed some ancient turret, long ago taken by assault, and then left to decay." From a distance she looked like a "whitewashed monastery" with "throngs of dark cowls" looking over the bulwarks and "Black Friars pacing the cloisters." Although the "ship's general model and rig appeared to have undergone no material change from their original Froissart pattern," there were no guns visible. Thus the general appearance was sinister, but there were no indications of the violence which lay concealed on the ship.

Symbolically Delano's boat approaches this ship from the *stern,* whose "relic of faded grandeur was the ample oval of the shield-like stern-piece, intricately carved with the arms of Castile and Leon, medallioned about by groups of mythological or symbolical devices; uppermost and central of which was a dark satyr in a mask, holding his foot on the prostrate neck of a writhing figure, likewise masked."

The political significance seems clear. Spanish despotism, which has always been supported by religion and myth and faceless symbol, is rotting away. The parallel with *The Confidence-Man* is very close. In that book, at the very beginning while the crowds stand around a theater announcement, there are "certain chevaliers"—

swindlers and sharpers—there too. "Their fingers . . . were enveloped in some myth." In both works myth is maintaining status quo at the expense of the common people. And each work bolsters the symbolism in the other. In this short story Melville is saying that the institutions that prop up and perpetuate the old order are falling away, and, as we shall see, underneath them and ready to explode lie all kinds of unsuspected violence.

As Delano's boat moves to the prow of the ship, the political symbolism continues. Delano discovers that the prow is wrapped in canvas. Although we do not yet know it, this white canvas—the inscrutable mask—covers the place on which formerly resided the figure of Columbus. But the figure of the discoverer of the New World—of him who sailed as an extension of the king and queen of Spain—has been destroyed because the hope that he symbolized for mankind has been subverted. His place has been taken by a new symbol, as yet unrevealed, which is in effect "death to the oppressor!" Although perhaps Delano cannot be expected to suspect any of the facts cloaked by the canvas, Melville is obviously ironic when he has the captain guess that it is there "either to protect it while undergoing a refurbishing, or else decently to hide its decay." In retrospect we know that Melville is actually saying that Delano is too innocent, too prejudiced in favor of the status quo, even to consider the possibility of a new order.

Upon boarding the ship Delano is surrounded by a mass of black and white bodies, who indiscriminately, "in one language, and as with one voice, all poured out a common tale of suffering." Melville's message is that all people, regardless of race or color, are the same under the skin, as he had said in *Moby-Dick* and was to say in *The Confidence-Man*, when the man with the wooden leg insists that a white man can look like a Negro.

On board, although Delano glances over the faces of all and sundry, the first individuals his look rests on, the first of the mass who become human beings, are the black oakumpickers. The next are the hatchet grinders, who symbolically have the edges of their hatchets pointing out toward the whites. Stylistically these two groups are obviously theatrical, even melodramatic. As such they reveal to the reader that Delano is more an observer of life than a participant—most acutely attuned to the theatrics in life, as Melville shows at the beginning of *The Confidence-Man*. The weakness of Americans, Melville is saying, is their non-participation in life, their innocence and lack of experience. They have not suffered. For too long they have been disengaged. They are, in the full use of Melville's word, *bachelors*. Therefore when they are forced to join in the hard actualities of life—as Delano must on this ship— they cannot distinguish between the false and the true, as the various persons on the *Fidele* cannot.

Melville, however, does not over-simplify the task of distinguishing between the real and the bogus. There is strong reason to suspect that the account of the voyage given by Cereno, and accepted by most critics, is incorrect. As Delano stays on the ship, gradually the sad story is related of how the ship came to her present condition. Cereno tells the American that the vessel sailed from Buenos Aires for Lima with a general cargo, fifty Spaniards and three hundred slaves, but was hit by storm and plagued by calm and disease until nearly all the whites and half the blacks died. Later, however, when freed from the ship, he repudiates his former tale, saying that the Negroes had threatened to kill him if he did not recount the story as he had told it. But just as Delano at the time suspects the captain as much as the Negroes, Melville throws some doubt on the authenticity of the later story about the revolt of the slaves, though obviously the revolt did take place. It must be remembered that the whites tell the repudiation. We do not hear from the Negroes. Babo never says a word after being captured. In the deposition of the court proceedings, no voice of a Negro is heard. There is only a little hearsay evidence reported through Spanish retelling.

173

More strikingly, at the beginning of the story, as Delano is about to board the *San Dominick* for the first time, Melville inserts a paragraph which clearly is intended to be significant: "As, at last, the boat was hooked from the bow along toward the gangway amidship, its keep, while yet some inches separated from the hull, harshly grated as on a sunken coral reef. It proved a huge bunch of conglobated barnacles adhering below the water to the side like a wen— a token of baffling airs and long calms passed somewhere in those seas." Delano says he could have made Cereno's trip in a few days, "but this ship has been in these waters for a long time."

There are strong political overtones in Cereno's physical appearance, which throughout the story is unfavorable. In the midst of the misery of the ship he maintains not a true dignity but a pose. He is richly dressed in velvet, white small-clothes and stockings, with silver buckles at the knee and instep; a high-crowned sombrero of fine grass; a slender sword, silver mounted, hung from a knot in his sash —the last being an almost invariable adjunct, more for utility than ornament, of a South American gentleman's dress. The irony here is that although we do not know it yet, the scabbard which carries the sword, which is "more for utility than ornament," is empty and artificially stiffened and can be only for show. However inappropriate the dress might seem, Melville says, Cereno's clothes "might not, in fashion at least, have gone beyond the style of the day among the South Americans of his class." South Americans were the most ruthlessly despotic of all Americans, and Melville urges political interpretation by contrasting Cereno's dress with Babo's, who supports him, which is "nothing but wide trousers, apparently, from their coarseness and patches, made out of some old topsail." The contrast between the apparent and the real strength, between appearances and reality, is terrifyingly obvious.

Delano though an innocent is a snob. But he believes in opportunity for all, and he cannot fail to remark, in one of his periods of vacillation, on the old custom of stuffing important offices with the highborn. He says that it is obvious that Cereno "had not got into command at the hawse-hold, but the cabin-window; and if so, why wonder at incompetence, in youth, sickness, and gentility united?" But Delano's bias lies with the wealthy, fight it as he may, and later when because of Cereno's bad manners the American doubts his authenticity, Delano thinks the Spaniard must be an "imposter," "some low-born adventurer, masquerading as an oceanic grandee." He could not be of the real Cereno family, a "sort of Castilian Rothschild." But Delano changes his mind again, when looking at Cereno's profile "whose clearness of cut was refined by the thinness, incident to ill-health, as well as ennobled about the chin by the beard. Away with suspicion. He was a true off-shoot of a true hidalgo Cereno."

Delano's snobbishness, his reverence for caste, his typical Americanism that Melville despised, is perhaps seen most clearly in his attitude toward the Negroes on the Spanish ship, and his treatment of them. Delano is, first of all, like Captain Vere in *Billy Budd*, a stern disciplinarian, believing completely in the necessity and virtue of discipline. When he sees the disorder on the *San Dominick* he almost jingoistically likens it to an emigrant ship, which has and needs "stern officers." He is quick to think of punishment and apparently quick to mete it out on the *Bachelor's Delight*. He is, further, "somewhat annoyed" at Babo's "conversational familiarities" with his master. Delano makes no effort to treat the Negroes like human beings. Although he knows the names of both Babo and the giant Atufal, he refers to them generically. They are "blacks," "your black," "fellow," "slaves." He even offers fifty doubloons to purchase Babo. Like many Americans of his day—both North and South—he believes that "most negroes are natural valets and hairdressers." Negroes are minstrel darkies: "God had set the whole negro race to some pleasant tune." He has a "docility arising from the

175

unaspiring contentment of a limited mind, and that susceptibility of blind attachment sometimes inhering in indisputable inferiors." [13]

Negroes are "stupid," the whites "the shrewder race. Therefore, despite all appearances, Cereno could not be in "league with negroes against whites." The Negro children under the worthless longboat are "like bats." Delano takes to Negroes "as other men to Newfoundland dogs," [14] "not philanthropically but genially." When he sees a Negro woman lying asleep on the deck, exposing her privates and having her baby suckle at her paps, he thinks that the Negress is a doe, the baby a fawn—but not human beings. As if they were animals, he is not startled by the nakedness of the woman, though he remarks on "naked nature." When the Negroes clap hands as Cereno bows over the water that has been delivered to the ship, consecrating it—and the Negroes parodying the consecration—Delano calls them "sight loving Africans," obviously, he thinks, mindless. When Babo impudently uses the flag of the Spanish king for a shaving cloth for Cereno, Delano says, "It's all one, I suppose, so the colors be gay."

Delano's treatment of the Negroes, Melville is asserting, is typical of that of many Americans, both southern and northern. He is on "half-gamesome" terms with them. He treats them as he would a dog. He pushes them around with a "half-mirthful, half-menacing gesture." He speaks "pleasantly" to them. He very nearly suffers dreadful

13. It is significant that Delano fell into the same potentially fatal error as many other Americans of that day, who believed that Negroes were all singers and storytellers and always contented while they were singing and storying. Actually the songs they were singing, as well as the folk tales they were telling, although apparently sunny on the surface, were bristling with underlying symbolism which had it been understood by the whites would have made their hair stand on end and would have electrified them into even greater apprehension about a slave uprising. For examples, see any collection of Negro folk songs, and reread Uncle Remus. See also Louis Filler, *The Crusade against Slavery* (New York, 1960), p. 13.

14. Despite what Elizabeth Foster says in her introduction to *The Confidence-Man* about the similarity of Melville's use of the symbol of Negro as dog in "Benito Cereno" and in *The Confidence-Man*, there is a great difference. In the short story the symbol is Negro as animal, whereas in the novel it is Negro as devil.

consequences. But the mutineers do not kill him because they recognize that his mistakes are more clumsiness and thoughtlessness than malice. But the warning to this nation as a whole seems quite plain.

In his treatment of Francesco, the "rajah-looking mulatto" steward, Delano again typifies American attitudes. His ambivalent feelings about England, for one thing, come out when he remarks that the mulatto "has features more regular than King George's of England," and he is a king, "the king of kind hearts and polite fellows." Then, in the second place, Delano reveals typical feelings about miscegenation. With an arch and naive superiority that would surely infuriate both full-blooded blacks and mulattoes, Delano is delighted that Francesco is living proof of the white man's superiority, "for it were strange, indeed, and not very creditable to us white-skins, if a little of our blood mixed with the African's should, far from improving the latter's quality, have the sad effect of pouring vitriolic acid into black broth; improving the hue, perhaps, but not the wholesomeness."

On this subject of miscegenation, Melville reveals the extent of the decay to which Cereno and his type of nation have slipped. The Spaniard insists that the subject is alien to him: "I know nothing of the matter," he says. To him clearly sex of any kind would be of no importance, since he is feminine, passive, lacking in virility. He and his kind are without future.

In fact Melville makes it quite clear that both Cereno and Delano are singularly deficient in virility, because the former is passive and the latter a "bachelor," in Melville's full sense of that word. The cabin in which they dine symbolizes both a sterile womb and a tomb. "Without companions, host and guest sat down, like a childless married couple, at opposite ends of the table." Old World superiority cannot continue to exist, nor can the American nation grow, Melville insists, until the male of each has taken unto himself a different kind of spouse. The common whites and the Negro must be brought into

177

useful productivity. Here somewhat extended is one of the salient beliefs of Hawthorne, who was deeply influencing Melville these days, especially in *The House of the Seven Gables.*

But Cereno for one will resist the change. In this womb and tomb he makes "reference to the different constitution of races, enabling one to offer more resistance to certain maladies than another. The thought was new to his companion." Melville is here paralleling the white—and American—practice of advancing theories demonstrating the inferiority of the Negro—here adding the biological to the existing ones of religion, morality, mentality, and so forth—to rationalize and defend slavery.[15]

In this context Delano provides one obvious key to the story—though it has been made perfectly clear elsewhere. When he looks upon Babo, who has just been slashed in the face, he says to Cereno, who he thinks cut the Negro: "Ah, this slavery breeds ugly passions in man." Again, Melville's development is significant. Fully believing that Cereno had inflicted the wound—in a "sort of love-quarrel" —Delano is *about* to "speak in sympathy to the negro" but fails to take any action and allows the apparently abused Negro "with a timid reluctance" to re-enter the cuddy, to a fate unknown. Melville had only the deepest scorn for those persons who for one reason or another will not commit themselves to life, those who are always *about* to live.

"Benito Cereno" is beautifully divided into two parts. The first is a still life, a static setting. The second is dynamic. It is as though during the first half of the story everybody and everything is dead and buried. Not a breath of air stirs, there is a minimum of movement, the tide is running out, all is a picture of the past, and all are dissemblings, lies, perversions, and falsifications.

The second—the dynamic—half begins at precisely two o'clock. As the hour is sounded, there are stirrings of labor pains, and there is indeed a birth of physical

15: See Filler, *The Crusade Against Slavery.* Ch. 6.

activity if not of spiritual maturity. The symbolic references are undeniable. Delano emerges from the cabin and discovers that Atufal, the "ex-king," is guarding the door, "like one of those sculptured porters of black marble guarding the porches of Egyptian tombs." With the wind rippling the waters, Delano gives the proper orders—with both Negroes and Spaniards responding with a will and a song, and with Babo assuming his post as captain of the slaves and thereby proving "valuable." Once the ship is taken care of, Delano descends again to the cabin. After trying to talk to the strangely indifferent and ambiguous Cereno, Delano starts to leave.

He has already marked the presence of Atufal at the door, and Cereno has admitted that the Negro stands there by his orders. For the twentieth time—at least—Delano's ambivalent reactions to the situation assert themselves. Now he feels that the Spaniard and the Negro are in league to do him harm. As he rushes down the narrow corridor "dim as a tunnel," the "sound, as of the tolling for execution in some jail-yard fell on his ears. It was the echo of the ship's flawed bell," and instantly his mind "swarmed with superstitious suspicions," and "all his former distrusts swept through him." "The Spaniard behind—his creature before: to rush from darkness to light was the involuntary choice." Then he burst from the corridor, with fists clenched, unscathed, into the presence of "benign nature," with "the screened sun in the quiet camp of the west shining out like the mild light from Abraham's tent."

Thus symbolically, though the American cannot make up his mind—because of inexperience—as to the real nature and source of evil, Melville shows that the Spaniard's ship, representing the old order, is flawed. This old order is sterile, incapable of progress, with no future, no matter how much it might want to advance. It will be acted upon but cannot—under its present philosophy—be the actor. Atufal represents both the institution of slavery and the Negro race itself. The institution is despicable and must be

179

destroyed. The Negro himself, for any of several reasons, might strike terror into the breasts of some white people, but, Melville is saying, this is an unwarranted and unreasoned fear and must be fronted, proved, and thereby overcome.

The religious implications of this story have generally been recognized. Upon Delano's first approach to the ship, the *San Dominick* had resembled a monastery, and the Negroes looked like friars. Some "melancholy old rigging" looked like a "heap of poor friars' girdles." Cereno's manner was "in its degree, not unlike that which might be supposed to have been his imperial countryman's, Charles V, just previous to the anchoritish retirement of that monarch from the throne." [16] Just before leaving Cereno and having to pass by Atuafal, "his creature before," Delano had wondered "if the Spaniard was less hardened than the Jew, who refrained not from supping at the board of him whom the same night he meant to betray." Plainly, then, this is a religious parable, too, and the message seems to be that religion sanctions and condones slavery.

But this sanction is more apparent than real, the illusion of only a moment's duration. The higher religion welcomes all colors and nationalities as brothers, and blends into a mysterious union with nature. This becomes manifest in the extremely significant passage in which Delano breaks out of the corridor with "the screened sun in the quiet camp of the west shining out like the mild light from Abraham's tent." The symbol has the same importance here that a similar one has in the crucifixion scene in *Billy Budd*, where "the vapory fleece hanging low in the East, was shot through with a soft glory as of the fleece of the Lamb of God seen in mystical vision," and Billy "ascending, took the full rose of the dawn." Delano can now deprecate his momentary "atheist doubt" of a moment before, for he sees that there is an "everwatchful Providence above," and

16. See H. Bruce Franklin. "'Apparent Symbol of Despotic Command: Melville's Benito Cereno'," *New England Quarterly* 34 (December 1961): 462-477.

Melville says that with this Providence America can solve the slavery, and the "Negro" problem, and all her children can prosper in the light from Father Abraham's bosom.

But America and Delano do not fully realize yet that the issue can be solved. Melville therefore continues his examination. Delano still vacillates between naïveté and experience. When he prepares to board his boat and leave the *San Dominick*, Cereno comes from his cabin, speaks to Delano, and the two walk toward the gangway. Babo is walking alongside Cereno, ostensibly supporting him but actually trying to prevent his escape. Delano steps to the other side of the Negro. Then the two white men hold hands across the black, symbolizing in startling vividness how both—Old World and New—contribute to the black man's enslavement.

One of Delano's troubles is that he never sees the problem whole. When, for example, Cereno jumps into the boat, followed by Babo, and "the scales dropped from his eyes" and Delano saw the Negroes "with mask torn away" in "piratical revolt," he still does not understand fully what is going on. He is now too hurried and harried to comprehend.

The Negroes left on the *San Dominick* cut the anchor line in their attempt to escape. The rope swings up and knocks off the canvas from the figurehead in a scene which again brings *Billy Budd* to mind, and the white skeleton of Cereno's dead friend is exposed, with the chalked inscription beneath it: "Follow your leader." The edge of this quotation cuts several ways. The Spaniards on board would surely like to follow their captain. The Negroes would certainly like to follow their leader, Babo, who is in the hands of the whites, as they would like to get at their former captain, Cereno, and kill him. And, as we shall see, there are more overtones in this scene.

Cereno after his rescue, it is obvious, is a broken man. But the implication is that he has always been a spiritual as well as a physical coward. He was courageous only as long as his position protected him. Like Captain Vere in *Billy Budd*, Cereno could not cope with a situation when forms

181

did not prop him up. On the *Bachelor's Delight* there is a great flurry of activity about capturing Cereno's ship, which is now floating out to sea. Here, too, there is significant symbolism. The ship has floated so far astern of Delano's ship that only one gun can be brought to bear on her, and this one fires ineffectually. Here the author is demonstrating how useless it is to attack so great a problem as Negro slavery with a single, simple solution.

When Delano prepares to lead a boarding party personally, the cowardly Cereno tries to dissuade him, but the American persists in his determination until reminded by his officers, "for reasons connected with their interests and those of the voyage," of "a duty owing to the owners." Then he desists, but he fires up the enthusiasm of the sailors by playing on their greed, by telling them that "no small part" of the loot from the ship "should be theirs." Here again is a close tie-in with Melville's criticism of American society in *The Confidence-Man,* the "myth" of American *laissez-faire* enterprise.

The ruthlessness of the whites in the fight which occurs when the sailors overtake the *San Dominick* is generally overlooked by critics. The battle is far from even. The sailors have all the advantage. They have guns; the Negroes have only hatchets. Lying out of range of the thrown hatchets and handspikes, the whites could pick off the Negroes one by one. But they want to board the ship, apparently to a large degree only so that they can hack and slaughter the blacks. Their military superiority and greater bestiality is terrifyingly revealed in Melville's figure of speech: "there was a vague, muffled, inner sound, as of submerged sword-fish rushing hither and thither through shoals of black-fish. Soon, in a reunited band, and joined by the Spanish seamen, the whites came to the surface, irresistibly driving the negroes toward the stern."

Fogle, it seems to me, is at least partially wrong about what Babo symbolizes. The ringleader of the revolt is

surely the "symbol of the slaves," but he is not, as Fogle
urges, "everything untamed and demoniac—the principle
of unknown terror," and he is not "the shark beneath the
waters."[17] The quotation from *Moby-Dick* that Fogle uses to
substantiate his argument can better be used *against* it. In
"Stubb's Supper"(CH. LXIV) Melville says:

> Amid all the smoking horror and diabolism of a
> seafight, sharks will be seen longingly gazing up to
> the ship's decks, like hungry dogs round a table
> where red meat is being carved, ready to bolt down
> every killed man that is tossed to them; and though,
> while the valiant butchers over the deck-table are
> thus cannibally carving each other's live meat with
> carving-knives all gilded and tasselled, the sharks
> also, with their jewel-hilted mouths, are quarrelsomely
> carving away under the table at the dead meat; and
> though, were you to turn the whole affair upside
> down, it would still be pretty much the same thing,
> that is to say, a shocking sharkish business enough
> for all parties; and though sharks also are the
> invariable outriders of all slave ships crossing the
> Atlantic, systematically trotting alongside, to be
> handy in case a parcel is to be carried anywhere, or a
> dead slave to be decently buried, and though one or
> two other like instances might be set down,
> touching the set terms, places, and occasions, when
> sharks do most socially congregate, and most
> hilariously feast; yet is there no conceivable time or
> occasion when you will find them in such countless
> numbers, and in gayer or more jovial spirits, than
> around a dead sperm whale, moored by night to a
> whale-ship at sea. If you have never seen that sight,
> then suspend your decision about the propriety of
> devil-worship, and the expediency of conciliating
> the devil.

Sharks to Melville are white—not black. Elsewhere he
says "the shark/Glides white through the phosporous sea"

17. A sensitive interpretation of the story is R. H. Fogle's, in *Melville's Shorter Tales*;
the quotation is on p. 137.

("Commemorative of a Naval Victory"). And they can be
substituted for white sailors maddened for revenge and it will
be "pretty much the same thing." Only when you have
seen this white devil devouring the defenseless—as the
swordfish slashes the blackfish—can you understand
the ultimate in evil. The battle between the whites and the
blacks was about as equally matched as that between the
swordfish and blackfish. In taking the ship the whites
killed nearly a score of the Negroes. Exclusive of those hit by
the cannon balls, many were mangled; their wounds were
inflicted by the long-edged sealing-spears, "resembling those
shaven ones of the English at Preston Pans, made by the
poled scythes of the Highlanders." Not a white was slain,
though a few were wounded, one seriously.

The Negroes had not, in fact, engaged in what they
would have considered unnecessary violence at any time in
their activities. They had used force to overthrow their
master and get out of fetters. But most of their subsequent
violence can be explained as the result of nervousness in
wanting to avoid being put back into chains. The treatment
accorded the corpse of Aranda, their master and Cereno's
friend, which has been seized upon by many critics as the
wildest bestiality, can be attributed partially to this
nervousness and partially to the Negro leader's realization
of the importance of a symbol in their battle. Compared
with the frenzied activities of the white sailors, the
violence of the Negroes is weak indeed. The murder of
Raneds, the mate, was undoubtedly due mainly to the
nervousness arising from a five-day calm, "from the heat,
and want of water," "that republican element." And the
Negroes were remorseful immediately after the murder.

The savagery of the whites is emphasized elsewhere,
before the battle on deck. After the sailors from the
Bachelor's Delight have overtaken the *San Dominick* and
the Spanish sailors aboard her have dropped the sails, the
Spanish ship turns slowly around, with the skeleton and
the words "follow your leader" facing the Americans. "One

extended arm of the ghost seemed beckoning to the whites to avenge it," says Melville. Then ironically Melville watches as these whites cast off all their veneer of civilization. Their leader uses the words of the Negroes when he leads the attack over the bulwarks into the melee that follows on board the *San Dominick*. Melville's irony is cutting.

In "Benito Cereno," as in all of Melville's works, form is fundamental. There is no wasted or misused wordage; all is functional. The legalese deposition near the end of the story, though soundly criticized by many readers from the day it was submitted to *Putnam's*, is highly artful. It begins to work up to the climax. Fogle is quite right in saying that it is purposefully cast in this language. In this form the words raise the level of the preceding and following events from the human and historical to the legal, therefore to the more nearly timeless, universal, and—to many readers—more important. Thus it points out the significance of the few paragraphs which follow. Melville asserts: "If the Deposition has served as a key to fit into the lock of the complications which precede it, then, as a vault whose door has been flung back, the *San Dominick's* hull lies open to-day." The truth lies revealed. What is this truth?

After the ship has been retaken and the mutineers destroyed, all should be secure and happy for the whites. But it is not. Cereno, who had the most to be thankful for and who should become revitalized, cannot. He pines away, shuns the world, and takes to the monastery on Mount Agonia, to be cared for by his confessor Infelez. Melville's feeling about this representative of the Old Order seems clear. Cereno, like Captain Vere in *Billy Budd*, cannot live without the protection of the forms of the past. When questioned about the cause of his decay, Cereno answers simply, "The negro." For that statement read "the slave," and you will come nearest Melville's meaning. For Melville is speaking generically. The slave symbolizes the old order, that which must pass away. Cereno is the wearer of the regalia he did not willingly put on, and he lives weighed down by the "silver-mounted sword, apparent symbol of despotic command," which is only the ghost of its former self, a scabbard that must be "artificially stiffened" because it is "empty."

Cereno might have lived had he been as innocent and uncommitted as Delano was, or in other words, if he had been the American New Order instead of the European Old. After Cereno's escape from the *San Dominick* the American superficially assures him that the "past is passed; why moralize upon it?" Like the typical, unthinking, optimistic American, Delano feels that life in this new country is an ever-renewing flower, blooming without obligation to the roots of the past. Melville, like Hawthorne, felt that the sins of the past cannot be ignored. America has been lucky so far because she has the "Prince of Heaven's safe-conduct through all ambuscades." But Melville turns his message into a warning to his country about slavery. He asks for forbearance and understanding from slavers and non-slavers alike, realizing himself the complexity of the problem and appreciating both sides of the argument, as he was to do, for example, throughout his poems about the Civil War. The burdens of the past are heavy upon us: "To such degree may malign machinations and deceptions impose. So far may even the best man err, in judging the conduct of one with the recesses of whose condition he is not acquainted. *But you were forced to it, and you were in time undeceived. Would that, in both respects, it was so ever, and with all men*" (my italics).

The deposition points up another explicit and equally important statement by Melville. Having cast these extracts in legal language, he makes it quite plain that such people as Cereno are not legally responsible. Cereno would not identify the chief malefactor, Babo, at the trial. Twice Melville points out that legal justice must depend on the "sailors" of the world, that is, on democracy, as distinguished from the captains, that is, aristocracy. The court believed that Cereno "raved of some things which could never have happened," but "subsequent depositions of the strangest particulars, gave credence to the rest." And, Melville insists, "On the testimony of the sailors alone rested the legal identity of Babo." In making only the "sailors" legally responsible, Melville implies a great burden and caution.

The most terrifying and probably the most significant paragraph in the whole story is the final one. Here Babo is subjected to far greater cruelty than he or the other Negroes ever imposed on the whites on the *San Dominick*. This cruelty, established earlier by the whites' ruthless slaughter of the Negroes on the ship, is with legal sanction. Babo was "dragged to the gibbet at the tail of a mule," his "body was burned to ashes." Inevitably Melville's use of the mule here raises in the reader's mind another similar use of roughly the same time, that of the ass, in "Sketch Eight" of "The Encantadas," in the magnificent tribute to the female Christ: "The last seen of lone Hunilla she was passing into Payta town, riding upon a small gray ass; and before her on the ass's shoulders, she eyed the jointed workings of the beast's armorial cross." The Chola widow's suffering and patience triumphed in life. Babo too triumphs, though in death. After his death "for many days, the head, that hive of subtlety, fixed on a pole in the Plaza, met, unabashed, the gaze of the whites; and across the Plaza looked towards St. Bartholomew's church, in whose vaults slept then, as now, the recovered bones of Aranda: and across the Rimac bridge looked towards the monastery, on Mount Agonia without; there, three months after being dismissed by the court, Benito Cereno, borne on the bier, did, indeed, follow his leader." It seems clear that legally and religiously sanctioned slaveholding had been defeated by the mere naked existence of the slave.

The profoundest significance in this symbol-packed story, which must rank with "Bartleby" as Melville's grandest achievement in the genre, seems underscored by the author's ending his account with the words "follow his leader." Cereno followed his—the Old Order—to his destruction. The Negroes on the *San Dominick* followed theirs, to their apparent failure but actual triumph. Melville draws his moral clearly and unflinchingly. The Negro, though essentially docile, is capable of destruction when pressed too hard too long. Contrary to all the propaganda being circulated and believed during the 1850's, the Negro did not prefer to be enslaved, and is not an unthinking animal. Slavery—both black and white—must be abolished. Touching on the numerous political questions of the day— the question of "bleeding Kansas," for example—he urges that Americans must not blindly and unthinkingly follow their leader, especially when he is wrong. National—and universal—suicide lies in such a course.

Though the scope of this examination is narrower than Melville ordinarily used, clearly his concern is the same—that man's problems are man-made and can and must be solved by man. The solution rests in man's realization that full-scale democracy must be a reality, not a dream. In the realization and implementation of this political and moral concept America represents the hope and salvation of the world.

SIX

THE OTHER SHORT STORIES

The other short stories, written through 1855, do not reach the artistic accomplishment achieved in "Bartleby" and "Benito Cereno." At their lowest, in perhaps the weakest of them all—"The Happy Failure"—these stories do not, in fact, rise above the mediocre. Others, however, such as "The Bell Tower," and certain sketches of "The Encantadas," are only slightly lesser accomplishments than the earlier great stories.

More important in our concern, however, is the fact that all the pieces regardless of artistic quality are clear statements advancing and elaborating on Melville's thesis of man's ultimate triumph. As such all are indispensable.

SOURCE AND SATIRE OF "COCK-A-DOODLE-DOO"

"Cock-A-Doodle-Doo" (*Harper's Magazine,* December 1853) is so extravagant, so obviously a burlesque, there can be little doubt that the easy and other-wordly optimism of Transcendentalism is the author's broad subject. Melville had examined this philosophy in *Moby-Dick* and condemned it in *Pierre;* more recently he had studied it in "Bartleby," and had found at least that he admired Thoreau's "majority of one" philosophy of *Civil Disobedience.* In "Cock-A-Doodle-Doo" it was the *extremes* of Transcendentalism that Melville found stupid and dangerous, and condemned. In particular it was Thoreau as spokesman for this philosophy whom Melville attacked; it was the Thoreau of the first edition of *Walden* who was quoted on the title page: "I do not propose to write an ode to dejection, but brag as lustily as chanticleer in the

189

morning."[1] Offensive though such a statement must have been to Melville, it was probably more specifically the stimulus provided by a section of the "Monday" chapter of *A Week on the Concord and Merrimack Rivers* and the essay "Walking" that triggered Melville's diatribe, as has been discussed by Egbert Oliver and William Stein. [2]

There are close parallels in those two works to Melville's story. Oliver and Stein erred in searching too narrowly, one in seeking parallels to Thoreau's comments on the Indian philosophy of Menu (Manu), and the other in simply overlooking the most obvious stimuli.

Melville's story is about a man who is deeply in debt and despair until he hears the wonderful crowing of a rooster. Searching the countryside he finally discovers that the cock is owned by one Merrymusk, the narrator's sometime woodsawyer. Though desperately poor and ill, the woodsawyer and his family feel themselves wealthy because of the cock; they would rather hear him crow than do anything else. The narrator's spirits also are lifted to unscalable heights by the crowing. In the end, the woodchopper and his family die to the uplifting strains of the rooster's crow, and the narrator under the rooster's influence crows "early and late with a continual crow."

If the story is flawed, the fault lies in the frenetic, almost manic, tone which pervades it from the beginning. The technique is like that in "I and my Chimney"—a technique very similar to Swift's in his "Modest Proposal," though more extravagant—in which the speaker assumes and maintains a position the absurdity of which becomes immediately apparent when the reader examines it in the light of common sense and Melville's known attitudes. In this tone Melville begins his burlesque of

1. Reaction against such obvious silliness came from none other than Emerson, who in his *Journal* for 1849 wrote, "We try to listen to the hymn of gods, and must needs hear this perpetual cock-a-doodle-doo and ke-tar-kut right under the library windows."

2. Egbert S. Oliver, " 'Cock-A-Doodle-Doo' and Transcendental Hocus-Pocus," *New England Quarterly* 21 (June 1959): 204-216. William B. Stein, "Melville Roasts Thoreau's Cock," *Modern Language Notes* 74 (March 1959): 218-219.

Thoreau, especially the two essays mentioned. In the *Week*, Thoreau said, "Enthusiasm is a supernatural serenity." In "Walking," which is more directly relevant here, he said, "I wish to make an extreme statement, if so I may make an emphatic one." Melville also meant to be emphatic.

"Cock-A-Doodle-Doo" begins, as R. H. Fogle correctly says, as a rough parallel to *Moby-Dick*. As Ishmael went to sea with bleak November in his soul to escape a pistol and ball, so the narrator in this story sallied out for a walk in spring, "being too full of hypoes to sleep." As Ishmael remarked on the tempestousness of the world, so the narrator comments on how many people have been thrown into the grave, and on "what a slight mark, after all, does man make on this huge earth. Yet the earth makes a mark on him." At this point Melville in fact almost begins to burlesque *Moby-Dick*.[3] He catalogues catastrophe after calamity, piling one on another. The narrator even lives in the *October* mountains. And the resignation of the narrator is the opposite of that of Ahab. Though this is scarcely the best of all possible worlds, nothing can be done for man's troubles.

As the narrator continues to brood, he says that if he were dictator he would set the world straight. He would retrogress. He is against progress of all kinds. What was good enough for grandfather is good enough for him. Grandfather "was no fool." Here is another example of Melville's satiric use of conservatism and the past, as he used it in "I and My Chimney" and "The Apple-Tree Table," to blast political conservatism as well as Transcendentalism.

With this introductory shot at over-enthusiasm, Melville turns to specific criticism of Transcendentalists. As the narrator walks along, he meets a group of two-year old calves, just turned out to pasture: "What a miserable-looking set, to be sure! A breaking up of a hard winter, that's certain: sharp bones sticking out like elbows; all quilted

---

3. In Chapter XCIX, "The Doubloon," Ahab stands before the doubloon speaking in a strutting soliloquy. Among other things he characterizes himself as "the courageous, the undaunted, and victorious fowl, that, too, is Ahab."

with a strange stuff dried on their flanks like layers
of pancakes."

This passage is a criticism of those Transcendentalists
who retire to Utopian communities like Brook Farm, only
to emerge the poorer for their stint. The conclusion of
Melville's paragraph parallels Hawthorne's comment on his
experiment of living at Brook Farm, when he said it was
not easy to think deep thoughts while shoveling manure.
Here the manure is caked on the backs of the calves.
Melville's story was probably written sometime after May 6,
1853; it was published in December of that year. This was
the period of Melville's most intimate association with
Hawthorne, and surely he would have heard of the older
man's Brook Farm experiences and feelings.

Melville may have been stung into his comments from
reading passages in the *Week*, where Thoreau made such
statements as: "To one who habitually endeavors to
contemplate the true state of things, the political state can
hardly be said to have any existence whatever. It is unreal,
incredible and insignificant to him." "Most revolutions in
society have not power to interest, still less alarm us." Such
irresponsible views would surely infuriate such a politically
sensitive person as Melville. That he was thinking of
politics at this time is evidenced by the fact that "I and
My Chimney," a deeply political story, was submitted to
Putnam's Monthly in July 1855, and may have been
conceived considerably earlier.

As the narrator stands in his reverie looking at the calves
he first hears the "triumphant thanksgiving" of the cock's
crow: *"Glory be to God in the highest,"* it says. The
"hair-trunks prick their ears at it, and stand and gaze
away down into the rolling country yonder." In a moment
the narrator discovers that he "had been addressing the two-
year-olds—the calves—in (his) enthusiasm; which shows
how one's true nature will betray itself at times in the most
unconscious way. For what a very two-year-old, and calf, I
had been to fall into sulks." Here Melville may well
have been attacking Thoreau's sentiments later published

in "Walking," where he says, "in their reaction to Nature men appear to me for the most part, notwithstanding their arts, lower than the animals." [4]

The narrator immediately begins to feel better. "Did ever such a blessed cock-crow so ring out over the earth before! It plainly says *'Never say die!!'*" Melville could have drawn his inspiration from Thoreau's statements in the *Week* where he touts the superiority of Indian philosophy. More likely, however, he was reacting to one of Thoreau's statements in "Walking":

> The merit of this bird's strain is in freedom from all plaintiveness. The singer can easily move us to tears or to laughter, but where is he who can excite in us a pure morning joy? When, in doleful dumps, breaking the awful stillness of our wooden sidewalk of a Sunday, or perchance, a watcher in the house of mourning, I hear a cockerel crow far or near, I think to myself, 'There is one of us well, at any rate,'—and with a sudden gush return to my senses.

It is a Shanghai because in "Walking" Thoreau had referred to such a rooster. Thoreau deprecated the thoughts of his contemporaries—great thoughts, like great men, no longer lived around him: "Our winged thoughts are turned to poultry. They no longer soar, and they attain only to a Shangai and Cochin-China grandeur. Those *gra-a-te* thoughts, those *gra-a-te men* you hear of!" If Thoreau is the cock of this story, Melville should indeed turn his sarcasm against the Transcendentalist and hoist him on his own petard.

The narrator then refers again to the cattle: "My friends the hair-trunks, fairly alarmed at last by such clamorously-victorious tones, were now scampering off, with their tails flirting in the air, and capering with their legs in clumsy enough sort of style, sufficiently evincing that they had not

4. Henry D. Thoreau, *Excursions* (Boston and New York, 1893). Page references are given in the text.

freely flourished them for the six months just past." These lines parallel and burlesque several passages in "Walking":

> Something like the *furor* which affects the domestic cattle in the spring, and which is referred to a worm in their tails, affects both nations and individuals, either perenially or from time to time. (p. 268)

> I love even to see the domestic animals reassert their native rights,—any evidence that they have not wholly lost their original wild habits and vigor. (p. 287)

> The seeds of instinct are preserved under the thick hides of cattle and horses, like seeds in the bowels of the earth, an indefinite period. (p. 287)

> Any sportiveness in cattle is unexpected. I saw one day a herd of a dozen bullocks and cows running about and frisking in unwieldly sport, like huge rats, even like kittens. They shook their heads, raised their tails, and rushed up and down a hill, and I perceived by their horns, as well as by their activity, their relation to the deer tribe. (p. 287)

When the cock crows again, the narrator is indeed possessed with the *furor* which Thoreau says "affects both nations and individuals." The crow makes his "blood bound." "I feel wild," he says. He continues: "What? on this rotten old log here, to flap my elbows and crow too. And just now in the doleful dumps." If any clincher were needed, this repetition of Thoreau's words "the doleful dumps" would rivet Melville's satire to Thoreau.

This tie-in is artfully continued. In the ten sketches of "The Encantadas," Melville had used quotations from *The Fairie Queene* as introductions and comments. The last of those sketches he had concluded with some lines from Porter's *Journal*. These sketches were probably being conceived and written about the same time as "Cock-A-Doodle-Doo." Melville therefore had this technique definitely in mind. Naturally, then, he used it in this story. When he is in his own *furor* he quotes some rooster-talk from a poem: "Of fine mornings, we fine lusty cocks begin our crows in gladness." Then Melville adds: "The poet had this very Shanghai in his mind when he wrote that." The satiric thrust is obvious.

The Shanghai crows all morning. But such is natural. The narrator wonders whether he can crow all day. At mid-day therefore, wondering if he will crow, the narrator "again ascended the hill," to listen. Here again, Melville is probably burlesquing another of Thoreau's remarks in "Walking" (p. 222) when he says, "There is something in the mountain air that feeds the spirit and inspires."

This is not a "sophomorean cock," but a "wise crow," a "philosophic crow," "a crow of all crows." Having heard this glorious noon crow, the narrator returns home but means to seek out this cock. He is determined to walk the country round if necessary to locate him. Here again Melville burlesques Thoreau's love of walking:

> I think I cannot preserve my health and spirits, unless I spend four hours a day at least—and it is commonly more than that—sauntering through the woods and over the hills and fields, absolutely free from all wordly engagements. (p. 207)

Thoreau says that one is not ready for this divine afflatus until he has risen into a kind of natural *furor:*

> If you are ready to leave father and mother, and brother and sister, and wife and child and friends, and never see them again,—if you have paid your debts, and made your will, and settled all your affairs, and are a free man, then you are ready for a walk. (p. 252)

Melville carries this philosophy one step further. He is so indifferent to the world that he ignores mortgages, piles one upon another, and denies their existence, and even chases the mortgagor with threats of bodily violence.

Exhilarated with his walk, the narrator thinks over the world, over his "debts and other troubles, and over the unlucky risings of the poor oppressed *peoples* abroad," and decides that he can face anything, "in pure overflow of self-reliance and a sense of universal security." Again, Thoreau provided more wood for Melville's fire, when he says that while walking, he sometimes broods on mechanics and shopkeepers "who stay in their shops, not only all the forenoon, but all the afternoon too," and thinks "they deserve some credit for not having all committed suicide long ago."

The narrator, having heard the cock crow also in the evening, decides the next morning to scour the countryside seeking him. Thoreau had said: "Unless our philosophy hears the cock crow in every barnyard within our horizon, it is belated." Melville's narrator can indeed hear the crow "in every barn-yard." He asks himself where it comes from. "There is no telling, further than it came from out the East." Thoreau had also said that when he was walking in the woods he could think of nothing else. "What business have I in the woods, if I am thinking of something out of the woods? I suspect myself, and cannot help a shudder, when I find myself so implicated even in what are called good works." Melville brushes against both these attitudes in the first two people the narrator meets in his search. The first is an old man who is plowing. In reply to the narrator's question whether he has heard "an extraordinary cock-crow of late," the old man— consistent with Thoreau's philosophy—replies that there are cock-crows in every barnyard: "The Widow Crowfoot has a cock—and Squire Squaretoes has a cock—and I have a cock, and they all crow." But the narrator dismisses this man because he has not "heard the crow of the Emperor of China's chanticleer." Then he meets another old man who is "mending a tumble-down old rail-fence." Here Melville thrusts at Thoreau's indifference to "good works." The old man is trying to repair rotten fences and is forced to fight, further, against "a set of young steers, possessed as by devils" (with, in other words, Thoreau's *furor*) that butt the rotten timbers down as fast as the old man repairs them. "What a fool," thought the narrator, "to have asked such an uncheerful creature about a cheerful cock!"

The search continues unsuccessfully for several weeks. Meanwhile the narrator becomes more and more imbued with the furor of the "celestial crow" and more contemptuous of and indifferent to the world.

Finally, however, a woodsawyer who had cut some wood for the narrator comes to collect his bill. This man, named Merrymusk, is a caricature of Thoreau himself. "His air seemed staid, but undepressed. He wore a long, gray, shabby coat, and a big battered hat," almost exactly paralleling a caricature of Thoreau, in which he is called "The Knight of the Umbrella."[5] Merrymusk's diet is as simple as Thoreau's was at Walden: "He had a hunk of stale bread and another hunk of salt beef, wrapped in a wet newspaper, and washed his morsels down by melting a handful of fresh snow in his mouth." He does not want "to gabble." If Melville did not have Thoreau's own person in mind, he might well have got his inspiration for this woodcutter from "Walking," where Thoreau devotes two pages to a reading of the signs left by a woodchopper on the stump of a log: "This one chip contains inscribed on it the whole history of the woodchopper and of his world." There is, also, the "deserted woodman's hut."

Merrymusk's hut is almost a caricature of Thoreau's cabin at Walden. On one side of it there is a hill, on the other a swamp. If not the Walden shack, Melville surely has in mind Thoreau's combined preferences for the afflatus of the hill and his love of the swamp. About the latter Thoreau says in "Walking": "Hope and the future for me are not in lawns and cultivated fields, not in towns and cities, but in the impervious and quaking swamps." He is always "attracted soley by a few square rods of impermeable and unfathomable bog." "That was the jewel which dazzled me."

In his use of Merrymusk, Melville exposes a contradiction in Thoreau's philosophy. The Law of Menu, Thoreau wrote in *Week*,

5. See the picture in Sherman Paul, *The Shores of America* (Urbana, 1958).

has such a rhythm as the winds of the desert,
such a tide as the Ganges, and is as superior to
criticism as the Himmaleh mountains. Its tone is of
such unrelaxed fibre, that even at this late day,
unworn by time, . . . its fixed sentences keep up their
distant fires still like the stars, by whose dissipated
rays this lower world is illuminated.[6]

When the narrator first heard the cock's crow, the
only sure thing he could detect about the direction from
which it came was that it emanated from the East. He
assumes it must be a Shanghai because no domestic
bird could sing so beautifully. Further, the cock is a
"bird of cheerful Socrates—the game-fowl Greek who
died unappalled." For Socrates read Plato, and remember
that Transcendentalism, as Emerson said, was only Plato
on American shores.

But the narrator discovers the cock in Merrymusk's yard.
Further, it is an American bird: "It chipped the shell here."
Here then Melville shifts his burlesque to some of
Thoreau's chauvinistic statements in "Walking":

If the heavens of America appear infinitely higher,
and the stars brighter, I trust that these facts are
symbolical of the height to which the philosophy and
poetry and religion of her inhabitants may one day
soar. At length, perchance, the immaterial heaven
will appear as much higher to the American mind, and
the intimations that star it as much brighter. . . Will
not man grow to greater perfection intellectually as
well as physically under these influences? (p. 222)

As a true patriot, I should be ashamed to think that
Adam in paradise was more favorably situated on
the whole than the backwoodsman in this country. (p. 223)

When the narrator discovers the fowl, named Trumpet,
his *furor* is so extreme that no one can take him seriously.
The cock is "more like a Fieldmarshal than a cock. A cock,
more like Lord Nelson with all his glittering arms on,

6. Henry D. Thoreau, *A Week on the Concord and Merrimack River*, ed. by Walter
Harding (New York, 1963) p. 120.

standing on the *Vanguard's* quarter-deck," "more like the Emperor Charlemagne."

Through Merrymusk and his family are ill, hungry, and desperately poor, he thinks himself not unlike Thoreau's "Adam in paradise." They all believe themselves wealthy because he has "refused five hundred dollars" for the cock. On the narrator's second visit to the family, the rooster is more aggravatingly cocky than usual. In his enthusiasm over the mighty power of Trumpet, Merrymusk drops dead, apparently the result of too much enthusiasm, a stroke of afflatus. The cock crows again, and Mrs. Merrymusk dies, "through long-loving sympathy."

The cock then "shook sparkles from his golden plumage," and "seemed in a rapture of benevolent delight." He stands beside the sawyer and his throat heaved far back, as if he meant the blast to waft the wood-sawyer's soul sheer up to the seventh heavens." He makes the same gesture beside the wife. Trumpet then crows again and again, and the children's faces are "changed to radiance," and they die. The cock then "flew to the apex of the dwelling, spread wide his wings, sounded one supernatural note, and dropped at [the narrator's] feet."

Melville's conclusion sums up all that has gone before, all the satire, and in fact points conclusively to the object of that satire—Transcendentalism in general and the Thoreau of "Walking" and "Monday" in particular.

The narrator out-cocks the cock, which was the most blindly stupid animal or man in the story. The cock crows over the dead people. His "Glory be to God in the highest," his "Never say die!" are the utterances of a benighted fool refusing to see the world around him. The acceptance of this philosophic moonshine by the pauperized Merrymusk marks the degree of his foolishness. But as though this were not lesson enough, the narrator becomes an even bigger fool. He buries the family and the rooster in a common grave. Their epitaph is a "lusty cock in act of crowing, chiseled on it, with the words beneath: *O Death, where is thy sting?*

O grave, where is thy victory?'' The narrator, for his part, spends the rest of his life without the "doleful dumps, but under all circumstances crow late and early with a continual crow."

The epitaph is from 1 Corinthians, of course. But the Beatitudes say blessed are the meek, the poor in spirit, those who mourn. These people and the cock are just the opposite. They are stupidly and blindly cocky. They represent exactly the opposite of Melville's comment in *Moby-Dick*: "The truest of all men was the Man of Sorrow, and the truest of all books is Solomon's and Ecclesiastes is the fine hammered steel of woe." These creatures are blindly manic. Merrymusk is the half-horse, half-alligator of Thoreau's west, the native home-grown Socrates of America who is enthusiastic to the point of witlessness.

The story is so strident that is is almost a burlesque of itself. Yet in no way is it artless and without merit. It is indeed an excellent example of Melville's philosophic reaction to the excesses of Thoreau's Transcendentalism, and is therefore another statement, though left-handed and oblique, of Melville's affirmation of man's innate individual worth—individual man, to be sure, but of greater importance in the mass than in the individual.

"THE TWO TEMPLES": THE SHAM AND THE REAL

These two sketches, "The Two Temples," were refused by the editor of *Putnam's Monthly* in 1854 because although they contained, he felt, "some exquisitely fine descriptions and some pungent satire," they would probably offend the "religious sensibilities of the public" and might call down upon the magazine "the whole power of the pulpit." The editor indeed had cause for apprehension, for the attack on the church is direct, heavy-handed and unrelentingly pitiless. But the topic of the two sketches broadens out from the difference between the bogus and the genuine in religion to embrace other topics that were always close to

Melville's heart, especially man's treatment of man and the desperate need for improvement in this treatment.

The first piece, "Temple First," pictures a young physician on a Sunday morning in New York, "prayer-book under arm," trying to gain admittance into an elegant church but being refused because he is obviously poor. He feels, however, that if his new coat had been delivered the night before, as the "false tailor promised," and he had "tickled the fat-paunched, beadle-faced man's palm with a bank-note, then, gallery or no gallery" he would have been admitted though, as the beadle plainly said in actions if not in words, they do not "entertain poor folks" in that particular church.

Melville's social criticism bristles. The people entering the church are all wealthy and elegant, with "gold hat-bands . . . and other gorgeous trimmings," all looking like English "royal dukes, right honourable barons, etc.," although they are "only lackeys." The narrator concludes that he does not want to "get into their aristocratic circle."

So "excommunicated," he decides he had "best move back to the Battery again, peeping into (his) prayer-book." Suddenly, however, he discovers a "very low and very narrow vaulted door" and decides to enter it. Clearly there is a parallel here with the Biblical teaching about the entrance to heaven being small. But there is also firm political warning also. Here, as in numerous other stories— for example, "Rich Man's Crumbs"—Melville points out the threat of political revolution. The Battery serves as the symbol, especially when only two pages later, although in a statement about being deprived of the right to worship, Melville echoes the words of Jefferson and Paine: "I will not be defrauded of my natural rights."

Entering the side door the narrator remembers that usually in these back entrances there is a "curious little window high over the orchestra and everything else, away up among the gilded clouds of the ceiling's frescoes; and that little window, it seems to me if one could but get there, ought to command a glorious bird's-eye view of the

201

entire field of operations below." Here Melville adopts the symbol of God's vantage point of view that he will use in the opening canto of *Clarel* and in other short stories, especially "The Apple-Tree Table."

He ascends until he reaches a "blank platform forming the second story of the huge square tower." At this height he is on an exact level with Bannadonna in "The Bell-Tower." In that story, written the following year, Melville will picture Bannadonna climbing the tower to pretend to be God, to play like God, and to despise and use the people below him. Here, however, Melville is using the height to comprehend and fully understand the rich people in the church below and, like Jonathan Swift, to comment on their true natures.

But the narrator is not yet high enough to understand the scene, not yet really out of the influence of these rich earthlings. At this height the tower is still merely a "gorgeous dungeon," for he cannot "look out, any more than if [he] had been the occupant of a basement in 'the Tombs.'" He seems "inside some magic-lantern" with "Gothic windows of richly dyed glass" which fill the "otherwise meagre place with all sorts of sunrises and sunsets, lunar and solar rainbows, falling stars, and other flaming fireworks and pyrotechnics."

The narrator climbs higher than this earth-bound sham heaven by means of a Jacob's Ladder until he reaches a "small round window in the otherwise deadwall side of the tower, where the tower attached itself to the main building." This added ascent and the little window must be compared in symbolism to the similar passage in "The Apple-Tree Table," where the speaker is baffled by the cobwebs of Cotton Mather's cold, formal religion until he opens a window in the ceiling above him and lets in the pure air and light of heaven and earth.

This church tower window provides the narrator with God-like omniscience. He is directly connected with the congregation below, for no pane stands between him and them. From them there blasts, as from "the mouth of a furnace" a "forceful puff of strange, heated air, blown, as by a blacksmith's bellows." Clearly their religion is false, their church the temple of Baal. This religion although it makes the people "feel so snug and cosy in their padded pews" is inadequate in the eyes of heaven, for it scorches the narrator's face while his back remains frozen. Those rich people are in too low a spot to be truly religious: "Height, somehow, hath devotion in it. The archangelic anthems are raised in a lofty place. All the good shall go to such an one. Yes, heaven is high."

The falsity of the religion in the church below is further emphasized by the fact that the "white-robed priest, a noble-looking man," after having given out the "hymn before the sermon," vanishes from the scene to reappear momentarily, "his white apparel wholly changed for black." Melville seems to be saying that the hymns might ascend to heaven because they are not the personal creation—the teachings—of the individual minister. They belong to everybody, rich and poor, are a common possession of man. But the words of the preacher, now turned to Satan, cannot be true and therefore must be hell-bound. Melville points up his feeling by parodying the sermon. From his God-like position the narrator cannot "so distinctly hear [the preacher] now as in the previous rites" [that is, the singing], though he does distinguish the theme of the sermon, often quoted: "Ye are the salt of the earth." Melville's satisfaction with this bit of irony must have been great.

After the congregation departs, the narrator is locked in the deserted church. Although the "Pharisee" has departed, the place of false-worship still retains the atmosphere he generated. The imprisoned man wants to escape. But as he ponders what to do he sets the stage here for the contrast the second sketch will provide. In that tale he will go to the London theater; here he ascends to his open window three times, the acts the play will be divided into. Further, the floor in this tower from which he viewed the

congregation below is a "magic-langern platform." The
"theatric wonder" was some "sly enchanter's show." Thus
Melville has firmly bridged the gap between the two
sketches and pointed up what does not need to be
emphasized, that one sketch is to be contrasted with the
other.

When the narrator is released from the church he steps
out, continuing Melville's theme of godliness in an unholy
world, like Christ into the hands of Roman justice and
of Pilate:

> Represented as a lawless violator, and a
> remorseless disturber of the Sunday peace, I was
> conducted to the Halls of Justice. Next morning, my
> rather gentlemanly appearance procured me a private
> hearing with the judge. But the beadle-faced man
> must have made a Sunday night call on him. In spite
> of my coolest explanations, the circumstances of the
> case were deemed so exceedingly suspicious, that
> only after paying a round fine, and receiving a
> stinging reprimand, was I permitted to go at large,
> and pardoned for having humbly indulged myself in
> the luxury of public worship.

The second temple is the opposite of the first. It is a
London theater. Melville is concerned in this sketch with
morality in the theater and with actors, with the
difference between, in the larger sense, bogus and real
acting. In a sense this sketch is an oblique tribute to
Shakespeare, on whom Melville had fattened in 1850 and
whose works thereafter influenced him profoundly. But it
is more; it is a defense of the theater against its critics
and an attack on the church as a theater, as, for example,
Henry Ward Beecher's theatrics in church at the same time
he was condemning the theater as being immoral. In this
examination of the true value of the church and the theater,
the latter wins overwhelmingly.

The narrator is in London a few weeks after having
visited the church in New York, penniless because he was
brought overseas by a rich young lady and then "cavalierly

dismissed." Unwilling to go to his rooms early on a
Saturday night the narrator is thrown loose into the
"three millions of (his) own human kind." Here, as often
he does, Melville assumes the role of the naive young man
in order to make his comments more biting. He is
frightened by London, and paints scenes that bring to mind
immediately similar descriptions in the later *Israel Potter*:
"The unscrupulous human whirlpools eddied in the Norway
Maelstrom. . . . Better perish mid myriad sharks in mid-
Atlantic, than die a penniless stranger in Babylonian
London."

He then wishes it were Sunday when he "might
conciliate some kind female pewowner, and rest . . . in
some inn-like chapel upon some stranger's outside bench."
But realizing it is only Saturday, he strolls along until
he comes to a building that reminds him of Sunday. It is
the theater, but Melville's criticism is direct: "Thinking it
might prove some moral or religious meeting, I hurried
toward the spot." The theater is appealing to Melville
because he anticipates in it all that was denied him in
America at the church. What he wanted was "not merely
rest, but cheer; the making of many pleased and
pleasing human faces; the getting into a genial humane
assembly of my kind." True religion to him is here equated
with that humanism, the joining of high and low, true
democracy, that he discussed in numerous works, the
association of man with man "such as, at its best and
highest, is to be found in the unified multitude of a
devout congregation."

Melville's social criticism, especially of Americans, comes
out as the narrator is approached outside the theater by a
"man who seemed to be some sort of a working man" to
give him a ticket to the play inside. The beadle-faced
commoner in New York had given him nothing but rebuffs
and condescension. The need for cooperation among all
people is urged by the narrator's response to the ticket
given him here. Accepting it is taking charity, and his

American independence rebels at the very thought. But he soon concludes that such scruples are indefensible: "All your life, naught but charity sustains you, and all others in the world. . . . And to the charity of every man you meet this night in London, are you indebted for your unattempted life. Any knife, any hand of all the millions of knives and hands in London, has you this night at its mercy. You, and all mortals, live but by sufferance of your charitable kind."

Inside the theater, when he enters, there is an exact contrasting parallel with the American church. The narrator "gained a lofty platform" and observed "a fixed human countenance facing me from a mysterious window of a sort of sentry-box or closet." But unlike the crabbed-faced beadle in New York, this ticket-taker is surrounded by a halo, as is St. Peter: "Like some saint in a shrine, the countenance was illuminated by two smokey candles." The American is greeted by a "sudden burst of orchestral music" which "revived the memory of the organ anthems" he had heard in the New York church. The height of the gallery in which he finds his seat is "in truth appalling." He is greeted by the same "hot blast of stifling air" that had burned him in New York. Down below he sees "just such a packed mass of silent human beings." There is, however, a major difference. The theater audience below are silent but are not bent as the church audience was, a "mass of low-inclining foreheads." In the theater the narrator "had company. Not of the first circles, and certainly not of the dress-circle; but most acceptable, right welcome, cherry company, to otherwise uncompanioned" him. His company was "quiet, well-pleased working men, and their glad wives and sisters." Later, the more he looks at "this lofty gallery," the more he is delighted. Not spacious, constructed "where very limited attendance was expected," it still embraced the "very crown of the topmost semicircle," and thus commanded "with a sovereign outlook, and imperial

downlook, the whole theater . . . at the very mainmast-
head of all the interior edifice."

The *true* religion in the atmosphere is emphasized. The
rail of his gallery is low, and he can easily see the
"sparkling arms of crowds of ladies in the semicircle."
In the American church, acts were performed for the sake
of form. After the benediction was pronounced there was
"hushed silence, intense motionlessness followed for a
moment, as if the congregation were one of buried, not of
living men; when, suddenly, miraculously, like the general
rising at the Resurrection, the whole host came to their
feet, amid a simultaneous roll, like a great drumbeat,
from the enrapturing, overpowering organ." The difference
in the theater is significant; here the heart directs action:
"In the interval of two acts, again the orchestra was heard;
some inspiring anthem now was played. As the volumned
sound came undulating up, and broke in showery spray and
foam of melody against our gallery rail, my head
involuntarily was bowed, my hand instinctively sought my
pocket. Only by a second thought did I check my
momentary lunacy, and remind myself that this time I had
no small morocco book with me, and that this was not the
house of prayer." What a world of difference between the
ritualistic actions of the American church and the
involuntary and instinctive religious motions in the theater!

Whereas the narrator was "excommunicated" in the
New York church, here he is given the sacrament, by a
"ragged, but good-natured-looking boy," who gives to the
penniless man "a small mug of humming ale," saying, with
unintended irony to this American: "Dad's gone to Yankee-
land, a-seekin' of his fortin; so take a penny mug of ale, do,
Yankee, for poor dad's sake." The American's response is a
toast, in which is contained all of Melville's hope for the
future of Americans, America, and all of mankind: "Here's
immortal life to him!"

The third act in this theater is far from the action at the
same time in the church in New York. Macready, playing
Richelieu, "looks every inch to be the self-same stately

priest" the narrator "saw irradiated by the glow-worm dyes of the pictured windows from my high tower-pew" back in America. Macready has the "same measured, courtly, noble tone" as the minister had, "the same imposing attitude." Like the minister, Macready "disappears behind the scenes." But instead of returning changed from heavenly garb to Satanic, Macready reappears only "somewhat changed in his habiliments," which only vaguely reminds the narrator of the earlier experience.

The conclusion of the play does not parallel the New York event. "Starting to their feet, the enraptured thousands sound their responses deafeningly, unmistakeable since right from the undoubted heart. I have no duplicate in my memory of this. In earnestness of response, this second temple stands unmatched."

There is no matching here either of the narrator's fate after the performance. Instead of being locked up, finally tried and condemned, as happened to him earlier, now here, in an impulse ever close to Melville's mind, he goes out to the street, to the surge of music, and joins "all the gladdened crowd," and is "harmoniously attended to the street."

Although it is unnecessary, Melville labors his point in order to draw his moral. His criticism of America, in her snobbishness, her sham, her crassness, her forced isolation of people—all are summed up in the final comment in the sketch, which becomes a plea for the opposite: "I went home to my lonely lodging and slept not much that night, for thinking of the First Temple and the Second Temple; and how that, at home in my own land, I was thrust out from the one, and, a stranger in a strange land, found sterling charity in the other." The key word is *charity*. Always with Melville *charity* is the key word.

POTENTIAL REVOLUTION IN TWO WORLDS:
"POOR MAN'S PUDDING" AND
"RICH MAN'S CRUMBS"

These two stories—"Poor Man's Pudding" and "Rich
Man's Crumbs," (*Harper's*, June 1854)—are among the
baldest and boldest of Melville's socio-politico-humano
documents. The obvious subject of satire is foolish and
dangerous ignorance of political facts. But there are more
immediate subjects of satire also. In the first story, for
example, the poet Blandmour clearly represents Thoreau,
whose easy optimism had been a subject for condemnation
in "Cock-A-Doodle-Doo." Also clearly satirized is the
general romanticized picture of life in America, as well
as the evils of life in England. If the New World comes
off better in Melville's hands than the Old, the whole
matter is comparative. Here, as in "Benito Cereno,"
Melville directly pictures and advances the thesis that the
social and political order of the day, although it can
suppress rebellion for a time, clearly invites revolution both
in this country and in England.

Each sketch is a complement to the other. In the first,
as in the second, the time is 1815, the age of revolution
and combat against tyranny. The narrator of the first sketch,
as we discover in the second story, is not rich though he
seems to have money. He recognizes the optimism of the
poet Blandmour to be the sheerest foolishness. To Blandmour
this is the best of all possible worlds. March snow is "Poor
Man's Manure," and if it drifts off the poor man's acres
and onto the rich man's, this is only because a benevolent
nature recognizes that the poor man's land is "sufficiently
moist without further moistenings. Enough is as good as a
feast, you know." This is a sly dig at Benjamin Franklin,
who is going to be even more smartly stung in *Israel
Potter.* "Winter's snow—that of December—is even better
than March snow because the Psalmist said 'The Lord
giveth snow like wool'; meaning not only that snow is
white as wool, but warm, too, as wool." "So, you see, the

winter's snow *itself* is beneficent; under the pretense of frost—a sort of gruff philanthropist—actually warming the earth, which afterward is to be fertilizingly moistened by these gentle flakes of March.''

"Poor Man's Manure" is also "Poor Man's Eye-water" because melted March snow makes "the best thing in the world for weak eyes." And the "poorest man, afflicted in his eyes, can freely help himself to this same all-bountiful remedy. Now, what a kind provision is that!''

"And what could be more economically contrived? One thing answering two ends—ends so very distinct." Here Melville is closely satirizing Thoreau of *Walden*, with his insistence on the benevolence of nature and the virtue in economy itself.

Rain is even better for the poor man, for it is "Poor Man's Egg." In this passage, too, Melville is satirizing Thoreau's philosophy of make-do in *Walden*, the section where he lists his various acts of economy. Rich people sometimes use this egg, but only when they are out of real eggs, Blandmour acknowledges. Rich men also often use "Poor-Man's Plaster," but again only after having consulted a physician.

But these are all parenthetical uses of snow and rain. The main use is in the staff of life, food. For it also makes "Poor Man's Pudding," which is "as relishable as a rich man's.''

With this beginning, the narrator is then introduced by Blandmour to a typical poor family, the Coulters. Members of this family are the cousins of those in "Cock-A-Doodle-Doo." Though poor, they are happy. They have lost two children from poverty and disease. Martha, the wife, is pregnant again. The husband comes home at dinner time to eat because his wife thinks he needs sociability. She likes her husband home because she seems afraid for him to be alone too much.

The fare of these people is poor indeed. The "Poor Man's Pudding" is made from rice, milk, and salt boiled together. In addition they have salt pork and rye bread. But the pork is last year's which Squire Teamster let them have because it was cheap. But the narrator cannot eat it. In fact, the only food that he—and the wife—can eat and enjoy is the bread, the Biblical staff of life. Finally, unable to abide the dire poverty of these people any longer, the narrator takes his leave.

As he departs he comments on the political implications of the sketch. He says that the American poor suffer more than the European paupers because the Americans will not accept "random relief charity." Here a contrast must be drawn with the comments of the narrator in the Second Temple, who as an American in England refuses to accept charity until he realizes that charity is not degrading, but rather is an affirmation of man's brotherhood and glory: "Charity. Why these unvanquishable scruples? All your life, naught but charity sustains you, and all others in the world."

The American political system is largely the cause of the sufferings of the poor. Squire Teamster, Coulter's boss, represents the haves, the rich, who conspire against the Coulters of this world. Teamster is not a hard boss, as both Coulter and his wife admit. But "his time-piece is true," and although he does not spy on his laborers, "he's particular" about their promptness. And the system of which he is a part is relentless. Unless one can work according to Teamster's time-piece he is fired. In other words, unless he can advance himself in the cutthroat practice of American laissez-faire, he will remain poor. Teamster is willing to foster religion to keep the masses happy. He even gives Martha a ride to church on Sunday. But during the other six days of the week, he lets the Coulters shift for themselves.

Melville directly criticizes the Teamsters of this world: "Of all the preposterous assumptions of humanity over humanity, nothing exceeds most of the criticisms made on the habits of the poor by the well-housed, well-warmed, and well-fed." He then blisters Blandmour, the Thoreau-like

211

Transcendentalist, by saying that although he is not rich and therefore not automatically evil, he simply does not know what he is talking about.

So much for the obvious statements in the sketch. But there is more. This story is more closely tied in with the second sketch than meets the eye. And both are more definitely revolutionary documents than is instantly manifest. To Melville the hearth, here as in "The Lightning-Rod Man," represents the common bond of humanity, around which man—common man—unites to fight both god and devil. The hearth brings out the real nature of man and his heritage of faith, courage, and dignity. The fire of the hearth is an especially important symbol in this story.

When the narrator first enters the house he notices that there is an "ineffectual low fire." The woman tries to make it burn out but cannot because the fuel is "old and damp; pick-up sticks in Squire Teamster's forest, where her husband was chopping the sappy logs of the living tree for the Squire's fires." The sticks are "inferior," "some being quite mossy and toad-stooled with long lying bedded among the accumulated dead leaves of many autumns. They made a sad hissing, and vain spluttering enough." These are the dead trees, unlike the Squire's "living tree," which in "The Lightning-Rod Man" contains the iron of life. Thus Melville here points out that the sticks by which the poor are forced to warm themselves are bits of old and rotten philosophy and political beliefs which no longer will suffice. They are a part of the old constitution of things. Melville makes it quite plain that old things cannot survive. In the house of the Coulters, the narrator sat in "an old-fashioned chair of an enfeebled constitution." Again he says, "The house was old, and constitutionally damp."

The air of change is about. Though Coulter—the word equals *plower* and *knife*—is yet fumbling and does not see what he is doing, he, like the mobs in England in the second sketch, is starting a conflagration. For the wife says: "I must sweep these shivings away; husband made

him a new axe-helve this morning before sunrise,
and I have been so busy washing, that I have had no time
to clean up. But now they are just the thing I want for the
fire. They'd be better though, were they not so green." The
husband is still shaping his tools in the dark and is
politically naive, but now that his wife recognizes the
need to use him, he is moving toward progress.

The narrator's editorializing highlights the point: "Now
if Blandmour were here, thought I to myself, he would call
those green shavings 'Poor Man's Matches,' or 'Poor Man's
Tinder,' or some pleasant name of that sort." But the
narrator, although he does not explicitly say so, recognizes
that they are in fact sulphur matches flaring to light a
cannon. Though the narrator's words are comment on the
Transcendentalists' ignorance of the real needed
revolution, in a way he hits upon the truth of "civil
disobedience." For the poor, now tired of passive
resistance and acceptance, will stop and begin active
rebellion.

"Rich Man's Crumbs," more obviously concentrating on
politics, demonstrates Melville's great concern with the
area of revolution—that of the American Revolution, as
studied in *Israel Potter,* and the French Revolution, as
analyzed in *Billy Budd,* and touched on in "Benito Cereno"
and in *Clarel.* In his study of the latter period Melville was
deeply troubled by the threat of beneficial revolution
gone astray and galloping into tyranny. But he was not
frightened by the impulses toward liberty. Despite what
critics have said about Melville's period of quiet submission
and acceptance following the failure of *Pierre,* he was in
fact just as much concerned with man's ultimate triumph
over tyranny as he had ever been. *Billy Budd,* his last
work, demonstrates this triumph more effectively than
any other single work.

In "Rich Man's Crumbs" he is concerned very much
with this problem. He projects this story back to 1814, as he
had the companion "Poor Man's Pudding," when
democracy was undergoing a great stress. In America the

gap between the rich and the poor was growing greater, with threats to democracy advancing from all sides.

In *Billy Budd* he was later to study the French Revolution after it had begun to abuse its original impulse. In "Rich Man's Crumbs" he brooded over England after the defeat of Napoleon, in other words, after true democratic impulses had been subverted by tyranny in the person of Napoleon and had been defeated by a coalition of democratic nations. But he was concerned with the "democratic" nations that had tumbled tyranny. What kind of democracy existed in England, supposedly the most democratic nation of the powers triumphing over Napoleon? What promise of the future existed?

In the story the narrator reaches England in the summer of the "year 1814" after the defeat of Napoleon at Waterloo. Melville's date is a slip on his part or by *Harper's Magazine*, in which it was pulished, for 1815 was when Waterloo occurred.

This story was based on an incident in Melville's life, and the fact that he reworked it putting it back into the Napoleonic era makes it all the more politically significant. On November 9, 1849, in London, Melville recorded that he "went into Cheapside to see the 'Lord Mayor's show' it being the day of the great civic feast and festivities. *A most bloated pomp*, to be sure" (my italics). The next day "unsolicited chance and accident threw in his venturous way" an event which he recorded in his journal:

> Thro' the influence of the Fire Officer, I pushed my way thro cellers & anti-lanes into the rear of Guildhall, with a crowd of beggars who were going to receive the broken meats & pies from yesterday's grand banquet (Lord Mayor's Day).
> Within the hall, the scene was comical. Under the flaming banners & devices, were old broken tables set out with heaps of fowls, game, etc, etc, pastry in profusion—cut in all directions—I could tell who had cut into this duck, or that goose. Some of the

legs were gone—some of the wings, etc. (A good
thing might be made of this) Read the account of the
banquet—the foreign ministers & many of the
nobility were present. [7]

For purposes of the story Melville elaborates and distorts
for his own ends.

The narrator arrives in London "at the time the
victorious princes were there assembled enjoying the
Arabian Night's hospitalities of a grateful and gorgeous
aristocracy, and the courtliest of gentlemen and kings—
George the Prince Regent." The narrator omits all other
events which happened to him in London "to recount one
hour's hap." Thus again he points up the political significance of this story. The guide, whose "discourse was
chiefly of the noble charities of London," is the English
equivalent of the American optimist Blandmour. He can think
only of the glories of the rich and well born. He mentions
"the event of yesterday." To which the narrator, being an
American democrat, replies: "That sad fire on the river-side,
you mean, unhousing so many of the poor?" But this is
distinctly not the event the guide is referring to: "No. The
grand Guildhall Banquet to the princes. Who can forget
it? Sir, the dinner was served on nothing but solid silver
and gold plate, worth at least £200,000—that is,
1,000,000 of your dollars, while the mere expenditure of
meats, wines, attendence and unholstery, etc., can not be
footed under £25,000—125,000 dollars of your hard cash."

After this orgy the poor are called in for their alms. To
witness this event the narrator and his guide avoid "the
main entrance of the hall, which was barred," and enter
"through some private way," and found themselves "in a
rear blind-walled place in the open air." It is "packed with
a mass of lean, famished, ferocious creatures, struggling
and fighting for some mysterious precedency." But the
narrator and his guide must dirty themselves in this
filthy crowd. "There is no other way," says the guide, "we

7. Leyda, *Log*, 1:328.

215

can only go in with the crowd." The political comment is obvious. Melville is indicating, as he did in numerous other stories, that the commonness of man make it necessary for all people to go together. But a religious parable is also being developed on another level. There is only one way to heaven, says Virgil to Dante. The religious symbolism is carried on immediately. A basement door is thrown open, "and the squalid mass made a rush for the dark vault beyond." The narrator and guide "drove, slow and wedge-like, into the gloomy vault," while, in an obvious perversion of the religious services, "the howls of the mob reverberated," and the narrator "seemed seething in the Pit with the Lost." After continuing on and on they ascend "a stone stairway to a wide portal; when, diffusing, a pestiferous mob poured in bright day between painted walls and beneath a painted dome," in other words, under their vault of heaven.

Political symbolism again comes to the fore. The narrator thinks "of the anarchic sack of Versailles," by, that is, the oppressed Frenchmen. The brotherhood of man is demonstrated when "a few moments more" and the narrator "stood bewildered among the beggars in the famous Guildhall." They are now standing where only twelve hours before all the uniformed and mighty sat. The English mob is no better than the uncivilized cannibals from the islands, for the narrator in going through the vault felt it was "just the same as if I were pressed by a mob of cannibals on some pagan beach." But the crowned heads of the world are no better; they are merely "a mob of magnificoes."

Melville's prejudice in favor of the American way of life—its effort toward democracy, despite its shortcomings—comes out when he compares the poor of London with the poverty-stricken of America. In London "misery but maddens." In the country it softens: "As I gazed on the meagre, murderous pack, I thought of the blue eye of the gentle wife of poor Coulter." Part of the maddening aspect of the London misery is its suppression. Here it is symbolized by the guide's symbol of power, "some sort of curved glittering steel thing," which "before worn in his belt, was now flourished overhead . . . menacing the creatures to forbear offering the stranger violence." It is similar to the symbol of despotic power that Benito Cereno wears in the story of the same name. Benito's is an empty scabbard "artificially stiffened." Here also it is vague and indefinite. It is "not a sword"; in fact, the narrator does "not know what it is."

The hall of Guildhall is politically significant. All the windows are so high above the ground that no one can see out. All that the mob can see, in fact, is the walls: "The walls swept to and fro, like the foliage of a forest, with blazonings of conquerers' flags. Naught outside the hall was visible." The world outside the sight of the insular and myopic Englishman, that is, and by extension, anybody who believes in this kind of political system, went unseen.

As the feast of the poor progresses, the "something comical" that Melville thought could be made of the situation is developed. He rather shamefully puns about the food. In one he is as brazen in his sexual allusion as he was in "The Tartarus of Maids." When it is pointed out that a pheasant, in which "the two breasts were gouged ruthlessly out," might have been eaten by the Prince Regent, the narrator responds: "I don't doubt it . . . he is said to be uncommonly fond of the breast."

The potentially revolutionary aspect of the setting is underlined more and more. The guide boasts that England is the only country "which feeds her very beggars with golden-hued jellies." To which the narrator responds that what these people need is "plain beef and bread." In the guide's comment that the emperors, kings, and other great personages do not eat plain beef and bread and consequently their leavings are superior to such rough fare there is plainly an echo of the French Revolution and the popular story of the condescension of Marie Antoinette who when told that the poor had no bread to eat replied, "Let 'em eat cake."

217

A "red-gowned official" orders the narrator away from the board, mistaking him for one of the mob. He represents the church, and the reprehensible role he plays is in aiding and abetting aristocracy, which here becomes satanic, for the guide is referred to by this official familiarly in one of the numerous references to Satan: in "The Tartarus of Maids," he was "Old Bach"; here he is "old lad."

The banners hanging on the wall have now become a leading symbol, changed from one of oppression to one of leadership, the flags of the revolutionaries. "The yet unglutted mob raised a fierce yell, which wafted the banners like a strong gust, and filled the air with a reek as from sewers." Here obviously Melville goes back to the "anarchic sack of Versailles" that he had been reminded of earlier and sees the mob rising to overthrow the dynasty which to them represented tyranny and oppression. Now it is open rebellion.

> They surged against the tables, broke through all barriers, and billowed over the hall—their bare tossed arms like the dashed ribs of a wreck. It seemed to me as if a sudden impotent fury of fell envy possessed them. That one half-hour's peep at the mere remnants of the glories of the Banquets of Kings; the unsatisfying mouthfuls of disembowelled pastries, plundered pheasants, and half-sacked jellies, served to remind them of the intrinsic contempt of the alms. In this sudden mood, or whatever mysterious thing it was that now seized them, these Lazaruses seemed ready to spew up in repentant scorn the contumelious crumbs of Dives.

Not all the English poor are in rebellion and some are still impressed and controlled by appearances, even approving of the English snobbishness. When the narrator is put in a cab to be taken away from the disastrous scene of carnage, his guide tells the cabby, "Mind, Jehu . . . this is a *gentleman* you carry." Jehu is the conventional name of a 19th century cab driver in England, but it is also the name of a 9th century Jewish king who, like Ahab in *Moby-Dick*, was a cruel and heartless wretch.

If the political implications of the two stories in this diptych have not been clear before, Melville makes them obvious in his concluding paragraph. Melville has handled the American scene gently because he realizes that the evil of poverty there, and its condonement by Blandmour— Thoreau—is not viciously motivated. The criticism of England is less restrained. In tying together the two worlds, the new and the old, he demonstrates the widespread aspect of poverty. He recognizes the "misery and infamy which is, ever has been, and ever will be, precisely the same in India, England, and America," and throughout the world as a consequence of poverty. But poverty and its resultant degradation will be rebelled against sooner in America than throughout the rest of the world. The difference between the American and the English resistance to the demands of the poor is symbolized, as in Swift, in clothes. During the sackings of the Guildhall the American's clothes are torn to tatters, but the Englishman's "close-bodied coat and flat cap" defied all tumbling and tearings.

Melville ends the sketches with the prayer, "Heaven in its kind mercy save me . . . equally from the 'Poor Man's Pudding' and the 'Rich Man's Crumbs'." This is precisely the same cry he utters in another study of gluttony and want, riches and poverty, "Jimmy Rose," where his "God guard us all," is an affirmation of his faith in and hope for the triumph of democracy.

TWO VIEWS OF COMMITMENT:
"THE PARADISE OF BACHELORS" AND
"THE TARTARUS OF MAIDS"

"The Paradise of Bachelors" (which with "The Tartarus of Maids" appeared in *Harper's* for April 1855) is one of Melville's three studies in the contrasts between English

219

and American life, or between two forms of life one of which he thinks is decidedly superior. This story is most closely associated with the diptych "Poor Man's Pudding" and "Rich Man's Crumbs," for food figures vary largely here—as in those stories—as an actuality as well as a symbol in the study of the rich and the poor.

The setting is the Temple of London, formerly the seat of the Knights Templars but presently the location of one of the great inns of court. The story had its genesis in an occurrence when Melville while in London dined with Robert Francis Cook and his brother. Though Melville had thoroughly enjoyed the actual occasion, his tone in the story he created from the experience, as in "Cock-A-Doodle-Doo," is so obviously forced and exaggerated in its heartiness that the reader knows he cannot take Melville's approval at face value. This is a story of the shirkers of the responsibilities of life, Melville's "bachelors," who fail to commit themselves to life and thereby do evil.

Melville's criticism of "bachelors" begins with the first paragraph of the tale. Going to this paradise "by the usual way," he begins indicating the habitual sloughing off of responsibility by the frequenters of the quarters. They avoid the "Benedick tradesmen" of life who must because of their commitment shoulder responsibilities. Melville's criticism is religious as well as social, as he indicates at the very beginning. These quarters are a "Paradise," and they are reached by turning a "mystic corner" and gliding down a "dim, monastic way, flanked by dark, sedate, and solemn piles, and still wending on, giving the whole careworn world the slip," until one stands "beneath the quiet cloisters" and "in mild meditation pace" around, perhaps finally to "worship in the sculptured chapel."

Melville is concerned, as he is elsewhere—in *Clarel* for example—with man's depth in history, with his memory. This paradise extends back in time past the Knights

Templar to Eden itself. It is still, geographically at least, the Original Garden. It is "quite sequestered from the old city's surrounding din"; "No part of London offers . . . so agreeable a refuge." "The Temple is indeed a city by itself . . . A city with a park to it, and flower-beds, and a river-side—the Thames flowing by as openly, in one part, as by Eden's primal garden flowed the mild Euphrates."

But since the days of the original dwellers in this Eden, a "moral blight" has set in. The monk-knights of old degenerated to what Melville calls the present good-fellows. The earlier ones were "but gruff and grouty at the best," their times and institutions cased them in "Birmingham hardware" and prevented them from joining in a fraternal handshake. Their nominal descendants are "like many other tumbled from proud glory's height—like the apple, hard on the bough but mellow on the ground—the Templar's fall has but made him all the finer fellow." Melville's seeming approval of the modern man is tempered with irony. Unlike his predecessor who was dedicated to "carving out immortal fame in glorious battling for the Holy Land," the present-day Templar is given to the "carving of the roast mutton at a dinnerboard."

Further, he has turned from "the monk-giver of gratuitious ghostly counsel" to someone who "counsels for a fee":

> The defender of the sarcophagus (if in good practice with his weapon) now has more than one case to defend; the vowed opener and clearer of all highways leading to the Holy Sepulchre, now has it in particular charge to check, to clog, to hinder, and embarrass all the courts and avenues of Law; the knight-combatant of the Saracen, breasting spear-points at Acre, now fights law-points in Westminster Hall.

The present Templar is, in other words, a sower of discord, a person who inhibits the smooth flow of life at large; "the Templar is today a Lawyer."

221

Melville's true feeling for the paradise of bachelors can be inferred by comparing what he seems to say here about the Knights Templar with what he explicitly stated about them in *Israel Potter*, published at the same time. When Israel is holed up in the squire's wall, in the room formerly used by the Templars in torturing their prisoners, Melville says: "The domestic discipline of this order was rigid and merciless in the extreme." "It was deemed a good sign of the state of the sufferer's soul, if from the gloomy recesses of the wall was heard the agonised groan of his dismal response." "Sometimes several weeks elapsed ere the disentombment, the penitent being then usually found numb and congealed in all his extremities, like one newly stricken with paralysis."

Melville criticizes further by saying that the men attending this particular meal are "sort of Senate of the Bachelors, sent to this dinner from widely-scattered districts . . . Nay it was, by representation, a Grand Parliament of the best Bachelors in universal London." Melville's dislike and criticism are pinpointed when we remember that in *Billy Budd* and *Clarel* the parliament of all nations were truly representatives of all people—common, Benedicts, not the uncommitted bachelors.

These bachelors are not religious men even if they hallow themselves with religious memories. The apartment in which the dinner takes place is "well up toward heaven," but the "ceiling of the room was low." In the first of "The Two Temples" Melville says: "Height somehow hath devotion in it. The archangelic anthems are raised in a lofty place." There is a significant difference between the two high places. Among the London bachelors Melville ironically rhapsodizes: the only hymn that can be sung is that to another kind of low-ceilinged heaven—"Carry me back to old Virginny."

The bachelors are stomach-oriented. "Who wants to dine under the dome of St. Peter's?" they ask, not favoring austerity. The meal these men enjoy here is scarcely any different from that luxuriated in by the kings in "Rich Man's Crumbs," which was obscenely over-plentiful. They indulge themselves without restraint. By the time they begin to eat, all are tipsy, and they continue to drink more and more. But although very gay, they are entertaining only to their drunken companions. One of Melville's more amusing comments is that a sick man in an adjoining parlor was so bored that he went to sleep and "enjoyed his first sound refreshing slumber in three long, weary weeks."

Though it has its overtones of religious disapproval, the story is primarily social criticism, condemnation of the bachelor's non-commitment with life. They know nothing of pain and trouble: they would not "suffer themselves to be imposed upon by such monkish fables," "as well talk of Catholic miracles," or of pain and woe. They care nothing for anyone but themselves, and not even for one of themselves if he is not well. For example they would not aid in any way their invalided fellow bachelor in the adjoining chamber.

Melville makes it quite plain that all non-bachelors, those people not participating in the feast, condemn it roundly. Especially is this true of the "venerable man," the waiter whom they call Socrates: "Amidst all the hilarity of the feast, intent on important business, he disdained to smile." He is a "surprising old field-marshal." The implications are that what the narrator mistakes for Socrates' decorum is actually disgust. This conclusion is strengthened by the fact that from this point on in the story Melville speaks of the feast in military terms; not the terms of the knights in their olden battles, but the language of present-day military campaigns, that needed to overthrow these bachelors. This military theme is climaxed near the end of the story when Socrates steps into the banquet room with an "immense convolved horn, a regular Jericho horn." This Jericho horn is in every way a bugle calling the dispossessed and poor to arms. The walls of this bastion are bound to come tumbling down. The vul-

nerability of these people is demonstrated by the fact
that the horn contains only snuff; only a smoke screen of
power is needed to topple them.

The horn does, of course, also symbolize sex. It has two
"lifelike goats' heads, with four more horns of solid silver,
projecting from opposite sides of the mouth of the noble
main horn." It is a satyr's symbol. The snuff in the horn
becomes then an unequivocal condemnation of the lack of
virile masculinity of the bachelors.

The story has been from the beginning a remarkable
mirror-image of the other half of the diptych, "The Tartarus
of Maids." "The Paradise of Bachelors" begins, as the
later story will, with a trip which is "like stealing from a
heated plain into some cool, deep glen, shady among
harbouring hills." After sexually suggestive development all
along, the sexual references at the end build up and
lead into "The Tartarus of Maids." The nine bachelors,
after sniffing their snuff from the satyr pipe, take their
several ways home. Some go individually, some "two by
two and arm-in-arm," "some going to their neighbouring
chambers to turn over the *Decameron* ere retiring for the
night." The hint of sex given here, homosexual and
consequently only faintly alluded to, is clear. Melville
condemns these bachelors for their unfulfilled potential
participation in life as strongly as he does the sailors on
the ship called the *Bachelor* in *Moby-Dick*. This condemnation is strengthened by the companion piece, which
is on a major level concerned with sex and is "the very
counterpart of the Paradise of Bachelors, but snowed
upon and frost-painted to a sepulchre."

Melville has no hesitation in the last statement of this
"Paradise of Bachelors," the *coup de grace* of the story.
When asked by his host what he thinks of the temple, the
narrator replies, "Sir this is the very Paradise of Bachelors."
But the full irony of this assertion can be understood only
at the ending of "The Tartarus of Maids."

"The Tartarus of Maids," the companion piece to "The

Paradise of Bachelors," to which it is connected throughout, was apparently extraordinarily subtle, as is revealed by the fact that it was published, without public outcry, in a magazine as an interesting but innocent story when it in fact is replete with sexual symbols that had they recognized them would have shocked its readers. The story is also one of Melville's most compactly symbolic. It operates on several levels at the same time.

Although it is difficult now to see how, it can be taken, on the first level, as it was apparently by the readers of *Harper's*, as a mere journey. As such it records an actual trip taken by Melville to Carson's "Old Red Mill" in Dalton, not far from Pittsfield. It is vividly and agonizingly recounted as a journey taken by sleigh in the dead of winter over the "Woedolor Mountain in New England" to visit a papermill.

The tie-in with "The Paradise of Bachelors"—through contrast—is immediately apparent. The former story is situated in a paradisiacal refuge in the city, with a room that seems close to heaven. The setting of this "Tartarus," as the name designates, is approached through a "Dantean gateway" that has a "sort of feudal, Rhineland and Thurmberg look, derived from the pinnacled wildness of the neighboring scene." The owner of the paper mill is Satan, called "Old Bach." The narrator, like Dante on his trip, has his Virgil, a youngster named "Cupid," who, although he adds his part to the unfortunate fate of the girls working in the factory, ironically has about him a "strange innocence of cruel-heartedness." Also, as Fogle has noted, the ninth circle of *The Inferno* is one of bitter cold, paralleling the forced virginity of the maids in this factory.

The sexual symbolism begins almost immediately. The paper mill is approached through a pass called "The Mad Maid's Bellows'-pipe." There is a hollow called "the Devil's Dungeon," through which runs "this strange-coloured torrent Blood River." As he approaches, the author details vividly the actual defloration of the giant vagina.

225

Horse and cataract are rushing into the Devil's Dungeon together: "With might and main, quitting my seat and robes, and standing backward, with one foot braced against the dashboard, I rasped and churned the bit, and stopped him just in time to avoid collision, at a turn, with the bleak nozzle of a rock, couchant like a lion in the way—a roadside rock."

The papermill, when the narrator finds it, is staffed only by girls, pale of face and blue with cold. He sees such a girl standing before a "vertical thing like a piston periodically rising and falling," stamping on "half-quires of rose-hued note-paper;" ironically, the wreath of roses is a symbol of virginity. Cupid, the narrator's guide, shows the visitor a "dark colossal water-wheel, grim with its one immutable purpose," over which runs Blood River, setting "our whole machinery a-going, sir; in every part of all these buildings; where the girls work and all."

This symbol of menstruation, and the beginning of the procreative process, is carried on, partially at least, in the rags all the girls handle, and would use in this biological process. Before each girl stands a vertical scythe which looks exactly like a sword. Across these phallic symbols which are turned away from and therefore forever prohibited to these virgins, the girls drag "long strips of rags, washed white." Cupid and the visitor go into another room which is "stifling with a strange, blood-like abdominal heat." The room contains a "great machine," "with two great round vats in it, full of a white, wet, wooly-looking stuff, not unlike the albuminous part of an egg, soft-boiled." The pulp from this machine requires exactly nine minutes to be developed into paper.

In addition to the sexual level, the story is on another plane clearly a comment, as "The Bell-Tower" is, on man's serving the machine that will eventually destroy him. The scythes before which the girls stand stripping their rags are "immovably fixed at bottom." Working them will cause death because the air the girls breathe swims "with the

fine, poisonous particles." And "through consumptive pallors of this blank, raggy life, go these white girls to death."
Every once in a while the girls take whetstones and sharpen "the very swords that slay them."

The "great machine" that manufactures the paper, "humming with its play," strikes the author "as well by the inevitability as the evolvement-power in all its motions." It must always "go." "The pulp can't help going," Cupid says. Melville continues: "Something of awe now stole over me, as I gazed upon this inflexible iron animal. Always, more or less, machinery of this ponderous, elaborate sort strikes, in some moods, strange dread into the human heart, as some living, panting Behemoth might. But what made the thing so specially terrible to me was the metallic necessity, the unbudging fatality which governed it." The girls, like the engineer in "The Bell-Tower" who is destroyed by the clock he creates, are ruined if not by the machine they create then by the machine they have become: "Slowly, mournfully, beseechingly, yet unresistingly, they gleamed along, their agony dimly outlined on the imperfect paper, like the print of the tormented face on the handkerchief of Saint Veronica."

Melville's social criticism cries out. The machine age not only destroys mankind but turns people into mere automatons before destroying them. The narrator describes the girls: "At rows of blank-looking counters sat rows of blank-looking girls, with blank, white folders in their blank hands, all blankly folding blank paper." The paper these workers turn out is nearly all foolscap. To the narrator's query as to whether any other kind of paper is made, Cupid replies: "Oh, sometimes, but not often, we turn out finer work—cream-laid and royal sheets, we call them. But foolscap being in chief demand, we turn out foolscap most." Melville's anguished protest rings out against the deadening weight of the machine and against blind chance, with an appeal for the uplifting of the democratic mass. He remembers "All sorts of writings would be writ on those vacant things [the Lockeian *tabula rasa*]—

sermons, lawyers' briefs, physicians' prescriptions, love-letters, marriage certificates, bills of divorce, registers of births, death-warrants, and so on, without end." He continues: "Then, recurring back to them as they here lay all blank, I could not but bethink me of that celebrated comparison of John Locke, who, in demonstration of his theory that man had no innate ideas, compared the human mind at birth to a sheet of blank paper; something destined to be scribbled on, but what sort of characters no soul might tell."

Finally, this story is on another level one huge grinning, leering sexual joke, in the nature of Davy Crockett and other frontier heroes. Melville was fond of these jokes both because he liked them, apparently, for their intrinsic value and because they tied in his subject with folklore and through it with the common people. We have already seen how the defloration of the gargantuan vagina is accomplished. The scythes before which the girls work but which are denied them are oversized phallic symbols. The narrator asks Cupid if among the rags the girls cut up there are not some "old shirts, gathered from the dormitories of the Paradise of Bachelors. But the buttons are all dropped off. Pray, my lad, do you ever find any bachelor's buttons hereabouts?" Cupid, strangely dense for the moment, misunderstands, and replies that there are no *flowers* in this vicinity. But the narrator meant semen.

The reference is strikingly close to one in *Moby-Dick,* when in the chapter named "Ambergris" (XCII) Melville builds on the "adverse winds" in the dead whale, saying, "It's the first foul wind I ever knew to blow from astern." He then builds on the unnatural sexual relations among sailors, joking about copulation between man and whale! "I have forgotten to say that there were found in this ambergris, certain hard, round, bony plates, which at first Stubb thought might be sailors' trousers buttons." Later, in the same vein, as the *Pequod* sinks, Stubb affirms by sexual allusions his desire to live: "For me, off shoes and jacket

to it; let Stubb die in his drawers! . . . .cherries! cherries!
cherries!" The scale of sex in "The Tartarus of Maids" is
that of "the grandissimus" of the whale which is "longer
than a Kentuckian is tall."

All levels of symbols merge at the end of this short story
to reveal Melville's social protest. It is a story told on a
grand scale; as such it represents humanity. It is a cry for
improved living and working conditions. Also it dramatically contrasts Melville's uncommitted person with
those who were very much committed, the male bachelors by
choice as opposed to the female bachelor against her will.
There is no doubt about which group Melville's sympathy
lies with. Here, as in his cry at the end of "Bartleby,"
Melville's choice is pointed out by the order of presentation
of the concluding words. In the other story the ending was
"Ah Bartleby, Ah Humanity!" with the greater concern
being placed on the second. Here it is "Oh! Paradise of
Bachelors! and oh! Tartarus of Maids!" Clearly Melville's
sympathy lies with the second group and all they symbolize.

"THE LIGHTNING-ROD MAN": HEAVEN AND EARTH

"The Lightning-Rod Man" (*Putnam's*, August 1854) is a
study in pagan-Christian mythology and man's relationship
to God and his fellow men. Futher, it is a study of the
confidence man that Melville was going to analyze much
more deeply in such works as *The Confidence-Man, Israel
Potter*, and *Billy Budd*. Chase called this short story a study
of a celestial confidence man. Clearly it derives directly
from Hawthorne's "Young Goodman Brown."

The dimensions of the story are set immediately, almost
with a jolt. This is a story of heaven and earth, and all that
dwell therein. It opens with supernatural manifestations,
immediately recognizable by reader and perceptive
participant as the prelude to a supernatural event, "grand

irregular thunder'' (my italics) in the Acroceraunian hills.[8]
Mountains for Melville are the home of giants on the earth,
heroes. Acroceraunia, as Egbert Oliver has pointed out,
is a part of ancient Greece which is noted for its wild
thunderstorms and is not far from the reputed throne of
Jupiter. Additionally, Jay Leyda noted that Mather's
Magnalia Christi Americana, a copy of which was in
Melville's library at Arrowhead, contains under ''Ceraunius.
Relating remarkables done by thunder'' (Sixth Book,
Chapter III), among others the following entry: ''IV. A
fourth voice of the glorious God in the thunder, is *make
your peace with* God *immediately, lest by the stroke of his
thunder he take you away in his wrath.*'' With these three
forces converging, this is naturally the proper setting for a
tug-of-war for the souls of men between Satan and a
humanistic earthman, who snug in his home, on top of
which ''swift slants of sharp rain . . . rang, like a charge of
spear-points,'' can resist the devil and live amicably with
God. Here, as in *Israel Potter*, great men abide, for
mountains intervene between God and the common people
in the valleys: ''The mountains hereabouts break and churn
up the thunder, so that it is far more glorious here than
on the plain.''

The resident is not so much surprised that there would be
a visitor making a call during this ''time of thunder'' as
that he does not ''man-fashion, use the knocker, instead of
making that doleful undertaker's clatter with his fist against
the hollow panel.'' That the visitor is Satan is revealed, as in
''Young Goodman Brown,'' by the implement he carries, a
''strange-looking walking-stick.''

Like all of Melville's dangerous men—for example,
Claggart in *Billy Budd*—the visitor is Cassius-like, a

8. Melville's great interest in and powerful use of thunder and lightning can be illustrated
in *Moby-Dick*. Father Mapple while preaching is possessed of the elements. Ahab, who
calls himself ''Old Thunder,'' has a ''slender rod-like mark'' running down his face, and
looks like a tree that has been struck by lightning. Stubb criticizes Flask for wanting
every man to go around ''with a small lightning rod running up the corner of his hat.''
Tashtego inquires ''What's the use of thunder?'' But we know the answer to that question.
In leading up to one of the highlights of the work, Melville has the compass turned
by thunder.

"lean" figure. He is a satire of himself: "Hair dark and lank, mattedly streaked over his brown face. His sunken pitfalls of eyes were ringed by indigo halos, and played with an innocuous sort of lightning: the gleam without the bolt." This man is clearly a con man, a fraud, shadow without substance, the empty scabbard of Benito Cereno. It becomes clear in a moment that he is out to scare people for his own profit. The profit motif is established by the fact that the walking-stick is made of copper (money). The lack of genuineness of his ware is highlighted by the figure at the end of the stick, which terminates "tripodwise, in three keen tines, brightly gilt." In the end, this instrument is converted into a murderous implement when the frustrated con man leaps at the heart of the householder.

The narrator is a hero who clearly is foremost a humanist. He dearly loves his hearth and fire because they symbolize human warmth and fraternity, as they do throughout Melville's works. The imposter, however, shies away from the fire because he cannot be exposed to human scrutiny and human standards.

The narrator recognizes the imposter immediately. He asks if the visitor is Jupiter Tonans, "he who stood in the Greek statue of old, grasping the lightning bolt." And he asks the Olympian to sit in the "rush-bottomed arm-chair," here signifying the narrator's, hence man's feeling of safety in the world.

Jupiter Tonans responds belligerently to being recognized: "the stranger eyed me, half in wonder, and half in a strange sort of horror."

He uses all the external tricks of religion. Clearly he is a revivalist, a religious con man. He calls upon the name of heaven at every opportunity. "Good heavens!" is his favorite appeal. Further, he narrowly resents any association with other religions. "Call me not by that pagan name. You are profane in this time of terror," he tells the narrator when he insists on calling the visitor "Jupiter Tonans." Melville may well have been satirizing a local fire-eating preacher possibly, as Oliver says, the Reverend John Todd, pastor of the First Church (Congregational) of Pittsfield, 1842-1873. But Melville is also broadening out to condemn those, even like Father Mapple, who automatically exclude all other religions, even the pagan, from the approved list.

The visitor insists that the only safe place in a storm is the center of the room; in other words he is a man of no extremes, with equal space to move to any side as expediency demands and tactics warrant. Here Melville is obviously condemning such moderation, while in other works, especially *Clarel*, he seems to approve of at least some aspects of moderation. Here when the visitor seems almost on the verge of pushing the narrator to the center, this humanist seeks his symbol of brotherhood and pride in *Homo sapiens*—"I stepped back upon the hearth, and threw myself into the erectest, proudest posture I could command!"

The strength and strategical situation of this stance is made clear by the visitor's alarm at the narrator's position. His remark reveals even more conclusively his Satanic character: "Know you not, that the heated air and soot are conductors;—to say nothing of those immense iron fire-dogs?"

This Satanic character of the visitor is further revealed when he is asked his trade. That he is evil is demonstrated by the fact that heaven will not allow him to name it. "My special business is_____." Then, for the first time he admits to heaven his imposture and calls for mercy. But immediately recovering, he reaffirms his own magical power and his isolation from man: "Say but the word, and of this cottage I can make a Gibraltar by a few waves of this wand."

The narrow, bigoted, and anti-social character of this Satanic religion is developed more fully. The visitor remarks that he has "the best of references." He "put up three-and-twenty rods on only five buildings . . . in Criggan last month." The narrator questions whether in Criggan "about midnight on Saturday . . . the steeple, the big elm, and the assembly-room cupola were struck?"[8] The con man answers that he had not put any rods on the elm or the assembly-room. In other words, he had had nothing to do with the elm, which represents nature, or the cupola, which symbolizes human companionship. The falsity of his product is clearly revealed by the fact that the place of worship, though protected by the rod, was destroyed. Perhaps Melville's finest comment to this point is his balancing the con man's false religion with the true, as revealed in the Twenty-third Psalm, a parody of which the con man had made in his twenty-three rods in Criggan. Melville points it up by having the narrator ask: "Of what use is your rod, then?" The rod of the true religion is one of peace and security, not fear and trembling. But God's wrath against the irreligious is swift and sure. Though the con man[9] insists that it was not his fault that the church steeple was struck, as a workman had installed the rod badly—thus revealing his real anti-humanistic bias—we know that a righteous God had blasted the imposter.

The narrowness and bigotry of the con man's kind of religion is further satirized in the narrator's remarking that a servant girl in Canada was struck by lightning with a rosary in her hand, to which the con man responds that the rods in use there (Catholicism) are not as good as his; they are iron, as distinguished from his copper. With unqualified bigotry he affirms categorically: "*Mine* is the only true rod." As Oliver says, Melville may have had specifically in mind the Reverend Todd.

The real nature of Melville's message becomes intensified. The con man flourishes in sham danger and distorts all happenings to his end. When the thunder nears the earth and them, the con man checks his pulse—his life-blood—and in an incantation on the magic numbers, counts three pulses between the time the lightning strikes and the time he hears the report. Capitalizing on this created terror, the

9. Oliver is correct in saying that inspiration for this touch came from the fact that the assembly-room of the First Church in Pittsfield, the Reverend John Todd's church, was struck by lightning.

con man builds on his earlier statement that his is the only
true rod. He reports that he earlier passed "three stricken
oaks" in the woods, "ripped out new and glittering."
Melville's message seems to be that in the Trinity there is
ever-new and vital religion, whereas the con man would
report the death of true religion and the life of his only.
True religion is the oak of life, which, according to the
con man, "draws lightning more than other timber, having
iron in its sap." When the con man notices that the
narrator's floor is oak, the message seems to be that true
religion, having the iron of resistance to falsity, does
indeed draw criticism but can resist it. But, more important, this "heart-of-oak" represents the author's
humanistic impulses, true concern for the common people.
The narrator points this out by insisting that the time of
travel for the con man is unusual. "Common men chose fair
weather for their travels: you choose thunderstorms!"
he observes.

Melville's attack on bogus, solitary, and anti-humanistic
religion continues. The narrator wants to step to the
window in order to close out the rain, but the con man,
reminiscent of his earlier fear and Melville's symbol of the
window as a vantage point for gaining wisdom, as well as
of communicating with other people, tries to frighten him
away. Next when the narrator asks the con man to "touch
the bell-pull," we hear echoes of the "First Temple," as
well as of "The Bell Tower" and immediately recognize in
the visitor's refusal his fear of real religion and of the
community of people that the bell would summon.

The evangelical aspect of this false religion is emphasized
still further. The con man insists that the center of the house is the
safest, as we have seen. Then in an ardor which is meant to
overcome all resistance, in reply to the narrator's question
about which is the safest part of the house, he urges: "This
room, and this one spot in it where I stand. Come hither."
His zeal rises: "Come hither to me!" "Come hither to
me!" he insists. But it is not to the safety of the center

of the room but to him personally that he invites the other man. His presumption is now equal to that of Bannadonna in "The Bell-Tower," and the lightning-rod man's attempted overthrow of all opposition is clearly revealed.

The Devil sometimes quotes scripture, and sometimes the truth. Here, speaking to another purpose, he reveals that "Lightning sometimes passes from the clouds to the earth, and sometimes from the earth to the clouds." The latter part of this statement gives the narrator "confidence." One of Melville's strongest affirmations of faith in the human being, in humanity, in man's dignity and real worth comes in the narrator's finding "strangely inspired confidence" in the con man's assertion that lightning does sometimes rise from earth to heaven.

But Satan is not interested in any true symbols. He wants only the show of religion, the trappings. Thus his insistence that being wet (that is, baptized) is the safest condition, for if "lightning strikes, it might pass down the wet clothes without touching the body." The falsity of this doctrine— its attempt to crucify the true religion—is emphasized by the fact that upon this announcement by false religion, the skies blacken—"it is dusk at noon"—precisely as happened at the crucifixion of Christ, the symbol of true religion. A moment later the con man parodies, or tries to profit by, the words of Christ on the cross. In answer to the narrator's desire to hear the con man's "precautions in traveling during thunder-storms," the latter replies: "Wait till this one is passed." ("Let this cup pass from me.")

But Christ was crucified under the old laws, those of the Old Testament, not those of true Christianity. Melville extends this true Christianity to include more humanism— as he did in "The Apple-Tree Table."

Man's innate dignity and greatness—tinged here with the Prometheanism that Melville always had hovering just on the edge of his powerful nature—enters the argument. The con man urges that the narrator should "avoid pine-trees, high houses, lonely barns, upland pastures, running water, flocks of cattle and sheep, a crowd of men." "But of

235

all things . . . avoid tall men." Thus he equates nature in
all her aspects with man. To the injunction that it is safest
to avoid tall men, the narrator explodes: "Do I dream? Man
avoid man? and in danger-time, too?" The con man
responds, naturally, that men are dangerous, being good
conductors of electricity, and tall men, Kentuckians,
mountaineers, being exceptional men, are especially
susceptible.

The con man further reveals his crassness by returning
to his subject of copper (his lightning-rods) and trying to
sell them for twenty dollars. His contempt for the people
he is ostensibly trying to save and his belief in the lack of
immortality for any one is revealed in his remark: "Think
of being a heap of charred offal, like a haltered horse burnt
in his stall; and all in one flash!"

The narrator, finally exasperated, cuts the con man down
to man size and emphasizes his falsity: "You mere man
who came here to put you and your pipestem between clay
and sky." He turns his satire to Johan Tetzel (c. 1460-1590),
who according to the *Encyclopedia Britannica* (quoted in Oliver)
"combined the elocutionary gifts of a revivalist orator
with the shrewdness of an auctioneer." Then he blisters
the self-annointed preachers peddling their "indulgences
from divine ordinations." He takes great comfort in the
care that God exercises over man and sees in the rainbow
the Creator's promise that He will not "of purpose, make
war on man's earth." Thus frustrated, the con man gives up
his disguise, becomes uncamouflaged Satan: "The scowl
grew blacker on his face; the indigo-circles enlarged
round his eyes as the storm-rings round the midnight moon.
He sprang upon me; his tri-forked thing at my heart." But
the narrator, strong in the power of God, seizes the
impostor, breaks his equipment, and throws him out the
door.

Melville's real message in the story becomes clear in the
last paragraph. Here as in most of his other works, Melville's main concern is not with himself, not with re-

ligion as such, not with God, but with people. This concern he clearly voices in the final sentence: "But spite of my treatment, and spite of my dissuasive talk of him to my neighbors, the Lightning-Rod man still dwells in the land; still travels in storm-time, and drives a brave trade with the fears of man."

"THE HAPPY FAILURE": SUCCESS THROUGH DEFEAT

"The Happy Failure" (*Harper's*, July 1854) is an Aesopian fable of America which discusses the political situation during the 1850's, points out the impossibility of conditions continuing as they were then, and ends with a prayer and a hope.

This is the story of an American inventor who after ten years of concentrated labor has invented the Great Hydraulic-Hydrostatic Apparatus to be used for draining swamps and marshes "and converting them, at the rate of one acre the hour, into fields more fertile than those of the Genessee." Here indeed is the promise of America, the land of hope and opportunity. The inventor is Uncle Sam, the typical old Yankee, who believes that he lives in the best of worlds in the best of ages, as he says: "The world has shot ahead the length of its own diameter" since the times of the Roman Emperor who tried to drain the Pontine marsh, but failed. "If that Roman emperor were here, I'd show him what can be done in the present enlightened age."

Like a typical American also, uncle is greedy. He thinks there is a fortune in his invention, and if it is successful he can "boldly demand any price for its publication." A child of his age, he believes in the solitariness, the isolation, of America. "Solitary in my scheme, I go to a solitary place to test it. If I fail—for all things are possible—no one out of the family will know it." He is afraid of foreigners, of snoopers. Before beginning to test the machine, he has his nephew and his servant scan the countryside for any spies. Overly suspicious, he will not

237

begin his test until a distant horseman has disappeared, and he mistakes a "withered white bough" for an observing boy.

Melville's most important comments in the story, however, are made on the general state of American thinking and on society. They are contrary to nature and to the movement of the times. Too commercial and outdated, the invention is housed in a "battered old dry-goods box." Uncle determines to pull ten miles up the river "against the stream" to test his invention, though the nephew, pointing up Melville's belief in the urgency of the situation, protests that "ten mortal miles in this fiery sun" are foolish and useless. Melville's symbol of the world is always a ship; here it is a skiff, and it "settles down under" the weight of uncle's monomaniacal nonsense.

American society and philosophy are complicated. The machine is a "surprising multiplicity of convoluted metal pipes and syringes of all sorts and varieties, all sizes and calibres, inextricably interweaved together in one gigantic coil. It looked like a huge nest of anacondas and adders." Despite the fact that all kinds of adjustments are made, accommodating "a leetle" this way and "a leetle" that way, the machine will not work. In anger, then, uncle rends it apart violently: "Running at the box he dashed his bare foot into it, and with astonishing power all but crushed in the side. Then seizing the whole box, he disembowelled it of all its anacondas and adders, and, tearing and wrenching them, flung them right and left over the water."

Melville here extends his symbolism to the question of slavery, over which he was darkly brooding during the grim fifties, and his apprehension over the possible consequences if the nation were split asunder because the American system, the invention, would not work. The youthful nephew here, after the destruction of the machine, urges his uncle to put it back together again: "It is not yet wholly ruined, dear uncle; come put it together again, and try it once more. While there is life there is hope." And he urges that if the whole nation cannot be saved, at least part of it, the

North, can be: "Do, do now, dear uncle—here, here, put these pieces together; or; if that can't be done without more tools, try a *section* of it—that will do just as well."

That Melville is thinking of the slavery question is demonstrated by his development of Yorpy, uncle's Negro slave. Melville thought that slavery was the work of Satan. In *Clarel* Ungar the ex-confederate officer always felt slavery was evil. More definitely, "Benito Cereno" clearly demonstrates what demons slavery makes of human beings. Here Yorpy, not nominally a slave but one in fact, automatically thinks of the devil when as a "drunker-headed black" he is commanded to handle the box: "'Duyvel take to pox!' muttered old Yorpy, who was a sort of Dutch African. 'De pos has been my cuss for de ten long 'ear.'" Later uncle, in his frustration over the failure of the invention, addresses Yorpy as the devil: "You, Yorpy, take your black hoff from under the box!"

The uncle, after the failure of his machine, falls back upon expediency, thus revealing one excuse of the pro-slavery people: "Never try to invent anything but—happiness."

Melville's humanistic impulses, never far from the surface, rise in this story. Uncle was an individualist, superior to all other people: "The natural tendency of man, in the mass, is to go down with the universal current into oblivion." But the nephew, here voicing the author's attitude, disproves this philosophy. The "woeful box," even after it has been reorganized with a few of its former parts and is being tested, is dropped and abandoned after uncle has turned white and nearly fallen, and the boy and Yorpy spring forward to save the human being at the cost of the loss of the machine. Thus unencumbered the nephew philosophizes: "How swiftly the current now swept us down! How hardly before had we striven to stem it! I thought of my poor uncle's saying, not an hour gone by, about the universal drift of the mass of humanity toward utter oblivion." But the uncle was wrong. The new drift is toward salvation. The abandoned box is recovered because the uncle in his new ways of thinking has become a new man: "It will make a good wood-box, boy. And faithful old Yorpy can sell the old iron for tobacco-money." Yorpy comments on the new sanity of his master after the passing of the insanity of the slavery question: "Dear massa! dear old massa! dat be very fust time in de ten long 'ear yoo so kindly. Yoo is yourself agin in de gen long 'ear."

The conclusion of the story is far from the reading that R. H. Fogle gives it, a study in "the value of failure." On the contrary, it is a study in the value of success. The failure of the machine, mellowing and enlightening him, "made a good old man" of him. He is "glad" he failed. Melville's conclusion to this "Aesopian" story is a fervent prayer that America will understand the lesson. The failure of the old man—America's old way of thinking—made a wise man of the youngster. Example sufficed for experience. Melville's concluding paragraph is a projection of the future of America, peaceful *in toto*, with the former slave a faithful and useful member of society: "When some years had gone by, and my dear old uncle began to fail, and, after peaceful days of autumnal content, was gathered gently to his fathers—faithful old Yorpy closing his eyes—as I took my last look at his venerable face, the pale resigned lips seemed to move. I seemed to hear again his deep, fervent cry— "Praise be to God for the failure!"

"THE FIDDLER": "SOMETHING OF AN ORPHEUS"

"The Fiddler" (*Harper's*, September 1854) is in many ways the least satisfying of Melville's short stories. Stridently overstated, like "Cock-A-Doodle-Doo," it misleads the reader about the author's point.

It concerns itself with a foolish young versifier who thinks he writes immortal poetry but really composes trash. An egoist, he is snobbish, fatuous, and given to irrational extremes. He is a great deal like the early versifying Pierre. But unable to feed his egotism in this medium, he wants to throw away everything to become a fiddler, being taught by the prodigy Hautboy who is "something of an Orpheus," "*with* genius but *without* fame."

The story is then a study of the difference between feckless snobbishness and true genius, in a very narrow way another of Melville's many case studies of monomania as opposed to humanism. Helmstone, the versifier, is autocratic and condescending. To him, Hautboy, the true genius, has "average abilities." "Nothing tempts him beyond common limit; in himself he has nothing to restrain. By constitution he is exempted from all moral harm. Could ambition but prick him; had he but once heard applause, or endured contempt, a very different man would your Hautboy be." In a statement very similar to naive Clarel's feelings about Derwent's superficiality, Helmstone says of Hautboy, "Acquiscent and calm from the cradle to the grave, he obviously slides through the crowd." Helmstone thinks himself a giant standing among pygmies.

Hautboy, the real genius, is indeed very much a common fellow, as Melville stresses several times. "His person was short and full, with a juvenile, animated cast to it," Helmstone sneers, and "Genius, like Cassius, is lean." Hautboy delights in circuses and clowns. At the performance of the clown that he, Standard, and Helmstone attend, "his eye twinkled, his hand wavered, his voice was lifted in jubilant delight."

Hautboy and his two friends sit "among crowds" at the restaurant they dine at after the circus. And the crowd which Hautboy likes to be a part of approves of the clown's performance with "claps, thumps, deafening huzzas; the vast assembly seemed frantic with acclamation."

Melville turns Hautboy into Everyman at the end of the story by having Standard whisper his name to the incredulous Helmstone.

Melville seems, therefore, in every way to approve of Hautboy. One must therefore seriously consider the terms of approval even when voiced by Helmstone, who is generally a questionable observer. Hautboy has "deep good sense":

> Good sense and good humour in him joined hands.
> As the conversation proceeded between the brisk
> Standard and him . . . I was more and more struck
> with the excellent judgment he evinced. In most of his
> remarks upon a variety of topics Hautboy seemed
> intuitively to hit the exact line between enthusiasm
> and apathy. It was plain that while Hautboy saw the
> world pretty much as it was, yet he did not theoretically
> espouse its bright side nor its dark side. Rejecting
> all solutions, he but acknowledged facts. What was sad
> in the world he did not superficially gain-say; what
> was glad in it he did not cynically slur.

Melville makes it clear that every man must be his own
guide, his own genius, and should not be led off by Orpheus.
Though Helmstone says precisely this, he still forgets his
own advice and throws himself wholeheartedly under
Hautboy's tutelage. But Standard, the Rolfe-like man of
moderation, is Melville's model. Standard admires Hautboy
and recognizes his genius. But Standard has not become a
pupil of the genius. Helmstone, however, the immoderate,
the extremist, to whom something must be all or nothing,
casts away his past, tears up his manuscripts—his "genius"
of yesterday—to begin taking lessons from Hautboy tomorrow.

   Melville's disapproval of this extremism, here as
throughout his works, is clearly demonstrated.

"JIMMY ROSE": "GOD GUARD US ALL"

The anger, criticism, and affirmation in "Jimmy Rose"
(*Harper's*, November 1855) are so involuted that they
sometimes go undetected. Yet this story, like the poem
Clarel, which it resembles in scope of subject and development, contains in an epitome powerfully and artistically
crafted many of Melville's comments on the world.

   The setting is an old New York house built "ninety
years ago." In other words, in the 1760s, before the
American and French revolutions. Life is elegant,
commercial, crass, superficial, vapid. Jimmy Rose, the

most successful of the business men, is the most gentlemanly of all the gentlemen and lives in a world of elegance. He is also the most sycophantic of all. Jimmy's cliches are worse than anybody else's. The implication is that wealth, like power, corrupts, and absolute wealth corrupts absolutely, for it turns Jimmy Rose into a complete dandy. All the wealthy people are without ethics, religion, or morality. Jimmy is sought after while wealthy but despised and merely tolerated after he loses all his money.

The narrator of the story now lives in the house that Jimmy lived in before he lost his money. The rooms in the mansion still stand as they did before the fall, opulent throughout. One room in particular is noticeable because "the paper hangings were in the most gaudy style." It "could only have come from Paris—genuine Versailles paper—the sort of paper that might have hung in Marie Antoinette's boudoir." The decorations in the paper are "all rubies, diamonds, and Orders of the Golden Fleece." The gaudiness of these rooms rests on cellars that "were full of great grim, arched bins of blackened brick, looking like the ancient Tombs of Templars," and they were arched over by great timbers "so thickly ranked, that to walk in those capacious cellars was much like walking along a line-of-battle ship's gun-deck."

The political symbolism is clear. The room resting on this foundation represents the sensuality and wickedness of pre-Revolutionary France, planted on the tyranny and religious fervor of olden times and augmented by the weight of the club of the military. These were the comments Melville was making in various other works during these years, especially as they applied to the American scene. The gaudy room is divided by decay, as America was. "The north side of this old apartment presented a strange look: half mossy and half mildew, something as ancient forest trees on their north sides, to which particular side the moss most clings, and where, they say, internal decay first strikes." This is not the delightful north side of the house pictured in "The Piazza." Rather the political comment is

243

that on the American North that Melville made in *Mardi*, "The Tartarus of Maids," and "Benito Cereno," among other works.

There is also much social criticism. Here, as in "I and my Chimney," the voice of the people is represented by Biddy, the narrator's maid. The roses which divide the lozenges in the elegant room are to this commoner "onion." The peacocks on the wall paper with their "princely plumage" make the room look to Biddy like a "hen-house."

Melville's picture of this "internal decay" is amplified. After his fall from wealth Jimmy is at first hounded into hiding by his own shame, by indifferent former friends, and by vicious creditors. But after a proper period he emerges from hiding to beg crumbs at the rich men's tables. This story must be compared with "Rich Man's Crumbs," in which during a demonstration of English charity the wealthy feed the poor on scraps. But the wealthy in American cities, Melville urges, are just as vicious.

The viciousness of the situation is further demonstrated. Jimmy does not mind being treated as a beggar at the tables of the affluent. Worse yet, they find nothing personally degrading in treating one of their former equals or superiors in this demeaning fashion. Again, this is the American version of the scene in "Rich Man's Crumbs." In that story Melville makes it perfectly clear that the poor will eventually rise against their oppressors. In this story Melville makes it obvious that he is writing primarily about man's inhumanity to man; and buttressing his comments here, as he does later in *Billy Budd*, on the despotism of France before the revolution, he promises changes in this country.

Here as in the "Two Temples" Melville also uses religion very obviously to develop his story, drawing a clear distinction between proper use and vicious abuse of it.

After Jimmy's crash the narrator comes in from the country and tries to learn of his fate and whereabouts. But everybody seems indifferent to both. Finally the narrator locates one person who takes him "close to Trinity Church rail, out of the jostling of the crowd," and tells of Jimmy's living quarters. The symbolism seems clear. Not *in* the church because formal religion is indifferent to man's real needs, but close to it, and "out of the jostling of the crowd" because the crowd in their haste are likewise indifferent to the true meaning of religion. But Christ, as He preached about the good Samaritan, represented the true meaning of religion and human brotherhood.

Wealth's use and abuse of religion is made clear. When Jimmy Rose is dying the rich send him religious books and pamphlets as a solace. But although he accepted their condescension when he was well, now "whether it was repugnance at being considered next door to death, or whether it was but the natural peevishness brought on by the general misery of his state," he rebels against it. He pitches the books into the "furthest corner," and says of the girl who tends him in his last days, "Why will she bring me this sad old stuff? Does she take me for a pauper? Thinks she to salve a gentleman's heart with Poor Man's Plaster?" One is reminded of the incident in *Huckleberry Finn* when Boggs, having been shot by Colonel Sherburn, has a heavy Bible placed on his chest to insure his trip to heaven, but surely to kill him here.

Melville's main theme in the story is the brotherhood of man, as touched on in the paragraph where the narrator is finally directed to Jimmy Rose's house. In this story the brotherhood theme is more strengthened by religion than it is in many other stories. Though Jimmy Rose is badly abused by man, unlike the numerous monomaniacal haters in various other stories—Ungar in *Clarel* for example—he does not become a misanthrope: "Perhaps at bottom Jimmy was too thoroughly good and kind to be made from any cause a man-hater." But here as in other stories, religion supports a more important item. Therefore "doubtless it at last seemed irreligious to Jimmy even to shun mankind." Like Rolfe, again in *Clarel,* Jimmy Rose is the moderate

245

man who serves as the nexus between opposites, between the rich and the poor: "Though in thy own need thou hadst no pence to give the poor, thou, Jimmy, still hadst alms to give the rich. For not the beggar chattering at the corner pines more after bread than the vain heart after compliment. The rich in their craving glut, as the poor in their craving want, we have with us always."

Melville's comprehensive concern with man and God, or with God's protection of man, is manifest throughout in a *leitmotif* which occurs, set off each time as a separate paragraph, four times: "Poor, poor Jimmy—God guard us all—poor Jimmy Rose!" Though emphasis is placed on *God*, at least double emphasis weights on *us all*.

In this story, as in numerous others, Melville uses a kind of detached ending to conclude and emphasize his point. Here he hesitatingly mentions "one little incident connected" with Jimmy's death, that of Jimmy's throwing the religious books away, and then leads into his moral. The moral is an affirmation of humanism. Hope for mankind is symbolized in the young lady, the "lovely ministrant" who cares for Jimmy during his last illness. Though she is one of his many naifs and as such allows the wealthy to degrade Jimmy in his last moments, she is somewhat like the Chola widow in sketch eight of "The Encantadas," and is a good Samaritan and cares enough for mankind to help one of its members, even when he is lowly.

Melville broods on the closeness of the rich and poor, on the brotherhood of us all, and the ease with which one can change his status. Jimmy Rose sank from high to low apparently without much trouble and discontent. Melville says: "I still must meditate upon his strange example, whereof the marvel is, how after that gay, dashing, nobleman's career, he could be content to crawl through life, and peep about among the marbles and mahoganies for contumelious tea and toast, where once like a very Warwick he had feasted the huzzaing world with Burgundy and venison."

Finally, to tie together the several themes of the story, and to emphasize his hope in America as well as in Americans, Melville stands as the narrator at the end of the story in the "parlour of the peacocks," which is on the north side of the house and has been allowed to decay. As he looks at the "wilted resplendence of those proud peacocks" he thinks of the "withering change in Jimmy's once resplendent pride of state," and he receives consolation and hope from the "undying roses which bloomed in ruined Jimmy's cheek." In mankind, in America, in every one of us, "God grant that Jimmy's roses may immortally survive!"

"THE BELL-TOWER": LEVELS OF TYRANNY

"The Bell-Tower" (*Putnam's*, August 1855) is a rich, organ-toned, baroque story developing three levels of tyranny—that of the pride of the superman, that of the machine, and that of politics. In working out all three, Melville emphasizes, though subtly and obliquely in places, his firm affirmation of the importance of the human being. In style and references he calls on several authors, for example, Poe Shelley, and Milton. But he calls most importantly on Hawthorne, especially in "Ethan Brand," and—much more importantly—"The Artist of the Beautiful" and "The Prophetic Pictures."

Most overtly the story concerns itself with man and superman, with Prometheus and the Olympians, with God and a Miltonic Satan. In the beginning paragraph, remarkably similar to the steel-like irony of Shelley's "Ozymandias," Melville begins his sad picture of the inexorable wash of time. In "south Europe" (Italy), "nigh a once frescoed capital" stands "what, at distance, seems the black mossed stump of some immeasurable pine, fallen, in forgotten days, with Anak and the Titans." The story is clearly an abject lesson against man's presumption, as much as *Moby-Dick* is a direct statement against the folly of Ahab's. One of the three statements prefacing "The Bell-

247

Tower," given as "from a private MS," asserts: "The world is apoplectic with high-living of ambition; and apoplexy has its fall." The story is concluded with a framing statement in the swelling final paragraph: "And so pride went before the fall." The parallel with Hawthorne's "Ethan Brand," the theme of which is also pride going before a fall, is immediately evident.

Man's pride manifests itself in the ambition of Bannadonna, a machinist and architect, to build a high tower, a new tower of Babel. The time is ripe for a new assertion of man's ambition and of his presumed greatness. It is a "high hour of renovated earth, following the second deluge, when the waters of the Dark Ages had dried up, and once more the green appeared." Bannadonna, a Renaissance Ahab, determines to build a tower hitherto unequalled by man.

Bannadonna is clearly pictured as a superman. Like Celio, the monomaniac in *Clarel*, Ahab, Claggart and Billy in *Billy Budd*, and numerous other Melvillean creations, Bannadonna is a "foundling." The foundling is in Melville, as in folklore and mythology in general, supernaturally good or evil. Here, as with Jackson, Bland, and Claggart, he is supernaturally evil.

As the tower rises, "snail-like in pace but torch or rocket in its pride," so does Bannadonna's god-like egotism. He resembles Ahab who finds "something ever egotistical in mountain-tops and towers. . . The firm tower, that is Ahab." The religious people of the town throng to watch the building, and their "homage not the less inspirited him to self-esteem." After it is finished, Bannadonna stands atop it like a Miltonic Satan—or Ahab—challenging God, in a stance echoed numerous times later in *Clarel*—"Erect, alone, with folded arms, gazing upon the white summits of blue inland Alps . . . sights invisible from the plain." And he is applauded (worshipped) though, or because, he is invisible: "Invisible, too, from thence was that eye he turned below, when, like the cannon booms, came up to him the people's combustions of applause."

His sense of greatness has swollen into monomania by the time the tower is finished and the "state-bell" must be installed. The magistrates of the city admit that the tower is titanic but caution Bannadonna that the bell must be limited by "dependent weight of its swaying masses," must, in other words, be limited by the human aspect of creator and workmen. But the proud architect ignores this earthly counsel, designs a more ambitious bell, even creating his own religious symbols, announced by Melville as denting the bell with "mythological devices."

So great and heedless are his zeal and ferver that when the workmen are frightened by the design of Bannadonna's ambition and shrink from the titanic forces about to be unleashed—when the "unleashed metals . . . bayed like hounds"—the architect rushes in and slays the chief worker. Though Bannadonna is unrestrained in assuming that he can create life, he is indifferent to taking it. With the homicide, "From the smitten part, a splinter was dashed into the seething mass, and at once was melted in," thus flawing the bell with human weakness, of which Bannadonna was a part though he would not admit it. Melville here is emphasizing his great belief in humanism, that the human being is much more important than the machine ordering him around, and much more important than the bell and what it symbolizes. Further, Melville condemns those persons, especially those who work in the religious and supernatural, who try to hide their imperfections, as is developed in his sketch of the First Temple; Bannadonna working in secret, "suffered no one to attend him in these inspections, he concealed the blemish by some preparation which none knew better to devise."

The marvelous state-bell is to chime the hours with a wonderful apparatus and mechanism never before used. After the clock-work has been raised to the tower, a heavy object "wrapped in a dark sack or cloak," and which might be statue or living man, is drawn up. A "shrewd old black-smith"—the type of which we remember as a "man-maker" in *Moby-Dick*—who should know, "ventured the suspicion that it was but a living man." This figure is seated in a kind of temple on his throne ("It seemed now seated upon some sort of frame, or chair, contained with the domino."). The living creature, if that is what it is, has "nigh the top, in a sort of square, the web of the cloth, either from accident or design, had its warp partly withdrawn, and the cross threads plucked out here and there, so as to form a sort of woven grating." This is precisely the same kind of grating which in the First Temple covers a vent which leads directly to hell. Thus this creature, created by Satan, breathes hell-fire. The Renaissance creator has also placed near the figure a symbol which is ambiguous. There is an "earthen cup, partly corroded and partly encrusted,"which, according to the observers, might "in mockery, be offered to the lips of some brazen statute, or, perhaps, still worse." Thus Bannadonna might feed his ego by offering in mockery this earthen cup to the statute; or worse, he might offer the "partly encrusted" cup which would literally be drunk out of by the living creation!

Bannadonna is a pagan god. To counter his obvious devilish power and creation, his "Vulcanic face hiding its burning brightness like a forge," one of the junior magistrates, a "kind-hearted man" who is "troubled at what in him (Bannadonna) seemed a certain sardonical disdain," advances Christian sympathy, "surmising what might be the final fate of such a cynic solitaire." It is this junior magistrate who recognizes that Una, the figure representing the hour of one among the "gay girls, garlanded, hand-in-hand, danced in a choral ring—the embodied hours," cannot be a party to the duplicity of Bannadonna. The facial expression on Una, who in the *Fairie Queene* represents truth, proclaims a "fatal" end, as the junior magistrate recognizes.

Bannadonna in an unguarded moment forgets his humble station and reveals his feeling of superiority over the magistrates. The younger one recognizes the revelation, and remarks to his elder that Bannadonna "so superciliously replied, his walk seemed Sisera's, God's vain foe."

During the last night before the first exhibition of the mechanician's art, the devilish art is practiced further. There are sounds, "not only of some ringing implement, but also—so they said—half suppressed screams and plainings, such as might have issued from some ghostly engine, overplied."

Next day at one, the hour when the first stroke was to peal, only a mangled sound is heard. As the soldiers rush up to investigate the silence in the tower, a spaniel follows and "stood shivering as before some unknown monster in a brake; or rather, as if it snuffed footsteps leading to some other world." The spaniel, which in folklore ordinarily represents the devil in dog form, is apparently frightened at the domino which "had limbs, and seemed clad in a scaly mail, lustrous as a dragon-beetle's." The figure of Banna-donna is lying at the feet of Una, the first hour. The shivering spaniel introduces two possible symbols. One is that Bannadonna, a creative devil, built a Frankenstein monster that not only destroyed him but was also capable of frightening the devil himself. The other is that the figure is a devil, and the spaniel, as in "Ethan Brand," senses his presence and reacts. There is no doubt that the domino is a devil, because when shot with an arquebuss, from it "thin wreaths of smoke were curling." The rehooded figure is taken out to sea and buried. The mystery of the whole business leads people to think that the fate of Bannadonna was caused by supernatural means. Melville agrees. It is another of his numerous statements of belief in the people which drives him to agree with the only explanation which "tradition has explicitly preserved." To strengthen his bias, he sneeringly comments that "some few less unscientific minds pretended to find little difficulty in otherwise accounting for it."

From watching the function of conventional bells, Bannadonna got his first intimations of monomania. For

"Pearched on a great mast or spire, the human figure, viewed from below, undergoes such a reduction in its apparent size, as to obliterate his intelligent features. It evinces no personality." But Bannadonna had determined that his creation would possess "the appearance, at least, of intelligence and will." His enterprises stopped not, however, on the creation of a good machine. He proceeded from "comparatively pygmy aims to Titanic ones." He tried in fact to create "the universal conveniences and glories of humanity; supplying nothing less than a supplement to the Six Days' work." In his creation, "All excellences of all God-made creatures, which served man, were here to receive advancement, and then to be combined in one."

It was decreed that the great state-bell should be rung at Bannadonna's funeral. A "powerful peasant, who had the bell-rope in charge, wishing to test at once the full glory of the bell, had swayed down upon the rope with one con-centrate jerk," and dragged it from its fastening. Here there is a direct assault upon the appearance of the supernatural, as there was in *Israel Potter* when the clod advances with his pitchfork and threatens the eyes of the "supernatural" scarecrow. Bannadonna's bell tumbled and "buried itself inverted and half out of sight." This inversion is of course a parody of the proper order, and this parody is substantiated in the following lines, when Melville points out that the presumption of Bannadonna in trying to become something he is not, that of aspiring toward the superhuman, is revealed by the fact that "upon dis-interment, the main fracture was found to have started from a small spot in the ear; which, being scraped, revealed a defect, deceptively minute, in the casting; which defect must subsequently have been pasted over with some unknown compound." Thus man, Melville seems to be saying, although he may mask and cover his defects, cannot escape from his humanity.

This criticism, significantly, Melville had leveled against Emerson upon first hearing him lecture: "I could readily see in Emerson, notwithstanding his merit, a gaping flaw. It was the insinuation that had he lived in those days when the world was made, he might have offered some valuable suggestions. These men are cracked right across the brow. And never will the pullers-down be able to cope with the builders-up." [9]

This story closely parallels various aspects developed by Hawthorne. The spaniel that sensed the living devilish soul of Talus is from the same litter as the dog in "Ethan Brand." But the similarity to two other Hawthorne stories is closer—"The Artist of the Beautiful" and "The Prophetic Pictures." In the former, to examine it first, Owen Warland, the creator of things of beauty, builds a clock on which "he would take upon himself to arrange a dance or funeral procession of figures across its venerable face, representing twelve mirthful or melancholy hours." Failing in his efforts to create beautiful things, he becomes, like Bannadonna, a master of the utilitarian. He is "invited by the proper church authorities to regulate the clock in the church steeple," and in this job succeeds completely. "The heavy weight upon his spirits kept everything in order, not merely within his own system, but wheresoever the iron accents of the church clock were audible." He finally creates a beautiful butterfly which seems to possess life, and might have been even more successful, and earlier, but for the "clogs" imposed upon him by mere plebeian craftsmen, such as the blacksmith. Warland's butterfly almost absorbed his "own being into itself." But it was destroyed by the overenthusiastic grasp of a child.

Another apparently influential work was "The Prophetic Pictures." The artist in this story, a European, some people thought offended "against the mosaic law" and even indulged in "a presumptuous mockery of the Creator to bring into existence such lively images of his creatures. Others, frightened at the art which could raise phantoms at will, and keep the form of the dead among the living, were

9. Merrell E. Davis and William H. Gilman, *The Letters of Herman Melville* (New Haven, 1960), p. 79.

inclined to consider the painter as a magician, or perhaps the famous Black Man, of old witch times, plotting mischief in a new guise. These foolish fancies were more than half believed among the mob." Several other paragraphs of this story are relevant.

> "The old women of Boston affirm," continued he [Ludlow] "that after he has once possession of a person's face and figure, he may paint him in any act or situation whatever—and the picture will be prophetic."
> Like all other men around whom an engrossing purpose wreathes itself, he was insulated from the mass of human kind. He had no aim—no pleasures—no sympathies—but what were ultimately connected with his art. Though gentle in manner and upright in intent and action, he did not possess kindly feelings; his heart was cold; no living creature could be brought near enough to keep him warm.

Hawthorne's conclusions are as explicit as Melville's: "Is there not a deep moral in the tale? Could the result of one, or all our deeds, be shadowed forth and set before us, some would call it Fate, and hurry onward, others be swept along by their passionate desires, and none be turned aside by the Prophetic Pictures." The artist might insist " 'O glorious Art!' thus mused the enthusiastic painter as he trod the street, 'thou art the image of the Creator's own.'" But Hawthorne's feeling is infinitely less egotistical and more humanistic: "It is not good for man to cherish a solitary ambition. Unless there be those around him by whose example he may regulate himself, his thoughts, desires, and hopes will become extravagant, and be the semblance, perhaps the reality, of a madman."

Bannadonna had created a face that was prophetic though he was so blinded by his monomania that he could not read the prophecy in Una's face. But Bannadonna was on purpose tinkering with creation.

The second strand in the rope of the story is that of the tyranny of the machine over man, developed here as especially in "The Tartarus of Maids." As Charles A. Fenton in "The Bell-Tower: Melville and Technology"[10] suggests, this story is a study of the relationship of the technological revolution of the 19th century and man. Melville is here keenly aware of the analogy between rising America and other risen nations of the past; this awareness informs other such stories as "The Happy Failure," "Jimmy Rose," and others.

As Fenton says, Bannadonna is enabled to build his tower because his state is "enriched through commerce." The workmen who are casting the bell are terrified by the power of the machine they are using, and consequently panic. But Bannadonna, more interested in the result than in the condition of the laborers, strikes one. Industry forgives him. Bannadonna despises metaphysicians. Instead, he is "a practical materialist," and believes that all power lies in "plain vice-bench and hammer":

> "In short, to solve nature, to steal into her, to intrigue beyond her, to procure some one else to bind her to his hand;—these, one and all, had not been his objects; but, asking no favors from any element or any being, of himself, to rival her, outstrip her, and rule her. He stooped to conquer. With him, common sense was the urge; machinery, miracle; Prometheus, the heroic name for machinist; man, the true God."

As we have noted, "what seemed his fancifulness was but his utilitarian ambition collaterally extended." The figure he created was "an original production."

The mechanism Bannadonna creates in the belfry is intricate a "cunning mechanism." The domino will issue from a sentry-box every sixty minutes, "sliding along a grooved way, like a railway; advancing to the clock-bell, with uplifted manacles; striking it at one of the twelve junctions of the four-and-twenty hands; then wheeling, circling the bell, and retiring to its post, there to bide for another sixty minutes, when the same process was to be repeated."

10. *American Literature* 23 (1951) p. 220.

When the domino is shot by the arquebuss there is a striking resemblance both to the terribly intricate mechanism of the invention in "The Happy Failure," and to the terrible impotence and evil of the swords in "The Tartarus of Maids"; there is a "report, followed by a fierce whiz, as of the sudden snapping of a main-spring, with a steely din, as if a stack of sword-blades should be dashed upon a pavement." Most terrifying, of course, is the inevitability of the working of the machine once it is set in motion, with its grooves oiled, its course infallibly set. The creature "true to its creation, and true to its heedful winding up, left its post precisely at the given moment," and "not oblivious" of Bannadonna struck and killed him. Thus the machine, once created, takes a nature and morality unto itself and wilfully destroys its creator. In "The Tartarus of Maids" the similarity is close. As Melville describes the assembly-line: "Not a syllable was breathed. Nothing was heard but the low, steady overruling hum of the iron animals. The human voice was banished from the spot. Machinery—that vaunted slave of humanity—here stood menially served by human beings, who served mutely and cringingly as the slave serves the Sultan. The girls did not so much seem accessory wheels to the general machinery as mere cogs to the wheels." These factory workers are "so many mares haltered to the rack."

The third strand—the political tyranny—is of course inextricably woven into that aspect of the social criticism discussed above.

"The Bell-Tower" is a close examination of political responsibility and the consequences of political irresponsibility. More narrowly it is a study of the American political scene and of Melville's apprehensions and fears about the future in this country, especially during the decades which lay immediately ahead. The story is like *1984* and other futuristic novels which paint the picture of what might happen if politics fall into the hands of irresponsible leaders. The very style of the story in its slow-paced, Poesque sledge-hammer pounding beats out with irresistible force the lesson of tyranny. No other story by Melville—not the grandiloquent rhetoric of *Moby-Dick* or the danse macabre bareness of "The Lightning-Rod Man," which it closely resembles—so appropriately fits the message as that in this work.

R. H. Fogle in his *Melville's Shorter Tales* has hinted at the similarity of Bannadonna to the wider problem of dictatorship. But Melville's concern was both more profound and more immediate than Fogle suggests. It is clear from the introductory words prefixed to the story, in the "private MS," that this story is another chapter of the problem Melville had been examining in "Benito Cereno," which he had submitted to *Putnam's Monthly* only some two months before sending this story to the same magazine. In the earlier work Melville had examined the relationship between the despotism of the Old World—symbolized by Spain—and the commercial and human despotism of the New World—epitomized in New England shipping interests and Southern slavery. The Negro in the New World was caught in the same mesh of forces that had always held most people in the bonds of slavery. These forces were almost beyond the correction of the citizens of the New World who practiced them. But "the Negro," as Benito Cereno admitted, was the cause of his destruction—signifying rebellion against the Old World—and as slave, threatened to precipitate the destruction of the New. Melville could only conclude that the problem of "the Negro" had to be resolved. America, the land of Columbus, symbolized the land of hope for the future of all mankind. But the promise in this country to a certain extent had died a-borning.

In "The Bell-Tower" Melville returns to another time and another land of great promise. The land is Italy, the time the Renaissance, "the high hour of renovated earth, following the second deluge, when the waters of the Dark Ages had dried up, and once more the green appeared. No wonder that, after so long and deep a submersion, the jubilant expectation of the race should, as with Noah's sons, soar into Shinar aspiration." Overlying the Old World is America, the land rich in expectation.

In this country "the Negro" symbolizes the slave, "Benito Cereno" pictures what happens when slaves revolt. Led by the powerful intellect of Babo, they mutiny and revenge themselves by killing half of the whites on the *San Dominick*. The introductory words of "The Bell-Tower" tie this story in with the earlier: "Like negroes, these powers own man sullenly; mindful of their higher master; while serving, plot revenge." The name given by Bannadonna to his mechanical monster at first is Haman, as thin a disguise as possible for the Biblical name of Ham, the father of the Negro race. In these introductory words, as in the earlier story, Melville seems to be saying that slaves everywhere and at all times owe it to a "higher master" to rebel against enslavement.

In this context the other two quoted sentences from the "private MS" are significant. The first says, "The world is apoplectic with high-living of ambition; and apoplexy has its fall." This is then a plea against over-ambition. The next extract is even more of a caution and plea: "Seeking to conquer a larger liberty, man but extends the empire of necessity." Though a seeming declarative statement, the sentence is more a hopeful prayer, a prayer for man to transcend his pygmy nature and grow to the possibilities of his birthright.

"The Bell-Tower" is then, like Hawthorne's "The Prophetic Pictures," and other stories, and like Melville's works in general, a plea for the development of democracy and an affirmation of humanism. Bannadonna tried to atomize and disintegrate society, as is symbolized by the fact that he created the giant and directed him to strike the hours—the continuum of time, the past, present and future—where the hands joined, thus destroying society and brotherly love.

In order to point up the significance of Talus' destruction of Bannadonna, Melville says that what happened after the killing is uncertain. Thus Melville is resorting to his

usual technique, used in "Benito Cereno," *Billy Budd,*
and in other works, of universalizing, of broadcasting to
the world at large.

"I AND MY CHIMNEY": THE ANTIC POSE

"I and My Chimney" (*Putnam's,* March 1856) is in many
ways the least satisfactory of the stories that Melville felt
should be preserved. It is too long and rambling, and,
perhaps more important, its meanings are difficult to
fathom because they are imprecisely delineated.

Biographical explanations for the story have been
forwarded. R. H. Fogle says that it reveals Melville
"fighting to preserve what is best in himself and his
life's work at a time when it seems to be threatened
seriously."[11] Various critics, including Jay Leyda, have
explained at least one episode, that of searching for the
treasure in the chimney, as the examination of Melville
by Dr. Oliver Wendell Holmes the preceding year.[12] Both
explanations and lines of inquiry fail to develop various
rather obvious lines of progression.

The story involves an old conservative man and the
gigantic chimney that monopolizes the center of a country
house. Both man and chimney are content with things as
they are and resist change. The narrator has an active wife
here, as in "Jimmy Rose" and "The Apple-Tree Table," and
two daughters, as in the latter story. Determined to renovate
and therefore improve the house, these people go through
various exercises, and try to use several deceits to get the
chimney removed, even to bringing in and bribing an
architect to say that there is treasure in the chimney. But
all fail. At the end the conservative owner of the house
declares, "I and my chimney will never surrender."

The story is a gigantic symbol, that of the chimney as a
block to progress. That the chimney means more than the
one which, coincidentally, happened to be at Arrowhead
while Melville was writing the story seems manifest. In

11. Fogle, *Melville's Shorter Tales,* p. 78.
12. Leyda, *Log,* 2:502-3.

Moby-Dick, written also at Arrowhead, Melville had used the same kind of chimney. At the Spouter-Inn, where Ishmael begins his education into humanism, Melville describes precisely the same chimney, which had been cut through to allow progress: Ishmael describes how "Crossing this dusky entry, and on through yon low-arched way—cut through what in old times must have been a great central chimney with fireplace all round—you enter the public room" (CH. III).

The short story signifies a conflict between conservatism and liberalism. It fairly bristles with political references. The narrator and his chimney symbolize unchanging, even stupid, political attitudes, and the wife obviously represents the urge to change. By slight extension the story represents the conflict between America and England in particular, and such opposing points of view in general. It may be extreme to say that Melville had particular individuals in mind in this conflict, such people as Tom Paine as American liberal and Edmund Burke as English conservative. Yet Hiram Scribe so clearly typifies Burke, or the popular conception of him, and the name so patently sounds like the popular idea of Burke's renting his pen to support royalty, and the wife so clearly talks like a female Tom Paine, that Melville could easily have had the Burke-Paine controversy in mind. He would surely have been familiar with this conflict from his general knowledge, as numerous references throughout his works indicate. If he did have this political conflict in mind, then Melville advocates the opposite of what he seems to foster, and in showing the intransigence of the narrator clearly reveals how he must and will lose his monomaniacal attachment.

In the light of this interpretation the story becomes a clear statement, like "Benito Cereno," about the proper political attitude for people who are deeply concerned about the condition of man in this world.

The story begins with the ornate embroidery of conservatism. The narrator says, "'*I and my chimney,*' as

Cardinal Wolsey used to say, 'I and my King.'" But his taking precedence over his chimney "is hardly borne out by the facts; in everything, except the above phrase, my chimney taking precedence of me." "In the presence of my betters," he says, "I hope I know my place." His chimney is a "huge, corpulent old Harry VIII. of a chimney." It "receives the first-fruits of the season." It is his superior, which he ministers to, but it never ministers or inclines to him. It is the "grand seignior—the one great domineering object" of the house.

Such statements can hardly be taken straight from the pen of Melville. The man who while writing *Moby-Dick* only six years earlier was telling Hawthorne about how furiously democratic he was, the man who in *Israel Potter*, published the year before, admired the king as a person but despised him as a symbol, the same person who throughout his writing attacked aristocracy and royalty in various short stories—this man could hardly be saying here and expecting us to believe that the chimney is his superior, that in the presence of his betters he knows his place.

The political symbolism strikes close to a picture of America during the 1850's, the time of the threatened schism over slavery. "In those houses," Melville says,

> which are strictly double houses—that is, where the hall is in the middle—the fireplaces usually are on opposite sides; so that while one member of the household is warming himself at a fire built into a recess of the north wall, say another member, the former's own brother, perhaps, may be holding his feet to the blaze before a hearth in the south wall—the two thus fairly sitting back to back. Is this well? Be it put to any man who has a proper fraternal feeling. Has it not a sort of sulky appearance? But very probably this style of chimney building originated with some architect afflicted with a quarrelsome family.

Though mildly stated this attitude is precisely Melville's during the days before and during the Civil War. Before the split over slavery he hoped it would not occur. During and after the war, he prayed that the South, though wrong, would be welcomed back into the nation and the reunited country could march ahead.

Melville further demonstrates that the tide of history is against his single chimney.

> Almost every modern fireplace has its separate flue— separate throughout, from hearth to chimney-top . . . . Does not this look egotistical, selfish? But still more, all these separate flues, instead of having independent masonry establishments of their own, or instead of being grouped together in one federal stock in the middle of the house—instead of this, I say, each flue is surreptitiously honey-combed into the walls, so that the last are here and there, or indeed almost anywhere treacherously hollow, and, in consequence, more or less weak.

Though Melville seems to condemn these individualized flues and chimneys, he is in fact approving of them. He demonstrates this approbation by his comparison. These flues are built to "economise room." In cities, that is in the modern world, "where lots are sold by the inch," people must adjust to their surroundings.

Against his approbation of modernity Melville pits, with ironic seeming approval, symbols of the old political order and despotism. That "stylish gentleman, Louis Le Grand of France," built a palace for his "lady friend, Madame de Maintenon" at Versailles. He was indifferent to the need to economise, and built the house "spacious, and broad—horizontal acres, not vertical ones." The political contrast is high-lighted: "Any man can buy a square foot of land and plant a liberty-tree on it; but it takes a king to set apart whole acres for a Grand Trianon."

His irony continues. His house, like the Grand Trianon, is built in open country. Unlike the situation in the city, where people aspire towards heaven, and in doing so try to outreach their neighbors, country people spread out. All common people, farmers, have room to move around.

Although they seem indifferent to Christ's maxim about caring for the mustard seed, they all prosper, the crops as well as the weeds. "As for grass, every spring it is like Kossuth's rising of what he calls the peoples." This political reference, like that in *Billy Budd* to Anacharsis Clootz's "parliament of the world," reveals Melville's real purpose in the story.

The architect of the chimney was a conservative. He "must have had the pyramid of Cheops before him," for the chimney is modeled after that structure. But the chimney has had to be altered because of the exigencies of time. The roof became leaky and some temporary proprietor sawed off the roof and replaced it with a modern one, "more fit for a railway wood-house than an old country gentleman's abode." Beheading the chimney, Melville says, was "a regicidal act, which, were it not for the palliating fact that he was a poulterer by trade, and, therefore, hardened to such neck-wrings, should send that former proprietor down to posterity in the same care with Cromwell." Melville is obliquely condemning his narrator's point of view. In "The Apple-Tree Table," published only two months after this story, he satirizes the uninquiring mind by stating that the attic of the house of Calvinism had not been investigated for years because the "roof was well slated, and thoroughly tight." Conversely, he is demonstrating that leaky roofs, that is, political ideologies, must be modified to fit occasions. Melville's sentiments lay more with Cromwell than with Charles I, whom he overthrew. Melville's feelings, as well as the topical nature of the story, are emphasized in the next paragraph, when he asserts that his chimney "as a free citizen of this free land, stands upon an independent basis of its own."

The alteration of the chimney, mentioned above, brought dire consequences. "The chimney, though of a vigorous constitution, suffered not a little, from so naked an exposure; and, unable to acclimate itself, ere long began to fail—showing blotchy symptoms akin to those in measles." Though Melville has before been talking about politics in general, here he particularizes England. "I've often thought that the proper place for my old chimney is ivied old England," because that country to him generally equated with aristocracy, kings, and tyranny. Thus, the narrator reveals that his chimney is not suited for democratic America. Increasingly, in fact, it becomes clear that the chimney not only represents conservative order, but in fact represents the British constitution.

Melville's pose about "old myself, I take to oldness in things," is so palpably absurd and a contradiction of his real feelings that it is silly to accept it as being anything but ironic. He loves "old cheese, and old wine," and this can be sensible enough. But these statements must be contrasted with his opposing hates, in which he catalogues "eschewing young people, hot rolls, new books, and early potatoes." Such a listing is frontier exaggeration given as an obvious tipoff to the comicality of the whole listing.

The narrator's wife is just opposite to the man, She is forever wanting new things. She is forever hopeful, "liking Swedenborgianism and the Spirit Rapping philosophy." It is useful to note that this woman is exactly the opposite of the wife in "The Apple-Tree Table," who hates the mysteries; here she loves it. Melville, always the broad humanist, was saddened by the struggle between science and religious faith, believing that there is not much in the world that science cannot explain.

The wife tells the narrator that she should take over and manage his affairs. She is paralleling American cocksuredness and its commitment to manifest destiny. She proposes that the narrator, like Charles V, retire. It should be remembered that when in "Benito Cereno," Melville refers to Charles V, it is to point out how cowardly he was. The narrator's wife is then demonstrating that he is cowardly, weak, negative, and therefore should step out of the way of progress.

Progress, according to the wife, demands that a tunnel be built through the chimney which would extend back to the dining room where travelers could be given food. The figure is exactly the same as in *Moby-Dick* at the Spouter-Inn, where a passage-way has apparently been cut through a large chimney thus allowing entrance into the area of sociability and fraternizing, the bar and dining room. The wife next wants to extend her alterations to the second floor and the attic. Even the husband admits that the wife has a point: "Perhaps there was some small ground for her discontent with things as they were. The truth is, there was no regular passage-way up stairs or down, unless we again except that little orchestra-gallery before mentioned."

Then the narrator reveals the inadequacy of his own thinking and of the house he so treasured:

> The consequence was, almost every room, like a philosophical system, was in itself an entry, or passage-way to other rooms, and systems of rooms— a whole suite of entries, in fact. Going through the house, you seem to be forever going somewhere, and getting nowhere. It is like losing one's self in the woods; round and round the chimney you go, and if you arrive at all, it is just where you started, and so you begin again, and again get nowhere. Indeed— though I say it not in the way of fault-finding at all— never was there so labyrinthine an abode.

So complex was the house that guests sometimes perforce tarried for "several weeks" because they were unable to find their way around in the house.

The described philosophical system is by analogy a political system, and in the light of the numerous references to England must be viewed as the British constitutional maze that though defended stoutly by its proponents, Edmund Burke being an excellent case in point, was roundly criticized and condemned by opponents, Tom Paine, for example.

The wife is one of the two important persons in the story. Generally the feeling, suggested by the story teller, is that she is a shrew, and the plague of the narrator's life as well as that of ours. But in truth she is merely the extreme of a sensible point of view. Here, as he had done in "Cock-A-Doodle-Doo," Melville is exaggerating in order to be emphatic. It is the wife who first notices and insists that the chimney be corrected before it burns the house down. The foolishness of the narrator is made clear when he insists: " 'Wife,' said I, 'far better that my house should burn down, than that my chimney should be pulled down.' " Here the political implications are plain. And indeed increasingly it becomes clear that what we have here is the American Revolution all over again. The narrator is a Tory, arguing all the Tory arguments. The wife is a radical, a Tom Paine, insisting on complete separation from England. This parallel becomes increasingly clear in the story. The narrator is willing to repair only those parts insisted upon by the mortgagee. In other words, he is sticking only to expediency. In precisely the way politicians did—Burke, for example—he calls upon precedent and buttresses his position on various types of history— classical, biblical, and druidical.

The narrator will reluctantly do what expediency demands, but he wants his changes to go unnoticed. When he is caught in the basement puttering away at the base of the chimney, he does not want to admit that he has been digging. To admit that would be to evidence that there might be need for change. And even to admit the possibility would be to invite changes.

As the Tories and Anglophiles said about the English Constitution during the American Rebellion and especially during the French Revolution—which Melville discussed in *Israel Potter* and at least touched on in *Billy Budd*— the whole was more than the sum of the parts. And "an adequate conception of the magnitude of the chimney" can be arrived at only through an act of the spirit, by osmosis, by a process "in the higher mathematics."

In a burlesque which is a *reductio ab absurdum*, Melville justifies the chimney by talking of the comfort it brings. When people are sitting around it or sleeping around it, they all face the center, or have their feet to the middle. Then, as Iroquois Indians in the woods are protected from the wild animals by the fire around which they sleep, so are the sleepers in this building protected, but not by the fire; they are protected because no burglar would enter a house from whose chimney issues such smoke! In other words the contents of this house are protected by the impenetrable fog cloaking them.

The narrator is willing to admit that the chimney is an inconvenience. "Were it not so mighty in its magnitude, my chambers had been larger." But whereas he is unwilling to give up seeming security for comfort, his wife is not. She recognizes her husband's weakness. Her tone and references are significant. The chimney "like the English aristocracy," casts a contracting shade all round it," and from its contracting shade all kinds of domestic inconveniences arise. Here she represents not only the modern man of progress, but also the American. The English Constitution plainly got in the way of "domestic" progress. She would do something about the situation; he would merely excuse its presence.

Melville goes to great length to describe the house around the chimney. What he describes is in fact the Houses of Parliament in England, with the King's private and "mysterious" chamber just off the Commons. The narrator's use of "mysterious" demonstrates how addled he is, like his silly eggs.

That the story represents the conflict between England and America is seen in the contrast between the narrator and his wife. She may not know much about architecture—a charge leveled against the political architects of America— but she is energetic. She is as old as her husband is: thus America is geologically as old as England. Both she and he come of an afflicted family (the sons of man); but being an American she is young in spirit and energy. She fills England with consternation. Further she wants to break away from conservative English thinking. She believes in the newness of America, its freedom from English oldness. Therefore, her maxim is "Whatever is, is wrong." She is a projector, a planner, a looker into the future. She should have been the wife of Peter the Great, the narrator chides. In other words, Melville is saying that she could have prevented the revolution against Peter by moderating his despotic control over his country. She does not believe in her own end, but in the everlastingness of America.

Melville is not blindly sympathetic to this American. He examines her faults as well as the narrator's. He chides her for impatience "of present and past," here stressing, as he did in numerous stories, that people cannot live without awareness of the past, one of the strictest criticisms he leveled against Thoreau. But the rightness of her point of view is emphasized when Melville describes the great bewilderment that ensues when guests try to find their way to their chambers—their proper living positions. To direct them by finger-posts—that is, clear pointers—could look queer; "and just as queer in him to be knocking at every door on his route, like London's city guest, the king, at Temple Bar." The wife decides because of the chimney's aspects to abolish it. The husband protests: "To take out the back-bone of anything, wife, is a hazardous affair. Spines out of books, and chimneys out of houses, are not to be taken like frosted lead-pipes from the ground. Besides the chimney is the one grand permanence of this abode. If undisturbed by innovators, then in future ages, when all the house shall have crumbled from it, this chimney will still survive—a Bunker Hill monument." Here are obvious political overtones. This is a parallel to the English argument over their Constitution, which was the only real aspect of their continuity as a political unity. Just as Bunker Hill monument stood as the American symbol of freedom, so here Bunker Hill is the equivalent of 1688 in England, which in the Restoration was a monument to English freedom.

An architect is called in to consider redoing the chimney. Significantly, his name denotes his character: Hiram Scribe, definitely an expedient, is for hire.

Automatically one thinks of Edmund Burke, or the popular image of him. Scribe finds the chimney not only ugly but expensive. He says it seems that the house was built for the convenience of the chimney, not vice versa—in other words, the nation exists for the convenience of the constitution, not the other way around.

Scribe is at first chased away. But half convinced that the chimney should be removed, the narrator again calls the architect, who says that he will destroy the chimney for $500. Like King George, the narrator sees that expediency demands that he thinks about changing the constitution. But he decides that he cannot go forward with the alterations.

Taunted beyond endurance, his wife and daughters decide upon other approaches. The wife knows that her husband might be susceptible to bribe. So she has Scribe hint that probably the chimney contains treasure. The husband agrees for a while. Politically here is the English liberal's appeal to the king to alter the government of America in order to keep the colonies because their presence is a source of great wealth. But the narrator is too obstinate to brood long on the alteration. He thinks his family is taking advantage of his credulity, but he does agree to have Scribe come again for further examination. First, however, he writes a letter refusing his offer to locate the treasure.

Scribe is obviously a tinkerer, a destroyer. In figuring out the dimensions of the chimney he did not include all calculations. Therefore when he demonstrates that the chimney must contain secret closets, he is easily tripped up by the more conservative owner, who points out that there must be room for walls, etc. Scribe demonstrates his lack of philosophical conviction by the fact that for money he will do anything, even sign a note saying that there is no treasure in the chimney. He does sign such a note. There is an obvious parallel with Edmund Burke, who was also an expedient.

But this does not satisfy the wife and daughters, who engage in eternal tapping of the chimney to expose its hollowness. Then Melville makes a significant reference: "Not more ruthlessly did the Three Powers partition away poor Poland, than my wife and daughters would fain partition away my chimney." But in partitioning "poor Poland," the Three Powers acted or thought they acted in the best interest.

The narrator's defense of conservatism continues: "Infinite mischief has resulted from the profane bursting open of secret recesses." What he is saying is that what was good enough for my father is good enough for me. Why examine a system when it seems to work? The universalizing political implications of the battle between progress and lack of progress are made clear when the narrator clearly outlines his and his wife's positions: "She is incessantly . . . besetting me with her terrible alacrity for improvement, which is a softer name for destruction." But he admits that nobody understands his attitude: "The truth is, my wife, like all the rest of the world, cares not a fig for my philosophical jabber."

The narrator will die fighting change. But Melville demonstrates that change must come. The wife and daughters, as well as the neighbors, as well as a "meddlesome architectural reformer, who, because he had no gift for putting up anything, was ever intent upon pulling down." And even others connived continually to destroy or renovate the chimney. The narrator cannot leave the house for a minute because once he did and returned to discover somebody on the chimney tearing away the bricks.

The narrator's obstinacy is so blind and extreme that Melville obviously means him as a study in stupidity. He resolves not to give an inch, will not allow any reform; therefore the only thing for those who will not relent is to destroy. Instead of needed gradual change, this man is causing total extermination. The man is so different from Melville's own attitude of moderation, of belief in the merit of the demands of antagonists, that clearly Melville disapproves of him. Though the wife and daughters—and

others—may be extreme in their demands, they have some
rights. In blindly resisting all modernization, he will
cause total destruction.

"THE APPLE-TREE TABLE":
SCIENCE AND RELIGION

"The Apple-Tree Table" (*Putnam's*, May 1856) is another
of Melville's many examinations of the essential nature
and validity of religion. The questions of man's death,
resurrection, and immortality were very much on Melville's
mind during these years. Though Hawthorne reported that
Melville had "pretty much made up his mind to be an-
nihilated," he was, as Bezanson has said, a compulsive
mythmaker, trying to create a heaven and God where he
was afraid none existed. Honesty drove him, however, to
examine the possibilities.

The original version of the story was in Dwight's
Travels in New England and New York, which in his
essay "Hawthorne and His Mosses" Melville says he
read. But probably a more immediate and profound
stimulus for Melville's writing his version of the story was
Thoreau's *Walden*. The easy optimism of Transcendentalism
was being closely studied by Melville during these years, in
The Confidence-Man, in "Cock-A-Doodle-Doo," and various
other works. Generally Melville's conclusions were derogatory
and negative. But he condemned only after impartial and
wide examination. Thus, though the easy optimism of *Walden*
stimulated the criticism in this story, the "Sunday" chapter
in *A Week on the Concord and Merrymack Rivers*, which
Melville borrowed from his friend Evert Duyckinck in 1850,
influenced its development, as William Braswell has demonstrated.[13] Thoreau, in this chapter, is skeptical of conventions
and of the narrowness and bigotry of Christianity and of
Christians. He pleads for universality in religious attitudes,
employing, as we shall see, some of the phraseology that
Melville, often a flagrant borrower of other authors' terminology,
later uses.

13. William Braswell, *Melville's Religious Thought* (Durham, N.C., 1943) p. 16.

"The Apple-Tree Table" involves substantially the same characters as the stories "Jimmy Rose" and "I and My Chimney." There are a rather eccentric, passive husband brow-beaten by his aggressive, realistic, shrewish wife, two daughters who are overly superstitious, and a democratic Irish Catholic maid named Biddy. The husband discovers an old table in the garret of his house and brings it down to the parlor. Soon he hears ticking sounds coming from the table, and eventually two beautiful insects emerge, to the consternation of all members of the household. A naturalist is brought in to examine one of the insects and explain the appearance, and he gives a reasonable and natural explanation. Neither of the insects survives; one is burned by Biddy and the other quickly dies and is embalmed by the two daughters. The story is, however, richer than this synopsis reveals.

It is foremost an examination of religion in general and of Calvinism in particular. The setting is an "old garret of a very old house in an old-fashioned quarter of one of the oldest towns in America." Clearly this age reaches back almost to the beginning of time. The religion of this age-old house needs no examination. It is as good now as in its pristine days: "The roof was . . . thoroughly tight." Further, authority discourages examination. "The company that insured the house, waived all visitation of the garret," since there is sufficient room below to accommodate all kinds of living. The key to the doorway leading above is lost, to further discourage seekers. Finally, the attic is sacrosanct: the garret is said to be haunted.

By chance—which as usual plays an important role in Melville's works—the narrator discovers a "rusty old key," and ascends to the attic. Significantly the garret "embraced the entire area of the mansion." The setting is strongly similar to that in the short story "The First Temple." There are "innumerable cobwebs" everywhere and "on every hand, some strange insect was seen, flying, or running, or creeping, on rafter and floor." This is clearly one level of the supernatural, the superstitious only, the lowest rung of the ladder of belief of God. The narrator ascends to the higher level on a "Gothic pulpit-stairway, leading to a pulpit-like platform from which a still narrower ladder—a sort of Jacob's ladder—led somewhat higher to the lofty scuttle." This situation, reminiscent of Father Mapple's ascent to his private pulpit in *Moby-Dick*, is a strong parallel with the setting in the First Temple from which the narrator in that sketch views man and his concept of God. Here, as in the earlier sketch, there is this "scuttle," the slide of which is about "two feet square, all in one piece, furnishing a massive frame for a single small pane of glass, inserted into it like a bull's eye." The light in the First Temple came through a wire covering the hole; here it is "filtered through a dense curtain of cobwebs." These cobwebs are indeed the graveyard, the "funeral accumulations," the "aerial catacombs," of "myriads of all tribes of mummied insects." If Melville's symbolism has not been explicit before, it is now: he has universalized his examination of the plight of man.

This plight is explicitly pictured. A "curious scene" is presented when the narrator ascends to the window. The sun is "about half-way up." Though, then, the light of God is only about half developed in this benighted world, there is ample illumination to reveal man's aspirations. "Millions of butterfly moles" are swarming in the "rainbowed tunnel" piercing from the window "across the darkness of the garret." "Against the skylight itself, with a cymbal-like buzzing, thousands of insects clustered in a golden mob."

Man's plight is even more crushing. The window of light, aspirations and hope is closed, "No sign of latch or hasp was visible" to the inquirer. Finally, however, after searching long, the inquiring mind does discover "a little padlock, imbedded, like an oyster at the bottom of the sea, amid matted masses of weedy webs, chrysalides, and insectivorous eggs." But the inhabitants of this world, in this case especially these people claiming to have the key to heaven, resent and resist any invasion of their domain. As the narrator picks the lock, "scores of small ants and flies, half-torpid, crawled forth from the keyhole, and, feeling the warmth of the sun in the pane, began frisking around me. Others appeared. Presently I was overrun by them. As if incensed at this invasion of their retreat, countless bands darted up from below, beating about my head, like hornets." Clearly, endarkened religion receives support from endarkened masses. The symbol of the opened window seems to offer hope: "But ah! what a change. As from the gloom of the grave and the companionship of worms, men shall at last rapturously rise into the living greenness and glory-immortal, so, from my cobwebbed old garret, I thrust forth my head into the balmy air, and found myself hailed by the verdant tops of great trees, growing in the little garden below—trees, whose leaves soared high above my topmost slate." Here, as elsewhere in Melville's works, the message seems explicit. Though the hope of salvation seems to lie in the sky, it actually is based on earth, or on a mixture of heaven firmly seated on earth, as the conclusion of the story will emphasize.

In the "least lighted corner of all, where was a profuse litter of indescribable old rubbish—among which was a broken telescope, and a celestial globe staved in—stood the little old table," on which rests Cotton Mather's *Magnalia*. It is a weird table, just such a "necromantic little old table as might have belonged to Friar Bacon," with "two plain features . . . significant of conjurations and charms—the circle and tripos." It has hoofed feet like those belonging to the Evil One, and all in all is "a very satanic-looking little table, indeed."

Melville's symbolism seems to say that in the darkest corner of this world, the limitations of which are perhaps created by and surely imposed by the ants and flies that practice the ministry, amid the wrecks of two examples of man's investigation of and hope for heaven, stands religion—the *Magnalia*—solidly resting on the support of conjurations, charms, superstition, and Satanism.

The narrator decides to rehabilitate the table and book, to bring them down to the "kindly influences of warm urns, warm fires, and warm hearts," and to have the "dislocations of the one and the tatters of the other repaired"; in other words, to subject Calvinism—and religion in general—to the test of pragmatism in the unbiasing light of everyday life. There might be some practical use for them, which would be appreciated by the modish wife who, although she at first resented the intrusion of the obviously out-of-place piece of furniture, changes her mind when she discovers that it can enhance her parlor.

Melville's ambivalence, his attraction toward the mystical and revulsion by it, his compulsion to subject all phenomena and attitudes to the test of rationality, becomes obvious. One night while reading Mather, the narrator is preternaturally sensitive and sensible. He realizes that Mather had tried to be fair, sensible, and just in his examination of various aspects of religion. He was not a "romantic Mrs. Radcliff," but "a practical, hard-working earnest, upright man, a learned doctor, too, as well as a good Christian and orthodox clergyman. What possible motive could such a man have to deceive? His style had all the plainness and unpoetic boldness of truth." Mather had reported the "detailed accounts of New England withcraft, each important item corroborated by respectable townsfolk, and, of not a few of the most surprising, he himself had been eye-witness. Cotton Mather testified himself whereof he had seen." Could the world of true religion and Satanic evil lie close together, Melville broods, or could so honest a man deceive for his own purposes?

The Mather of scientific investigation into the nature of religion and of reality is, however, apparently too strong a medicine for man. The same night that the narrator realizes that Mather was a pragmatist he first hears the ticking in the table and spends a sleepless night. The next morning,

275

as he lies "in bed watching the sun in the panes," he begins to think "that much midnight reading of Cotton Mather was not good for man; that it had a morbid influence upon the nerves, and gave rise to hallucinations." The practical-minded wife, however, is determined to get at the bottom of the business, knowing perfectly well, in her shallow-minded way, that since all the investigators are "good Christians" nothing can harm them. She determines to learn the truth. The activity of life—"the uproar of the street," "the continual rubbing against . . . practical men in the street"—seemed to confirm his wife's easy optimism.

This too-easy optimism, Melville's distrust of and contempt for those people who merely skim through life, is further attacked. The narrator turns from interest in the deep aspects of life to the superficiality of Democritus, whose philosophy teaches "that any possible investigation of any possible spiritual phenomena was absurd; that upon the first face of such things, the mind of a sane man instinctively affirmed them a humbug, unworthy of the least attention." A moment after affirming Democritus' wisdom, however, Melville reveals that it is not sufficient for this world, for the profounder questions will not so easily be put down, and the practical mind must be joined to the mystical.

Thus, comforted by the realism of Democritus and energized by the profounder impulses of religion, the narrator is present when the ticking is explained by the emergence of an insect that "shone like a glow-worm," which, in an obvious tie-in with the attic from which the table came earlier, Melville describes as "like a butterfly escaping its chrysalis." Melville again blends the empirical and mysterious frames of mind, Democritus and Mather: "Once again, Democritus befriend me. Supernatural coruscation as it appeared, I strove to look at the strange object in a purely scientific way."

Here is "a live bug come out of a dead table," "a fire-fly come out of a piece of ancient lumber." Here is, in other words, a supernatural birth, like those witnessed earlier in the garret, though more mysterious and more powerful because coming from older surroundings, from the very bed-rock of history. The fate of this supernaturally-born bug is significant. The narrator preserves it under a glass tumbler, determined "not to let the occasion pass without reaping some credit from it." But the next morning the Irish Catholic Biddy," Put the bug in the fire . . . and rinsed out the tumbler ever so many times."

Melville does not distinguish between the two bugs. Both are mysterious, beautiful and equally "supernatural." He is therefore pointing out the Satanic impulses of super-stitious people who put to the flame the gods and practitioners of other religions. And, as we shall see in a minute, he is demonstrating the closeness between the spurious and the real, the supernatural birth that is not accepted as such and such an "advent" that is proclaimed as the birth of a savior.

The emergence of the first bug is not the end of the supernatural manifestations of the table. When more ticking emanates from it, the narrator and wife determine that all the family—himself, his wife, and their daughters—will witness the appearance of the second bug, the "first advent of the thing." Melville's language here points up the increasingly religious nature of these births. After its "advent" the bug flashes in the "room's general dimness, like a fiery opal," it "was a beautiful bug—a Jew Jeweller's bug—a bug like a sparkle of a glorious sunset." "This was a seraphical bug; or rather, all it had of the bug was the B, for it was beautiful as a butterfly." The symbol of the birth of Christ and Christianity need not have been more explicit.

During the night before the birth of the bug, the narrator, "gently oscillated between Democritus and Cotton Mather," though to please his matter-of-fact-minded wife and to reassure his daughters, he "assumed to be pure Democritus— a jeerer at all tea-table spirits whatever." He carries on this pose of assurance when after the birth of the bug his wife wants to consult "Professor Johnson, the naturalist." To the suggestion, the narrator replies, "Bravo, Mrs. Democritus!"

277

The man of science, after hearing all the particulars, explains how eggs might lie for one hundred fifty years and then quite naturally be hatched. He dismisses all suggestions of spirituality "with a slight sneer." In this sneer, Melville undoubtedly deprecates the lack of cooperation between science and spirit. The narrator says he does not "exactly understand" the scientist's explanation, but he is convinced that though the phenomenon is not spiritual, "it is very wonderful as it is."

The superstitious daughter Julia insists on seeing the birth of the bug as a symbol "which teaches a spiritual lesson. For if, after one hundred and fifty years entombment, a mere insect comes forth at last into light, itself an effulgence, shall there be no glorified resurrection of the spirit of man?" Julia's words are a restatement of Thoreau's optimism in *Walden* in his telling of the story: "Who does not feel his faith in a resurrection and immortality strengthened by hearing of this?"

Melville had already voiced his opinion of such false optimistic analogical thinking, as Frank Davidson has pointed out. In *Mardi* (I,244), Babbalanja, Melville's philosopher, answers the question of whether larva changing into a butterfly is not "but illustration of the miraculous change to be brought in man after death?" Babbalanja replies: "No . . . for the analogy has an unsatisfactory end. From its chrysalis state, the silkworm but becomes a moth, that very quickly expires. Its longest existence is as a worm. All vanity, vanity . . . to seek in nature for positive warranty to these aspirations of ours."

This statement seems to be substantiated by the length of life of Melville's beautiful bug. "The mysterious insect did not long enjoy its radiant life; it expired the next day."

But the narrator's "girls have preserved it. Embalmed in a silver vinaigrette, it lies on the little apple-tree table in the pier of the cedar-parlour." And like the angel at the entrance of Jesus' tomb stationed there to point out to women where He lay and thus demonstrate that He had arisen from the dead, the narrator's daughters "will be happy to show (any doubting lady) both the bug and the table, the two sealing-wax drops designating the exact place of the two holes made by the two bugs, something in the same way in which are marked the spots where the cannon balls struck Brattle Street Church."

Melville's irony is heavy. The darkness, the cobwebs, the ignorance which covered the attic in the old, old house has not materially improved after the symbol of old and outmoded religion, Mather and the Satanic table, was brought to the light of the world, given a pragmatic test and subjected to the scrutiny of men of science. Such enlightenment has attacked and destroyed old and established religion only in the same way that two cannon balls destroyed Brattle Street Church. Now the new religion rests on the old table just as comfortably as Mather's did. In this symbol Melville seems to be affirming Thoreau's words in *A Week on the Concord and Merrimack Rivers,* although often he was critical of Thoreau: "You can hardly convince a man of an error in a life-time, but must content yourself with the reflection that the progress of science is slow. If he is not convinced, his grand-children may be."

Melville's hope for the future seems to be real. Characteristically throughout his works his hope for the salvation of man is long-range. He realizes that to substitute hope in man for hope in God is such a shattering process that great time will be needed for reassembling the pieces. He has patience since he has no alternative.

SEVEN

THEME AND TECHNIQUE IN
"THE ENCANTADAS"

"The Encantadas" are unusual in subject matter and method of
presentation even for an author who changed as freely as Melville
did. The ten pieces, all of which in one way or another contribute
to a comprehensive travel sketch of the Galapagos Islands, are a
mixed bag of artistic accomplishment. Some are mere crayon
outlines, scarcely long enough for real development, and
stylistically as flat and colorless as the scenes they depict. Some,
however, develop with great power. And one—sketch eight,
"Norfolk Isle and the Chola Widow"—is almost equal in overall
strength, if not in art, to Melville's best short works. The Chola's
story is a South American Indian spiritual song equal in
tragedy and poignancy to almost any of North America's Negro
spirituals—a quiet crooning of degradation, unbelievable terror
and suffering, but of firm hope and expectation.

All ten are pieces of a jigsaw puzzle picturing islands and sea
and the people who dwell among them which adds up to much
more than the sum of the parts. The completed picture reflects in
the sky above, projected there because of the great meanings of
the individual pieces and of the greater significance of the whole.

The theme of these sketches (which appeared in *Putnam's*
during March, April, and May 1854) is that which we have seen
in all of Melville's works, to one degree or another, and will
see in the remainder—the ordeal and triumph of humanity. The
technique Melville uses here is that of having the author view in
various ways man's degrading and heroizing qualities, his attempts to triumph over his surroundings, and, most important,
his isolation from man and his accursed though necessary association with man.

Though sections of the total picture seem bleak, the conclusions more tentative than firm, altogether they add to the quiet certainty of Melville's conviction of man's ultimate victory.[1]

I. STATIC DECAY

The first sketch is a superb picture of static decay, of a setting of the stage for the pieces that follow. The Enchanted Islands, "five-and-twenty heaps of cinders dumped here and there in an outside city lot," which look "much as the world at large might, after a penal conflagration," are unparalleled in desolateness. They are "abandoned cemeteries of long ago." They lack the "thoughts of sympathy" which "all else which has but once been associated with humanity" arouses in us. This last sentence provides the key to understanding all the sketches: *sympathy* is one of the most important words in Melville's works.

The "special curse" of the islands is that "change never comes; neither the change of seasons nor of sorrows." They are, in other words, denied the ennobling experience of challenge and triumph which mankind enjoys, the theme of which is to be rounded off in the last published work of the volume in which these sketches appeared, "The Piazza." Only sloth, decay, desolateness, death, and eternal curse can result from the unchanging physical situation of these islands.

Another of the terrors is these islands' "emphatic uninhabitableness." The "chief sound of life here is a hiss." It is the complete absence of all things that have been "associated with humanity" which renders these islands accursed. Here is the pathos found later in *Clarel*. In these islands the flora and fauna are unworldly. The coast is "clinker-bound," flights of "unearthly birds" heighten the "dismal din." And "in no world but a fallen one could such lands exist." Again, it is the despair that

1. The best single study of these stories is that of R. H. Fogle, *Melville's Shorter Tales* (Norman, Okla., 1960).

will be restated in *Clarel*: "There is a hell over which mere hell/Serves—for—a—heaven." These islands have fallen below the eye of God and also of living nature. They are thrown into the other-worldliness characterized by the hiss, the hiss which in *Moby-Dick* accompanied the demoniac gesture of the harpooners when, misled by Ahab, they drink ritualistically from the socket of the harpoon, and their drinks are "quaffed down with a hiss."

Melville examines the islands from all sides, compares the flora and fauna, intensifies their loneliness by references to the Bible, to cemeteries, to history and archeology. The setting is static. The dynamic is the development which provides the theme, the *raison d etre* for the stories that of Melville's concern for man, for man living with men, for man's concern with society; in other words, Melville's firm belief in humanism.

This theme is at first planted subtly, with the super-stitions of the sailors. Melville humanizes experience by anchoring it in folklore, in the Jungian collective un-conscious. Common sailors hold the belief that these islands are the hell of their wicked superiors: "They earnestly believe that all wicked sea-officers, more especially commodores and captains, are at death (and, in some cases, before death) transformed into tortoises; thence forth dwelling upon these hot aridities, sole solitary lords of Asphaltum." Melville thus criticizes the difference in rank between the commodores and captains and the sailors. He who was always content to sail before the mast as a common sailor and who severely criticized officers in various books is here voicing the protests of the sailors and demonstrating his, and their, desire to feel the commonalty of men, the need to associate freely.

The isolation and social commentary themes are climaxed in the last paragraph of this sketch, in a scene which baldly summons up Coleridge's "Ancient Mariner." In "scenes of social merriment, and especially at revels . . . in old-fashioned mansions . . . I have drawn the attention of my comrades by my fixed gaze and sudden change of air, as I have seemed to see, slowly emerging from those imagined solitudes, and heavily crawling along the floor, the ghost of a gigantic tortoise, with 'Memento . . .' burning in live letters upon his back."

Human association is necessary, Melville insists. But he emphasizes that the sailors, the common people, curse the rich, the inhabitants of this mansion, by delegating them to the greatest possible hell, the Encantadas, in the form of the tortoise. The reminder of our common mortality is "burning in live letters" upon the back of the earthly great and powerful.

II. DIMENSIONS OF LIFE

The second sketch, "Two Sides to a Tortoise," is one of Melville's most masterful vignettes. Its subject is the depth and superficiality, the sadness and humor, the history and lack of history of the world, and by extension of the human being.

Having overstated the gloom of the islands in the earlier chapter, he here mitigates it. The islands have their bright side, as symbolized in the "calapee or breast-plate" and the underside of the tortoise. In a tone that he tries to make light but obviously is intended to be serious, Melville says that everyone ought to enjoy the bright side of life if he can, but he must not deny the black.

He then recounts how once his ship put in at the Galapagos and brought three "huge antediluvian-looking tortoises" on deck, that "seemed hardly of the seed of earth." Thus he universalizes tortoises in time and space. They inspired the feeling of age, "dateless, indefinite endurance."

These animals represent the past, but they also represent other things. They call forth more of the social criticism Melville began in the first sketch.

When the tortoises are first thrown onto the deck of the ship, Melville thinks of the symbol of ageless tyranny that he used in "Benito Cereno"—Spain. He revives his memory of his own reception in the Marquesas after he had jumped ship and descended to the valley of the Typees, where, he later says in *Clarel*, he was welcomed as a god. But though received as a god he was treated in a curiously naive, democratic manner: "Had three Spanish custom-house officers boarded us then, it is not unlikely that I should have curiously stared at them, felt of them, and stroked them much as savages serve civilized guests." These men are "civilized guests," the natives' superiors, but they are officers and represent ageless tyranny, as they do in the first sketch—the tyranny of Eastern religion and of Roman emperors of the time of the colosseums.

One of the neatest bits of irony is introduced in the apostrophe to the tortoises, in which Melville asks for the keys to the cities: "Ye oldest inhabitants of this or any other isle, said I, pray give me the freedom of your three-walled towns." As he will demonstrate in the last paragraph of the sketch, he and the other sailors of the ship—his symbol of the democrats of the world—simply destroy the walled towns and convert them to their own practical uses.

An even stronger political statement is made when Melville describes how, as he lay in his hammock the night after the tortoises were brought aboard, he heard them on the deck above his head. The "impregnable armour of their living mail," their "citadel wherein to resist the assaults of Time" suggest that they are aristocrats. Though he has grudging respect for their endurance, he points out their lack of intelligence. "The stupidity of their resolution was so great, that they never went aside for any impediment." Politically they do not adjust. "Their crowning curse is their drudging impulse to straightforwardness in a belittered world." One of the tortoises jammed against the foremast and stayed there all night unable to get through it and unwilling to go around. Like Captain Vere in *Billy Budd*, who is unwilling or unable to alter the forms of life, these tortoises cannot change age-old patterns of behavior. Other tortoises adjust a little, but still persist in driving forward. As Melville thinks of these monsters he sees them "century after century, writhing through the shades, grim as blacksmiths." The reference to blacksmiths is immediately reminiscent of that in *Moby-Dick*, where the blacksmith is a man-maker, and the maker of Ahab's leg, servant therefore to a monomaniacal tyrant.

Next Melville dreams that he is "sitting cross-legged upon the foremast, a Brahmin similarly mounted upon either side, forming a tripod of foreheads which upheld the universal cope." This "univeral cope" is the universality of man, and it is significant that Melville is surrounded by Brahmins; he represents Christianity and Western man, they Eastern man and pagan religion. So here, as in *Moby-Dick*, the two sides of the world, the two sides of man, the practical and the mystical, join to triumph.

The concluding paragraph of the sketch is artful in the extreme. In the first place it clearly represents the lighter side of man's nature, and Melville always felt that man should recognize the light as well as the dark. But the paragraph also carries political—and universal—symbolism. Those mighty Spanish and Roman grandees who have persevered through the centuries and whose permission Melville prayed for earlier have now fallen to his knife. Though the metaphor is different, the message here is the same as in various other works: the triumph of the sailors of the world. In this story, they simply eat the aristocrats.

III. AQUATIC TOWER OF BABEL

The third sketch, "Rock Rodondo," parallels in development the initial power of "The Piazza." First the rock is seen from a distance. Melville says that from its peak, as from the mountain around his favorite porch, there is a superb view more than that of mere human beings. The mountain stands "solitary and alone," and "occupies, on a large scale, very much the position which the famous Campanile or detached Bell Tower of Saint Mark does with respect to the tangled group of hoary edifices around it." It has, in other words, exactly the same kind of eminence as the roof of the house in Jerusalem that Clarel ascends in order to view, god-like, the world of man below him. The rock, from the base, is seen surrounded with mysteriousness and magic especially when, like religion which it symbolizes, it is imperfectly seen.

Melville first visited the place during the gray of morning when "its aspect was heightened, and yet softened, by the strange double twilight of the hour," when "the twilight was just enough to reveal every striking point, without tearing away the dim investiture of wonder."

The rock is an aquatic Tower of Babel. It rises "in entablatures of strata to a shaven summer," and all is throbbing to the "demonic din created by the birds." All birds are sea-birds, for though the rock is "terra-firma," no land birds ever touch down here, and wisely: "What a falling into the hands of the Philistines, when the poor warbler should be surrounded by such locust-flights of strong bandit birds, with long bills cruel as daggers." Here is the contrast between sea life and land life. The land, as in *Billy Budd*, represents steadfastness, human society, docility; the sea, its opposite.

Melville next comes closer to the rock and ascends, describing the bird life existing thereon. There is an analogy with human life. "Birds light here which never touched mast or tree; hermit-birds, which ever fly alone; cloud-birds, familiar with unpierced zones of air." Also lowly birds, perhaps demonic birds. Next, bachelor birds: these are isolated, uncommitted, undemocratic, and perhaps Emersonian birds. Then the high-level birds that fly above all. Melville further distinguishes. On the lowest shelf, "which is the widest too," is the penguin, neither fish, flesh, nor fowl, "merely the most ambiguous and least lovely creature yet discovered by man." On the shelf above are the pelicans, "sea Frairs of Orders Grey." Higher up is the gony or gray albatross.

286   "THE   ENCANTADAS"

Melville's language, which so far has been flecked with references and tones reminiscent of the Scripture, becomes more Biblical as he goes further up the rock. "As we still ascend from shelf to shelf, we find tenants of the tower serially disposed in order of their magnitude:— gannets, black and speckled haglets, jays, sea-hens, sperm-whale-birds, gulls of varieties:—thrones, princedoms, powers, dominating one above another in senatorial array." High above all flies the stormy petrel, "this mysterious humming-bird of ocean," whose "chirrup under the stern is ominous to mariners as to the peasant the death-tick sounding from behind the chimney jamb."

The religious symbolism is carried further when Melville likens the deafening din of the birds to celebrating "matins." "Each moment, flights push from the tower, and join the aerial choir hovering ahead, while their places below are supplied by darting myriads." Then he looks up, in further development of the religious analogy, and beholds a "snow-white angelic thing," the boatswain's mate.

From this heavenly vantage point, Melville, as he would later do in *Clarel*, looks down at the world and sees tiered below him in a "full counterpart" of the bird life of Rodondo various levels of fish which "people the waters at its base." Whereas the heavenly birds are always in com-motion and making noise, the fish are tame and unwary. They too compete for food, and if you drop a hook into the water the fish on the lower levels cannot get at it so eagerly do those on the upper levels grab at it. There is much religious, political, and social symbolism in the tiered wold, as Melville makes clear in his remark, paral-leling the theme of *The Confidence-Man* but *vis a vis* heaven: "Poor fish of Rodondo! in your victimized con-fidence, you are of the number of those who inconsider-ately trust, while they do not understand, human nature," Looking up at God who is looking down on man, Melville here, as in various places, criticizes God for taking advantage of human nature. He undoubtedly finds reason for people in the presence of the Being banding together for protection.

Melville carries on his religious symbolism, as well as the contrast between appearance and reality: "This moment," he says, "doubtless, while we know it to be a dead desert rock, other voyagers are taking oaths it is a glad populous ship." The view is roughly that of those people who see Israel from a distance as the Holy Land but who when seeing it close up must change their minds into calling it the blasted and desolate land.

IV. PREPARATION FOR HEAVEN

In sketch four, "A Pisgah View from the Rock," the narrator ascends the rock. In ascending, Melville breaks into frontier humor, exaggeration, as he had in *Moby-Dick* and other works. He cautions the person who would climb this rock to "take the following prescription. Go three voyages round the world as a main-royal man of the tallest frigate that floats; then serve a year or two apprenticeship to the guides who conduct strangers up the Peak of Teneriffe; and as many more respectively to a rope-dancer, and Indian juggler, and a chamois." But there is a serious symbolism behind this humor. All these jobs are those of the common man, the democrat. Thus the best preparation for heaven is working at a common man's task.

The symbolism of the rock as heaven is developed further. Melville reaches the summit and asks: "Does any balloonist, does the outlooking man in the moon, take a broader view of space? Much thus, one fancies, looks the universe from Milton's celestial battlements. A boundless watery Kentucky. Here Daniel Boone would have dwelt content." This is the heaven of God and of the folk hero, both being one and the same. From this height Melville points out the distances from here to other sections of the world, naming and locating the other various islands of the Enchanted group.

The frontier humor expands in Melville's statistics about the population of one of these isles, Albemarle. There are ant-eaters (number unknown), man-haters (number unknown), lizards (500,000), snakes (500,000), spiders (10,000,000), salamanders and devils (numbers unknown), "making a clean total of 11,000,000 exclusive of an incomputable host of fiends, ant-eaters, man-haters, and salamanders," but of "men . . . none." The humor is jovian and grim. The God and hero of Melville's and Daniel Boone's heaven seems to be laughing at man's world and plight. The enumerated beasts are all hissers and enemies of man. The whole universe seen from the rock is one of desolateness, as though this Superior Being looked down upon a creation—or mis-creation—of "tormented lava."

In particularizing the islands, Melville uses Biblical references with demonic effect. The real trouble with these islands in general is that they constitute "for the most part an archipelago of aridities, without inhabitant, history, or hope of either in all time to come."

Melville then suggests that we turn to the remaining islands which have some ground for "notability." That is, they are lands on which people live or have lived, and therefore have some hope of history, some chronicles of life.

V. ROIL OF LIFE

Sketch five, "The Frigate, and Ship 'Flyaway'," is the weakest of the sketches, but its symbolism is terrifying. Melville descends from Rodondo, the heaven of the gods, and immediately steps into the roil of life. The scene is a water-reflection of the cannibalism existing above. Man is out to destroy man.

The time is 1813, and the American frigate *Essex*, with David Porter as its captain, is engaged in war activities. The ship is becalmed one morning when no doubt the birds on the rock are celebrating their "matins," and a strong tide is pulling her toward the rock, when another ship is seen in the distance. Porter is convinced that the ship is an Englishman though she hoists American colors. The strange ship finally indeed raises her English flag, but in the chase that follows eventually escapes the fury of the *Essex.*

Melville undoubtedly liked this brief sketch because it pictures yet further his development of the theme of the ambiguity, the two-sidedness, of man, this world, and religion.

Man's nature can be seen in the behavior of the Americans. Saved from destruction on the rocks, the *Essex* "now made use of that salvation to destroy the other vessel." Though she does not capture the vessel, she does in later engagements triumph over "the furthest wandering vessels." Finally she "valiantly gave up the ghost fighting two English frigates in the harbor of Valparaiso." Further, the "enigmatic craft" that the *Essex* chases— "American in the morning, and English in the evening"— reveals Melville's belief in the closeness of America and England, though he particularly criticized England in numerous other works. The fighting between these two nations was here, as it was in the Civil War, a form of fratricide.

On a larger, more cosmical, scale the sketch is even more terrifying. The atmosphere surrounding the whole business is one of mysteriousness and enchantment. The *Essex* lies becalmed "as if spell-bound." The strange ship sighted—"not out of keeping with alleged enchantments of the neighbourhood"—seemed to be staggering under a violent wind." The escape of the *Essex* from the rocks toward which she was headed "was so critical as to seem miraculous." The other vessel is "an enchanted ship."

Melville thus in every way points out that all these aspect of man's destructive proclivity take place directly under the eye of and in the presence of the heaven of God and hero. As observer, Melville looks both ways, seeing not only the mountain but also the people below it. Here, as in *Clarel* later, he wonders about the nature of a divinity that allows such viciousness in creatures supposedly created by Him. But, perhaps most important, Melville clearly demonstrates that although man is capable of such inexplicable and dastardly behavior, Melville is concerned with man, his nature and activities. Thus the sketch is an oblique affirmation of Melville's humanism.

VI. TWO SIDES OF MAN

"Barrington Isle and the Buccaneers," the sixth section, is a continuation of Melville's main theme, that men, like life, are two-sided; they can look up to heaven with prayer in their eyes and hearts while their hands are at the throats of their fellowmen.

Melville tells of Barrington Isle which 200 years ago "was the resort of that famous wing of the West Indian Buccaneers," who "ravaged the Pacific side of the Spanish colonies." But "after the toils of piratic war," the pirates came to this island and "lay snugly out of harm's reach" in this "harbour of safety" and "bower of ease." They here assumed the "tranquility" that they had "fiercely denied to every civilized harbour in that part of the world."

Melville then quotes at great length "a sentimental voyager of long ago," One symbol of the civilized aspect these buccaneers assumed was "seats which might have served Brahmins and presidents of peace societies." The seat to Melville, it must be remembered, symbolized companionship, brotherhood, and humanism. In a famous letter to Hawthorne he pictures the ideal heaven, in which he and Hawthorne can sit and sit and sit and drink and drink while they talk on and on forever.

> If ever, my dear Hawthorne, in the eternal times
> that are to come, you & I shall sit down in Paradise,
> in some shady corner by ourselves: and if we shall by
> any means be able to smuggle a basket of
> Champagne there (I won't believe in Temperance
> Heaven), and if we shall then cross our celestial legs

291

in the grass that is forever tropical, and strike our
glasses & our heads together, till both musically ring
in concert,—then O my dear fellow-mortal, how shall
we pleasantly discourse of all the things manifold
which now so distress us. . . . [2]

In this sketch Melville seems to be asking if the buccaneers, who not only pray but also build seats for themselves
and for their followers, can be all bad. Much earlier Melville
had asserted that he felt that a "thief in jail is as honorable
a personage as Gen. George Washington." Here his conclusion must be that even the lowly can be high. This is the
firm voice of his democratic impulse.

VII. STUDY IN MIS-USED FREEDOM

In reading sketch seven, "Charles's Isle and the Dog-King,"
one must be careful to detect Melville's irony. He seems to
be saying one thing when in fact he means the opposite.
The story is a study in misused freedom and in the explosive danger of tyranny. In many ways it is a parable of
the colonizing and rebellion of America, though set in the
Encantadas. But the lesson is clear even without
translating the story to a parallel with the United States.
A certain Creole adventurer from Cuba fought with Peru
against Spain. The adventurer "by his bravery and *good
fortune* . . . advanced himself to high rank in the patriot
army." Then he was given Charles's Isle for his services. He
sought to get people to colonize the island, but he planned
to rule them with a "disciplined cavalry company of large grim
dogs." These are politically symbolic dogs. On the passage
to the island, they, "it was observed . . . refusing to consort
with the emigrants, remained aristocratically grouped
around their master on the elevated quarter-deck, casting
disdainful glances forward upon the inferior rabble there;
much as, from the ramparts, the soldiers, of a garrison,

2. Jay Leyda, *The Melville Log* (New York, 1951), 1:412-413.

thrown into a conquered town, eye the inglorious citizen-mab over which they are set to watch."

Melville's long-standing concern with tyranny is immediately apparent. These dogs are the lady and gentleman passengers on the emigrant ship in *Redburn* who refuse to associate with the Irish emigrants, they are Fedallah and his fellow ghosts remaining aloof from the other whalers on the *Pequod* while they serve the aloof Ahab, they are the whites in "Benito Cereno" tamping the cannon of rebellion until it bursts, and they are the magistrates in "The Bell-Tower" serving the tyrannical Bannadonna. Aristocrats everywhere often serve tyrants.

These people brought to colonize Charles's Isle were not much different from other pilgrims, for example, those poor Irish brought over in *Redburn*. The ruler, nervous in his abuse of power, had no reason and no legal excuse for shooting these people. After he had killed many of his original eighty people, the ruler gave up his sport and set about recruiting new citizens.

Melville makes several statements heavy with political message. He says that "the history of the king of Charles's Island furnishes another illustration of the difficulty of colonizing barren islands with unprincipled pilgrims." Here he means that tyranny has difficulty surviving in lands where precedent has not set the reins of control, and he means that man's basic drive to survive will eventually break bonds of artificial control, as it did with the Negroes in "Benito Cereno."

Melville does, however, issue a firm caution. Here as in numerous other works he pulls back from extremism in political organizations and deeds.

The land of these deserted sailors became "the unassailed lurking place of all sorts of desperadoes, who in the name of liberty did just what they pleased." As such the land became a dangerous Siren land to ships passing by. The dwellers thereon keep "a beacon burning" to entice other men to the shores.

The parable of the United States, hinted at earlier, thus reasserts itself. The beacon is analogous to the Statue of Liberty in Vivenze discussed vividly in *Mardi.* People in Vivenze act wildly, at cross purposes one to another, and in the imminent Civil War in the early 1850's, when Melville wrote these sketches, are about to knife themselves into a *riotocracy.* The sketch thus grew out of Melville's keen political sensitivity and his hope in the future of the human race.

VIII. HUMANIZATION OF THE SAVIOR

By far the strongest sketch of the ten is number eight, "Norfolk Isle and the Chola Widow." In it the theme that has run through all pieces—the commonalty of the human race—is given its strongest articulation.

The sketch is of a Chola lady, her husband, and her brother who go off to a lonely island to work for tortoise oil. Soon after they arrive, she witnesses the drowning of her husband and her brother. The husband's body is washed ashore, and his widow buries him. Then for a long time, abandoned by the French ship that had brought the three and had promised to return to pick them up, and alone now except for some dogs the three had brought with them, she ekes out an existence, and through sheer power of will manages to survive until she is rescued by the ship of the narrator. The story is rich in the awe and reverence that the narrator holds for this symbol of the perseverance of the human race.

She is a superwoman, a heroine. Her heroic qualities are made clear at the beginning of the story. The narrator's boat is beginning to pull away from Norfolk Isle when one of the sailors causes it to stop. He is the most unusual man on the boat. He saw the white object on the shore because he was "high lifted above all others . . . and this elevation of his eye was owing to the elevation of his spirits."

Interestingly, although this is a religious sketch from the very beginning, since it is the third day that the boat is leaving the island—the day therefore when the widow rises from her grave—the sketch is also very earthy. Although the sailor is a high looker whose spirits and eyes are on elevated things, his elevation of spirits resulted from "a dram of Peruvian pisco," which had; in accordance with Melville's insistence of the superiority of non-white people, been given him by the "mulatto steward." Further, Melville makes it explicit that the island "through sympathy . . . has become a spot made sacred by the strangest trials of humanity."

The widow had been staying on the side of the island opposite to that visited by the boat that rescued her. Although she seldom or never visited this side of the island, on this particular day she had been told to look to it by "something" that "came flitting by" her and touched her cheek and heart, something that "came through the air." The narrator then suggests that it was the "echoing chorus of the windless song." In other words very likely it was the song that summoned her. Thus the super-natural elements are humanized and the natural elements raised to the power of the supernatural, for this savior was raised from the grave by a folk song sung by sailors, not a hymn sung by God.

The power of humanism is made explicit in another instance. Before leaving the island the Chola widow visits the grave of her husband. Good Catholic that she was at his death, she buried him. Now, however, the narrator witnesses her farewell to the grave, and in so doing points out the powerlessness of the whole ritual. The grave is covered with sand, like that "found at the bottom of an hour-glass run out." The cross at the head of the grave is fraying bark and is "forlornly adroop in the silent air." The crucifix she fingers while on the grave is "worn featureless, like ancient graven knocker long plied in vain." The last four words are terribly and terrifyingly significant. Though her religion was without avail, the widow is being saved by

men whose folk song she replied to because of her extra-
sensory perception of it.

To Melville the "most direful fate" is that of being
separated from humanity. This is stated explicitly and
illustrated further. When, for example, the widow must
leave several of her dogs behind on the island because of
lack of space on the ship for them, Melville says, "Had they
been human beings, hardly would they have more vividly
inspired the sense of desolation" of that world cut off
from mankind.

That this story is the humanization of the Savior, or the
humanity of the Savior, is clear from the beginning. God's
voice, works, and charity are missing. Heaven is deaf, blind,
and indifferent. Melville editorializes about the widow's
being left alone on the island: "Ah, Heaven, when man
thus keeps his faith, wilt Thou be faithless who created the
faithful one? But they cannot break faith who never
plighted it." The comment is an early version of the feelings
that he will voice more directly when in visiting the Holy
Land later he will see only desolation and godless hopelessness.

Being forced then to turn from a powerless and
indifferent God to man, Melville asserts his true feeling,
speaking about "Hunilla, this lone shipwrecked soul, out of
treachery invoking trust. Humanity, thou strong thing, I
worship thee, not in the laureled victor, but in this vanquished one." Hunilla had recognized that "pain seemed
so necessary, that pain in other beings, though by love
and sympathy made her own, was unrepiningly to be borne.
A heart of yearning in a frame of steel. A heart of earthly
yearning, frozen by the frost which falleth from the sky."

There is hope in humanism, expectation even of triumph.
Hunilla is probably modeled to a large extent on Hester
Prynne, Hawthorne's female Christ in *The Scarlet Letter*.
The two women are strikingly similar, especially in their
bearing of sins of and atoning for the sins of man. In one
of the most felicitous and effective symbols he ever devel-

oped, one which brought tears to the eyes of James
Russell Lowell, Melville ends his sketch of hope for
humanity, a symbol and hope which in bringing God down
from heaven to earth also drags man upward toward
heaven. Hunilla is taken to the mainland and: "the last
seen of lone Hunilla she was passing into Payta town,
riding upon a small gray ass; and before her on the ass's
shoulders, she eyed the jointed workings of the beast's
armorial cross."

IX. DEGRADATION FROM OVERAMBITION

"Hood's Isle and the Hermit Oberlus," sketch nine, is
another study in humanism and in political and social
ambition. As the sketch of the dog-king had been to a
certain extent a study in ambition run to tyranny, this story
is of the degradation resulting from overambition, Melville
makes it clear from the start, however, that the cause of
the degradation in the hermit Oberlus is his isolation from
humanity. Melville also makes it clear that men are all the
same, both the aristocrat and the commoner. Melville has
several other points, all of which join in the rope of humanism on which all aspects are strung.

The hermit Oberlus is driven to Hood's Isle, where
Melville says, the European was capable of sinking much
lower than the heathen, a point made in virtually all his
books. Oberlus is "a European bringing into this savage
region qualities more diabolical than are to be found among
any of the surrounding cannibals." Here he grows vege-
tables for ships that put into the harbor to augment supplies.

The story obviously derives somewhat from Hawthorne's
"Minister's Black Veil," for this monster refuses as long
as he can to show his face to visitors. But in having him
present his backside to captains, Melville is again call-
forth the practice he revealed in *Redburn* and *Moby-
Dick* of having men return up their rears in a gesture of

297

contemptuous humor. Oberlus also derives from "Young Goodman Brown" because he is so evil that the hoe handle he uses has been influenced by the serpent in him; it writhes and coils, becoming in its own way a writhing serpent. But most vicious of all, the trouble with Oberlus is that he is a misanthrope: "He acted out of mere delight in tyranny and cruelty. . . ." He shares with "noble minds" the degradation of "no mind at all" and "selfish ambition."

The misanthrope tries to revenge himself upon humanity by subjecting people to his will. He first tries to capture a Negro, but Melville with his usual insistence that non-whites are superior to whites, demonstrates how the Negro, at first frightened, regains his wits and overcomes his would-be enslaver. Finally however, Oberlus captures four sailors, and becoming his slaves "these wretches were now become wholly corrupted to his hands." He tyrannizes over them, finally providing them with cutlasses, though thereafter he fears their uprising against him.

Having smashed the boats of some sailors he lured to his harbor, and stolen one of the boats, Oberlus leaves behind on the isle a note which is subsequently found and read to us by two ships' captains. This letter, a lie from start to finish as is the news report at the end of *Billy Budd*, is Oberlus's admission of several things: of the false ends politicians—tyrants—profess to achieve their ends; of the alleged beatings he took from Christians, an allegation which is to a certain extent correct, for the smugglers who once beat him were Christians.

The most significant comment about the import of the story is, as usual with Melville, in the concluding paragraph. Having arrived in Payta and married a girl whom he wants to take back to his edenic island, Oberlus is caught about to burn a ship that is ready to be launched—thus in Melville's symbol trying to cut off communication between people—and is thrown into a South American jail.

Melville's message is that since hating and acting

against mankind are the most detestable of sins, the opposite, loving and acting for the good of mankind, are the noblest. All people, great and small, noble and poor, are bound together by their suffering, and are fragmented and injured by their hate and ambition. Therefore to practice virtue is the great good.

X. APOTHEOSIS OF HUMANITY

The tenth sketch, "Runaways, Castaways, Solitaries, Grave-Stones, Etc.," to a certain extent brings to a conclusion though it does not round out Melville's concern with the islands, not with all the possible themes; but it does rather logically end the subject, because it reaches a point from which an author cannot go forward or retreat. Though the sketch begins in the bleakest doom, it seems to end with a danse macabre which is either inappropriate or manic. But it is this ending, in fact, that provides the philosophical conclusion to all ten sketches.

Using the hut of Oberlus of sketch nine as a point of departure, Melville describes how horrible it is to be solitary, especially on these islands. There are several reasons why people take to them. Some go to escape tyrannical ships' captains. Though it is terrible to be left alone in these islands, it is immediately safer than to desert ship on either civilized islands or those inhabited by primitives who through association with whites have been corrupted in morals and humanity and will therefore return the escaping sailor to the ship from which he fled.

Another reason sailors wind up on these islands is that they are deserted by the ships that brought them there, perhaps even abandoned there by inhuman captains. Sometimes accidents force people to try to eke out a living on these piles of clinkers. But regardless of how the people got to these islands, and regardless of their social, political, or martial rank (one lieutenant was buried on the island after having engaged in a duel—in this land of eternal death!), all receive virtually the same treatment in this Potter's Field.

Melville then ends his sketch with a bit of a "doggerel epitaph" that is a sample of the kind often found on the wooden boards marking the graves on the island. Melville's technique here is precisely a parallel of that he was later to use in *Billy Budd*, a resort to folk verse in an effort to democratize all levels of humanity, and to show that the final word is the people's and that they are the longest lasting and the hope of humanity. This is one of this most explicit statements of his humanism.

His bit of doggeral is a rattling of skeleton bones:

> Oh, Brother Jack, as you pass by,
> As you are now, so once was I
> Just so game, and just so gay,
> But now, alack, they've stopped my pay.
> No more I peep out of my blinkers
> Here I be—tucked in with clinkers!

Melville's is a paraphrase of some lines taken from David Porter's *Journal of a Cruise to the Pacific Ocean,* which reports the same setting for the verse:

> Gentle reader, as you pass by,
> As you are now, so wonce was I;
> As now my body is in the dust,
> I hope in heaven my soul to rest.

But Porter's is merely another folk poet's paraphrase of a epitaph known by all:

> Behold you, sir, as you pass by,
> As you are now, so once was I.
> As I am now you soon shall be
> Prepare to meet me in eternity.

Melville's resorting to folklore to express his hope in humanity is one of his subtlest but truest statements. There is significance in Melville's variation. The folk and Porter's versions are addressed to "Sir," and "Gentle Reader." But Melville's is addressed to "Brother Jack." This is Jack-the-sailor, everysailor, who can be apotheosized in Jack Chase, or Bulkington, the "Jack" capable of soaring to the heights of Billy Budd—the apotheosis of humanity.

EIGHT

THE CONFIDENCE-MAN:
THE SHADOW OF HAWTHORNE'S FORM

The Confidence-Man: His Masquerade (1857), after
suffering from the day of publication from the charge of
being obscure, is finally coming into its own as one of
Melville's major works. Designated by Richard Chase as
"what one is tempted to call [Melville's] second-best book,"
the work has recently received excellent critical attention.
Elizabeth Foster, in her admirable introduction to the
Hendricks House edition, traces the growth of this
appreciation, and adds superb critical comments of her
own, and the remarks of James E. Miller, Jr., are further
revealing.[1] Despite these three admirable studies and
others, however, the book remains, with the exception of
Clarel, by far the most demanding of Melville's works
because its complicated and intentionally difficult style—its
irony and inversion—requires unfaltering critical attention.
To mine some more, but by no means all, of its secrets,
three veins of inquiry suggest themselves for further
study: the relationship of this book to Hawthorne's works;
the relationship of this book to Melville's other works; and
further examination of *The Confidence-Man* itself. All three
veins can best be explored concurrently. All three develop
in one way or another Melville's belief in the ultimate
triumph of humanity.

The influence of Hawthorne (as well as Shakespeare),
which had been so extensive and profound in the early
1850's, was still pervasive when Melville worked on this
book, and was in fact probably more far-reaching on this one

---

1. Herman Melville, *The Confidence-Man*, ed. Elizabeth Foster (New York, 1954);
James E. Miller, Jr. "*The Confidence-Man:* His Guises," *Publication of the Modern
Language Association* 124 (1959): 102-111.

than on any other except *Moby-Dick* and *Clarel*. The story, as
John Shroeder has demonstrated, derives considerably from
Hawthorne's "Celestial Railroad," and through that from
Pilgrim's Progress.[2] It derives also from "The Intelligence
Office" and "Young Goodman Brown," and other Hawthorne stories, far more than has been demonstrated. But
of all Hawthorne's works probably the single most influential on this book was *The Scarlet Letter*. For Melville form
was always extremely important, and on the form of this
book *The Scarlet Letter* had profound influence.

The opening scene in both books is strikingly similar.
Hawthorne's opens on a still-life of what transpires after
a sin is committed. Hawthorne is interested in the results
of sin, the consequence on the sinners as well as on the
people around. He begins his study outside the jail in
Boston. "A throng of bearded men . . . intermixed with
women" is assembled. Hawthorne is especially interested in
the women, who in their examination of a fellow woman
are startlingly without charity. "This woman has brought
shame upon us," one says about Hester Prynne, "and
ought to die. Is there not a law for it? Truly there is, both
in the Scripture and the statute-book." This is the tenor of
the words spoken on the *Fidele* by the people criticizing
the mute.

There are other strong parallels between the two books.
Hester is examined by the townspeople. Hester is genuine;
she openly admits her guilt and pays the price. But these
judges of character—the townspeople—completely
overlook and misread the real fraud in their midst, the
real confidence man, the Reverend Arthur Dimmesdale:
"'People say,' said another, 'that the Reverend Master
Dimmesdale, her godly pastor, takes it very grievously to
heart that such a scandal should have come upon his
congregation.'" Again, the parallel with the rejection of the
mute is close. Melville's people also cannot distinguish

2. John W. Schroeder, "Sources and Symbols for Melville's *Confidence-Man*," *Publication of the Modern Language Association* 116 (1951): 363-380.

between the real and the bogus, the mute and the con
men.

Like Hawthorne, Melville is interested in showing the result
of an action, not the action itself. In order to be explicit,
however, he pictures the actual rejection of the mute—who, as
we shall see, represents the Savior of the world—and then the
result of this rejection.

The *Confidence- Man*, further, is much more thematically
related to Melville's other works than has been generally
recognized. James E. Miller, Jr. has pointed out that there
is nothing radically new in this book—except style. As
Miller says, Melville had demonstrated the confidence
man—representative of evil—at work in most of his
earlier works: he is the missionary in *Typee* and *Omoo*,
spreading contagion along with his selfish "Christianity";
he is omnipresent in *Mardi*. Furthermore, though Miller
does not mention it, he is in *Redburn, White- Jacket,
Moby- Dick*; he is the lightning-rod salesman in the story of
the same name, the architect in "I and my Chimney," and
to a certain extent Derwent in the later work *Clarel*. With
less intensity and for different reasons he is the masquerading figure of Israel Potter. Most important of all, he is
split into two persons in *Billy Budd*, appearing as both
Captain Vere and Claggart.

Equally dependent upon Melville's other works is the
figure of the mute. Although there is little doubt of what
such a figure represents when he appears in other works—
in the person of of Billy Budd, for example—there is strong
feeling among some critics that in *The Confidence- Man* he
must be damned with the company he seems to be keeping.
Thus many readers see the mute as the first of the
confidence men, or if not one himself, then guilty of
softening the public and thus paving the way for the
workings of the real con man who follows. But such
criticism ignores some obvious points. Melville means the
mute to be separated from the confidence man. The mute
is **not** listed by the Negro cripple—the first disguise of

the con man—as being one of his friends; in fact, the Negro clearly knows nothing of the mute. Further, he is not mentioned in the list of characters to be developed as con men that Melville drew up and kept working over. Instead the mute is tied in with the white savior who is common in Melville's works. The mute is another in the long line of saviors who will be most fully developed in Billy Budd. More immediately he is closely similar to Bartleby, the Christ figure in the story written only four years before this book.

In the earlier story Melville had shown the Savior in his Passion. In the final scene Bartleby lies down in the pose of a crucified Christ awaiting rebirth: "Strangely huddled at the base of the wall, his knees drawn up, and lying on his side, his head touching the cold stones, [was] the wasted Bartleby." His "dim eyes were open," and to touch him made the skin "shiver." That story, in other words, concerns itself with the actual rejection of the Savior and the promise of His resurrection. *The Confidence-Man* in effect begins where the other story leaves off. It starts with the resurrected Savior. We see him rejected immediately, and them we observe what happens in the world that has cast him off.

The first two chapters of the book are used to build up the genuine Savior. It should perhaps be pointed out that to Melville the Savior did not necessarily mean Jesus Christ, although he had a great respect for Christ the individual; instead *savior* symbolizes the universal savior, the genuine hero, the true man. In *The Confidence-Man* the mute, the Savior, is the "man in cream-colors" (not white, as many critics misread); his "cheek was fair, his chin downy, his hair flaxen, his hat a white fur one." He appeared "at sunrise," and his coming was an "advent." He was "in the extremest sense of the word, a stranger." He "appeared, suddenly as Manco Capac at the lake Titicaca." Further, Melville does not use about him the usual words of equivocation that he carefully utilizes

throughout the remainder of the book to suggest
the imposter.

Another significant aspect is that the mute comes
aboard the "ship of fools" at St. Louis. Although this is
obviously a possible logical point of embarkation for a
Mississippi River voyage, there is greater importance.
Melville is picking up a motif that he has touched on
before and will develop more obviously later, in, for
example, *Clarel* and *Billy Budd:* the contrast between what
the French Revolution expressed in its original manifestations and the excesses it fell into when extremism
usurped power from moderation. Melville's reference to
Anacharsis Cloots and his "congress of all kinds of that
multiform pilgrim species, man," which significantly comes
at the end of Chapter Two, after the mute has disappeared,
presages similar references in other works. In none is
Melville deprecating Cloots, but is rather pointing out the
difference between the noble ideal represented by Cloots
and the evil that excesses can produce.

Further, St. Louis means more than a mere city. It
symbolized true faith, as in *Clarel.* In *Billy Budd* the
French ship *St. Louis* is renamed the *Atheiste* when the
excesses of the revolution carry the French into extremes.
In *The Confidence-Man* the *Fidele* makes its regular run
from St. Louis—genuine faith—into extremes when it
becomes the "ship of fools" by rejecting the genuine
Savior. Eden, it will be remembered, is up-river from
St. Louis, in a colony founded by two people who swam
naked across the river. The true nature of this Eden is not
reversed by the fact that the confidence man tries to sell
stock in this colony. Satan has before used heaven for his
own ends. Down-river from St. Louis is away from faith.
Thus develops Melville's irony in having his "ship of fools"
on a down-river voyage from faith into the waters of
atheism on a ship named the *Fidele.*

On the ship the mute does not act suspiciously, although
the people around him choose to suspect him. The only

doubtful aspect is Melville's placing him in juxtaposition to a "theatre-bill" which announces the recent arrival of some imposter from the East. But the setting must be kept carefully in mind. Standing around the poster is a cross-section of American life. These people are being given the opportunity to choose between the real and the phony. This is the first of many tests Melville gives these people to choose between the genuine and the spurious. The situation exactly parallels that in *The Scarlet Letter* when the citizens of Boston are given the opportunity to distinguish between the genuineness of Hester Prynne and the fraudulence of Arthur Dimmesdale. In both instances the wrong choice is made.

These people standing around the poster are too busy in other activities. Primarily they are motivated by greed. They would like to get the reward for the capture of the imposter. But the chevaliers—the swindlers and sharpers— are the most active and are benefiting most concretely. Their fingers "are enveloped in some myth," that is, the practice of taking money from their fellow-passengers, pocket-picking. They myth is that of *laissez-faire,* in which, as Melville says in *Moby-Dick* and "Benito Cereno," the sharks devour the defenseless fish. This theme is emphasized by the other activities going on among these chevaliers. They are buying money-belts and selling fraudulent literature dealing with the lives of other great robbers, such men as Samuel Meason, John A. Murrall, and the Harpes.

The irony here is that all people standing at the poster—the crooks and non-crooks—are self-deluding. The reasonably honest would seem to be interested only in capturing the imposters from the East; the crooks ap- parently think they are safe among their kind and the objects of their search. But in fact in "new countries, where the wolves are killed off, the foxes increase." Apparently, however, very few are aware of this axiom. Here, as Hoffman points out, Melville is restating a theme from American popular lore and belief—that is, "myth"—the theme of Simon Suggs, the arch swindler of his day: "It pays to be shifty in a new country." [3]

It is in this setting that the mute stands before the bill and preaches this gospel of charity, quoting from 1 Corinthians. But his message is "inappropriate to the time and place." The people make fun of him and jostle him. One "flattened down his fleecy hat upon his head." In other words, his crown, his airiest part, is beaten, its symbol parodied. One theme of the mute's message and of 1 Corinthians is the need for unity among people. They must stick together in charity. Thus it is a cry for democracy. As Melville says about the white cripple who accuses Black Guinea of being a fraud: "That these suspicions came from one who himself on a wooden leg went halt, this did not appear to strike anybody present. That cripples, above all men should be companionable . . . should have a little sympathy in common misfortune, seemed not to occur to the company." But this cry for companionship is alien to the American psychology of the time, its *laissez-faire*, atomistic philosophy. Therefore the world is predisposed against the mute. Christianity is out of place in materialistic America.

This picture of charity being out of date in Melville's America is given undeniable vividness in the paragraph with which Melville ends the mute's quotations from the Bible. On the slate on which he had been writing his gospel, he had left the word *charity* untouched: "The word charity, as originally traced, remained throughout uneffaced, not unlike the left-hand numeral of a printed date, otherwise left for convenience." Melville's message seems to be that charity, though it is an alien in some societies, does not disappear, and that in America the blank temporarily left will someday be filled in, and charity will be welcome. This is indeed a dignified, quiet hope.

The easy dismissal of the teachings of Christ by the people inevitable draws comparison with a similar passage,

3. Daniel G. Hoffman, *Form and Fable in American Fiction* (New York, 1961). p. 72.

again, from *The Scarlet Letter*. As Hester Prynne is standing upon the scaffold before the hard-hearted people who are hooting her, Hawthorne develops at great length how Hester had been taken "out of the ordinary relations with humanity" and enclosed "in a sphere by herself." He says further, "Had there been a Papist among the crowd of Puritans, he might have seen in this beautiful woman, so picturesque in her attire and mien, and with the infant at her bosom, an object to remind him of the image of Divine Maturity." The fact that no one saw the comparison for Hester casts light on the mute and the real Savior.

The Scarlet Letter casts more illumination on the rest of Melville's passage. The mute in moving about through the crowd to get to the poster had used some "persistence, of a mildly inoffensive sort," and the crowd, "perceiving no badge of authority about him, but rather something quite the contrary," has resented his behavior. But these same people distrust others because they know they themselves cannot be trusted. Everyone is out to con those he can. The barber's commanding presence takes us back to Hawthorne, where the beadle, with his staff of authority, opens a lane through the crowd so the Hester can be taken to the scaffold, meanwhile stating: "I promise ye, Mistress Prynne shall be set where man, woman, and child may have a fair sight of her brave apparel . . . . A blessing on the righteous Colony of the Massachusetts, where iniquity is dragged out into the sunshine."

As if this were not enough evidence to demonstrate that the mute is real, and rejection of him catastrophic, Melville builds much more to make his point explicit. The mute is in fact both deaf and mute. Two porters approach him from behind, and give a "loud" warning to him, but he does not hear, and they swing their trunk against him "nearly overthrowing him." Though deliberately abused, the mute remains undisturbed by his ill treatment, as though he were used to it, and just as Bartleby in the earlier story had remained unresentful about his severe treatment. The mute

309

finally wanders to the foot of the Jacob's ladder which connects with the deck above, stretches out, and goes to sleep. Melville tries to be as unironic as possible in giving this scene a lyrical, almost reverential, and surely significant description:

> Gradually overtaken by slumber, *his flaxen head drooped, his whole lamb-like figure relaxed, and half reclining against the ladder's foot,* lay motionless, as some sugar-snow in March, which, softly stealing down over night, with its white placidity startles the brown farmer peering out from his threshold at daybreak (my italics).

With his tragic flaw—deafness and muteness—the mute, like Bartleby and Billy Budd with theirs, ascends to heaven.

The beginning of the second chapter is very important. It starts with the various comments of the upper-deck passengers on the sleeping mute. There is a wide difference of opinion. To some he is an "odd fish," or a "humbug." To others, a minority, he is the apparently sleeping Savior and is immortal. One calls him "Casper Hauser," referring to a mysterious German youth (Kasper Hauser, 1812?-1833) who appeared, as Elizabeth Foster notes, at Nuremberg suddenly in 1829 and could not or would not reveal anything of his past. Another calls him "green prophet from Utah," thus tying him in with the Latter Day Saints. Another picks up and develops a motif just used. The mute had lain down "at the foot of a ladder there leading to a deck above, up and down which ladder some of the boatmen, in discharge of their duties, were occasionally going." As Miss Foster points out, this is a reference to Jacob's vision of the ladder to heaven with angels going up and down and through that to heaven. This implication of heaven is substantiated by the statement of one of these travelers, when he says simply, "Jacob dreaming at Luz." All these comments, the derogatory as well as the commendatory, are "epitaphic comments," spoken by "a miscellaneous company, who,

assembled on the overlooking, *cross-wise* balcony at the
forward end of the *upper deck* near by, had not witnessed
preceding occurrences" (my italics).

There is social comment in this passage. Melville seems
to be saying that the mute took his place in "this humble
quarter" because he "was not entirely ignorant of his
place," and therefore belongs to the lower deck and
the people on it. He is the would-be savior of the common
people; though they, like the commoners in their rejection
of Jesus Christ, will not accept him. Those people on the
upper deck, above the cross, have not been witness to his
mistreatment by the common people. They are separated
from the commoners and from their savior. This savior
apparently has no desire to go up to their deck; thus
apparently is not for them. These upper-deck people give
their "epitaphic comments" because they recognize that
the mute has departed this world. But he went directly to
heaven, indifferent to those persons who would write his
epitaph. While the comments of these people were
"conflictingly spoken or thought," the mute, "like some
enchanted man in his grave, happily oblivious of all
gossip, whether chiseled or chatted," "still tranquilly slept."

The significance of this layered aspect of the book into
two levels is given more force later when Frank and
Charlie, the cosmopolitan and the metaphysician, are
talking together and look down to the lower deck and see
a poor boy there. Charlie laughs at the poor wretch, to the
chagrin of even the diabolical cosmopolitan. This situation
strengthtens Melville's criticism of Emerson's Transcendentalism. Emerson, Melville thought, always remained above
and uncommitted to the issues of this world, looking down
from his Olympian heights in indifference and contempt.

The consequence of man's rejection of the savior becomes immediately manifest. After "two or three random
stoppages" have been made "and the last transient memory
of the slumberer vanished, and he himself, not unlikely,
waked up and landed"—

311

the crowd, *as is usual,* began in all parts to break
up from a concourse into various clusters or squads,
which in some cases distintegrated again into
quartettes, trios, and couples, or even solitaries;
involuntarily submitting to that *natural law* which
ordains dissolution equally to the mass, as in time
to the member (my italics).

Melville seems here to be hammering home the point
he has established before. Charity is what holds the
common people together. But Americans are not sticking
together. Instead, under the influence of the "myth" about
them they are resorting to individualized actions. Ruled by
natural law rather than a superior love, man is doomed to
fragmentation, Melville says, which can result in the
solitary pioneer and, without charity to temper his
extremism, the Indian hater.

The next paragraph in the work points out, again, the
result of these people's choice. "As among Chaucer's
Canterbury pilgrims, or those oriental ones crossing the
Red Sea towards Mecca in the festival month, there was
no lack of variety." These people constitute "a piebald
parliament, an Anacharsis Cloots congress of all kinds
of that multiform pilgrim species, man." But these people
are not to journey toward the shrine of Thomas Becket or
Mecca. Instead they turn from Christ to paganism, to the
West: "Here reigned the dashing and all-fusing spirit of
the West, whose type is the Mississippi itself, which,
uniting the streams of the most distant and opposite
zones, pours them along, helter-skelter, in one cosmopolitan
and confident tide." Here then the difference between the
cohesiveness of the pilgrims on the road to Canterbury,
and the "cosmopolitan and confident tide" of the American
West, a West which Melville always felt was the very
essence of America, her future and hope, but which as he
shows in *Israel Potter,* that is itself concerned with a
masquerade, and with some stories of this kind, he also
feared as being superficial and crass.

The shift from the world in which the mute might have had some influence to that of the "all-fusing spirit of the West" is startling, from one to its opposite. Melville's technique is precisely that of Hawthorne in *The Scarlet Letter*, in which at the beginning of the third chapter, as in Melville, the spotlight is turned from Hester and Dimmesdale on the scaffold and the platform above it, the latter about to perform his masquerade, to the satanic Roger Chillinworth, standing on the ground.

"Black Guinea," to whom Melville turns, the first of the confidence men, is clearly Satan, and Satan is of course a parody of God, goodness perverted. As Satan he represents the "natural" and "pagan" aspects of humanity. He is cut down to the stature of a Newfoundland dog, and his "honest black face" is always "rubbing against the upper part of people's thighs."

Literature is filled with examples of the folk belief of the devil appearing in the form of a dog. Further, Guinea is Satan in being a dog "widout messa," for there is no God in the world in which he runs free. The symbolism which must be attached to the name *St. Louis* is enriched by the fact that Satan cannot pronounce the name of anything holy; therefore he is unable to pronounce the name of the city in which he asserts he lives. All he can say is that he "libs in der city." It is the inquiring "purple-faced drover" who infers—and is allowed to believe—that the city is St. Louis, the holy city. But Guinea will not allow close inquiry about his habitat. When quizzed too closely he shuffles "off into the thickest of the crowd, like a half-frozen black sheep nudging itself a cozy berth in the heart of the white flock."[4] But before escaping he introduces one of the significant themes of the book. He claims that it is the sun shining over St. Louis that keeps him warm. Thus, in Biblical terms, sunshine—like the rain—comes to the just and the unjust. But in many ways this book is a study

4. Chap. III. Because of the numerous editions, references will be to chapters rather than to pages, and will hereafter appear in the text.

in blindness, that despite the fact that there is light nobody can or will see clearly.

This theme is picked up later in the book when after having been rebuked by the Missourian the cosmopolitan is accosted by a stranger "with the bluff *abord* of the West," who tells the story of Colonel Moredock, Indian-hater. The setting might well be supposed to tip off the nature of his story, it being a lie raised to the power of legend in order to seduce in yet another way an unseeing and therefore credulous public. The cosmopolitan meets this stranger "in the semicircular porch of a cabin, opening a recess from the deck, lit by a zoned lamp swung overhead, and sending its vertically down, like the sun at noon. Beneath the lamp stood the speaker, affording to any one disposed to it no unfavorable chance for scrutiny; but the glance now resting on him betrayed no such rudeness" (CH. XXV). The point of significance at this moment is that the "zoned lamp" casts a narrow and circumscribed light, but one bright enough to reveal the speaker's true character if the other person had cared to read it. Later the amount of light is reduced, when the stranger, continuing his story of Moredock, reports that he in fact never saw the legendary colonel. Once he tried to see him in the loft of a cabin but could not because there was "not much light" there.

The motif is carried on in the account of China Aster. This story is told by Egbert, who represents Transcendentalism, about Orchis, who becomes a Come-Outer and ruins his friend Aster. Ironically Egbert does not recognize the evil of Transcendentalism although the Come-Outers were Transcendentalists. Orchis is a confidence man, like all people on the ship. He may not be on to the way to becoming a con man, but the evil he performs is just as vicious. Acting in what he may consider only the interests of his friend, he in effect forces China Aster to borrow money in order to enlarge his candle business. Orchis has become rich by chance. That is, he represents the American capitalist, who in a *laissez-faire* economy might win and might lose. He promises to purchase all of his candles from his friend Aster, and thus assure his success: "I'll buy all my light of you," he says, in what is obviously a parallel to Melville's other uses of the light-lamp references. Thus lured, China Aster takes the loan, though against his better judgment, and ultimately loses his new shop, fails in whatever he attempts, and finally is left without anything.

This theme concludes the book, when the cosmopolitan extinguishes the "solar lamp" that had been used by the old man in reading his Bible, and had thus to a certain extent lighted the world against Satan.

Though Satan is obviously the greatest con man on the ship, it must not be forgotten that since all or most of the passengers act under the philosophy of Simon Suggs—that it pays to be sharp in a new country—most feel that in one way or another, to one extent or another, they must try to trick the others. This is clearly demonstrated at the beginning of the scene with Black Guinea, when various persons play with and abuse the Negro, who seems to be at their mercy. The people soon tire of mere charity, but delight in it when it is mixed with "diversion." So in order to allow the people to toy with him, Black Guinea—Satan—acts like a dog, and opening his mouth allows the people to cast pennies into it. But ironically, although this game of extreme humiliation of an apparent fellow human is being played for mere pennies, some of the people are too cheap to play fairly. "Some of the apparent pennies thus thrown proved buttons." Thus the people trick the seeming helpless. Little wonder that they likewise should be fooled. The passage, which probably derives in part from the dog scene in "Ethan Brand," introduces perhaps one of the most important themes of the book: that all creatures, both human and Satanic, like to fool others, not for gain but for sport.

The most important theme is of course that of the need for but absence of *true* charity (love), that is, cohesiveness among the people of the world. In this connection four characters demand close study: the white cripple, who accuses Black Guinea of being a fraud; the "invalid Titan in homespun," who gets on the boat at a "houseless landing, scooped, as by a land-slide, out of sombre forests," and temporarily thwarts the confidence man; Pitch, the misanthropic Missourian; and Colonel Moredock, the diluted Indian-hater. All four have one thing in common: they are supermen. Three are super evil men; one, the "Titan in homespun," is a super good man.

The three evil supermen are extremes in suspiciousness, uncharitableness, and misanthropy. They vary in degree of intensity of their lack of charity and their importance in the book according to the order in which they appear. The book as a whole is in effect a battle of the gods before and among the people, with the latter being the battleground. At the beginning the savior is introduced and apparently loses to his Satanic adversary. On a slightly lower scale but actively engaged are the supermen.

The first white cripple, the least superman of the trio, might at first be mistaken for Melville's spokesman. He voices what is obvious to us when he suspects Black Guinea of being a fraud, and when he says of the passengers in general, "You flock of fools, under this captain of fools, in this ship of fools." But he lacks love for this "flock of fools," and that is his weakness. He condemns people "diabolically," and he *writhes* when caught. Melville emphasizes that this man is a kind of little Satan, a figure of folklore, by his use of a folktale here, as he uses folklore generally throughout the book to raise it from the merely human and to make it timeless.

The clergyman who went in search of one of the references Black Guinea gave for his character has found one, who indeed vouches for "poor Guinea." The clergyman then admits that he had begun to suspect the Negro. The cripple overhears the remark and relates a story which continues the theme of suspicion. The story he tells is obviously an earthy folktale which is "unpleasant to repeat." but "might, perhaps, in a good-natured version, be rendered as follows." The story of a beautiful Tennessee girl who when married to an old Frenchman of New Orleans was "liberal to a fault" is clearly the oft-told tale of the marriage of January and June. It could have come straight from Boccaccio, Chaucer, or from the lips of thousands of tellers of folktales. Its conclusion has the undeniable stamp of folktale: upon entering his apartment one night, the old Frenchman who had been told of his wife's liberality but would not believe, sees a "stranger burst from the alcove," and remarks, "Begar! . . . now I begin to suspect."

Miss Foster is surely correct in saying that Melville's message in the book is that humanism is the only mainstay on earth. In the scales of humanism this cripple is found wanting. As the militant Methodist minister accurately observes, the cripple's physical affliction is "emblematic of his one-sided view of humanity." He is, however, apparently in Melville's view, not as wicked as Pitch, the Missourian, to whom he is closely linked. When the minister urges the cripple to have charity, the latter replies, "To where it belongs with your charity! to heaven with it." Though he snaps this remark "diabolically," at least he knows that there is charity in heaven; and significantly the cripple is clear-headed enough not to be swindled by the confidence man.

Not so, however, with Pitch the misanthropic Missourian, who is a study of a larger-sized white cripple. Pitch, despite his extreme misanthrophy, is tricked. This cynic is thematically tied in with his earlier counterpart in several ways, obviously in his misanthropy. He is lacking in humaneness, as the confidence-man in the disguise of the herb-doctor charges, and the Missourian admits. When the herb-doctor has sold the poor man his bogus medicine and has tried to sell some to the Missourian, the latter snaps his rifle and declines. The herb-doctor rejoins to the charge that he has gulled the old man with a question: "For the gulling tell me, is it humane to

talk so to this poor old man?'' and soon Pitch admits,
''*gravely eyeing the old man*''—''Yes, it *is* pitiless in one like
me to speak too honestly to one like you''(CH. XXI). To Pitch
the ''only practical Christians'' are machines.

Pitch is also tied in with the earlier cripple verbally. The
former had replied to the minister, ''To where it belongs
with your charity! to heaven with it!'' Pitch makes a similar
statement. When the representative of the Philosophical
Intelligence Office is talking with Pitch attempting to
explain the principles on which his office is run, the
misanthrope exclaims: ''To the devil with your principles!''
(CH. XXII). One of Melville's fine ironies is that the
Missourian, despite his belief in the infallibility of his
wisdom, does not know at this point that he is in fact
talking to the devil. Since Pitch's remark is the reverse of
the white cripple's, and they are brothers under the skin,
and Pitch is gulled, whereas the other is not, Melville's
purpose seems to be to demonstrate that Pitch is a
greater evil than the other. He points more directly to the
greatest evil of all, Moredock the Indian-hater.

The white cripple and Pitch are demonstrably related in
yet another way. The former is, as we have seen, a
character with folk overtones and dimensions. So is the
latter, and much more fully developed. He is a Melvilleian
Davy Crockett.

Crockett, as both Richard Chase and Daniel Hoffman
have demonstrated, was omnipresent during the 30s, 40s,
and 50s in the American western mind, kept in the public
eye by the numerous Crockett almanacs. In them, as
Hoffman says, ''We find Crockett supernaturally hideous,
Crockett entering the animal world, Crockett displaying
Jovian and Promethean prowess, Crockett screaming his
brag, Crockett snapping fire and lightning from his
knuckles, Crockett climbing Niagara, Crockett saving the
earth from extinction with a kick and a daub of bear-oil
when the sun freezes fast on its axis.'' [5] Melville surely was

5. For more examples, see Hoffman, *Form and Fable,* p. 63.

not indifferent to folk and popular lore. He collected the
Agatha story that he sent to Hawthorne for his friend to
cast in literary form. He was himself a great teller of tales
and singer of songs in his youth, as his companion Toby
Green reported. Further, *Moby-Dick,* as we have seen, and
other works before and after *The Confidence-Man* pulse
with folklore.

Crockett the folk hero was almost surely in Melville's
mind when he drew Pitch. This fabulous folk creature—and
his later extensions—was half horse, half alligator. Pitch is
"a rather eccentric-looking person," "somewhat ursine in
aspect" (in other words, bearlike), "sporting a shaggy
spencer of the cloth called bear's-skin; a high-peaked cap
of raccoon-skin, the long bushy tail switching over behind;
raw-hide leggings; grim stubble chine; and to end, a
double-barrel gun in hand." He has an air "which would
have seemed half cynic, half wild-cat, were it not for the
grotesque excess of the expression, which made its
sincerity appear more or less dubious"   He makes
a sound, a "low, half-suppressed growl, as of Bruin in a
hollow trunk." He talks "like a snapping turtle"
He closely resembles a combination Crockett-Mike Fink
creature.

His talk, further, is strongly like that of the ring-tailed
roarer. Mike Fink bragged, in a typical fashion: "Hurray
for me, you scapegoats! I'm a land-screamer—I'm a
watchdog—I'm a snapping turckle—I can lick five times
my own weight in wildcats, I can use up injuns by
the cord." The Missourian's brag is in the same vein: "Yes,
sir, yes. My name is Pitch; I stick to what I say. I speak
from fifteen years' experience." The Crockett-Fink
frontiersmen loved the taste of words, rolling them around
in their mouths, then spewing them forth to overwhelm,
in the age-old folk demigod style, their enemies. Such
words as "tetotatious," "exflunticate," "absquatulate,"
"slantindicular" heavily weighted their vocabularies. Pitch
too clearly loves the sound of his own words, for
example:

319

... All thinking minds are, now-a-days, coming to
the conclusion—one derived from an immense hereditary
experience—see what Horace and others of the
ancients say of servants—coming to the conclusion, I
say, that boy or man, the human animal is, for most
work-purposes, a losing animal. . . . Carding machines,
horse-shoe machines, tunnel-boring machines, reaping
machines, apple-paring machines, boot-blacking
machines, sewing machines, shaving machines, run-
of-errand machines, dumb-waiter machines, and the
Lord-only-knows-what machines.

The folk characteristics of the white cripple and Pitch
("a sort of comprehensive Colonel Moredock") are further
developed in the person of the diluted Indian-hater.
Melville's purpose in using folklore here is to make this
Indian-hater larger than life, a demigod, thus to enlarge
and intensify the picture of him into, as Roy Harvey Pearce
has said, the most misanthropic and therefore most evil
aspect of the book.

Melville's source for the story of the Indian-hater was
Hall's "Indian-hating.—Some of the sources of this
animosity.—Brief account of Colonel Moredock." Melville
excluded or expanded as he chose in order to shape his
material to his own purpose. Melville begins with the
chapter "The Metaphysics of Indian-hating," in which he
gives the picture of Indian-hating *par excellence*. But there
is no such thing as a perfect Indian-hater; so he follows
with the story of Colonel Moredock, perhaps the nearest
thing that can be to the ideal hater of red men.

The purpose of Melville's book is to show what happens
to a world that has rejected the teachings of the Savior, the
need for true charity (love) and for living together, and has
fallen in to bogus Christianity, where everyone cons all
others. The purpose of this section on Indian-hating, as
Miss Foster correctly shows, is to demonstrate what happens in a world which carries to its logical conclusion
its rejection of love. Indian-hating is only a synonym for
man-hating.

Melville makes this perfectly clear at the beginning of
this passage, even before getting into the metaphysical. The
stranger telling the story begins by saying: ". . . You must
know that Indian-hating was no monopoly of Colonel
Moredock's; but a passion, in one form or other, and to a
degree greater or less of largely shared among the class to
which he belonged. And Indian-hating still exists; and, no
doubt, will continue to exist so long as Indians do"
(CH. XXV). But for Indian one must read *man,* says
Melville in one of his quiet extensions of meaning,
when the judge telling the story asks if the hate for the
red man is surprising:

> A race whose name is upon the frontier a
> *memento mori;* painted to him in every evil light; now
> a horse-thief like those in Moyamensing; now an
> assassin like a New York rowdy; now a treat-breaker
> like an Austrian; now a Palmer with poisoned arrows;
> now a judicial murderer and Jeffried, after a fierce
> farce of trial condemning his victim to bloody death;
> or a Jew with hospitable speeches cozening some
> fainting stranger into ambuscade, there to burk him,
> and account it a deed grateful to Manitou, his
> God (CH. XXVI).

Thus, the Indian is no more evil than the white, than a
horse-thief in Pennsylvania, a killer in New York, a political
liar in Austria, a legalized murderer in England. The
frontiersman's inability to see that evil is universal and his
insistence on singling out the Indian, who at least had
some initial reason for his animosity to the whites, as evil's
only source indicates the degree of his blindness.

Further evidence of the self-delusion of the Indian-
haters can be seen in the fact that though they practice
little Christianity—charity and love of fellowman—they
use it as a touchstone with which to test the red man's
iniquity. The Indian-hater says that when an Indian
becomes a Christian, "he will not in that case conceal his
depravity; and, in that way, as much as admits that the

321

back-woodsman's worst idea of it is not very far from true; while, on the other hand, those red men who are the greatest sticklers for the theory of Indian virtue, and Indian-loving-kindness, are sometimes the arrantest horse-thieves and tomahawkers among them." But Melville's irony in ending this statement is terrifying: "So, at least, avers the backwoodsman" CH. XXVI).

Melville points out, further, that having renounced the true spirit of Christianity, and having subverted it to their own uses, Indian-haters become friends in making hatred their religion. The hater "with the solemnity of a Spaniard turned monk," takes leave of his kin. "Indian-hating, whatever may be thought of it in other respects, may be regarded as not wholly without the efficacy of a devout sentiment."

Melville builds up the importance of the backwoodsman into the symbol with universal application by calling upon the concept of this man as symbol in popular and folklore like Crockett, Fink, Boone, and many others. Melville makes him ubiquitous in time and space:

> Though held in a sort a barbarian, the backwoodsman would seem to America what Alexander was to Asia—captain in the vanquard of conquering civilization. Whatever the nation's growing opulence or power, does it not lackey his heels? Pathfinder, provider of security to those who come after him, for himself he asks nothing but hardship. Worthy to be compared with Moses in the Exodus, or the Emperor Julian in Gaul, who on foot, and bare-browed, at the head of covered or mounted legions, marched so through the elements, day after day. The tide of emigration, let it roll as it will, never overwhelms the backswoodsman into itself; he rides upon advance, as the Polynesian upon the comb of the surf (CH. XXVI).

This is the idealized standard built up by folklore which makes Colonel Moredock a demigod. Though he is not an Indian-hater *par excellence*—there can be no biography of such a person—as diluted Indian-hater he represents a logical culmination of the picture of misanthrope developed successively in the white cripple and the Missourian.

His hate is monomaniacal. It began with cause, perhaps. His mother had been married three times and widowed each time by Indians. She and eight of nine children were killed by the red men on the banks of the Mississippi. Melville makes it plain, however, that the murderers were a "band of twenty renegades from various tribes, outlaws even among Indians." Moredock dedicates his life to tracking down and slaying all of these guilty Indians. In four years he has slain them all. But he is not satisified. "To kill Indians had become his passion," and he spent many years killing them, renouncing all worldly advancement, even that of becoming governor of Illinois. Giving up worldly glory, however, was no privation for him, since he knew "that to be a consistent Indian-hater involves the renunciation of ambition, with its objects—the pomps and glories of the world" (CH. XXVII).

Moredock, like the white cripple and the Missouri misanthrope, was an eccentric with cause. The white cripple probably owed his attitude to his misshapen body; the Missourian owed his to the fact that twenty-nine boys had proved unworthy of trust. Moredock became an Indian-hater because of the fate of his family. Without this hate—which grew in intensity into a monomania if not a religion—he might have been the ideal backwoodsman. He was surely a superman: "As an athlete, he had few equals; as a shot, none; in single combat, not to be beaten." He was "master of . . . woodland-cunning" and his "bravery, whether in Indian fight or any other was unquestionable." "Nearly all Indian-haters have at bottom loving hearts; at any rate, hearts, if anything more generous than the average," and Moredock "mingled in the life of the settlements" and showed himself "not without humane feelings" (CH. XXVII).

Bigger than life as he was, he pictures in greater magnitude the evil of obsessive hate, and demonstrates

323

how it overwhelms all. This hatred is as self- and world-destructive in its blindness as is the confidence which is fed upon by the confidence man.

Roy Harvey Pearce is too despairing in his conclusion about the picture presented by the Indian-hater. Melville does not necessarily point out that "only by becoming a hater *par excellence* can one resist the confidence-man," and consequently the conclusion of the novel is not that hope "virtually disappears after Chapter I." On the contrary, Miss Foster is more nearly correct when she says that "Melville, though a pessimistic moralist in this novel, is not . . . a despairing one."[6] In fact, as I shall point out at the conclusion of this chapter, the ending of the novel specifically opens the door a crack to admit a ray of hope.

Before that, however, one other aspect needs to be examined: the character of the "Titan in homespun," who with his daughter boards the ship at a landing in the forest and confounds the scheming quack doctor.

Along with the other supermen about whom we have been talking, this person is extraordinary, a "Titan," as Melville calls him. He is the opposite of the overly-suspicious and misanthropic white cripple, Missourian, and Colonel Moredock, and an answer to the jingoism and racism that was so much a part of nineteenth-century American and backwoodsman psychology.

His daughter "walking in moccasions" is "evidently of alien maternity, perhaps Creole, or even Comanche." She was wearing "an Indian blanket" which "appeared that morning to have shielded the child from heavy shower" (CH. XVII). He is clearly a lover of Indians—in two senses of the word. He is an Anacharsis Cloots representative of the nations of the American backwoods, bowed low under the burden of compassion for the knowledge of the human plight.

More important, he is the foil of Satan. The quack doctor, the present role of Satan, recognizes the "Titan"

6. Foster, *Confidence-Man*, p. 340.

instantaneously as his mortal enemy, a superman, a benign folk hero. Immediately he resorts to folklore in an effort to seduce the child and thus get at the father. The quack calls the little girl his "little May Queen," and sings to her the nursery rhyme "Hey diddle, diddle, the cat and fiddle." But the father's hatred, and protection of his daughter, is complete. He will not carry on a conversation with his enemy.

The significance of this giant is pointed up by his similarity to certain people in other books by Melville. The quack doctor is lying in order to sell his fake medicine, when suddenly the "Titan" strikes him a side-blow that all but fells him. Then he say to the quack "profane fiddler on heart-strings! Snake!" And Melville comments, significantly "more he would have added, but, convulsed, could not." Like all heroes in folklore, he has a tragic flaw, like Bartleby before and Billy Budd afterwards.

He is also Melville's enigmatic man, a parallel to Jeremiah in *Moby-Dick*, the Spanish sailor on board the *San Dominick* who hands Delano "the knot" and tells him to unravel it, the Dansker in *Billy Budd* who could have prevented the terrible destruction of Billy if only he had spoken out and told all he knew. Had the "Titan hit the quack doctor hard enough he would have been eliminated." But all these people were victimized by their tragic flaws. One of the most moving sentences in the book is that spoken by the quack doctor when the giant turns and walks away, undoubtedly voicing Melville's own deep tragic sense, "lost to humanity"(CH. XVII).

His personal life was filled with reversals, his literary future in doubt, but Melville's comment, like the message of the book throughout, is not of despair. Watching the rejection of the savior and all he represents, we witness the happenings in a world in which sham Christianity and bogus charity and confidence seduce one person after another, touching in one way or another and to one extent or another practically everyone. We sense Melville's rising anger. But we do not sense that bleak November is merging into black December. Indeed at the conclusion, despite the immediately preceding scene, where Satan turns out the "solar lamp" that has been used by the old man for reading his Bible and leads him into darkness, there is a hint of hope.

Form always is important in Melville, as we have seen. In *Moby-Dick*, he uses a short "Epilogue" to provide necessary explanation. More significantly in such works as "Bartleby," "Benito Cereno," and *Billy Budd*, the ending highlights or even pin-points and clarifies Melville's conclusion. So too in this story.

The work ends in a symbol-laden paragraph: "The next moment, the waning light expired, and with it the waning flames of the horned altar, and the waning halo round the robed man's brow; while in the darkness which ensued, the cosmopolitan kindly led the old man away. *Something further may follow of this Masquerade*" (my italics).

Without the concluding sentence this conclusion would be the bleakest despair. With it, however, there is hope. Various critics have assumed that this sentence indicates that Melville meant to add other adventures to this voyage.[7] Perhaps he did. In his *Journal up the Straits* he wrote "Pera, the headquarters of ambassadors, and where also an unreformed diplomacy is carried on by swindlers, gamblers, cheats, no place in the world fuller of knaves," and alongside this entry he noted, "For the Story." And other entries can be construed as being jottings for this particular story.

Regardless of what Melville's immediate intentions might have been, however, he never used these jottings for a sequel to *The Confidence-Man*. Melville's feelings at this time and his real meaning at the ending to this book can best be illuminated by a comparison with his general

---

7. Herman Melville, *Journal Up the Straits*, ed. Raymond Weaver (New York, 1935). For a summary of the evidence seeming to favor the sequel, see Howard C. Horsford. "Evidence of Melville's Plans for a Sequel to *The Confidence-Man*." *American Literature* 24 (1952): 85-89. For a brief comments, see Foster, *Confidence-Man*, p. 364.

feeling during these years as revealed in his other works, and especially by the endings of his other works.

Israel Potter (1854) is a study of a man of disguises, a masquerader, in one way at least a confidence-man. Though this story seems to end in gloom, the conclusion is in fact, like that of *Hamlet*, filled with promise and hope; the author of such a robustly humorous and muscular story was obviously not just short of darkest depression. So, too, with "Bartleby" (1853), and "Benito Cereno" (1855), in which the endings are pregnant with hope and promise. Further, the ending of *The Confidence-Man* must be read with an awareness of Melville's attitude during the Civil War, when sorrow was mitigated by a genuine hope in the future of man.

Melville's words "Something further may follow of this Masquerade," refer not to this book but to life, as the capitalized final word would seem to indicate. His message is that something yet may come of this journey called life by this creature called man. The sentence seems more the still quiet voice of hope than the death rattle of despair. As such, like the book in its entirety, it reveals another aspect of Melville's study of and hope in humanism.

NINE

CLAREL AND THE OTHER POETRY

CLAREL: MAN'S "COMPLEX MOODS"

Clarel: A Pilgrimage (1876) is, of all of Melville's works, the most complex in method and tentative in conclusion. The poem is the direct result of Melville's voyage to the Holy Land in 1857, when his family felt he was in desperate need of improved health and spirits. But it is a work which grew many years in the author's attic of ideas. For despite urgings by his family, Melville would not capitalize on his voyage for lyceum lectures or superficial literary exercises. The account of the voyage was not published until 1876, when it was privately financed by Melville's literary angel, Uncle Peter Gansevoort.

A long meditative poem of 18,000 lines in four parts and 150 cantos, in tetrameters generally rhyming in couplets, the work is not easy going for the reader who skims. It is diffuse and rambling and does not have the singleness and power of, say, *Moby-Dick* nor the simplicity and clarity of, for example, *Billy Budd*. But its skein of complexities can be unwound by careful study. And understanding of this work is vital to any full comprehension of Melville the man and of all his writings. It is one of the most important works in revealing his lifelong questions and tentative answers, for it contains aspects of most or all of Melville's earlier works— strengthened by many years of meditating—and a prediction of his last, *Billy Budd*.

Melville's experience in the Holy Land was sadly disillusioning. Always wracked by skepticism of man's hope in God and heaven, he became increasingly doubtful when he found in the land of the birth of the proclaimed Savior of the world nothing but bleakness and pettiness which overwhelmed him. In the *Journal Up the Straits,* the day-by-day account of his trip through the Holy Land, his certainties about God are burned on the terrible, bleak rocks: Jehovah is a "terrible mixture of the cunning and awful." About Palestine he asks the question and supplies his own answer: "Is the desolation of the land the result of the fatal embrace of the Deity? Hapless are the favorites of Heaven." In his candor and forthrightness, Melville sets forth the anomalies, paradoxes, and questions if he cannot discover answers and resolutions.

Clarel is a study of heaven and earth, East and West, Old World and New, past and present, myths and comparative religions, people, nature, man, and animal, all ways of life. It is, in other words, a study in humanity. In method, Melville is the omniscient author-narrator, yet he is also present to one degree or another in virtually all of the characters or at least the major ones. The result of this lack of consistency in development is greater ambiguity and lack of definiteness than is found in any other of Melville's works, even *The Confidence-Man,* otherwise Melville's most difficult work.

Because *Clarel* is filled with more questions than answers, because of its tentativeness and ambiguity, one hesitates to dogmatize on Melville's meanings, intentional or unintentional. Yet one thread, one message, does seem perfectly clear and intentional in the poem—Melville's insistence here, as in *The Confidence-Man* and *Billy Budd,* as well as in numerous other works, that man's fate, his future, his hope and consolation, lie not in heaven but on earth, not with God but with mankind. Man's immortality is bound up with the longevity of the race, not the fate of the individual. William Ellery Sedgwick described this growth as effectively as anyone has: "Melville's act was toward humanity, not away from it. He renounced all the prerogatives of individuality in order to enter into the destiny which binds all human beings in one great spiritual and emotional organism. He abdicated his

329

independence so as to be incorporated into the mystical body of humanity."[1]

Thus the poem is a study of the commitment of various individuals to mankind. Vine, the artist, though a genuis and therefore to a certain extent uncommitted to individuals, is nevertheless wholly pledged to the human race. Rolfe, the moderate man of no extremes, is very nearly the ideal person in the poem because he appreciates all forms of life. So does Derwent. The monomaniacs—Celio, Mortmain, Agath, Ungar, as well as Nehemiah and other religious zealots—are demoniac and unworldly insofar as they deny man. Foremost, the poem is about the humanization of Clarel. The other characters are generally static and experience no growth in the poem. Clarel, however, is dynamic and undergoes a profound transformation. He grows from a callow student who knows nothing but books to an adult who recognizes and feels the agony of the human predicament. This picture of the growth of Clarel into life, coupled with the obvious sanity of the normal characters and the aberrations of the monomaniacs, demonstrates convincingly Melville's belief in the necessity and power of humanism.

The poem begins with an epitome of the whole 18,000 lines. It is a static picture of still life, a device Melville had used successfully in the first half of "Benito Cereno" twenty years earlier.

Clarel is in a "chamber low" in Jerusalem. A callow young ex-divinity student, he suddenly realizes that he has been too long a mere reader of books, that the library does not contain all of life. He wants to know people—life—to give up books for nature. From his physical position, he cannot see any people. So he ascends to the roof of the building, and his eyes rise to the encircling hills and Mount Olive. From his high vantage point Clarel surveys Jerusalem like a god. Like God, Clarel is detached from the

1. William Ellery Sedgwick, *Herman Melville: The Tragedy of Mind* (New York, 1962), p. 566.

world. He sees life from a distance but cannot hear the
sounds of life, the suffering of man. He, like God, must get
closer, must be humanized in order to understand the
troubles of life, because "To avoid the deep saves not from
storm." So Clarel is "let to rove/At last among mankind."

Today life is complicated and "Man is heir/To complex
moods." Melville is deeply interested in comparative
religion, in "The intersympathy of creeds." Clarel sees
that all faiths have been corrupted since the days of the
founders, and he is terrified by the feuding sects in
Christianity. In one of his hasty and childish impulses,
Clarel becomes disgusted with society. His negative
attitude toward man makes the houses seem closed and
alien to him:

> In street at hand a silence reigns
> Which Nature's hush of loneness feigns.
> Few casements, few, and latticed deep,
> High raised above the head below,
> That none might listen, pry, or peep,
> Or any hint or inkling know
> Of that strange innocence or sin
> Which locked itself so close within.
> (I. vi. 1-8)

Because of his attitude he wanders out of Jerusalem,
through the Jaffa Gate, and "Along a vague and
houseless road" bordered by a Turkish cemetery. He
suddenly remembers that Christ after his resurrection
appeared on this road to two of his disciples, and Clarel,
aching for "Some stranger of a lore replete," meets
Nehemiah, the saintly monomaniac who lives in a dream
world of the New Jerusalem and the Second Coming.
Nehemiah's illusion appeals to Clarel because it offers an
escape from this world. Clarel's ambivalent attraction to
heaven and earth is revealed here, however, as well as
Melville's theme of the humanization of the student. For
despite the fact that Clarel reveres Nehemiah's "primal
faith," he is also "grateful for the human claim." The

student is led back into Jerusalem by the saint, and
Melville makes it clear that Clarel must learn to see
through man's windows into his troubles and joys if the
student is to live the full life.

Another comment on Clarel's growth into humanism is
made in the character of Celio, the monomaniacal
hump-backed ward of the Franciscan monastery of
Terra Santa who is revolting against the Roman Catholic
Church. Broken by doubt, he seeks some reason for faith
but finds none. The world and the Church have failed him.
He has excluded humanity, and he is shut out of humanity,
symbolically, when the gates of Jerusalem are closed
behind him, barring him from the city for the night. Though
he thinks another "Harbor remains," religion also fails him,
when the monks of Terra Santa file by him in the night
but bring no consolation.

Sympathy is one of the key words in the poem. There is
between Celio and Clarel "a novel sympathy" which deeply
influences the latter though they only see each other twice.
In Clarel's feelings for Celio, Melville demonstrates one
aspect of the main theme of the poem. After the second
glance with Celio, Clarel sees Ruth, the daughter of the
American Nathan and Agar, and is immediately attracted
to her,

> Whose air expressed such truth unfeigned,
> And harmonies inlinked which dwell
> In pledges born of record pure—
> She looked a legate to insure
> That Paradise is possible
> Now as hereafter.
> (I. xvi. 160-165)

But immediately all thoughts of Ruth were "strangely
underrun/By Celio's image." Melville is demonstrating
that Clarel is not fully awake sexually.

The development of Clarel in the poem is revealed by
the contrast between him and Celio when we see each for
the last time. Like Clarel at the end of the poem, Celio

enters the Martyr's Gate and plunges deep into the city,
where he dies. One of Melville's most poignant comments
on the theme of humanism comes when the wail of the
Syrians announces Celio's death: "Who young dies, leaves
life's tale half told" (I. xix. 35).

Clarel's lack of worldliness, his lack of humanism, but
his ambivalence about the matter is further revealed in his
association with Nehemiah, the monomaniacal religious
zealot. Though the older man is suffering from "illusion,"
he does have humanistic impulses. When he speaks of
"sweets that time should yet bring in, / A happy world,
with peace for dower," Clarel has a "vague disturbance" for
the "solitary man/Who such a social dream could fan."

Clarel's suspicion of Nehemiah's lack of interest in this
world is to a certain extent substantiated. Clarel
accompanies the older man to his quarters. On the way they
pass through a dismal street inhabited only by those
persons whose ties with humanity have been severed. They
are in some "degree / Of craze" "mastered by the awful
myth" which to a large extent now deludes Nehemiah and
temporarily Clarel. But these two pass by their fellow men
apparently without paying any attention to these outcasts.
They arrive at the older man's residence, in a peopleless
part of Jerusalem, which is cold and inhuman, "little there /
A human harbor might express."

After talking with Nehemiah for a while Clarel "slid into a
dream" of Ruth. His naiveté is further demonstrated by
Melville's picture of Ruth. She is never materialized as a
human being. Rather she is a dream of femaleness, a
symbol, in the same way that Yillah is in *Mardi* and Lucy is
in *Pierre*. She is half child. Her mother fondles her while
her head rests on her mother's lap like a child's. Ruth
thrills Clarel with puppy love, with "life's first romance." To
the young man Ruth's eyes are "Pure home of all we seek
and prize." She is a "bud" "with promise of unfolding hour."
She is "grace of Nature's dawn."

Melville's questioning ambivalence is further manifested.
Clarel's impulses are toward the earth but his heart drags

him toward heaven. When he and Nehemiah enter the
street of lepers (which in life had repelled Melville) both,
especially the younger man, are horrified. Time was,
Melville says, when the Church took care of these people.
When they were exiled, when "life's chain was riven" it
was done with love. Now, however, they are exiled and
ignored, locked out from human society with their huts
facing the wall. Clarel turns his eyes from these lepers
"in affright" and Nehemiah thinks of heavenly things, not
of the plight of these wretched human beings en masse.
"Is *he* of human rank?" Clarel asks when one "Horror
hobbling on low crutch/Draws near," and Nehemiah
responds in a way which demonstrates that his attitude is
superior to Clarel's though it is still unhumanitarian, in
wanting the leper to look for his happiness in heaven.
Melville's criticism at this point seems clear — the failure
of the Church and of religion in general, for the Church
"failed him [Nehemiah's friend] in the end."

A significant comment is made on the other-worldliness
of Clarel and Nehemiah with the introduction of Vine, the
character obviously modeled closely on Hawthorne.
Although Vine is an artist and possessed of some inner
greatness known only to himself, the fact that he is a
great humanitarian is made immediately manifest. He is no
saint. He has "blood like swart Vesuvian wine" though he
keeps himself under strict curb. He does not forget
"The beauty of the world, and charm:/He prized it
though it scarce might warm." "He communed with me."
He is "no monk": "Thronged streets astir/To Vine but
ampler cloisters were."

Vine is unapproachable because "Tradition, legend, lent
such spell/And rapt him in remoteness so." Melville uses
the traditions and legends of the past to bolster his point
of humanism:

On Salem's hill in Solomon's years
Of gala, O the happy town!
In groups the people sauntered down,

And Kedron crossing, lightly wound
Where now the tragic grove appears,
Then palmy, and a pleasure-ground
                    (I. xxx. 14-19).

Melville and Vine are not lovers of the past for its own
sake, but because in olden times there were fewer schisms,
more unity, and God walked the earth: "Yes, memory/Links
Eden and Gethsemane."

Melville introduces the third of his major characters
Rolfe—a partial self-portrait—immediately after the
appearance of Vine. Of the two, Rolfe is the more
important in the poem, and especially in the development
of the theme of humanism. He is met on "The hill above
the garden." He too is "keeping cheer/Apart." But
unlike the ascetic looking Vine, Rolfe is immediately
discernible as "Though given to study, as might seem,/Was
no scholastic partisan/Or euphonist of Academe,/But
supplemented Plato's theme/With daedal life in boats and
tents" (I. xxxi. 16-20). To him Melville applies one of his
greatest compliments: "Messmate of the elements."

Rolfe has returned to the Holy Land, "where evermore/
Some lurking thing he hoped to gain—/Slip quite behind
the parrot-lore/Conventional." He and Vine are to teach
Clarel humanism:

> If average mortals social be,
> And yet but seldom truly meet,
> Closing like halves of apple sweet—
> How with the rarer in degree?
>   (I. xxi. 53-57)

Of these two Rolfe does most of the talking, as the more
humanistic of the pair should. He converses on all aspects
of truth and error, religion and atheism, always questioning,
never revealing his true thoughts.

The pyramid of arguments for humanism continues to
rise. Melville tells the story of Arculf, the eighth century
French bishop who, returning from a pilgrimage to the
Holy Land, was wrecked in the Hebrides and was cared for

335

by Adamnan, the abbot of St. Columba, in order to
demonstrate obsession with heaven and indifference to
earth. Then Rolfe begins to tell of a mariner like
Nehemiah, and Vine shows, significantly, a "deep human
interest." Rolfe recounts the ship captain's failings and
eventual acceptance of God's goodness. But just as Vine,
Rolfe, and consequently Clarel are not sufficiently interested
in Nehemiah to accept his invitation to go to Bethany, they
are no longer interested in the sea captain when he is
likened to Nehemiah. Vine no longer has his "deep human
interest" and is "mute."

The theme of humanism is continued in Melville's condemning the Church for claiming Celio's corpse before it
was cold. He contrasts this "mistimed zeal" with Celio's
humanism despite his seeming despair. Clarel felt Celio's
poor petition from the ground:

Remember me! for all life's din
Let not my memory be drowned.

The evil of the friars and the poignancy of Celio's plea
are demonstrated when Clarel moves over in the cemetery
to others who "afar from kindred lie:/Protestants, which in
Salem die," and finds Rolfe standing over the grave of
"Poor Ethelward!" whom he knew. Ethelward "didst but
grope" and "hadst small hope." But he is remembered on
earth.

After this passage Rolfe's basic humanism, his desire
to be with people, with the living and not the dead, is reemphasized in his desire to leave the cemetery and get
back inside the gate of Jerusalem:

But home the sparrow flees.
Come, move we ere the gate they quit,
And we be shut out here with these
Who never shall re-enter it.

The canto "On the Wall" reveals Clarel tottering between
naiveté and sophistication, faith and doubt. Melville carries
on his criticism of religion by slurring the priests who love

wealth best, the humble but rich man, and will not have anything to do with poor men. Clarel is restive, cannot read the fathers. He is estranged from the evangelists. Thus "irresolute" he views the wall before him on which is written the poem by the departed "B.L.: Oxford: St. Mary's Hall." This poem is a desperate criticism of modernism and of revolutionaries, of "Atheists and Vitriolists of doom/ Faith's gathering night which rockets red illume." Melville makes it clear that Clarel is interested in the lines and in the author but does not necessarily agree with them and him. There are many ironies in the canto. When mentioning the Greeks "in starch/of prelate robes, kissed him on both cheeks," for example, Melville is obviously ironic. Also, by withholding any direct criticism of his own he probably makes clear that he does not agree with the Anglo-Saxon "B.L."

At this point in Clarel's naiveté, blind chance—as throughout the poem—plays an important role. By chance Clarel learns that Vine and Rolfe will go on the trip to the Dead Sea. "As chanced" he sees the messenger come to tell of the murder of Nathan, Ruth's father, by the Arabs. Though he realizes that he may as well go since custom denies him access to Ruth for a mourning period, he is still irresolute until by chance he witnesses an Armenian bier bearing a girl to her sepulcher. Clarel now becomes resolute. Hesitating only a moment he decides to make the trip. Though Clarel is sufficiently realistic to admit that "Biers need be borne," the speed with which he makes up his mind to leave Ruth suggests that he has not yet attained enough worldliness to know what love is and that he has merely been looking for an excuse to get away from her. The concluding stanza of this book makes clear this point. "Farewell to Zion's seat," concludes the author, and symbolically to faith and security. Life will change Clarel, will educate him; indeed this is a "profound remove." The stage is set for the humanizing of Clarel.

The theme of the education of Clarel is picked up immediately in Part II, beginning with Glaucon, the

Smyrniote, who rides with the Greek banker and is shortly to become his son-in-law. Rakish and atheistical in temperament, he speaks freely to Clarel, as the Lyonese youth is to do later. But Clarel, filled with "simpleness that comes/To students versed more in their tomes/Than life," cannot understand the bawdy songs that Glaucon sings. It is both ironic and a development of Melville's theme that Glaucon is going lightly to his marriage in a month, while Clarel plods heavily and painfully to his, if indeed he ever does achieve it.

The broader theme of humanism is also further developed. Clarel thinks that "the kindly Christ" was "man's fraternal Lord." Later as the travelers descend the terrible road to Jericho, Rolfe in a moment of brooding about his death verbally draws up his will, and in so doing reveals his outstanding concern for man:

> Bury me by the road, somewhere
> Near Spring or brook. Palms plant me there,
> And seats with backs to them, all stone:
> In peace then go. The years shall run,
> And green my grave shall be, and play
> The part of host to all that stray
> In desert: water, shade, and rest
> Their entertainment. So I'll win
> Balm to my soul by each poor guest
> That solaced leaves the Dead Man's Inn.
> (II. xv. 30-39)

This statement by Rolfe touches Vine's sometimes latent humanism:

> Where thrown he lay,
> Vine, sensitive, suffused did show,
> Yet looked not up, but seemed to weigh
> The nature of the heart whose trim
> Of quaint good fellowship could so
> Strike on a chord long slack in him.
> (II.xv. 42-47)

In the next canto Rolfe seems to inveigh against revolutionists, speaking apparently against the Septem-

338 *CLAREL* AND THE OTHER POETRY

berists and the Red Caps and Vitriolists. Against
Elijah and John the Baptist he balances Volney and
Chateaubriand, though one was a skeptic, the other a
Chaolic apologist, and Lamartine. But Rolfe praises
Lamartine's "fine social dream." Rolfe longs for the
good old days when *man* was better and God was
on earth:

> A god with peasants went abreast:
> Man clasped a deity's offered hand; . . .
> The 'world'—by Him denounced, defined—
> Him first—set off and countersigned, . . .
> Oh men ·
> Made earth inhuman; yes, a den
> Worse for Christ's coming, since his love
> (Perverted) did but venom prove//...
> Cut off, cut off!

This is the same desperate humanism of *The Confidence-
Man*. Rolfe does not like the state of the world, yet sense
tells him there is no other.

Rolfe's humanism is further demonstrated. In the
canto significantly named "The River-Rite," Rolfe urging
unity says:

> "Comrades, come!
> If heaven delight in spirits glad,
> And men were all for brothers made,
> Grudge not, beseech to joy with Rome."
> (II. xxiv. 31-34)

Rolfe, Derwent, and Vine, "Fraternal thus, the group
engage." They sing the *Ave Maria stella:*

> The triple voices blending glide,
> Assimilating more and more,
> Till in the last ascriptive line
> Which thrones the Father, lauds the son,
> Came concord full, completion fine—
> Rapport of souls in harmony of tone.

But, though it may seem a contradiction, these souls are
of this earth. The song is tied up with Rolfe's earlier

339

statement that in the good past God walked on earth. This medieval hymn is not of souls going to heaven. This is well proved by the fact that the saintly Nehemiah would not join in this concord. True and steadfast faith are Nehemiah's, Melville says, while the singers "but fulfill" "an esthetic glow," that restricts them to human desire and satisfaction.

Part II ends in a crescendo of significance. Both Mortmain and Nehemiah rail against Antichrist and extremism. Mortmain, whose name means "Death Hand" and who is one of the several monomaniacs in the poem, thinks he has every justification to curse extremism. He has oscillated between two poles, a family consisting of a father who gave him money but not love and a mother who, Medea-like, tried to destroy him, and a political philosophy or irresponsibility which drove him to the extremes of revolutionism in fighting for the French Revolution. Nehemiah has been victimized by myth which drives him "With throbbing brain" and "febrile musings, life's decay," to walk in his sleep, and he drowns in the Dead Sea.

Vine appropriately finds the dead saint because "To him, indeed, each lapse and end/Meet—in harmonious method blend." But it is Rolfe who works up and allows Melville's comment as author omniscient on the significance of the event. Rolfe wonders if Nehemiah's complete end is here, if there is "no more." Melville apparently provides the answer:

> He turned him, as awaiting nod
> Or answer from earth, air, or skies;
> But be it ether or the clod,
> The elements yield no replies.
> (II. xxxix. 87-90)

Melville continues to demonstrate his belief in humanism. The Bible is buried, at Rolfe's insistence, with Nehemiah, thus symbolizing the death of faith. There are convulsions of nature, with "a rush, a roar," "Flints, dust,

and showers of splintered stone,/An avalanche of rock
down tore." After these convulsions Melville asks what
heaven and God there are: "What works there from
behind the veil?" A sign appears, "The fog-bow," "A thing
of heaven, and yet how frail."

Significantly Melville turns from heaven to earth to
folklore, which humanizes the meaning and symbol:

> The rainbow
> Suspended there, the segment
> Like to the May-wreath that is swung
> Against the pole. It showed half spent—
> Hovered and trembled, pales away, and—went.
> (II. xxxix. 159-63)

Thus religious enthusiasm and religion itself are dead.
God's sign given in the avalanche is like that given at the
death of all of folklore's heroes. That given in the "slim
pencil" of a rainbow is of no greater significance than the
dance around a May-pole, and all are gone. The ending is
blackly gloomy. Nothing is left but desperate humanism,
belief in man, upon rationality and rationalism.

In Part III Melville begins his questions again. Will things
which here on earth seem so awry be set straight in
heaven? he asks. His answer is that such hopes are mere
wishes, "Exhalings! Tending toward the skies/By natural
law, from heart they rise." But the hope must be abandoned. Though hope of God seems to be held out by
the promise of the holiness of the monastery of Mar Saba
toward which they are now headed, the hope is grimly
illusory, for Melville will show that this monastery is evil in
being separated from the world and peopled by bigoted
monks and ruled by a blind abbot.

Melville's humanism is made clear as the pilgrims, before
they turn toward Mar Saba, give "one natural look" toward
Margoth, the Jewish geologist who scoffs at religion and
praises science. Rolfe the humanist provides this comment
on the departed man, not on his isolation from God but on
his seclusion from men:

So fade men from each other!—Jew
We do not forgive thee now thy scoff
Now that thou dim recedest off
Forever.
(III. i. 54-57)

Perhaps this is also an ironic comment on the pilgrims
who are departing for the monastery as they too are fading
from men.

The theme of humanism is continued in contrasts. As
the pilgrims mount the trail in single file toward Mar
Saba, one of the supersensitive horses, "one strange
steed," a "foal with snort and glard," locates and points
out to the pilgrims on the ledge below:

Two human skeletons inlaced
In grapple as alive they fell,
Or so disposed in overthrow,
As to suggest encounter so.
(III. i. 84-87)

Seemingly Melville's criticism is clearcut against this
"Cain meeting Abel." But as usual he is questioning, and
seems to use the contrast to point out further the grim
humanism that seems necessary. The pilgrims are still
seeking a "clue" to life. As they look down upon the valley
they think of mad Nehemiah "Single in life—in death, how
far apart!" Clarel remembers a story Nehemiah told him
about a carpenter, "A gentle wight of Jesu's trade." This
man lived alone, "Esteemed a harmless witless one" until
he made a single friend by working for a man for nothing.
Eventually however these two had a breaking up. In a
development very similar to that in his short story "The
Apple-Tree Table," Melville tells how this "witless one" was
deluded. An insect from "the rafter and the joist" ticked,
saying to the lone man, "Me fear only man." The man, like
Nehemiah, mistakenly became a recluse, made a monastery
of his house, and had no more social intercourse with man.

Rolfe "from Clarel's mention caught/Food for an
eagerness of thought." And he concludes that the
carpenter's behavior was wrong:

> It bears, it bears; such things may be:
> Shut from the busy world's pell-mell
> And man's aggressive energy—
> In cloistral Palestine to dwell
> And pace the stone!
>   (III. ii. 67-70)

Rolfe's sigh of regret is quite audible. Mortmain reacts to this humanism with a bitter look. But perhaps the most revealing commentary at this point is that of the ass. Melville uses this ass to reveal not only the wisdom of the animal world, but also to demonstrate the close intersympathy between man and brute, as well as to provide interesting comments and sometimes bits of grim high humor and laughs. Here the ass provides a profound comment on Rolfe's plea for humanism. It is "high o'er the bed/Late scooped by Seddim's borders there," but from this heavenly height it "As stupefied by brute despair,/Motionless hung the earthward head." But it must be observed that the despair is at least as much at a loss of hope with heaven as with a loss of faith with earth, and the head though earthward hung is also pointing to earthward consolation, as opposed to the madness of monomania.

Rolfe continues to brood on the fact that world-wide religions of the past, other than Christianity, did not promise "Christian hopes," and he concludes that Christianity's vision seems "Enslaved, degraded, tractable/ To each mean atheist's craft power." Mortmain at this point at least half takes a humanist's point of view. He admits that the theme of religion "dragged a god here down to earth," and concludes, "Religion oft times, one may deem,/Is man's appeal from fellow-clay." At this point at a general comment on the belief in higher things, of heaven, at this moment "from the crags above their view" comes the Cypriote's voice singing light love songs.

Significantly, the pilgrims ascend to "the High Desert," and there brood on the future of God and of religion. They comment on the opposition of contraries; of the Gnostics,

343

of Jehovah as evil, Christ "divine his contrary"; of whether
science and faith can unite; "Of Mammon and Democracy";
of the fate of the western world; of Protestantism. But Melville
always asks the questions, and does not give the answers.
To all this questioning, however, Vine remains indifferent.
He picks up bits of that "unchristened earth" and sends
them tumbling down the mountainside as though he is
tired of "That weary length of arguing/Like tale interminable told." Further making the point of the necessary
consolation of this world, the Arabs are unperturbed while
over them "Stretched the clear vault of hollow heaven."
Melville is showing either that the Arabs have not peopled
heaven and therefore do not hope for it, or, more likely,
that this indifferent and hollow heaven sits above the
concerned and the unconcerned equally, a joke and farce
to all who hope for its interest in them.

Vine points up again either his conclusion or a general
question about religion, by in effect framing the bells of the
monastery Mar Saba in his sensitivity and prescience.
During the debate between Mortmain and Derwent some
words of the Swede apparently open Vine's true nature to
the light, for he is "quivering." At this point the chimes of
Mar Saba peal out and all the pilgrims except Vine rejoice.
Vine, however, thoughout the chiming is engaged in too much
earthly activity to answer the message of the chimes. He is
building "A heap of stones in arid state," which Clarel
thinks is a cairn, "A monument of barrenness."

Vine's earthliness is carried on clearly in the next canto.
The travelers climb upward toward Saba "In Indian file."
"Man after man they labor on." Thus individually they pass
the skeleton of a camel which "worn out, down had laid"
and is now being circled over by a kite. Melville's symbolism
is clear: man individually tries to ascend to a heaven but
fails and is destroyed. Vine recognizes:

> But Vine, is mere caprice of clay,
> Or else because a pride had birth
> Slighting high claims which vaunted by

And favoring things of low degree—
From heaven he turned him down to earth,
Eagle to ass.
(III. vii. 19-24)

It is the ass, the commentator on mankind, not the eagle
that directs mankind. With this knowledge Vine gives an
"impish" glance. And Melville comments, "O, world's
advance:/We wise limp after." But it is we the race, not
the individuals.

Melville begins his description of Mar Saba, when the
pilgrims get there, with seeming approval but with actual
disapproval. Of all the lone and isolated monasteries of the
world, in the Alps, on Olympus, the Grand Chartreuse, Saba
is the loneliest. It is in fact too isolated from the world. The
monks, having ascended to their perch by ladder, are
indifferent to the needs and cries of the people below
unless they bear some letter of admittance from the
patriarch in Jerusalem.

With this religious pass, however, these travelers are
admitted and are, as Vine says, "imparadised," In their
activities they reveal the irresponsibility of heaven. A monk
lays out a bottle of wine for their night's "medicinal" needs
and all drink and jollify. All get slightly tipsy. In addition
to being a heaven separated from mankind, it is also a
militant heaven. Rolfe wanders around the hall and sees
various scimitars on the wall which, deadly weapons
though they are, carry such names as "In Name of God the
Merciful!" and "Hail, Mary, Full of Grace!" Melville's
further ironic comment on the peacefulness of heaven is
carried on in the story of Agath the Timoneer whose ship,
that on Friday set out from Egypt for Venice loaded with
old cannon for smelting into new artillery, was "Christined
by friar The Peace of God." Later, the ship that Agath is on
again (XIV) is called *The Apostles,* and during a battle,
"grand Paul and Peter" never moved, "Never blanched."

Melville continues his criticism of religion in the canto
"The Easter Fire" in Rolfe's condemnation of all religious

345

forgeries and fakery. Mar Saba aids and abets such fakery
in claiming that the Easter fire is sent down from God.
Melville's contempt for the Easter services is revealed in
re-use of the comic spelling "El Cods" for Jerusalem which
he found in Chateaubriand's book on the Holy Land
(III.xvi. 30), a device he had earlier used in his comic
treatment of "The Cassock" in *Moby-Dick*.

The criticism of religion, by implication, and of Mar
Saba explicitly, and a reaffirmation of the theme of humanism
is continued in the canto "The Masque," in the monks'
presentation of the age-old story of the wandering Jew.
The theme of this old story is separateness, as the Jew
attests: "Cut off I am, made separate" from man as well
as from God: "For man's embrace I strive no more";
"Some wrong/On me is heaped, go where I may,/Among
mankind." "For, human still, I yearn, I yearn," The irony
here is that the monks in this monastery perform this play
of separation without recognizing that they too are cut off
from mankind, though by their own choice, and in this act,
as well in their other fraudulent acts, they invite the wrath
of God. Mortmain, who is always being seen on the crags
and mountain tops presaging his final ascent at Saba, in a
scene strangely anticipating the crucifixion scene in
Billy Budd comments on the play the monks have just
completed. To the comment of "Bismillah!" ("In the name
of God") made by Belex, the Bethelehem guard, Mortmain
responds, "Dies Irae, dies illa!" the beginning lines from a
medieval hymn, "The day of wrath, that dreadful day."

The criticism of religion and of isolation continues with
beautiful symbolism in the canto called "The Medallion." In
a symbol which recalls Melville's use of the picture in the
Spouter-Inn in *Moby-Dick* (an obscure smoky picture of
a whale destroying a ship), he has Derwent pass before an
inner porch named "Galilee" in which is set a stone which
shows "Before an alter under sky,/A man in armor, visor
down,/Enlocked complete in panoply,/Uplifting reverent a
crown/In invocation." Though the "armed man" "showed
the dented plate" and "the right helm inviolate/Seemed

raised above the battle-zone—/Cherubic with a rare
device:/Perch for the bird of Paradise," Melville hints that
this device must not be taken at seeming value, for "The
art/So cunning was." It is Derwent, who has just revealed
his true nature to Clarel in the canto significantly named
"In Confidence." The inscription under the figure tells of a
miraculous intervention of God in a battle.

Fittingly this medallion was placed in Saba by a "count
turned monk" because he felt the monastery was the
"securest place,/For a memorial of grace/To outlast him,
and many a year." Melville builds on this placing and this
security. Derwent steps from this medallion to the abbot of
the monastery. This abbot is the living example of the
visored knight. He lives separated from the world, and
wants no communication with it, secure in his heaven-on-
earth. He is stone blind, as symbolized by the knight in
the medallion, and like the knight who named himself
Lazarus to indicate his Biblical counterpart, the abbot
seems to be humble but in fact is foolishly autocratic: he
retained "that toy/Dear to the old—authority." The
abbot seems to be candid and honest, but like Derwent (who
cons the abbot) he is a fraud and false.

A telling comment is made on the abbot and Derwent
by Clarel. Clarel in his education hangs on the fence
between asceticism and worldliness. After leaving Derwent
he is "Tossed in his trouble." He sees "a cenobite" "busy
at shuttle-hole in floor/Of rock, like smith who may repair/A
bolt of Mammon's vault." This monk hates his work,
though obviously since it is God's work done "in Paradise,"
and since done voluntarily should be happy toil; "he
toiled as in employ/Imposed, a bondman far from joy." But
the falsity of this whole concept of the monastery and
separation from the world is revealed by the true light;
the sun from the true heaven sends "A fiery shaft into
that crypt" and reveals the skulls of the "dim conclave
of the dead." These skulls are watched over by Cyril, a mad
monk, who demands the countersign *Death*, in which is

347

revealed the true fate of the workers in the monastery.
Clarel seeks some explanation from the seemingly
enslaved monk why Cyril is "unhinged." This monk's
answer reveals in his reply what also unhinged himself, the
abbot, and all others in this monastery, "Go/ask your
world," "and grim toiled on."

Clarel clearly refutes this monk. He is "Conscious of
seeds within his frame/Transmitted from the early gone." He
walks "in vision" and sees "in fright" "The spirits innumerable lie,/Strewn like snared miners in vain flight/
From the dull black-damp. Die—to die!" But it is all
spirits that have tried to escape mortality, especially,
apparently, those of the skulls he has just seen. And all is
"cowardice," Clarel admits. Significantly, here his thoughts
turn to Ruth, and reveal how his view of her is changing.
At first he thinks of her romantically, of her eyes which
"Abash these base immortalities." But soon

> . . .slid the change, anew it slid
> As by the Dead Sea marge forbid:
> The vision took another guise:
> From 'neath the closing, lingering lid
> Ruth's glance of love is glazing met,
> Reproaching him: *Dost tarry, tarry yet?*
> (III. xxiv. 101-104)

He realizes his and her mortality, and this feeling is a
premonition of her coming death, but most important,
Clarel realizes that he must live his life fully on this earth,
for there is no need to expect fulfillment in heaven.

Melville seemingly means to consign Derwent to hell:
but does he? Derwent parodies Mar Saba by saying that
the ass in the stables is in her nunnery, where like the
monks around her she is "pondering" "the asses' hell."
Derwent in his lighthearted usual way plays along with the
parody of true religion and feeds "your nun" that "fasts
overmuch." Then, in an obvious take-off on Dante, the
Lesbian becomes Dante's Virgil. Virgil-Lesbian points out
that the abbot's miracle, "St. Saba's fount" begins down

"Near where the damned ones den," that is, Cyril the
mad monk. They descend. Derwent and the Lesbian see
Mortmain on the crag point, and the latter says that the
monomaniac is mad. Derwent agrees that Mortmain is
strange but "as some esteem him not/not without some
wisdom to his lot." Lesbian replies that in the East anyone
who has lost his wits "For saint or sage they canonize."
They enter the grotto of "another crazed monk," Habbibi,
who has written the painful human words: "He heard a
call/Ever from heaven: O scribe, write, write!" Demented,
he wrote words of prayer to God to deliver him from
himself. "There is a hell over which mere hell/Serves—
for—a—heaven." Here Melville clearly is showing the
hellishness of heaven as well as the craziness of religious
people. In another parody of Dante, Melville has over the
door of Habbi's den, but Lesbian and Derwent see them
after they come out, the words: "Ye here who enter Habbi's den,/Beware what hence ye take!" Melville apparently
doesn't quite make his message clear. It is not clear that
Melville means to send Derwent to any hell other than we
all are in, that of the crazed monk who thinks that the religious suffer so much that they make a hell worse than
the hell of mere existence. Derwent is clearly a skimmer,
a con man, and not a deep thinker, but is that bad? Rolfe
and Vine like him. He admits: "We loiterers whom life can
please/(Thought he) could we but find our mates/Ever! but
no; before the gates of joy/lie some who carp and tease:/
Collisions of man's destinies!—" (III.xxvii. 181-185). But
he quickly gives up this "deep" thinking, which is humanitarian in tone, and turns to the Lesbian who talks to Belex
and Og about dancing. Virgil cannot lead Dante out of
Hades, but Melville seems to be saying that this is high
enough if one is to retain his sanity because clearly they
have said that Mortmain is the most saintly and the crazi-
est of the nonmonks.

After Derwent and Lesbian have been challenged and
passed by Cyril, custodian of the skulls, the eagle grabs and
drops Mortmain's skull-cap. The Lesbian then says that an

eagle once grabbed his hat and pecked at his skull while he was riding a dromedary and dozing. At this point the Agath Timoneer, who also has had his skull-cap taken by an eagle on the sea, comes by but refuses to answer the two men's hail, thus showing the isolation of individuals in hell, or on earth, especially after they have had their skull caps taken. Is there a difference between Mortmain and Timoneer and Lesbian, as demonstrated by the fact that he will talk, but the other two are silent and isolated?

The Palm of Saba is obviously a profound symbol. It provides a scene similar to the one concerning the doubloon in *Moby-Dick*, around which various commentators gather to reveal their various personal reactions. Melville is the commentator who points out where each of the other persons is situated in relation to the Palm. Melville begins at the highest observer and works down. Vince, the mystic, is highest up on the rung toward the Palm. He begins by regretting his isolation from his fellows: Do they leave him, or he them, he ponders. But wishing for them, he loves the past, "The further back the better," the future is "overcast," and "The present aye plebeian." Yet, though he loves Mar Saba, he will leave tomorrow "With right good will." In his invocation, which he tries now, he continues the theme of leaving tomorrow and denies the immortality of the Palm's symbol by pointing out that it is not the only one true symbol of religion and immortality. Though the tree would "win the desert here/To dreams of Eden," it "kinship claimest with the tree/Worshipped on Delos in the sea—/Apollo's Palm." Though the tree is kin to the pagan symbol of immortality, Vine questions the promise of either: The Palm though it "pledgest heaven" to him, hang'st suspended/Over Kedron and the night!" with strong likelihood of its mortality:

> Shall come the fall? shall time disarm
> The grace, the glory of the Palm?
> Tropic Seraph! thou once gone,
> Who then shall take thy office on[?]
> (III. xxvi. 49-53)

Then he turns from questioning to certitude, and in words which echo Tom Paine's in *The Rights of Man*, he accepts this certitude: "Every age for itself must care." "Let the grim/Awaiter find thee never dim!/Serenely still thy glance be sent/Plumb down from horror's battlement." Once having accepted the horror of death, he turns to humanism and is content: "He loitered, lounging on the stair:/Hobeit, the sunlight still is fair."

Mortmain, who is on a ledge below Vine and who is the next to comment on the Palm, is a sharp contrast to Vine in outlook. He sees the Lesbian dancing and curses him. Mortmain confesses he would be a misanthrope "did not the hate/Dissolve in pity of the fate." He is brotherless, and partially at least therefore his password is *despair*. He is brotherless, as is evidenced by his gnawed hand which he bit. He is also insane. Melville clearly points this out. As he looks at the Palm, he "soon in such a dream was thrown/He felt as floated up in cheer/Of saint borne heavenward from the bier." Melville shows that this intense feeling for religion throws Mortmain into a trance, as the Palm seems to say to him: "*Come over! be —forever be/ As in the trance.*" And Mortmain "lingered as in Lethe's snare." But his separation from man for heaven is reluctant, and he wishes he could repair that gnawed hand and clasp those of fellow mortals. Only reluctantly does he accept heaven: He appeals to the Palm:

> Yet hear me in appeal to thee:
> When the last light shall fade from me,
> If, groping round, no hand I meet:
> Thee I'll recall.
> (III. xxix. 88-91)

Rolfe is the last to soliloquize on the Palm. Since he is the most humanistic of the three observers he is where he should be, at the bottom of the three, "Small does he show /(If eagles eye), small and far off" from heaven and hope of heaven. He turns up here as everywhere in life, "By chance," and as he looks up the rocky stair of life "so crooked with turns" he wonders if it is "Man's work or nature's." Ascending only a little space, he remembers the Marquesas Islands, where Melville as a youth first sailed, and remembers how he (here Melville) descended from the mountains and was hailed by the natives as a god. That world, and the world at large, was all man needed: "Yea, much as man might hope and more than heaven may mean (?)" Rolfe further regrets the impulses, those of priest or people, which drive man from this happiness:

> But who so feels the stars annoy,
> Unbraiding him—how far astray!—
> That he abjures the simple joy,
> And hurries over the briny world away?
> Renouncer! is it Adam's flight
> Without compulsion or the sin?
> (III. xxx. 73-78)

Melville points out Rolfe's humanism by further tying his contemporary universalism with classical paganism, by saying that to Rolfe's mood, "Each swaying fan/Sighed to his mood in threnodies of Pan."

Part III ends with the theme of the final humanizing of Clarel. It sets the stage. The questions are posed, and Melville gives the promise of the resolution. Clarel's mind is filled with "But Ruth—still Ruth," but with more than Ruth, with in fact the question of sex, earth, and heaven. "Her image labored like a star," so she is herself heavenly. She represents heaven, for "Twas Ruth, and oh, much more than Ruth." This heaven is highlighted when Clarel steps out beside the Palm and comes upon the celibate, the "almoner of God," feeding the doves, in symbolism painfully like Christ, with his halo of doves.

Though Saba represents the good, peaceful life, Clarel is disturbed by its separateness and sexlessness. He is anguished because "No life domestic" is there and "Woman I miss," and here in the monastery he hears "a stifled moan/of lonely generations gone;/And more shall pine as more shall fleet."

He wonders if possessing Ruth he would not be worried
by not possessing Vine, a higher love. He continues
to brood upon the Virgin Mary. Why are all the saints
in heaven masculine? There is no marrying in heaven. But
"Can ever be riven/From sex, and disengaged retain/Its
charm?" He continues, "But if Eden's charm be not
supernal;/Enduring not divine transplaining—/Love
kindled thence, is that eternal?" And he concludes, "Ah,
love, ah wherefore thus unsure?" but questions whether
earthly love is unclean: "Linked art though—locked, with
Self impure?" This is the furthest Clarel has gone toward
questioning heaven's apparent attitude toward sex. This
feeling, though as Melville says will be further developed,
is, as the canto is entitled, "The Recoil." Although he does
not yet recognize it as such, he is awakening fully to Ruth
as woman, to sex, and to consequent humanism.

The last canto provides several interesting comments.
Entitled "Empty Stirrups," it reveals how the other people
are continuing their journey, but Mortmain, the monomaniac, is no longer with them. He has departed from
people, as he had felt earlier, while ironically yearning for
them. Appropriately Clarel finds him dead on his ledge
below Saba, as Mortmain had apparently looked at him last
the day before when Clarel was seeing all three viewers—
Vine, Mortmain, and Rolfe—in their separate niches.
Mortmain has apparently gone to heaven: "On those
thin lips a feather lies—/An eagle's, from the skies."
But is heaven superior to man's self-created image
of it?

Melville's criticism of religion is direct and savage.
Some of the people think Mortmain is demented and always
has been. More important, the monks bury Mortmain, but
not in consecrated ground. Then the monks leave him. Rolfe
is the only one who lingers around the grave, and to offer
an invocation, not a prayer. His invocation is to "Holy Morning," and he is disturbed by the fact that this holy
morning "viewest all events alike," not distinguishing

between good and bad, but Melville's severest comment is reserved for his statements made by the omniscient author. The friars buried Mortmain "without the walls/(Nor in a consecrated bed)," and without charity. Outside the walls "the beak and claw contend,/There the hyena's cub be fed." Then Melville distinguishes between real religion and that of Mar Saba. Heaven is not isolated as the friars at this isolated monastery are. "Heaven that disclaims, and him beweeps/In annual showers; and the tried spirit sleeps." True religion then decries the bigotry and isolation of Mar Saba.

Part IV begins with the irony, ambivalence, and inconclusiveness characteristic of the earlier parts. Melville says that if the legends of the "new-born Lord" are "fable," "Let man lament the foundered Star." Yet he continues one minute later by saying that the abbot, whom he severely criticized at the end of Part III, gave his benedictions to the departing travelers. Immediately, however, he switches to his theme of humanism in the poem and the continuity of the human race:

> For, ah, with chill at heart they mind
> Two now forever left behind.
> But as men drop, replacements rule:
> Though fleeing be each part assigned,
> The eternal ranks of life keep full.
> (IV. i. 32-36)

The Arnaut's horse and he seem brothers, and the Arnaut seems "complete," thus man and nature, the theme Melville has been developing all along.

Soon there is introduced Ungar, the last in Melville's sequence of monomaniacs. He shows the consequence of being alienated from people, from his "countryman" "estranged!" Rolfe has a "frater-feeling of the sea" for the Timoneer.

As the travelers ride away, the "convent's twin towers disappear," and they are alone on the "land of dust" where "few do tarry, none may live—/Save mad. possessed, or fugitive." But with nothing behind them there is still nothing ahead, but Jerusalem, which Agath dubs "Wreck, ho/the wreck," and this feeling Melville emphasizes with the comment of Djalea, "Keen-sighted art thou." Melville's feeling of man's necessity to be self-sufficient is made clear when he has his pilgrimage "alight/Upon the Promethean ledge," where the Druze—and man in general—stands with his only real companions:

> While sighs the sensitive creature fetched,
> As e'en that waste to sorrow moved
> Instinctive. So, to take the view
> See man and mare, lover and loved.
> (IV. i. 172-175)

Jerusalem is a shambles, as well any "Abandoned quarry mid the hills" "one's dreams fulfills/Of what Jerusalem should be."

Agath carries on him "the *Ensign:* palms, cross, diadems,/And star—the *Sign!*" as Rolfe describes it, which he had received as a sailor when the sailors had "naught to do." The worthlessness of Christianity is demonstrated when Agath says "This crucifixion, though, by some/A charm is held 'gainst watery doom." And Rolfe comments on the fact that men now use "The gold of legend." Derwent points up the humanism of the book in that, churchman that he is, he wants to follow the man-Christ:

> Follow the star on the tattooed man,
> We wise men here.

The universality of religion, and of humanism, is emphasized. Vine thinks that Agath bears "The impress bore of Nature's mint/Authentic." "Naught that slid between/Him and the elemental scent," and he asks if anything Agath has encountered can compare with the desolation of Judah. In comparing Judah with the Encantadas, Agath continues the theme that Rolfe has carried along, revealing Melville's interest in his early adventures, and the theme of the universality of man and of religion.

Ungar is an unwilling anti-humanist. With his mind warped by man's injustice to man, he says here, "A gun's man's voice—sincerest one. Blench we to have assurance here/Here is the waste, the kind is near?" Clarel now enlarges his point of view, commenting on the universality of religion: "Oh, heavens enlarge/Beyond each designated marge." Agath has "Nature's own look, which might recall/ Dumb patience of mere animal." Clarel further reveals his coming of maturity. "What may man know?" he asks. But more important he wonders if he has a mind or wrong attitudes. Does he but "lacquey" another's mind? Is he "Green and unsure?"

The incident of Agath starting at the sight of the scorpion demonstrates more fully humanism and the oneness of man and animal. Rolfe says "But speak not evil of the evil: Evil and good they braided ply/Into one cord." And after a moment Melville adds:

> In common-place here lightly blew
> Across them through the dessert air
> A whiff from pipe that Belex smoked:
> The Druze his sleek mare smooth bestroked,
> Then gave a sign. One parting view
> At Zion blurred, and on they fare.
> (IV. iv. 50-56)

Thus Melville turns from vanishing Zion to the world of animals and man.

The trouble with Ungar is lack of humanism:

> Reading and revery impede his pain,
> Confirmed, and made it take a flight
> Beyond experience and the reign
> Of self.
> (IV. v. 95-98)

Ungar would "eat thou thy cake of pride,/and henceforth live on unallied" with fellowman.

When Derwent and Clarel get to Bethlehem, Derwent enthuses about Mary and the Birth, but these three only lament the death of Nehemiah, thus showing their greater interest in man than Christ and religion.

The conflict between humanism and narrow, regular religion is dramatized when the pilgrims arrive in Bethlehem. Rolfe points it out when he says that he and his fellows though unworthy "welcome win/Where Mary found no room at inn." Then he carried on by wondering why Protestands do not hold dear enough to tend and care for a single sacred place in the Holy Land though they set apart Shakespeare's house. Ungar, monomaniac that he is, points out the contrast by overstating his urge for heaven: "the age, the age forget—There's something to look up to yet."

The climax—especially in sex—is building up as Melville highlights at the end of Canto xxv:

> And how—not wantonly designed
> Like lays in grove of Daphne sung,
> But helping to fulfill the piece
> Which in these cantos finds release,
> Appealing to the museful mind—
> A chord, the satyr's chord is strung.
>
> (IV. xxv. 56-61)

Clarel is now exposed to the licentiousness, the sensuality, the sexuality of the Lyonese, a young French Jew who travels for a merchant of luxuries in Lyons, whose talk of sexual matters stirs and scares Clarel. The young licentiate quotes the Song of Solomon: "Stay me with flagons, comfort me/With apples; thee would I enclose!/Thy twin breasts are as two young roes." And the young ex-naif is "not displeased," though he blushes. In fact his reaction is affirmative: "So young (thought Clarel) yet so knowing." When the Lyonese urges Clarel "Put up, put up your monkish thong!" Clarel seems willing, even eager to do so.

Clarel has the same kind of homosexual attraction for the Lyonese that he earlier had for Vine and Celio. But now there is a decided difference. Clarel has enjoyed the heterosexual word play of the youth so much that when

357

they both go to sleep he has an erotic dream. He stands "betwixt a Shushan and a sand," between voluptuous Shushan, the setting of the book of Esther, and the dry sand of sexlessness. In this dream he feels "the strain/Of clasping arms which would detain/His heart from each ascetic range," from, in other words, religion and bookishness and *in life*. When he awakes it is day and he is alone; "Vital he knew organic change,/Or felt, at least, that change was working—/A subtle innovator lurking." The departure of the Lyonese indicates that Clarel has turned to woman for his sexual desires, his vital "organic change." This change is emphasized by the next canto, "The Parapet," when Clarel standing on the roof is joined by Derwent, who comments on the physical charm of the Lyonese, his "warm/Soft outline," Which might well serve as a temptation even to the "staid grandees of heaven,/ Though biased in their souls divine/Much to one side— the feminine." But this hint of homosexuality or unusual sexuality repells Clarel, who speaks "a scare/Of incredulity. . . From eyes," and seems "home-sick," and "mum." And Clarel declines to "be led/Or cheered." Clarel-Melville concludes:

> Nor less in covert way
> That talk might have an after-sway
> Beyond the revery which ran
> Half-heeded now or dim: This man—
> May Christian true such temper wish?
> His happiness seems paganish.
> (IV. xxviii. 31-36)

Ungar departs with another train of travelers. He is still the loner, though touched by Melville's theme of humanity, comradeship. He felt that "Twas country-men he here forsook:/He felt it; and his aspect wore/In the last parting, that strange look/Of one enlisted for sad fight/ Upon some desperate dark shore."

> Who bids adieu to the civilian,
> Returning to his club-house bright,
> In city cheerful with the million.

But Nature never heedeth this
To Nature nothing is amiss.
(IV. xxviii. 14-18)

The theme is of humanism, and the oneness of nature.

The education-of-Clarel theme continues. At the
departure of Don, he feels "unto him, oppressed—/In
travail of transition rare,/Scarce timely in its unconstraint/
Was the droll Mexican's quirkish air." But Clarel is
"Swayed by love's nearer magnet now . . . Yet comradeship
did still require/That some few hours need yet expire."
But only a few hours. He had been nearly completely
humanized, or commonized, and he feels it and still
holds back afraid:

> But whither now, my heart? wouldst fly
> Each thing that keepeth not the pace
> Of common uninquiring life?
> What! fall back on clay commonplace?
> (IV. xxviii. 76-79)

In the midst of these clashing thoughts, he is greeted by the
Russian traveler, friend of the Lyonese, who tells him that
Greeks and Latin travelers are the same: "All's much the
same: many waves, one beach." And this Russian solves
another of Clarel's doubts. In what is admittedly a difficult
section—this as well as all in these few cantos—the Russian tells Clarel that there is still prejudice against Jews,
and that is why the Lyonese will not admit that he is a
Jew, even to speaking against them. The Russian:
"Society/Is not quite catholic, you know,/Retains some
prejudices yet— ." Though he has not admitted it even
to himself, Clarel has stayed away from Ruth because she is
Jewish. Now, however, having faced the problem he can
more readily solve it:

> They strolled, and parted, And again
> Confirmed the student felt the reign
> Of reveries vague, which yet could mar,
> Crossed by a surging element—

Surging while aiming at content:
So combs the billow ere it breaks upon the bar.
(IV. xxviii. 156-161).

Increasingly the cantos throb with sex and expectation.
"The-Night-Ride" shows that Clarel "Felt in every vein,"
the end of the trip. Djalea, though still "considerate and
prudent" muses of "The starry sequins woven fair/Into
black tresses."

For his the love not vainly sure:
Tis the passion deep of man mature
For one who half a child remains:
Yes, underneath a look sedate,
What throbs are known!

For Clarel, there is "new emotion, inly held,/That so the
long contention quelled—"

Was it abrupt resolve? a strain
Wiser than wisdom's self might teach?

The answer is a definite yes. Clarel will:

Yes, now his hand would boldly reach
And pluck the nodding fruit to him,
Fruit of the tree of life.

Melville in reversing the biblical saying from the tree of
life equaling religion to that of life, intensifies and makes
significant his message. Clarel's thoughts of Ruth are "(Now
first aright construed)." He hears Ruth telling him not to
become a religious zealot: "Ah, tread not, sweet, my
father's way." He has "pulse was this with burning heat?/
Whence, whence the passion that could give/Feathers to
thought." "Had he infected Clarel here?" Clearly yes.
And Clarel's thought become erotic:

Are the sphered breats full of mysteries
Which not the maiden's self may know?

Clarel's affirmation if complete:

At large here life proclaims the law:
Unto embraces myriads draw
Through sacred impulse. Take thy wife.

Melville is stating explicitly that individuals may suffer disaster but the race lives on in the embraces of the myriads.

When Clarel discovers that Ruth is dead, he is by himself and rages against the universe. He spends Passion Week alone, but on Easter the city bursts into life, with people all around—a cross section of all humanity. The people "issue, dot the hills, and stray/In bands, like sheep among the rocks." When Easter ceremonies are over, "Their confluence here the nations part." But Melville emphasizes life's continuation: "Sluggish, life's wonted stream flows on."

As the various threads of this main stream of humanism coalesce, Melville points out the oneness of man and nature: "A hint or dictate, nature's own,/By man, as by the brute, obeyed." Though the streets are depopulated of the Easter crowd, life's humanity goes on. Significantly Melville uses the "Via Crucis" to demonstrate this continuation. Both the high and the low, the rich and the poor— but mostly the poor—people this ancient street, for "Man and animal, 'tis one." Into this street comes Clarel "at close of rarer quest," that is, the quest for love.

He broods on his loneness:

> They wire the world—far under sea
> They talk; but never comes to me
> A message from beneath the stone.

But in pointing up Clarel's seeming despair Melville highlights his salvation or hope of it. Clarel turns to humanity since he cannot apparently have Ruth and religion:

> Dusked Olivet he leaves behind,
> And, taking now a slender wynd,
> Vanishes in the obscurer town.

Celio had buried himself in the crowds of Jerusalem but had been destroyed because he was still separate and alone. Clarel is turning to humanity for his salvation.

Form is all-important in Melville's works. Here, as in *Moby-Dick, The Confidence-Man, Billy Budd,* and in numerous other works, the final, detached statement, the

"Epilogue," is overwhelmingly significant. The final comment begins with a generality:

If Luther's day expand to Darwin's year,
Shall that exclude the hope—foreclose the fear?

It continues in this vein, concerned with people. Then in the last stanza it turns to Clarel in particular, as it should since this poem is about him. But Clarel is now one of the masses, and his fate will be that of all people. All may "prove that death but routs life into victory." Significantly, there is no mention of heaven or religion. It is life that may be triumphant, longevity. Though the concluding remarks are tentative and questioning, there is no despair there. Instead there is a quiet hope, a determined humanism, that life will truimph over death, that humanity will persevere and even conquer.

THE POETRY: "THE BONDS THAT DRAW"

Poetry was a great concern of Melville throughout his mature life, and was sprinkled throughout his prose works from *Typee* on, though he did not take to it as a major form of expression until after the publication of *The Confidence-Man* and its disastrous reception. Besides *Clarel*, Melville published three volumes of poetry. Another, his first, was still-born when a publisher could not be found for it in 1860, though the poems were apparently finally published as "Fruits of Travel of Long Ago" in *Timoleon*. His last volume, "Weeds, Wildings, and Roses," written especially for and to his wife, was left with his other papers at his death.

After his apparent failure to achieve artistic or financial success in prose, Melville hoped, though not very strongly, for greater accomplishment in verse. Acclaim, however, did not come then. The reasons are not obscure. Melville was not interested in adhering strictly to conventional prosody. Instead, as F. O. Matthiessen and Robert Penn Warren have observed, he structured his form to suit his purposes, and as his aims were personal and highly individualized, so was his poetry. Frequently it is not felicitous. In places it lumbers and stumbles, in others it is stretched so tightly that it breaks. Often words are ugly, discordant, and harsh. At times, also, swinging from the highly individualized, the style is too obviously imitative of other forms, especially of the ballad and song—in, for example, "Malvern Hill," with its rhythm of Burns' "Bonnie Doon."

But the artistic blemishes in the poetry are unimportant to the student of Melville interested in the development of his thinking and writing, for the poetry contains in bits and snatches many aspects of the author's mind which cast light on the themes that he discussed at greater length in prose works. Most explicitly the poems reveal further evidence of Melville's growth in humanism, his turning, as William Ellery Sedgwick said about *Clarel,* "toward humanity, not away from it."

This incorporation of humanism into the poems, as generally throughout his later works, is achieved with restraint, but always with firmness and definiteness, as examination will reveal.

Melville's first published volume of poetry was *Battle-Pieces and Aspects of the War* (1866). Besides *Clarel,* it is his best volume of poetry. Stimulated, as Melville said, by "an impulse imparted by the fall of Richmond," it was written and partially published during the Civil War, and was supplemented with descriptive material taken from the twelve-volume *Rebellion Record.*

The degree to which Melville is concerned with humanity in these poems is clearly stated in the *Supplement*: "Let us pray that the terrible historic tragedy of our time may not have been enacted without instructing our whole beloved country through terror and pity; and may fulfillment verify in the end those expectations which kindle the bards of Progress and Humanity." Like Lincoln, Melville felt no real malice toward the South. He felt it was enough to hope that the South had been taught that "secession, like Slavery, is against Destiny; that both now lie buried in one grave; and her fate is linked with ours; and that together we comprise the Nation," a nation that cannot exist or thrive "based upon the systematic degradation of man." Slavery was to Melville "an atheistical iniquity," and the future welfare of the Negroes is of paramount importance. But, he urged, we must realize that we have a responsibility to our fellow-whites as well as to our fellow-blacks, that is, to all our fellow-men. Thus "the future of the whole country. . . urges a paramount claim upon our anxiety." All must work toward the growth of democracy and mankind.

The approaches used in the poetry to make his points are those Melville had employed in his prose works. Like the other works, then, his poetry takes on several levels of investigation and affirmation. In a series of statements he emphasizes the terror of war, especially on youth, and especially when fought by the young. In "Apathy and Enthusiasm" (1860-61) he contrasts the seeming indifference of people during peace before the war with the wild and nonsensical enthusiasm generated by war, and the danger tied in with war when enthusiastic youth lead the surge:

> The young were all elation
> Hearing Sumter's cannon roar
> . . . . . .
> But the elders with foreboding
> Mourned the days forever o'er,
> And recalled the forest proverb,
> The Iroquois' old saw:
> Grief to every graybeard
> When young Indians lead the war.

In "The March into Virginia" (1861) Melville reiterated the warning against letting youth plan and execute wars: "All wars are boyish, and are fought by boys." In another poem of the same year, "Ball's Bluff," the poet is saddened by the foolish waste of youth, and the stark difference between appearance and reality—"Youth feels immortal, like the gods sublime," but "how should they dream that Death in a rosy clime/Would come to thin their shining throng?"

Throughout the war, however, Melville clings to hope in the people. Though at times concerned with their actions, he still has faith in the fruition of the hopes of man, democracy, and America, and ultimately in the preservation of mankind.

In "Misgivings" (1860) Melville outlines his worries about America's ills, "the world's fairest hope linked with man's foulest crime." In "Rebel Color-Bearers at Shiloh" he curses Southern reasons for renting the land asunder: Southern people are fighting for "the Wrong," and "Perish their cause!" Their cause, as he says in "The Armies of the Wilderness," is "Feudal fidelity." And Southerners are "zealots of the Wrong." "In this strife of brothers," Melville prays, "Let not the just one fall." He yearns for reunification of torn families and divided country, as in "Battle of Stone River, Tennessee": "Shall North and South their rage deplore,/And reunited thrive again."

But running throughout his war poetry is Melville's hope in the people and in the ultimate triumph of man. This hope for triumph does not progress on a straight line without detours or interruptions, and faith in democracy is not without momentary doubts. The people can do wrong, can be shortsighted and terribly unwise, in the North as well as in the South. No more powerful statement is made by Melville on this subject than that on the assassination of Lincoln in "The Martyr." "They" killed Lincoln "in his prime/Of clemency and calm." "But they killed him in his kindness,/In their madness and their blindness/And they killed him from behind:

> There is sobbing of the strong,
>   And a pall upon the land;
> But the people in their weeping
>   Bare the iron hand:

Beware the People weeping
When they bare the iron hand.

But despite these misquided errors into evil, the
people—democracy—can and must survive. Sometimes Melville doubts, and clings to desperate hope in
Christianity, as in "The Conflict of Convictions" (1860-61),
when he fears that the people may be headstrong and
overwhelmingly powerful: "The People spread like a
weedy grass,/The thing they will they bring to pass,/And
prosper to the apoplex." The poet fears that God has
deserted man: "But He who rules is old—is old;/Ah! faith
is warm, but heaven with age is cold." In this mood,
Melville can only fall back on hope: "But God He keeps the
middle way./None was by/When He spread the Sky;/
Wisdom is vain, and prosphesy."

Generally, however, Melville's hope is more terrestrial,
more human. His sympathy for the vast hordes of unnamed
men is profound: "There is glory for the brave/Who lead,
and nobly save/But no knowledge in the grave/Where the
nameless followers sleep" ("Sheridan at Cedar Creek"). In
"On the Photograph of a Corps Commander" Melville
admits man's limited vision and glories in it. "Man is
manly," he says. Though at the end of the poem he is
talking about a commander, a hero, the message is clearly
that there is no difference between the leader and man:

Nothing can life the heart of man
　Like manhood in a fellow-man.
The thought of heaven's great King afar
　But humbles us—too weak to scan;
But manly greatness men can span,
　And feel the bonds that draw.

Melville's primary concern with man on earth is tellingly
stated in "A Canticle," a celebration of the end of the war.
The nation "Moves in power, not in pride;/And is deep in
her devotion/As Humanity is wide." Therefore "Hosanna to
the Lord of hosts/The host of human kind":

The Generations pouring
From times of endless date,
In their going, in their flowing
Ever form the steadfast State;
And Humanity is growing
Toward the fullness of her fate.

The "fullness" of this fate is seen in "Formerly a Slave,"
the portrait of a slave mother who represents her race
which has been too late delivered from bondage. But there
is now hope: "Her children's children they shall know/
The good withheld from her."

John Marr and Other Sailors (1888), Melville's second
volume of poetry, is consistently less successful both
poetically and intellectually than the war pieces. As the
name states, these poems are about sailors, and are told
in ballad-like verse. Melville does not strike the notable
lines here he achieves in other poems. The first verse of
"John Marr" carries on Melville's familiar development
and theme about humanism.

Marr is a typical sailor and hero. With no knowledge of
his parents, he put to sea early, where he remained until
disabled in fighting with pirates. Then, like Israel Potter, he
began numerous wanderings, finally settling on the prairie,
which to him resembled the sea. Deprived of wife and
child, and thus precluded from further roaming, he settled
down permanently with the landsmen. This settling,
however, was a failure, and herein lies the poignancy of the
poem, and its message. Because of their dissimilar back-
grounds, the landsmen cannot understand Marr when
he can talk only of the sea. No communication develops
between this lonely man and other men; they have nothing
in common. Living with people Marr is nevertheless
isolated from humanity. He recognizes in his loneliness
that "A beat, a heart-beat musters all,/One heart-beat at
heart-core." And he sighs for reunification with humanity,
his kind, the sailors.

"The Maldive Shark" also works on the theme of
comradeship and friendship. Picturing the terror of the

Maldive shark's "serrated teeth," among which the
defenseless pilot-fish swim with no harm, Melville turns to
humanity, and likens the travels of himself and his former
sailor friends when they too, like the shark and pilot-fish,
were "friends."

"The Aeolian Harp" throbs with compassion for the
common sailor. Describing a drifting wreck on the sea,
Melville turns to and concludes with his main concern:

> O, the sailors—o, the sails!
> O, the lost crews never heard of!
> Well the harp of Ariel wails
> Thoughts that tongue can tell no word of!

Melville has the same concern in "Far-Off Shore,"
describing a raft afloat on which obviously there is no life:

> Cries the sea-fowl, hovering over,
>   Crew, the crew?
> And the billow, reckless rover,
>   Sweeps anew!

In *Timoleon* (1891), Melville's third and final volume,
published like *John Marr and Other Sailors* in private
printings of twenty five copies, the best poem by far is
"Monody," Melville's lament on the death of Hawthorne.
This piece is Melville's most effective short poem. It is one
of the most powerful and heart-rending statements of one
man's longing for friendship with another, of one soul
seeking a kindred spirit. The poem is charged with all the
emotion Melville had earlier poured out to Hawthorne in
joyful appreciation of their wonderful and invigorating
association during 1850-51. But the tenor of the poem is
quiet and restrained, articulating a regret so profound it can
hardly be faced. Filled with wonder over how two such
close friends could have spun off into two distant and
distinct orbits, Melville casts no blame:

> To have known him, to have loved him
>   After loneness long;
> And then to be estranged in life.
>   And neither in the wrong;

And now for death to set his seal—
Ease me, a little ease, my song!

Melville's poetry in general is then obviously not his
artistic triumph. At its best it is strengthened by its high
degree of individuality. At its worst it is perhaps individualism run to accentricity, and as such is interesting
more as curiosity than as artistry. At its weakest it is
scarcely more than mediocre, as even the most ardent
Melvilleophile must admit. However, in a dozen or so
poems—perhaps even a hundred—his unique style thrusts
his verse into the realm of genuine poetry. Regardless of
"poetic" achievement, though, all his verse is fundamental
for a full understanding of the way Melville looked at
life, what he expected from it, and to what degree and in
what way he committed himself to it.

TEN

BILLY BUDD: GOSPEL OF DEMOCRACY

Billy Budd: Sailor (An Inside Narrative) is without doubt second in greatness only to *Moby-Dick*, and must be considered one of the brightest gems, one of the most provocative and profoundly disturbing books ever written. The manuscript was left among the unpublished papers on Melville's desk at his death in 1891. Whether or not the story was in the finished state that Melville would have desired remains, and must always remain, an open question. He had brooded long over the problems raised in the work and had tinkered frequently with the story. He had begun the work with a ballad-like story similar to the type used in *John Marr*, then in two further reworkings had expanded the development, introducing the characters of John Claggart and Captain Vere, with all the complications consequent to the elaboration and enrichment.

Billy Budd, begun by Melville in 1886, was first published in 1924, in a text edited by Raymond Weaver that was far from faithful. A fuller and more carefully edited text was published in 1948, prepared by F. Barron Freeman, but one still far from Melville's last wishes. The 1962 text, edited by Harrison Hayford and Merton M. Sealts, Jr., with both a reading and a genetic text, undoubtedly presents as faithful and reliable a text as is possible. This version outlines in full detail the development of the various texts, thus providing raw material for critics' mining. More important, it modifies portraits of the characters, extenuates circumstances, and alters readings, thus eliminating some hitherto salient sections.[1]

1. Herman Melville, *Billy Budd: Sailor (An Inside Narrative(*, ed. Harrison Hayford and Merton M. Sealts, Jr. (Chicago, 1962). Other references will be noted by chapter number in the text.

But essentially the problems about the interpretations of *Billy Budd* have not been substantially changed. Sufficient seeming ambiguity still remains to force readers to argue over whether the story is a "testament of acceptance" or a "testament of resistance." But the ambiguity is, it appears to me, only seeming. Though Melville was profoundly aware of the apparent ambiguity of life, his conclusion about life was a quiet though firm affirmation. *Billy Budd* demonstrates that Melville ended life with the same attitude he had held all of his mature years. He realized that in this man-of-war world in which Christ cannot exist, or has been extracted by God or expelled by man, the only hope of and for man is mankind itself. This is essentially the same attitude Melville has been expounding, in one degree or another and in one way or another, in all of his works. The feeling may be one of quiet acceptance but not at all one of resignation. There is no sniveling, no regret, no remorse. If life is that way, he seems to say, so be it. One must walk with dignity and with hope. This hope lies in *Billy Budd,* as with Melville's other works, with the common man, the people, with democracy, with the heroic men who all together make up mankind.

This attitude, this affirmation, this basic humanism, thematically develops in two ways: in the same way that Melville has shown in most of his stories the conflict between supermen, their eventual destruction, and their descent to the bodies of common men; and the careful examination of political systems, the result of which is an explicit condemnation of arbitrary and tyrannical government and an espousal of humane democracy. The two threads must be examined separately.

I. CHANGING NATURE OF SUPERMAN

That the story deals on one level with supermen is made manifest at the very beginning. It is dedicated to Jack Chase, Melville's former friend on the frigate *United States* in 1843, "wherever that great heart may now be/Here on Earth or harbored in Paradise." He is the Titanic commoner in *White-Jacket*, who is apotheosized as Bulkington in *Moby-Dick* and thus shows the growth of the common man into a superman. Here in *Billy Budd* he sets the stage for a superhuman story.

The story develops from the start on this plane. The common sailors are shown surrounding "some superior figure of their own class" rendering him their "homage." This general picture of the heroic sailor is pushed one level higher in the particular picture of the "common sailor so intensely black that he must needs have been a native African of the unadulterate blood of Ham" that Melville remembers having seen in Liverpool "half a century ago." Thus he reiterates his numerous assertions that the non-white person is the superior of the pure white, a statement he has made in numerous works, in the person of Queequeg, for example.

The handsome sailor is further heroized. No dandy, he is "mighty boxer or wrestler," with both "strength and beauty." His form is "heroic," a "young Alexander curbing the fiery Bucephalus," a "superb figure, tossed up as by the horns of Taurus against the thunderous sky, cheerily hallooing to the strenuous file along the spar." Such a hero, though with "important variations," is Billy Budd.

In mythology and folklore the hero always has certain characteristics: 1) he has a supernatural birth or is illegitimate; 2) he is physically and mentally precocious or outstanding; 3) something about his appearance is uncommon; 4) often there is highlighted a contest between him and his arch antagonist; 5) there is something unusual about his death—there are convulsions of nature, or some kind of acknowledgment of the hero's passing. Billy fits all requirements.

He is a "foundling, a presumable by-blow, and, evidently, no ignoble one. Noble descent was as evident in him as in a blood horse." He is physically a Titan, and mentally an androgynous Adam before the Fall. His unusual appearance is cited in numerous ways: he is "welken-eyed," that is, "heavenly" eyed; he habitually wears an "adolescent expression in the as yet smooth face all but feminine in purity of natural complexion"; he has "small and shapely" ears, feminine feet, mouth and nose; he is in fact so feminine that several of sailors, among whom homosexuality was endemic, cast their "ambiguous" smiles upon him, and several of the "more intelligent gentlemen of the quarter-deck" were aware of his attraction, either to themselves or to the sailors. Spiritually Billy is one of Melville's numerous naifs, "with little or no sharpness of faculty or any trace of the wisdom of the serpent, nor yet quite a dove; he possessed that kind and degree of intelligence going along with the unconventional rectitude of a sound human creature, one to whom not yet has been proffered the questionable apple of knowledge." He is an "upright barbarian, much such perhaps as Adam presumably might have been ere the urbane Serpent wriggled himself into his company."

It is important also that despite the fact that Melville originally designed the story as a ballad that Billy would sing he left in the version as a significant aspect of Billy's character his development as Orpheus, medieval troubadour and modern folk song creator, with all the magic and other-worldliness ordinarily implied in the occupation: "He was illiterate; he could not read, but he could sing, and like the illiterate nightingale was the composer of his own song." Billy's most outstanding characteristic is, of course, his flaw of stuttering, and a fatal flaw of some kind has been characteristic of heroes since the beginning and universal in provenance.

Billy engages in two contests, one between himself and Claggart, which he wins, and one with Vere, which because of what the captain represents (the tyranny of forms of the world) Billy apparently loses, but in losing actually tri-umphs. At the climax of the second contest, the greater

373

one, there are the usual conventional convulsions of nature marking the death and triumph of the hero.

But Billy is more than merely the hero of this world. Melville makes it clear that this handsome sailor is a superman, and that the symbol is more that the usual one. His form is "heroic," but he is "not presented as a conventional hero . . . [and] the story in which he is the main figure is no romance." He is, in other words, an unconventional hero, and the story is which he figures is a super romance, a story more profound, more significant.

Having first introduced Budd and demonstrated clearly that the story in which he figures is about supermen and profoundly significant, Melville then continues the story, building up Billy. But as they are introduced, the other two important characters are shown to be worthy antagonists also.

Captain Vere was the last of the three characters to be introduced and developed in the story as Melville continued to work through the years. Vere is the least obvious of the three, neither pure white nor altogether black, as Billy and Claggart are. Vere is developed with an equivocation and tentativeness which asserts Melville's belief that the motivations and actions of most men are profound and subtle. But Vere is treated with an obvious irony which indicates that Melville, though understanding such a person as the captain, surely does not approve of him.

He is a bachelor of some forty years of age, "allied to the higher nobility." He is "an exceptional character," "engaged in . . . the world's more heroic activities." He is the right age to be Billy's father, and therefore more poignantly developed by Melville, but he is far from capable of fathering anything. In keeping with Melville's conventional use of the term *bachelor* throughout his works, Vere is detached from life, therefore living only half a life. He is thus anti-life, anti-women, anti-humanistic, a gentlemanly version of Ahab. He is nicknamed "Starry Vere" because of this detachment from life. There is irony in the "Starry" name. Nelson, to whom Vere is compared many times, is connected by this star; in Nelson's case a star was placed on the deck of the *Victory* "designating the spot where the Great Sailor fell." Melville's comments on Nelson at this point, though possibly equivocal, are surely sufficiently explicit to indicate that Melville thinks that Nelson may have been a vainglorious fool.

Nevertheless, Nelson was Vere's superior. Nelson was more relaxed, less slavish to form and precedents. Vere on the contrary, is narrow, inflexible, slavish in following precedent. He is a man of restraint or self-control. When interrupted in his reverie, he is more or less irascible for a moment but instantly controls himself. He is an avid reader, but of books "treating of actual men and events no matter of what era." He is a follower of "unconventional writers like Montaigne, who, free from cant and convention, honestly and in the spirit of common sense philosophize upon realities." He is then antipathetic to those persons who, in Melville's word, "dive," and as such, since Melville throughout life loved those men who "dive," could scarcely be winning Melville's unqualified approval. Vere is "at war" with all institutions that do not work toward what he considers the "true welfare of mankind." But, as we shall see, his notions of this true welfare support only persons like himself who want to be detached from mankind and who want only the "forms" of life to be perpetuated.

The results of Vere's behavior, no matter what the cause of his impulse, are best revealed in the scene depicting the confrontation between Billy and Claggart. Thinking that it would be the easiest and most practical way to test the validity of Claggart's accusation against Billy, Vere summons the innocent sailor and has the evil one charge him in Vere's presence. When Billy is unable to answer because of his stutter, the captain, though unaware of this affliction, understands and apparently with a fatherly kindliness places his arm on Billy's shoulder to reassure him and thus minimize the nervous affliction. But the result is the opposite. When Vere calls Billy "my boy," Billy apparently recognizes the falsity of Vere's pose, his sham

375

fatherliness, for his stuttering worsens, and his expression "was as a crucifixion to behold." At this moment he lashes out and strikes Claggart. Vere is then both indirectly and directly guilty of the homicide. In destroying Billy he is obliterating any evidence that might possibly be used in the future against him.

With Claggart dead at his feet, Vere's actions are not without suggestive taint. He stands with "one hand covering his face . . . to all appearance as impassive as the object at his feet." Melville asks significantly: "Was he absorbed in taking in all the bearings of the event and what was best not only now at once to be done, but also in the sequel?" Apparently Vere decides in this moment that the best course is one that assures his safety, for the face his hand uncovers has undergone a remarkable alteration: "The father in him, manifested towards Billy thus far in the scene, was replaced by the military disciplinarian." And whereas Vere in the past had referred to Billy as "boy," now the fated sailor is spoken of as "man." Vere has made up his mind that though Claggart has been "Struck dead by an angel of God! Yet the angel must hang!"

Though both Billy and Vere are "two of great Nature's nobler order," the nobler of the two must hang.

John Claggart, the second character developed by Melville in elaborating the story from the ballad, is more obviously a superman, with many of the age-old and universal characteristics blending into other traits. Like all of Melville's dangerous men, and Shakespeare's from whom he drew, Claggart is "spare and tall." His hands, like Billy's are feminine—"small and shapely." Phrenologically his brow is "of the sort . . . associated with more than average intellect." His "silken jet curls reveal that there is something sexually abnormal or perverse about him." His chin, freakishly "beardless as Tecumseh's," protrudes and is broad, thus indicating, folkloristically, an indomitableness which drives him to get his way at whatever the cost might be. His skin is of a color hinting of something defective or abnormal in the constitution or blood." Most indicative of his real character are his eyes, which "cast a tutoring glance" in casual life. When the will of their owner is challenged or questioned they become more openly Satanic. When, for example, Claggart is accusing Billy of his threatened mutiny, Claggart "mesmerically" looks Billy in the eye, and his own eyes reveal his real character: "Meanwhile the accuser's eyes, removing not as yet from the blue dilated ones, underwent a phenomenal change, their wonted rich violet color blurring into a muddy purple. Those light of human intelligence, losing human expression, were gelidly protruding like the alien eyes of certain catalogued creatures of the deep. The first mesmeristic glance was one of serpent fascination; the last was as the paralyzing lurch of the torpedo fish."

Claggart has a "superior capacity," is of "high quality." He is "like the scorpion for which the Creator alone is responsible," and when Vere and Billy move his corpse, Claggart handles like a "dead snake." Furthermore, and most important, like Billy, Claggart is a bastard, or might be, because he will not talk about his parentage. He is unqualified innate depravity. He is one of Melville's many studies in the confidence man; he is *chevalier*, a sharper, a crook.

Thus are set the three characters in the elemental struggle between positive evil and unsophisticated innocence; of moral responsibility and lack of it, of failure to act responsibly toward nature; of the blind worshipful following of forms and of adjustment to life; of separation from and contempt for humanity and of desire to live with and for humanity; of anti-humanism and humanism.

II. "BARBARIAN" AS SUPERMAN

Billy Budd is also extremely important on a strictly political level, as numerous critics have recognized. Among other philosophical-political messages, critics see the "doctrine

377

of worldly accomodation" in action,[2] the "sacrifice of self
to the historical moment,"[3] exemplification of the
"utilitarian principle of social expediency,"[4] and evidence
that a "judicious combination of instinct and reason can . . .
eventually produce a new set of objective conditions which
require less repressive forms for man's governance."[5]

Such critics generally agree that in the struggle between
Claggart and Billy, Captain Vere stands ground between the
two, forced by the power of evil to destroy that which he
loves, a Lincolnesque figure of great tragic proportions: the
spokesman for Melville.

Other critics however, find in Melville's treatment of Vere
an irony which turns all forms of "acceptance" into
"resistance," and makes of the captain a caricature of what
he appears to be.[6] These readers are much nearer Melville's
meaning. Instead of being the voice of the author, Vere is in
fact Melville's political antagonist.[7]

On a strictly political level Billy Budd is a search for the
best form of government—autocratic versus democratic—
a question Melville worried about all of his mature life,
especially during the writing of *Clarel*. On this level, as
Noone has shown, Claggart can be equated with Hobbesian
primitive man and Budd with the Rousseauvian "noble
savage," which had been one of Melville's preoccupations
since *Typee,* with Vere as a spokesman or apologist for and
manipulator of Hobbesian despotism as compromise.

2. Merlin Bowen, *The Long Encounter: Self and Experience in the Writings of Herman Melville* (Chicago, 1960), p. 215.

3. Milton R. Stern, *The Fine Hammered Steel of Herman Melville* (Urbana, 1957), p. 207.

4. Wendell Glick, "Expediency and Absolute Morality in *Billy Budd," Publications of the Modern Language Association* 68 (1953): 104.

5. John B. Noone, Jr., "*Billy Budd:* Two Concepts of Nature," *American Literature* 29 (November 1957): 262. See also Ray B. West, Jr., "Primitivism in Melville," *Prairie Schooner* 30 (1956): 369-385

6. Paul Withim, "*Billy Budd:* Testament of Resistance," *Modern Language Quarterly* 20 (1959): 115-117. See this article for a summary of arguments about acceptance, resistance, and irony. Though I agree with these findings as far as they go, I think the author stopped short of their possibilities.

7. A late identification of Vere with Melville is in R. H. Fogle, "*Billy Budd:* The Order of the Fall," *Nineteenth-Century Fiction* 15 (December 1960): 189-205.

But Melville had more immediate political references. As Bowen and Hayford and Sealts have suggested, Melville undoubtedly had steadily in mind the political developments associated with Edmund Burke and Thomas Paine, as references in the text point out. Though it may be riding a thesis to death to insist that Melville always had Burke and Paine in mind, the circumstances under which the novel was written and the references and development in it suggest that the analogy was clear to Melville. Thus this line of inquiry will be fruitful to the modern reader.

As Melville makes clear, his political concern is with reform and liberalism (as illustrated in the original impulse of the French Revolution, before its excesses) and with its archenemy, status quo and conservatism (as exemplified in the British government). Melville naturally chose as spokesmen for these opposing ideologies those authors and books that were contemporary with the setting of the story: Edmund Burke and his *Reflection on the Revolution in France* (1790); and Thomas Paine and his answer in the *Rights of Man*, Part I (1790) and Part II (1792). For around those two authors and books had generally polarized the basic views in the struggle between conservatism and liberalism, political expediency and principle, down to Melville's time. At that time, in fact, the battle was especially violent.

The novel becomes, then, a study in the conflict between those opposing ideologies. In this context the struggle is not between Claggart and Budd, but between Captain Vere as spokesman and apologist for authority (with Claggart serving only as prime mover) and Billy, who is on this level, Melville takes great pains to point out, representative of the common, ordinary sailor, the voice of the people in their insistence on their rights. Vere is the opponent of rights. He is, therefore, lossely identified with Edmund Burke. In his conflict with and ultimate triumph over Vere, Melville uses two voices, that of Billy the common sailor, and his own as author, both of which —or the sum total of which—loosely represent Thomas Paine.

379

My thesis is, then, that the novel instead of demonstrating the irresistible triumph of political evil, of conservatism, insists on the opposite; that the Veres (and Claggarts) prevail only in the short run, never in the long; that though the Budds seem to lose and are even destroyed personally, they ultimately prevail, not in themselves but in the political philosophy and in the people they represent. In the struggle for power Melville casts his hope with the people, here as he has done throughout his life. They will outlast all other persons. And they will inevitably inherit the earth.

In *Billy Budd* form is of paramount importance. Though Melville wrote several digressions here, as in his other works, he included no irrelevances. It is significant therefore that as soon as he has established the fact that the book is on one level concerned with supermen, he turns next to the political significance, with the first chapter.

That Melville had his eye on the political scene around him is not far-fetched. His mind was always politcally alert. Such a thinker and worrier as he was could hardly have been alive in the time and not be aware of the currents and cross-currents of political upheaval around him. Henry George's *Progress and Poverty*, for example, published in 1879, was creating great agitation among both conservatives and liberals. Edward Bellamy's *Looking Backward*, with its picture of a communistic-socialistic state, came from the press while Melville was working on his novel. Economically and politically the West was rebelling against the East and the rich. Anarchists, foreign and domestic, were terrifying the land with their potential threat.

Thomas Paine was also very much in the air. Two books on him had recently appeared.[8] Elihu B. Washburn, the United States Minister to France, had published in 1880 in *Scribner's Magazine* his study of Paine and the French

8. John E. Remsburg, *Thomas Paine, The Apostle of Religious and Political Liberty* (Boston, 1880); M. F. Savage, *Thomas Paine: Some Lessons from his Life* (Boston, 1883).

Revolution. The firebrand Robert Ingersoll had recently (1879) brought out his "vindication of Thomas Paine," and his "Mistakes" had been corrected by James B. McClure (1880). Ingersoll's "atheism," everybody knew, derived from Voltaire and Paine. The biggest bombshell of all had been Theodore Roosevelt's denomination (1887) of Paine as "the filthy little atheist," which words cost him in subsequent years "many moments of explanation and vexation."[9] The 151st anniversary of the birth of Paine was commemorated in Chicago in 1888. The centennial of the publication of Paine's *Rights*, as well as of Burke's *Reflections*, came as Melville was writing his novel.

Burke, too, was influentially on the minds of Americans. Increasingly from 1850 to the end of the century he "became the symbol of wise and heroic statesmanship" in America, as well as in England. His love of rhetoric and his pronouncements on the sublime had in the past influenced and still affected American oratory and literature. Men of letters such as Holmes and Emerson, although narrowly read in political classics, never tired of praising Burke. His works had recently been published twice in Boston (1861-1871, 1881).[10]

The Gilded Age was, then quite conscious of and concerned with the writings and philosophies of Paine and Burke.

Melville, too, was aware of these two antagonists long before he discussed their political philosophies in this book. His "Fragments from a Writing Desk," Sealts says, for example, "imply his youthful familiarity" with Burke. He also probably owned *The Philosophical Inquiry into*

9. Roosevelt's words were in his *Gouverneur Morris* (Boston, c. 1898), and were quoted in E. E. Morison, et al., *The Letters of Theodore Roosevelt* (Cambridge, Mass., 1951), 2: 1158, with this derogatory comment.

10. Quoted in Naomi Johnson Townsend, "Edmund Burke; Reputation and Bibliography, 1850-1954" (Ph. D. diss., University of Pittsburgh, 1955), p. 55. Melville's attitude toward Holmes was perhaps mixed, but he condemned Holmes' touting of everything European as being superior to anything American, which Melville thought was Bostonian flunkeyism. See Leon Howard, *Herman Melville*, p. 158. Though Melville admired some qualities of Emerson he sorrowed over others.

the Origin of our Ideas on the Sublime and Beautiful.[11] He
cites Burke in the excerpts preceding *Moby-Dick*. Thomas
Paine had been close to Melville's mind for years, and was
often quoted and paraphrased in his works, as we have seen.

But more important evidence of the closeness of the
Burke-Paine controversy is to be found in *Clarel*, Melville's
last major work before *Billy Budd*, which he probably
meditated on after his return from the Mediterranean in
1857 and began actively to write in 1870. A philosophical
poem probing the conflict between "heart" and "head," it
also vividly reflects Melville's interest in politics, in the
French Revolution, and in Thomas Paine. The doors of the
walls around Jerusalem, for example, "as dingy were/
As Bastille gates." Are "Mammon and Democracy"
inseparably linked, he asks in Part II, canto v. The "holy
and right reverend" abbot denounces change and those
people who espouse it as being worse than Paine. But the
abbot is "stone-blind and old" and longs to retain "that toy,/
Dear to the old—authority" (III. xxiii). Even more
revealing is a conversation between Ungar, the part-Indian
American, and Derwent and Rolfe, with Vine and Clarel
listening in. Ungar, thoroughly disillusioned with
materialistic America, writes off the country as a total loss:
without the past, with no regard for its value, the New
World will end up in the "Dark Ages of Democracy."
Derwent in answering bases his hope for America's future
on reform:

> Through all methinks I see
> the object clear: belief revised,
> *Men liberated—equalised*
> *In happiness.*
> . . . .
> . . . *True reform goes on*
> *By Nature; doing, never done.*
> Mark the advance: creeds drop the hate;
> *Events still liberalised the state.*
> (IV, xx. 28-31 and 64-67, emphasis mine)

11. Merton M. Sealts, Jr. "Melville's Reading," *Harvard Library Bulletin* 2)1948):
147.390.

Even Ungar admits that there was justice initially in the French Revolution:

> The mob,
> The Paris mob of 'Eighty-nine,
> Haggard and bleeding, with a throb
> Burst the long Tuileries. In shrine
> Of chapel there, they saw the cross
> and Him thereon, Ah, bleeding Man,
> *The people's friend,* thou bled'st for us
> Who here bleed, too!
> (IV. xxi. 117-124, emphasis mine)

Though *Clarel* is a series of questions without answers, it vividly reveals Melville's continued interests in the best government for man.

Overt political references, only hinted at before, become salient in the second half of the first chapter of the novel. Lt. Ratcliffe of the *Bellipotent* goes aboard the *Rights-of-Man* to impress a needed fighter. Melville draws his political lines of battle:

> The hardheaded Dundee owner [of the *Rights*] was a staunch admirer of Thomas Paine, whose book in rejoinder to Burke's arraignment of the French Revolution had then been published for some time and had gone everywhere. In christening his vessel after the title of Paine's volume the man of Dundee was something like his contemporary shipowner, Stephen Girard of Philadelphia, whose sympathies, alike with his native land its liberal philosophers, he evidenced by naming his ships after Voltaire, Diderot, and so forth. (CH. I)

The political aspects of the novel are continued. As Ratcliff and his crew leave the *Rights,* some of the men note the name of the free ship "bitterly" and some "with a grin." Here is a split reaction to Paine. Some of these sailors have not enjoyed their rights, but they know that they have been deprived of them and are bitter; others, however, forswear their natural rights easily, and are in fact merely amused by hints—or promises—of them. These people ally themselves with the lieutenant—one of the robots of the kind and of established authority—who "with difficulty" represses a smile when Billy salutes his former ship with his famous "And good-bye to you too, old *Rights-of-Man.*" The lieutenant, sensitive about what he is depriving Billy of, recognizes this apparent guileless farewell as "a covert sally on the new recruit's part, a sly slur at impressment in general, and that of himself in especial."

A political point of great significance is the fact that the *Rights-of-Man* is a merchantman. Here Melville is echoing Paineian philosophy that commerce is the proper business between nations: people who trade do not war; in this commercial intercourse there is great exchange of ideas from which proper alterations in political and social structure will grow. Also there has been on this ship a microcosmic parallel to the events which finally destroy Billy. On the *Rights* Red Whiskers, a mean sailor equivalent of the later Claggart, out of envy tries to pick on Billy, and once makes an obscene gesture "under the ribs." "Quick as lightning" Billy struck Red Whiskers, and "gave the burly fool a terrible drubbing," which thereafter made Red Whiskers really love Billy. Melville's point here is that in this *Rights-of-Man* world, Billy, the "peacemaker," can act naturally, without the suppression of forms that will be imposed on him in the man-of-war world of the *Bellipotent.* He can act without killing, without being destroyed by his fatal flaw. Captain Graveling is not the stickler for rules that Vere is. Thus Graveling's recounting the episode is another indictment of Vere's later behavior.

With Billy on board the *Bellipotent,* Melville emphasizes the date and political circumstances. It was summer of 1797, just after the mutinies at Spithead and Nore. The latter, the "Great Mutiny," was a "demonstration more menacing to England than the contemporary manifestoes and conquering and proselyting armies of the *French Directory.*" In the Nore Mutiny "*Reasonable* discontent growing out of *practical* grievances in the fleet had been ignited into irrational combustion as by live cinders blown across the Channel from France in Flames" (CH. III. my emphasis): in other words, Melville saw right demands fanned into flame by French example.

Even more unequivocally political was Melville's conclusion about these two mutinies: "Final suppression, however, there was," he said, then added a moment later: "To some extent the Nore Mutiny may be regarded as analogous to the distempering irruption of contagious fever in a frame constitutionally sound, and which anon throws it off." Here is dramatically mirrored one of the great · arguments between Burke and Paine. Burke insisted that the English had a constitution tacitly recognized by all—and followed by the king and the lawmakers. But Paine claimed that there was no English Constitution. Such a written agreement guaranteed protection of the people. It assured soundness to the body politic. Melville, then, was agreeing with Paine that within the framework of a sound constitution mankind could be assured of progress, but without such a guarantee nothing could be certain.

The irony in the portrait of Vere which Melville soon presents proves the author's hostility to him. It also makes the captain close relative to Burke. Vere does not owe *all* his advance to his "influences." Neither did Burke; he was very capable, but his rise resulted from his alliance with the Rockingham Whigs, and throughout life he had to cling to powerful political leaders. Vere and Burke are similar intellectually. Vere's "bias was towards those books to which every serious mind of superior order occupying any active post of authority in the world naturally inclines." And "his settled convictions were as a dike against those invading waters of novel opinion social, political, and otherwise, which carried away as in a torrent no few minds in those days, minds by nature not inferior to his own." Burke's political opinions, even when justifying the American Revolution, were always practical, expedient. Like Vere, he had grown more and more "intellectual" through the years, profoundly learned and superb as a reasoner. But as man in authority, or supporting authority, he became more and more politically illiberal. He would entertain only those notions which supported his own point of view, would read only those books which confirmed his feeling that he was correct.

Burke could easily have been in Melville's mind when he said of Vere: "While other members of that aristocracy to which by birth he belonged were incensed at the innovators mainly because their theories were inimical to the privileged classes, Captain Vere disinterestedly opposed them not alone because they seemed to him insusceptible of embodiment in lasting institutions, but at war with the peace of the world and the true welfare of mankind." (CH. VI). Burke, if narrow and conservative, was the sincerest man alive. He always felt that his views were held only in the best interests of mankind.

There is another strong similarity between Burke and Vere. The former's companions in Commons, like the latter's fellow-officers, found him, in Melville's words about Vere, "lacking in the companionable quality, a dry and bookish gentleman," with a "queer streak of the pedantic running through him." He was "apt to cite some historical character or incident of antiquity," some "remote allusion," without bothering to remember that his auditors were his inferiors in knowledge. So boring did Burke become, in fact, that he was called the "Dinner Bell": when he started to speak, regardless of the hour, many of the members of Commons went to dinner. [12]

More of Melville's political slant is seen in his effort to explain why Billy is so innocent. He does not know of evil intuitively. But, then, Melville points out, "as a class, sailors are in character a juvenile race. . . . Every sailor, too, is accustomed to obey orders without debating them; *his life afloat is externally ruled for him*" (CH. XIV. my emphasis). In

---

12. Thomas H. D. Mahoney, *Edmund Burke and Ireland* (Cambridge, Mass., 1960); p. 139.

thus pointing out the universal naiveté of sailors Melville is echoing the usual belief of the time,[13] but his real purpose is to contrast sailors with landsmen. The common sailor, he says, is in every way less prepared to combat life than is the common landsman. "The sailor is frankness, the landsman is finesse. Life is not a game with the sailor, demanding the long head" as it is with his counterpart on land. Thus he is easily imposed upon and advantage is taken of him. What is the cure for this gullibility? asks Melville: "promiscuous commerce with mankind," which will sophisticate him.

This re-introduction of the comparison of seamen with landsmen is important in the development of Melville's political purpose. Both kinds together make up the common man; only when both—*all* men—live together are they complete and prepared to combat evil, especially political evil. The pen is Melville's, but the sentiments are Tom Paine's.

All the above is, of course, background to the drama of the accusation of Billy, the consequences and the denouement. In this drama the action is rapid, the air electric. The circumstances surrounding the affair must be remembered.

The climax begins in a supercharged atmosphere. Vere's ship has just encountered a frigate, a sure prize, but the

13. In the search for sources of and parallels to *Billy Budd* not nearly enough attention has been paid to the numerous sailor songs of the time, especially to those of Charles Dibdin. Melville knew many of them, more than were in the only book containing Dibdin's songs that he is known to have consulted, Charles McKay's *Songs of England.* For example, two of the songs in *White-Jacket*—"True English Sailor" and the one sung to the tune "The King, God Bless Him"—which Melville calls Dibdin's, and which are his, are not in McKay. Melville drew heavily from these songs for the portraits of Billy and Claggart, and—by inverting Dibdin's extreme Tory sentiments—to develop his final political philosophy in the song which concludes the novel. Concerning the universal naiveté of sailors, one of Dibdin's pieces (*Sea Songs,* 3rd ed., [London, 1852], p. 102), "The Sailor's Maxim," contains the following lines:

> Of us tars 'tis reported again and again,
> That we sail round the world, yet know nothing of men;
> And, if this assertion is made with the view
> To prove sailors know naught of men's follies, 'tis true.
> . . . .
> How should Jack practise treachery, disguise, or foul art,
> In whose honest face you may read his fair heart:
> Of that maxim still ready example to give,
> Better death earn'd with honor than ignobly to live.

smaller ship has outrun the *Bellipotent*. Then "ere the excitement incident thereto had altogether waned away," Claggart, choosing his moment wisely, approaches the captain with his suspicions of Budd. Vere, "absorbed in his reflection," is caught off guard and off balance; he does not ever regain his equilibrium. Through the next few minutes the tension is intensified. Vere gest more taut, more nervous, less reliable. Claggart, on the contrary, remains always cold and calculating. After Claggart is killed, Vere's mind and nerve crack. He tries to be the strict "military disciplinarian" but cannot. He becomes more and more excited. His actions thereafter are always erratic. Melville spends several paragraphs analyzing the captain to determine if he is truly mad. The surgeon surely thinks he is, while Melville, speaking as author, implies that he is. In this breakup of Vere, Melville invalidates the captain's credentials as political philosopher. Vere has become, in fact, capable of great evil and perhaps of much destructiveness.

In his madness Vere can think only of self-protection. He wants to "guard as much as possible against publicity" by "confining all knowledge [of the event] to the place where the homicide had occurred." Does Melville approve of this action by Vere? Hardly! In being so secretive Vere "may or may not have erred," but surely "there lurked some resemblance" to the tyrannical policies "which have occurred more than once in the capital founded by Peter the Barbarian." In this denial of news to the general public—and its being equated with tyranny—there lie general political overtones and a striking similarity to the efforts of the British Government to strangle the *Rights of Man* by confiscation of the book and prosecution of the author.

The trial scene further highlights the political overtones. Throughout it Vere demonstrates his hatred of democracy. The captain of the marines was reluctantly appointed to the drumhead court because he was too much a man of "heart" rather than of "head." Furthermore, Vere

constantly condescends to the court as "men not
intellectually mature." Even more important, Melville,
speaking in his own person, says, "similar impatience as to
talking is perhaps one reason that deters some minds from
addressing any popular assemblies"—in other words,
impatience with the speed with which the common people
learn, and therefore contempt for their intelligence and for
their rights. Vere's feelings burst forth a few moments later
when the sailing master asks if the court might not
"convict and yet mitigate the penalty." Vere responds:
"The people (meaning the ship's company) have native
sense; most of them are familiar with our naval usage and
tradition; . . . they will ruminate," and will think the
"clement sentence . . . pusillanimous. They will think that
we flinch, that we are afraid of them (CH. XVIII).   Again,
though Melville was looking at Vere, he might well have
been seeing Burke.

   With Vere's statement to the sailors about the coming
execution of Billy, Melville begins to emphasize the theme
which has been present though somewhat subdued all
along: the overriding significance of the reaction of
common man. To their captain's announcement the sailors
listened "in a dumbness like that of a seated congregation
of believers in hell listening to the clergyman's announcement of his Calvinistic text." As Vere ended, "a confused murmur went up. It began to wax." It might have
grown into mutiny there had it not been quelled by the
boatswain's whistle. The importance of the passage lies in
the fact that the people were beginning to react strongly
to events. Just as most people had found intolerable the
unyielding doctrine of Calvinism and had forced it to be
modified, so most were finding unbearable the iron-
bound despotism—and conservatism—of Vere
(and Burke) and were beginning to insist that
it be changed.

   At the actual hanging the people's incipient rebellion
begins to run at higher tide. Though they echo Billy's
"conventional felon's benediction" ("God bless Captain

389

Vere!'')[14] they do not mean it. At the moment the sailors say these words; "Billy alone must have been in their hearts, even as in their eyes."

The absolute silence attending the hanging is followed almost immediately by a murmur which is scarcely audible at the beginning but which gains volume until it clearly emanates from the sailors on the deck. Melville continues, meaningfully: "Being inarticulate, it was dubious in significance further than it seemed to indicate some capricious revulsion of thought or feeling such as mobs ashore are liable to, in the present instance possibly implying a sullen revocation on the men's part of their involuntary echoing of Billy's benediction" (CH. XXIII). Melville's message seems to be that the masses are inarticulate, and therefore their intentions and actions are often misunderstood, their compliance misread. But he ties together the commoners of the sea and of the land and indicates that this total humanity condemns both the actions of the captains of the world and their own silent allowance of these actions.

The political theme continues as Vere, the "martinet," as the author suggests he is, has the men beat to quarters an hour early to get the decks cleared. "With mankind," Vere felt, "forms, measured forms are everything; and that is the real import couched in the story of Orpheus with his lyre spell-binding the wild denizens of the woods." On this statement Melville editorializes: "And this he once applied to the disruption of forms going on across the

14. Another of Dibdin's songs (*Sea Songs*, pp. 157-158) demonstrates further the conventionality of this kind of statement, and the degree to which Melville uses the songs of the common man to develop his political thesis. Entitled "Ben Block," this piece tells of a man sent to sea by his father, leaving behind his sweetheart Kate. A false friend reports that Kate is untrue, and the sailor commits suicide, as the last stanza chronicles:

Tho' sure from this cankerous elf
The venom accomplish'd its end:
Ben, all truth and honor itself,
Suspected no fraud of his friend.
On the yardarm while suspended in air,
A loose to his sorrows he gave—
"Take thy wise," he cried, "false, cruel fair!"
And plunged in a watery grave.

Channel and the consequences thereof." Only so superficial a person as Vere could equate himself with Orpheus, and only so blind a person could insist that the French Revolution was *only* a breaking up of forms.

In ending the novel Melville says that it should terminate with the death of Billy, but "truth uncompromisingly told will always have its ragged edges," and it is truth he is seeking. He writes three more chapters. The order in which they are presented is important.

In the first Melville switches to France and tells how the ship *St. Louis* was rechristened *Atheiste*. But he does not condemn the French. Although this renaming indicated a nasty turn from religion to atheism, the new name was the "aptest" that was "ever given to a warship," because it is applicable to all war, and it is war that Melville condemns. In having the French ship destroy the British captain, but not the *Bellipotent,* Melville is predicting the fate of all men like Vere (and Burke) and those countries whose political philosophy such men reflect.

Vere's death is no glorious Nelson's demise, and he was no Nelson. His death is ignominious. He is shot by a commoner (a marine, no doubt) from the port-hole of the enemy's main cabin. Then, if this is not sufficient ignominy, he is carried below and laid with the wounded commoners. After his ship has prevailed over the Frenchman, he is put ashore at Gibralter, the symbol of British militancy and tyranny.

In the shadow of this symbol of force, when Vere has been denuded of his own character by drugs, when these drugs have allowed the "subtler element in man" to speak, then and only then does he begin to think about Billy, and he calls his name twice. Melville is not precise whether Vere's words indicate remorse. But it is significant that Vere said them in the shawdow of Gibralter's strength, and that they were repeated to the "*Bellipotent's* senior officer of marines, who, as the most reluctant to condemn of the members of the drumhead court, too well knew, though here he kept the knowledge to himself, who Billv Budd was."

The death of Vere is his complete dissolution and dismissal. Throughout the story Melville has shown that Vere and his kind of people are interested only in facts; they read newspapers, official reports, and men like Montaigne, who "free from cant. . . . in the spirit of common sense philosophize upon realities." In the official report of the case, the last chapter but one in the book, Melville gives a "factual" and "true" report. It is, of course, a gross misstatement of truth. It reports that Budd was actually guilty, that Claggart was an honorable and worthy individual. But Vere is not mentioned. Hayford and Sealts feel that Melville's omission in this instance derives from oversight, from the fact that in finally introducing and working in Vere, Melville merely forgot to rewrite the report. Possibly so. More likely, however, Melville's intent is clear. The report mentions Vere only in the generalized term "the captain." His personality has been lost. In the chronicle of human events, Melville is saying, such a man does not deserve even being named.

The novel ends, as a book with such a message had to end, with the common sailors. These men preserve the chips of the spar on which Billy was hanged. There was something sacred about it. Such is the treatment accorded all heroes and saviors by such people. But even more important is the ballad which concludes the work. Though this song is written in the first person, and is actually a version of the ballad that Melville began to enlarge in constructing the fuller story of *Billy Budd,* significantly it was composed by other "tarry hands" "among the shipboard crew" than Billy's. The "I" in the song is more the sailor author than it is Billy personally. The singer, for example, thinks about the "ear-drop I gave to Bristol Molly." But Billy was surely as innocent of women as Christ and other heroes were. This is merely a stock statement in sailor songs. In other words, Billy is no longer an individual. He has been universalized. He is Every-Sailor. A variant reading of this ballad (CH. XXVI) points this up even more vividly:

In a queerish dream here I had afore
A queerish dream of days no more,—

> A general number from every shore
> Countrymen, yes and Moor and Swede,
> Christian Pagan Cannibal Breed.

There could be little more thorough mixing of the peoples of the world than here described: black, and white and in-between; religious, irreligious and indifferent. The novel has now returned to the handsome sailor—the universal savior—of the beginning, this time in a song.

Melville makes his point clear. There are no songs about Vere, none about Claggart. The song is not actually about Billy personally, but about the type of sailor he represents. He is not an unusual sailor. He is not being hanged unjustly. Rather, very much the average sailor under the circumstances, he is hungry and frightened; and once hanged he is slipped under the water in the usual way—the typical sailor of Charles Dibdin's songs. The conclusion should be compared with a statement (made by Derwent) in *Clarel:*

> Suppose an instituted creed,
> (Or truth or fable) should indeed
> To Ashes fall; the spirit exhales,
> But reinfunds in active forms:
> Verse, *popular verse,* it charms or warms—
> Belies philosophy's flattened sails—
> Tinctures the very book perchance,
> Which claims arrest of its advance.
>   (III. xxi. emphasis mine)

The political "truth uncompromisingly told" of *Billy Budd* is this ballad, this "popular verse": not the death of Billy, not even the dissolution of Vere. The subject of the novel is the common sailor. Melville has made it clear that this common sailor is inseparably attatched to the common landsman—together comprising "the people" throughout the world. The novel demonstrates that "the people" have outlasted all the others and everything else in the book. Here is Melville's reply to the Teddy Roosevelts of his age who cursed Tom Paine. Here is Melville's comment on the conservative-liberal controversy of his day and of all time. Here is his resounding affirmation of belief in the ultimate triumph of the rights of man and of democracy.

393

Most significantly, *Billy Budd* is a final affirmative statement of the single most powerful sinew in all Melville's works,
humanism. In this last work the supermen have on one level
fought their Titanic battle but also have descended, as in
numerous earlier works, to blend with Everyman, with the
common people of the world. Billy, who begins and ends
this story, is especially this hero descended to commoner.
He is more than mere Christ. This is clearly demonstrated
in an obvious echo of *Moby-Dick*. When the corpse of
Billy is slipped into the water, seafowl scream above the
spot and "kept circling it low down with the moving
shadow of their outstretched wings and the croaked requiem
of their cries." In *Moby-Dick* the circling of the seafowl
above the sinking *Pequod*, and his sinking with the ship,
signified the death of conventional Christianity, from
which, as it were, rose up the more universal Ishmael, the
Christian-pagan commoner. So too here, Billy Budd's reputation rises from sunken Christianity, as is indicated by the
parody of Christianity performed on deck after Billy has
been buried.

Billy is a "young barbarian," and drawn to a large extent
like the earlier Queequeg. He thus is superior to the
Christian sailor. The chaplain recognizes this quality when
he visits the condemned sailor before his death.

Most important is Melville's affirmation of humanism,
pictured through Billy. The chaplain, though serving Mars
as well as God, recognizes that Billy though a "barbarian"
is best prepared to face the hereafter. So while visiting
Billy before the hanging, the chaplain "kissed on the fair
cheek his fellow man, a felon in martial law." Later the
theme of the brotherhood of man, and man's longing for
this brotherhood—humanism—is taken up and reemphasized.
In *Moby-Dick* on the second day of the chase of the whale
Ahab, big with knowledge of his impending death, wants to
shake hands with Starbuck. Here in *Billy Budd* the singer
of the ballad, ending the account with the immortal version
of the whole affair, wants above all to "shake a friendly
hand ere I sink."